ASP.NET Core MVC 2.0 Cookbook

Effective ways to build modern, interactive web applications with ASP.NET Core MVC 2.0

Engin Polat
Stephane Belkheraz

BIRMINGHAM - MUMBAI

ASP.NET Core MVC 2.0 Cookbook

Commissioning Editor: Edward Gordon
Acquisition Editor: Chaitanya Nair
Content Development Editor: Zeeyan Pinheiro
Technical Editor: Ketan Kamble
Copy Editor: Safis Editing
Project Coordinator: Vaidehi Sawant
Proofreader: Safis Editing
Indexer: Rekha Nair
Graphics: Jason Monterio
Production Coordinator: Arvindkumar Gupta

First published: February 2018

Production reference: 1230218

Published by Packt Publishing Ltd.
Livery Place
35 Livery Street
Birmingham
B3 2PB, UK.

ISBN 978-1-78588-675-1

www.packtpub.com

mapt.io

Mapt is an online digital library that gives you full access to over 5,000 books and videos, as well as industry leading tools to help you plan your personal development and advance your career. For more information, please visit our website.

Why subscribe?

- Spend less time learning and more time coding with practical eBooks and Videos from over 4,000 industry professionals

- Improve your learning with Skill Plans built especially for you

- Get a free eBook or video every month

- Mapt is fully searchable

- Copy and paste, print, and bookmark content

PacktPub.com

Did you know that Packt offers eBook versions of every book published, with PDF and ePub files available? You can upgrade to the eBook version at www.PacktPub.com and as a print book customer, you are entitled to a discount on the eBook copy. Get in touch with us at service@packtpub.com for more details.

At www.PacktPub.com, you can also read a collection of free technical articles, sign up for a range of free newsletters, and receive exclusive discounts and offers on Packt books and eBooks.

Contributors

About the authors

Engin Polat has been involved in many large-scale and medium-scale projects on .NET technologies as a developer, architect, and consultant, and has won many awards since 1999.

Since 2008, he has been conducting training for many large enterprises in Turkey on Windows development, web development, distributed application development, software architecture, mobile development, cloud development, and so on.

> *I'd like to thank my dear wife, Yeliz, and my beautiful daughter, Melis Ada, for all the support they gave me while I was working on this book. I also want to give a warm welcome to the newest member of my family, my dear son, Utku Ege.*

Stephane Belkheraz is a professional software developer with over 16 years' web development experience. He spends his time developing, testing, and architecting exclusive ASP.NET applications with Web Forms, MVC, SQL Server, native JavaScript, AngularJS, and all open source frameworks around the ASP.NET ecosystem.

Stephane also develops, integrates, and creates multimedia applications with numerous technologies, including Flash, ActionScript, Java, PHP, JavaScript, and CSS.

About the reviewers

Gaurav Aroraa has completed an MPhil in computer science. He is a Microsoft MVP, lifetime member of the **Computer Society of India (CSI)**, advisory member of IndiaMentor, certified as a Scrum trainer/coach, XEN for ITIL-F, and APMG for PRINC-F and PRINC-P.

Gaurav is an open source developer and a contributor to TechNet Wiki. In over 20 years of working in the industry, he has mentored thousands of students and industry professionals. You can find him using his twitter handle @g_arora.

Gaurav is the founder of Ovatic Systems LTD, Innatus Curo Software LLC, and Shubh Computing LLP. He has also worked on other Packt books, such as *Building Microservices in ASP.NET Core*, *Learn C# in 7-days*, and *Building Microservices with .NET Core 2.0 Second Edition*.

> *I would like to thank my wife, Shuby, and my angel (daughter), Aarchi, who permitted me to steal time for this book from the time I was supposed to spend with them. I'd like to thank the entire team at Packt, especially Vaidehi Sawant, whose coordination and communication during the period was tremendous, and Denim Pinto, who introduced me to this book.*

Jason De Oliveira works as CTO for MEGA International, a software company in Paris. He is an experienced manager and senior solutions architect skilled in software architecture and enterprise architecture.

He loves sharing his knowledge and experiences through his blog and articles and by speaking at conferences. He even conducts software courses as an MCT and coaches his co-workers.

Jason is a Microsoft Most Valuable Professional (MVP C#), and has worked on numerous books on.NET, such as *Learning ASP.NET Core 2.0* and *.NET 4.5 Expert Programming Cookbook*.

> *I would like to thank my lovely wife, Orianne, and my beautiful daughters, Julia and Léonie, for supporting me in my work and accepting long days and short nights during the week and sometimes even during the weekend. My life would not be the same without them!*

Packt is searching for authors like you

If you're interested in becoming an author for Packt, please visit `authors.packtpub.com` and apply today. We have worked with thousands of developers and tech professionals, just like you, to help them share their insight with the global tech community. You can make a general application, apply for a specific hot topic that we are recruiting an author for, or submit your own idea.

Table of Contents

Preface

The ASP.Net Core 2.0 Framework is designed to meet the needs of today's web developers. It provides better control, support for test-driven development, and cleaner code. Moreover, it's lightweight and allows you to run apps on Windows, OSX, and Linux, making it the most popular web framework with modern day developers.

This book follows a unique approach to web development, using real-world examples that guide you through problems with ASP.NET Core 2.0 web applications. It covers VS2017 and ASP.NET Core 2.0-specific changes, and provides general MVC development recipes. It explores setting up .NET Core,
Visual Studio 2017, Node.js modules, and NuGet. Next, it shows you how to work with Inversion of Control data pattern and caching. We explore everyday ASP.NET Core MVC 2.0 patterns and go beyond ASP.NET Core MVC 2.0 , into troubleshooting. Finally, we will lead you through migrating, hosting, and deploying your code.

By the end of this book, you'll not only have explored every aspect of ASP.NET Core 2.0, you'll also have a reference you can keep coming back to whenever you need to get the job done.

Who this book is for

This book is for developers who want to learn to build web applications and make a career building web applications using ASP.NET Core.

If you're new to programming, this book will introduce you to the patterns and concepts used to build modern web applications.

This book is also for those who are working on other web frameworks and want to learn more about ASP.NET Core.

You'll learn how to build a web app from scratch; this book will give you a starting point so you can learn more advanced topics.

What this book covers

Chapter 1, *Cross-Platform with .NET Core*, dives deep into what .NET Core is, what its core components are, and creating ASP.NET Core web projects using the .NET Core CLI.

Chapter 2, *Visual Studio 2017, C# 6, IDEs, and Roslyn*, covers the use of Visual Studio 2017, Visual Studio Code, and Atom as C# editors. Also, we'll investigate the new features that come with C# 6 and use Roslyn compiler as a service.

Chapter 3, *Working with NPM, Frontend Package Managers, and Task Runners*, covers using and creating npm modules and using Bower, Grunt, Gulp, and Yeoman.

Chapter 4, *Reusing Code with NuGet*, guides you though manage NuGet packages, creating new NuGet packages, using previously created packages, and creating a new NuGet repository to privately list NuGet packages.

Chapter 5, *SOLID Principles, Inversion of Control, and Dependency Injection*, covers all SOLID principles, plus the inversion of Ccontrol and dependency injection libraries that come with ASP.NET Core and seperate NuGet packages.

Chapter 6, *Data Access - Entity Framework with Repository, SQL Server, and Stored Procedures*, covers implementing the repository pattern using Entity Framework Core. During implementation, we'll cover the IoC life cycle. Also, we'll investigate different providers of Entity Framework Core.

Chapter 7, *Data Access with Micro ORMs, NoSQL, and Azure*, covers creating DataAccessLayer with several libraries, such as Dapper and OrmLite. Also, we'll investigate MongoDB, Azure table storage, Azure blob storage, and SQL on Azure.

Chapter 8, *Cache and Session - Distributed, Server, and Client*, covers caching with several providers, such as InMemory Data Caching, Response Caching, Session Caching, and Distributed Caching. We'll use Redis on both on-premises and Azure.

Chapter 9, *Routing*, discusses the different aspects of ASP.NET Routing mechanisms, Route Constraints, and SEO-friendly routing.

Chapter 10, *ASP.NET Core MVC*, covers ActionResult types, creating and using POCO controllers, and managing Exceptions.

Chapter 11, *Web API*, discusses managing content-negotiation, handling cross-domain requests, auto-documenting controllers and actions using Swagger, and testing actions.

Chapter 12, *Filters*, covers how to create, manage, and use Global Filters for injecting tasks before and after the execution of actions, such as logging, caching, controlling authentication, and authorization.

Chapter 13, *Views, Models, and ViewModels*, covers creating and using ViewModels, and understanding and using the ModelBinding mechanism and ValueProviders.

Chapter 14, *Razor and Views*, talks about views, partial views, areas, HTML helpers, and dependency injection into views.

Chapter 15, *TagHelpers and ViewComponents*, dives deep into using Environment, Script, Form, and Link TagHelpers. We'll also create reusable ViewComponents.

Chapter 16, *OWIN and Middlewares*, describes OWIN and Katana, the new ASP.NET Core pipelines and middleware, along with creating and using ASP.NET Core middleware.

Chapter 17, *Security*, covers Authentication and Authorization mechanisms, managing Identity, and securing data with ASP.NET Core.

Chapter 18, *Frontend Development*, covers how to use Bootstrap classes, write maintainable and clean JavaScript code, and debug it. We will see what TypeScript is and write unit tests for JavaScript code.

Chapter 19, *Deployment and Hosting*, covers hosting ASP.NET Core web applications using IIS, Azure, and Docker. We'll also host ASP.NET web applications on Linux, Windows, and Mac environments using Kestrel.

To get the most out of this book

1. It's beneficial to have some web backend or frontend programming experience.
2. You'll need Visual Studio 2017, Visual Studio Code, Atom, SQL Server Management Studio, and a modern web browser installed. Don't worry, we'll guide you on how to install them when needed.
3. You'll need an active Azure subscription. The Microsoft Azure platform offers free trial accounts at http://www.azure.com

Download the example code files

You can download the example code files for this book from your account at www.packtpub.com. If you purchased this book elsewhere, you can visit www.packtpub.com/support and register to have the files emailed directly to you.

You can download the code files by following these steps:

1. Log in or register at `www.packtpub.com`.
2. Select the **SUPPORT** tab.
3. Click on **Code Downloads & Errata**.
4. Enter the name of the book in the **Search** box and follow the onscreen instructions.

Once the file is downloaded, please make sure that you unzip or extract the folder using the latest version of:

- WinRAR/7-Zip for Windows
- Zipeg/iZip/UnRarX for Mac
- 7-Zip/PeaZip for Linux

The code bundle for the book is also hosted on GitHub at `https://github.com/PacktPublishing/ASP.NET-MVC-Core-2.0-Cookbook`. We also have other code bundles from our rich catalog of books and videos available at `https://github.com/PacktPublishing/`. Check them out!

Download the color images

We also provide a PDF file that has color images of the screenshots/diagrams used in this book. You can download it here: `https://www.packtpub.com/sites/default/files/downloads/ASP.NETMVCCore2.0Cookbook_ColorImages.pdf`.

Conventions used

There are a number of text conventions used throughout this book.

`CodeInText`: Indicates code words in text, database table names, folder names, filenames, file extensions, pathnames, dummy URLs, user input, and Twitter handles. Here is an example: "Run `dotnet new mvc` from the command line. This command will create a new ASP.NET Core MVC project with the same name as the containing folder."

A block of code is set as follows:

```
public class Person
{
    public class Name {get;set;}
    public Person(){
        Name = "Stephane";
    }
}
```

When we wish to draw your attention to a particular part of a code block, the relevant lines or items are set in bold:

```
public class Person
{
    public class Name {get;set;}
    public Person(){
        Name = "Stephane";
    }
}
```

Any command-line input or output is written as follows:

```
$ apt-get install nautilus-open-terminal

$ killall nautilus && nautilus
```

Bold: Indicates a new term, an important word, or words that you see onscreen. For example, words in menus or dialog boxes appear in the text like this. Here is an example: "Select the **Subscription**."

 Warnings or important notes appear like this.

 Tips and tricks appear like this.

Sections

In this book, you will find several headings that appear frequently (*Getting ready, How to do it..., How it works..., There's more...,* and *See also*).

To give clear instructions on how to complete a recipe, use these sections as follows:

Getting ready

This section tells you what to expect in the recipe and describes how to set up any software or any preliminary settings required for the recipe.

How to do it...

This section contains the steps required to follow the recipe.

How it works...

This section usually consists of a detailed explanation of what happened in the previous section.

There's more...

This section consists of additional information about the recipe in order to make you more knowledgeable about the recipe.

See also

This section provides helpful links to other useful information for the recipe.

Get in touch

Feedback from our readers is always welcome.

General feedback: Email feedback@packtpub.com and mention the book title in the subject of your message. If you have questions about any aspect of this book, please email us at questions@packtpub.com.

Errata: Although we have taken every care to ensure the accuracy of our content, mistakes do happen. If you have found a mistake in this book, we would be grateful if you would report this to us. Please visit www.packtpub.com/submit-errata, selecting your book, clicking on the Errata Submission Form link, and entering the details.

Piracy: If you come across any illegal copies of our works in any form on the internet, we would be grateful if you would provide us with the location address or website name. Please contact us at copyright@packtpub.com with a link to the material.

If you are interested in becoming an author: If there is a topic that you have expertise in and you are interested in either writing or contributing to a book, please visit authors.packtpub.com.

Reviews

Please leave a review. Once you have read and used this book, why not leave a review on the site that you purchased it from? Potential readers can then see and use your unbiased opinion to make purchase decisions, we at Packt can understand what you think about our products, and our authors can see your feedback on their book. Thank you!

For more information about Packt, please visit packtpub.com.

1

Cross-Platform with .NET Core

This chapter is an introduction to explain all the new concepts and features included in **ASP.NET Core 2.0**.

Some of the following explanations are mandatory to understand all the options available in ASP.NET Core.

In this chapter, we will cover:

- Installing or updating .NET Core
- Managing NuGet packages in ASP.NET applications
- Creating and running an ASP.NET Core MVC application on Linux
- Creating and running an ASP.NET Core MVC application on Linux with Docker
- Creating and running an ASP.NET Core MVC application on macOS
- Creating and running an ASP.NET Core MVC application on Azure

What is ASP.NET Core 2.0?

This new version of ASP.NET is quite a revolution in the Microsoft ecosystem.

Before ASP.NET Core, ASP.NET was not open source, and ran only on Windows. To develop ASP.NET applications, most developers used Visual Studio as IDE. It was not mandatory, because we could use Notepad with CSharp or VB compilers (which were always free), but so much easier with VS even with an express edition. At that time, the only way to run .NET applications on Linux and macOS was to use Mono, an open source cross-platform version of the .NET Framework.

The ASP.NET Core version 2.0 is far more flexible. You can develop on any OS (at least Windows, Linux, and macOS), use various tools such as Visual Studio, Visual Studio Code, or even Sublime Text. ASP.NET Core is now modular, more maintenable, and has increased performance. By design, it is cloud-ready and middleware-based.

With the new version of ASP.NET, IIS is not the only possible host. You can host your ASP.NET applications on other web servers, such as **Kestrel** on macOS and Linux.

Among all the changes, some of the most important were the fusion of **MVC** and **Web API**, and the deletion of **WebForms**, **Service locator**, and **System.Web**.

All the duplicate libraries existing both in MVC and Web API, such as Controllers, Actions, Filters, Model Binding, and Dependency Resolver, are now the same unified classes.

The strong dependency on the heaviest library used in ASP.NET, System.Web, is now deleted to make ASP.NET Core MVC more modular, middleware-compliant, and platform-independent.

All the source code for ASP.NET Core MVC is available in its GitHub repository at `https://github.com/aspnet/mvc`.
We can find all the ASP.NET Core repositories at `https://github.com/aspnet`, and all the .NET Core repositories at `https://github.com/microsoft/dotnet`.

What's new in ASP.NET and CLR?

We now will use two frameworks, and have two options to develop web applications:

- The **Framework 4.6**, which offers us maximum compatibility with legacy apps and the previous .NET frameworks. Framework 4.6 only works on Windows. One of the most interesting new features of ASP.NET 4.6 is HTTP2, which gives us:
  - Asynchronous ModelBinding
  - Ability to always encrypt exchanges on the web
  - Pre-population of the browser's cache
  - Interruption of a TCP connection without closing
- The **.NET Core 2.0**, which is the modular and lightweight approach above the Core CLR to develop cross-platform applications.

We can use them independently, or both at the same time, in order to create a two-frameworks-compatible application, and the old DLLs of the legacy applications will have to migrate on .NET Core version 2.0.

Two versions of the .NET framework can also live side by side in the same application; for example, .NET Framework 4.6 and .NET Core 2.0.

 Before .NET Core, Mono was used as and open source cross-platform .NET Framework.

All the libraries outside the framework are optional, available in the form of packages.

Before .NET Core, a .NET application could only be executed under Windows, because only Windows could instantiate the CLR. If IIS was in charge of the instantiation, `WebEngine.dll` was responsible for instantiating CLR.

Now, we have a new SDK with a lot of tools to allow us to execute ASP.NET applications outside IIS and independently from any web server.

Installing or updating .NET Core

In this recipe, we will learn how to set up .NET Core. This recipe is pivotal if you are installing it for the first time.

Installing .NET Core is a relatively easy task. Microsoft did a great job to make it easy to install .NET Core to any computer. All we need is a clean computer and an internet connection.

How to do it...

The first step is to open a web browser and navigate to the `http://dot.net/core` site. It'll detect a host operating system, and will show downloading and installation steps.

- Installation for Windows:
  On the Windows platform, we can easily download .NET Core SDK installer by clicking the **Download .NET Core SDK** button and beginning setup. Once setup finishes, you're ready to develop/run .NET Core applications on the machine.

- Installation for Linux:
  On the Linux platform, there are different commands to install .NET Core on Ubuntu, RedHat, Debian, Fedora, CentOS, and Suse distribution. We should select the correct distribution on the page, and execute some Terminal commands by following preceding instructions.

- Installation for macOS:
  On the macOS platform, it's as easy as downloading the .NET Core SDK package.

- Installation for Docker:
  There is another platform available to deploy and run .NET Core applications: Docker. Docker is simply a virtualization platform. You may run Docker on the machine and deploy your .NET Core applications into Docker. Once you successfully deploy an application to Docker, it's easy to run more than one instance of it.

Docker usually helps developers to scale their applications with minimum management cost.

How it works...

After installing .NET Core 2.0 SDK, you can open the Terminal/Command Prompt window and run the following command:

```
dotnet --info
```

This command displays the installed and most recent .NET Core SDK version (2.0.2 at the time this book was written), Runtime Environment info (OS platform, architecture, version, and more), and .NET Core SDK installation path:

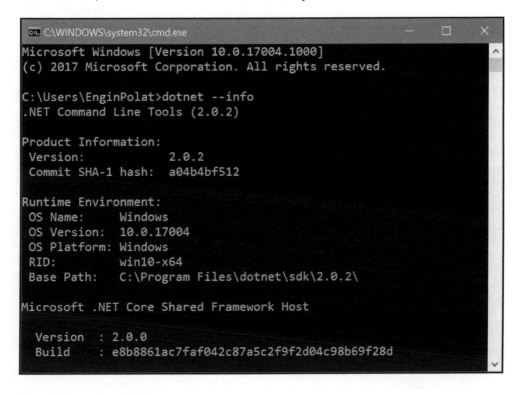

We can see `Base Path` includes the .NET Core SDK version. If we remove that version from the path and open that path in Finder/Explorer, we can see all the installed .NET Core SDK versions:

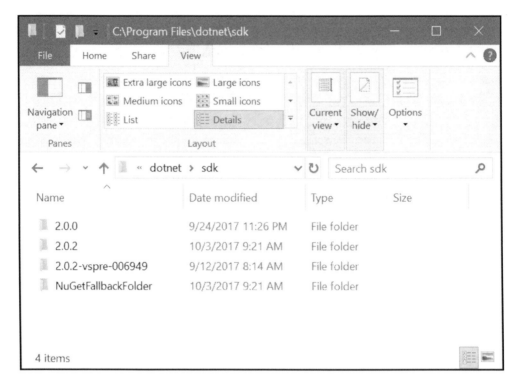

It's as easy as deleting a folder to remove any .NET Core SDK version on a machine.

Managing NuGet packages in ASP.NET Core applications

Now in ASP.NET Core, every dependency and every DLL is a NuGet package that can be managed with **dotnet CLI**.

How to do it...

With dotnet CLI, you will be able to:

- Install and uninstall packages
- Build an application
- Creating assemblies for an application
- Restore packages by downloading the entire graph of dependencies for the dependency asked
- Publish an application with all the necessary files to execute the application event if there is no .Net Core installed on the machine

Creating an ASP.NET Core MVC application on Linux

In this recipe, we will create an ASP.NET Core MVC application on Linux. In order to perform this feature, we will have to install all the necessary libraries, components, and IDE on Ubuntu.

Getting ready

For cost consideration, we may be interested in hosting our websites on a Linux infrastructure. With cloud possibilities, we can consider hosting a Linux VM with ASP.NET Core capabilities.

For this recipe, we will use Ubuntu 17.10, but you can use a different Linux distribution such as Debian, CentOS, Fedora or any Linux distribution that supports a Docker Engine.

Before .NET Core, there was the `Mono` Framework (`http://www.mono-project.com/`) to run a .NET application on Linux. `Mono` is an open source and a cross-platform port of the `.NET` Framework, which contains an `Apache` module to host ASP.NET applications.

For now, .NET applications always need `Mono` to run on Linux or OS X, because not all the BCL (The `.NET` Framework base class library) is fully ported on Linux.

To host our ASP.NET Core 2.0 application on Linux, we will use Kestrel (you can read more about this at `https://github.com/aspnet/KestrelHttpServer`) as a `WebServer`, which is a lightweight cross-platform web server able to execute ASP.NET Core code. Kestrel uses Libuv internally as a multi-platform asynchronous `IO` and `TCP` library, also used by Node.js.

For the moment, there's no other web server we could use to host ASP.NET Core applications on Linux or macOS, and Kestrel is not production-ready. We can also use IIS or `WebListener` as a web server to host ASP.NET Core applications, but exclusively on Windows.

How to do it...

After installing .NET Core on Linux, creating a new project is easy.

Let's start creating a new project:

1. Run `dotnet new mvc` from the command line. This command will create a new ASP.NET Core MVC project with the same name as the containing folder. If we want to give a different name to the project, `-n PROJECTNAME switch` should be added

2. Next, we need to run `dotnet restore` in the project folder. Most IDEs run `dotnet restore` in the background for us, such as Visual Studio and Visual Studio Code

How it works...

The dotnet CLI will generate all the necessary files you need for the project template we select.

The `dotnet run` command will be used to launch the ASP.NET Core MVC project:

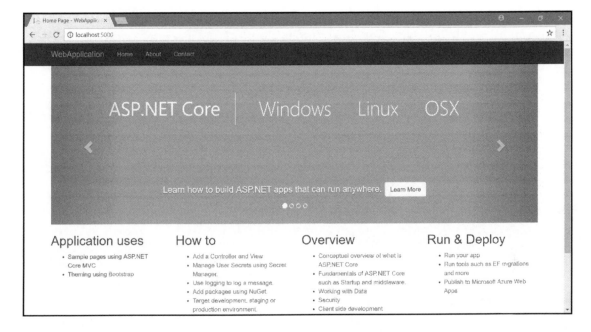

Creating an ASP.NET Core MVC application on Linux with Docker

In this recipe, we will learn how to create an ASP.NET Core MVC application on Linux with Docker, the new `Container` technology.

Getting ready

We also have the option to use Docker to create, host, and publish an ASP.NET Core MVC application on Linux. Docker is a piece of operating system and software you will use to run your applications as a server (generally used as a VM locally, or in the cloud). We use Docker Containers as a lightweight VM with only the necessary files (system, tools, runtime, libraries, and code) for running applications, which starts much more quickly and runs independently from the environment it evaluates.

How to do it...

In our recipe, we will locally create a Docker Container with a Linux Ubuntu 17.10 VM to publish and host our ASP.NET Core MVC application.

In this recipe, we will do the following:

1. Before beginning, you can install Nautilus, a file manager for a gnome-like explorer on Windows, which allows you to open the Terminal by right-clicking in a folder:

    ```
    $ apt-get install nautilus-open-terminal
    ```

    ```
    $ killall nautilus && nautilus
    ```

2. Download and install Docker on our Ubuntu VM:

    ```
    $ sudo apt-key adv --keyserver hkp://keyserver.ubuntu.com:80 --recv-keys 36A1D7869245C8950F966E92D8576A8BA88D21E9
    ```

    ```
    $ sudo sh -c "echo deb https://get.docker.com/ubuntu docker main > /etc/apt/sources.list.d/docker.list"
    ```

    ```
    $ sudo apt-get update
    ```

    ```
    $ sudo apt-get install lxc-docker
    ```

3. Add the current user to Docker group, then log out and log in again:

    ```
    $ sudo usermod -aG docker
    ```

    ```
    $ sudo service docker restart
    ```

     Note: We don't need to write `sudo` before the command lines anymore, because now we have enough rights to execute the command without writing `sudo`.

4. Download `project.json` and `Starup.cs` from the HelloWeb sample, at https://github.com/aspnet/Home/tree/dev/samples/latest/HelloWeb. These two files are the only mandatory files required to run our application.

5. Create a directory named `HelloWeb`, and place the two previous files inside.

6. Create a file without an extension inside called `Dockerfile`, and insert in the following code:

```
# This code will download and use the last ASP.NET 5 Docker
 # image based on Mono at
 # https://github.com/aspnet/aspnet-docker/blob/master/1.0.0-
 # rc1-update1/Dockerfile

FROM Microsoft/aspnet:latest

# This code copies the project into the folder and restores
 # the packages using dotnet CLICOPY . /app
 WORKDIR /app
 RUN ["dotnet","restore"]

# Open this port in the container
EXPOSE 5000

# Start application using DNX and the command from
 # project.json to call kestrel
ENTRYPOINT ["dotnet","run"]
```

7. Save and close `Dockerfile`.

8. Then, verify the existing containers (not mandatory):

```
$ sudo docker images
```

9. We can also check the running containers (not mandatory):

```
$ docker ps
```

10. You can build your application now:

```
$ docker build -t
```

11. Run it (port 5004 is the default port for Kestrel):

```
$ docker run -t -d -p 5004:5004
```

12. You can see the home page at `http:localhost:5004`.

How it works...

A web server usually uses port 80 for web applications, while Kestrel will use port 5000 or 5004. We know that we cannot open ports lower than 1024 with default user permissions on Linux. To host ASP.NET Core applications using port 80, and to be production-ready on Linux, we will have to use Nginx with Kestrel to bring us all the web server features we need that Kestrel doesn't have, like load balancing, caching, and security, among others.

We can think of Docker Container as a mini VM with the minimum OS and software components you need to run the applications, isolated from the other application containers. Docker is lightweight, open, and secure, isolating applications from each other. You can consult the Docker documentation at https://www.docker.com/.

We can create a Docker Container on Windows, macOS, Linux (Ubuntu, RedHat, Suse, Arch, Debian, and so on), and on the cloud (Azure, AWS, Google, and so on). It will generally run on Linux distributions, but Windows will also support it.

Creating an ASP.NET Core MVC application on macOS

In this recipe, we will learn how to install the .NET Core components in order to create an ASP.NET Core MVC application on macOS.

Getting ready

Because macOS is based on Unix, it is possible to run a .NET application on it with the Mono project. As mentioned in the previous recipe, for the moment, .NET application needs Mono to run on Linux or macOS.

To install Mono, we use Homebrew (http://brew.sh/), which is a package manager for macOS.

 We suppose that you have the necessary privileges to execute all these commands. If not, prefix sudo before all the command lines and you should be good to go.

How to do it...

In this recipe, we will do the following:

1. Install `Homebrew` by entering this command at a Terminal:

   ```
   ruby -e "$(curl -fsSL
   https://raw.githubusercontent.com/Homebrew/install/master/install)"
   ```

```
● ● ●                          ⌂ test — -bash — 140×51
MacBook-ProdeThom:~ test$ ruby -e "$(curl -fsSL https://raw.githubusercontent.com/Homebrew/install/master/install)"
==> This script will install:
/usr/local/bin/brew
/usr/local/Library/...
/usr/local/share/man/man1/brew.1
==> The following directories will be made group writable:
/usr/local/.
==> The following directories will have their owner set to test:
/usr/local/.
==> The following directories will have their group set to admin:
/usr/local/.

Press RETURN to continue or any other key to abort
==> /usr/bin/sudo /bin/chmod g+rwx /usr/local/.

WARNING: Improper use of the sudo command could lead to data loss
or the deletion of important system files. Please double-check your
typing when using sudo. Type "man sudo" for more information.

To proceed, enter your password, or type Ctrl-C to abort.

Password:
==> /usr/bin/sudo /usr/sbin/chown test /usr/local/.
==> /usr/bin/sudo /usr/bin/chgrp admin /usr/local/.
==> /usr/bin/sudo /bin/mkdir /Library/Caches/Homebrew
==> /usr/bin/sudo /bin/chmod g+rwx /Library/Caches/Homebrew
==> /usr/bin/sudo /usr/sbin/chown test /Library/Caches/Homebrew
==> Downloading and installing Homebrew...
remote: Counting objects: 3916, done.
remote: Compressing objects: 100% (3760/3760), done.
remote: Total 3916 (delta 30), reused 2263 (delta 19), pack-reused 0
Receiving objects: 100% (3916/3916), 3.40 MiB | 1.28 MiB/s, done.
Resolving deltas: 100% (30/30), done.
From https://github.com/Homebrew/homebrew
 * [new branch]      master     -> origin/master
Checking out files: 100% (3918/3918), done.
HEAD is now at 1cc74a1 cassandra: update 3.0.2 bottle.
==> Installation successful!
==> Next steps
Run `brew help` to get started
MacBook-ProdeThom:~ test$ brew tap aspnet/dnx
==> Tapping aspnet/dnx
Cloning into '/usr/local/Library/Taps/aspnet/homebrew-dnx'...
remote: Counting objects: 7, done.
remote: Compressing objects: 100% (7/7), done.
remote: Total 7 (delta 1), reused 2 (delta 0), pack-reused 0
Unpacking objects: 100% (7/7), done.
Checking connectivity... done.
Tapped 2 formulae (33 files, 136K)
MacBook-ProdeThom:~ test$ brew update
Already up-to-date.
```

2. Use `Homebrew` to get `DNVM`, `DNX`, and `DNU` using the commands as follows:

   `$ brew tap aspnet/dnx`

   `$ brew update`

   `$ brew install dnvm`

   `$ source dnvm.sh`

3. Install Node.js and npm (the npm will be installed automatically with Node.js):

   `$ brew install node`

4. Verify Node.js and NPM versions:

   `$ node -v`

   `$ npm -v`

   The version currently being used will be displayed on your screen as follows:

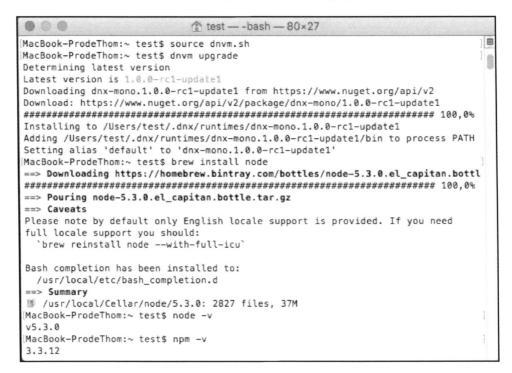

5. Install `Yeoman` with `Gulp` to help automate tasks:

```
$ npm install -g yo gulp
```

```
$ npm install -g generator-aspnet
```

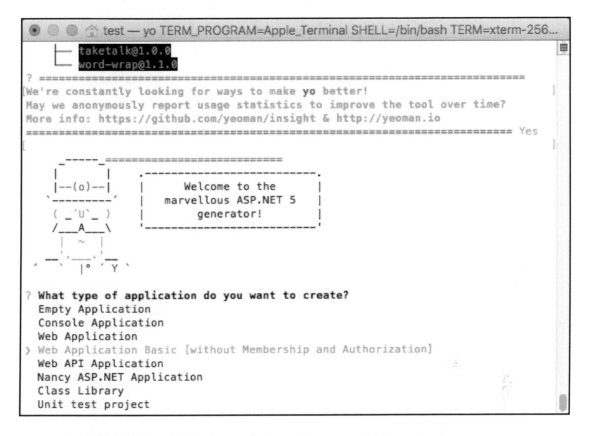

6. `Yeoman` asks us what type of application we want to create. In our case, we choose Web Application Basic.
7. After that, `Yeoman` asks us the name for the application to create, as shown in the following screenshot.
8. `Yeoman` will generate all the necessary files to run an ASP.NET Core MVC application. After the project is created, `Yeoman` shows us the different commands we can use to run the application.
9. With the command `cd "nameoftheapplication"`, we are placed in the application directory.

10. After that, we can run the `dotnet restore` command, which will restore all the dependencies needed to run the application. In the background, this command will connect to the `NuGet` online repository to download, as `NuGet` packages the missing dependencies:

11. Build and run `webapp1` typing the following command:

```
$ dotnet run
```

After executing the preceding command you get the following output at `localhost:5000`:

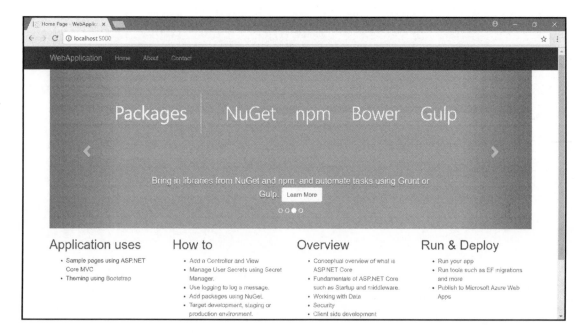

Creating and running an ASP.NET Core MVC application on Azure

In this recipe, we will create a web application and deploy it to Azure.

Getting started

We will use **Visual Studio 2017 Community Edition**, and create a web application using the ASP.NET Core templates in Visual Studio.

How to do it...

1. First, let's create a new project by clicking **New | Project | ASP.NET Core Web Application | Web application** to create a web application running with ASP.NET Core:

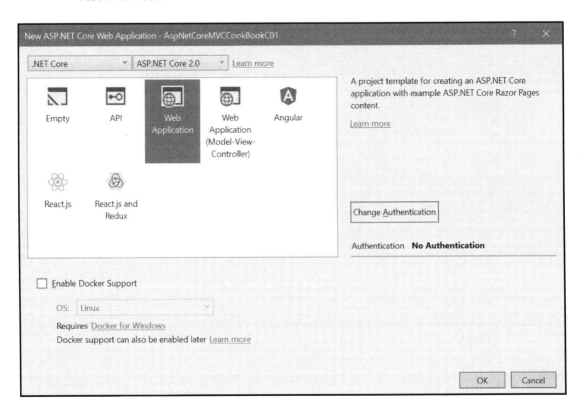

When you run a web application in Visual Studio 2017, you have the choice to develop, debug, and deploy a web application in two different runtime versions, which have themselves two versions for the processor architecture as follows:

- **CLR x86** (.NET 4.6 in 32 bits, only for Windows)
- **CLR x64** (.NET 4.6 in 64 bits, only for Windows)
- **CoreCLR x86** (.NET Core in 32 bits, cross-platform)
- **CoreCLR x64** (.NET Core in 64 bits, cross-platform)

2. Let's do our first deployment by creating a website on Azure. To do that, right-click on the root of the project and select **Publish...**.

3. The `Publish Web` dialog box will open:

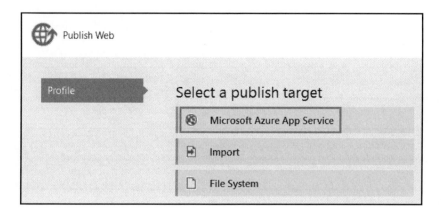

4. Click **Microsoft Azure App Service**. The **Create App Service** dialog box will open:

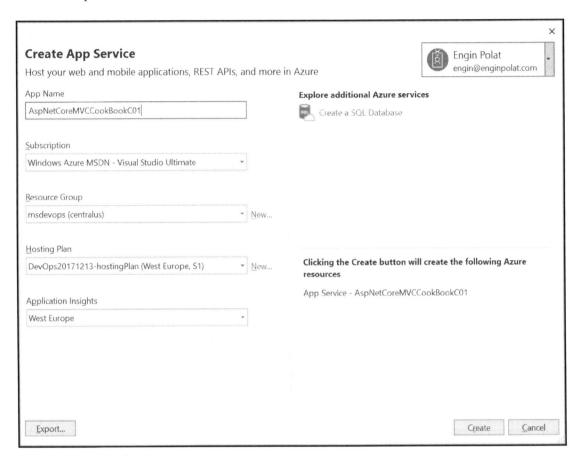

5. We have to give an **App Name.**
6. Select the **Subscription.**
7. Select an **App Service Plan**, or create one.
8. Select a **Resource Group** (optional).
9. Select a **Region** (optional).
10. Select or create a **Database Server** (optional).

11. Now the **Create** button is enabled, we click on it:

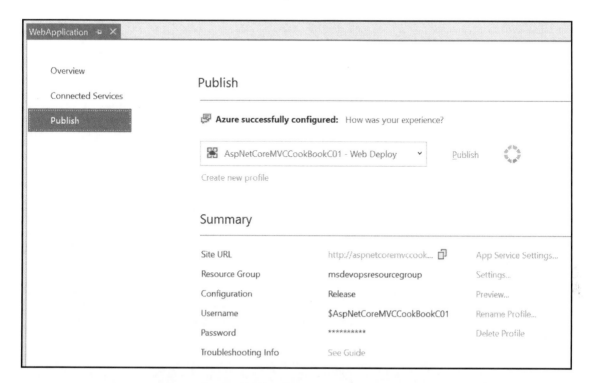

In the preceding screenshot, we can see a preview of the deployed files.

12. Click **Publish**:

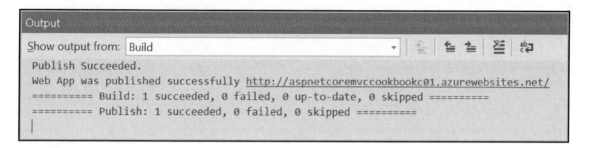

In the preceding screenshot, we can see the result of the build and the publishing in the output window.

In the following screenshot, we can see how our web application deployed on Azure:

Take a look at the screenshot below. We can see the publish settings for the web application in the PublishProfiles folder as one .pubxml file.

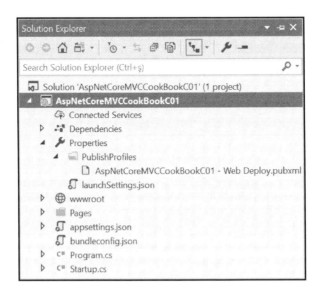

How it works...

We can publish the following applications to the Azure platform:

- .NET web application
- .NET Core web application
- Java web application
- Node.js web application
- PHP web application
- Python web application
- Ruby web application

Azure makes it very easy to deploy and run web-based applications.

2
Visual Studio 2017, C# 6, IDEs, and Roslyn

In this chapter, we will cover:

- Working with Visual Studio 2017
- Working with Visual Studio Code
- Installing and using OmniSharp on macOS
- Installing and using OmniSharp on Linux
- Working with Roslyn
- Using new C# 6 features

Introduction

In this chapter, we will learn about the most interesting new features of Visual Studio 2017. We will use Visual Studio Code as a cross-platform editor for C# and some other languages.

We will install the `OmniSharp` library to have the benefits of intellisense and language support, just as VS does, on other IDEs on macOS and Linux.

We will also discover the new open source and cross-platform compiler named Roslyn, and will understand what its different APIs will bring to us.

Finally, we will discover some useful and relevant new C# 6 features.

Working with Visual Studio 2017

There are many new or enhanced features in VS 2017. Let's have a look at a few of them.

How to do it...

1. Feature one—VS project templates:

   1. We will find a large number of project templates and samples by going to **Menu** | **File** | **New Project** | **Installed.**
   2. Select a project template related to the technology or language you want to develop with.
   3. We can also download a lot of project templates by going to **Menu** | **File** | **New Project** | **Online.**
   4. You can search for a template that matches with a technology.

   We want to use all the projects which are not necessarily reliable, so it's up to us to verify that. The **New Project** dialog box appears:

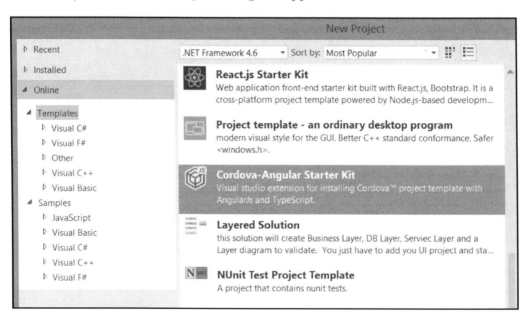

2. **Visual Studio Gallery** to add extensions:

   1. Let's go to **Menu** | **Tools** | **Extensions and Updates** | **Visual Studio Gallery**.
   2. We will find some awesome extensions and tools for many languages and technologies. We can go to **Visual Studio Gallery** (http://visualstudiogallery.com/) to browse all the available extensions:

   3. An extension can be a VSIX extension, but it can also be an MSI file.

4. Too many extensions installed make the usage of VS very heavy. You can disable or uninstall any extension you want in the **Tools | Extensions and Updates** window, shown as follows:

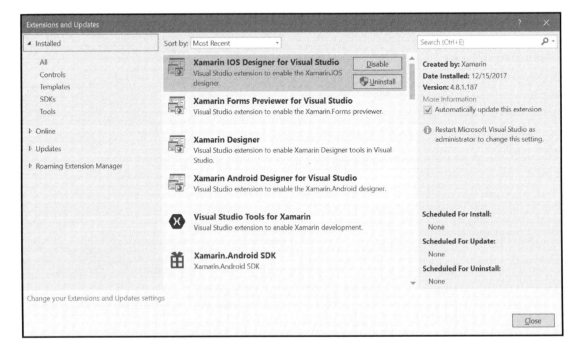

3. Searching (classes, methods, interfaces, and many others):

1. Many options are available for searching. One of the most relevant within VS is searching in the **Solution Explorer** panel:

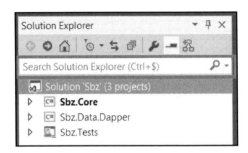

2. If it is not open, we can show it by navigating to **View** | **Solution Explorer**:

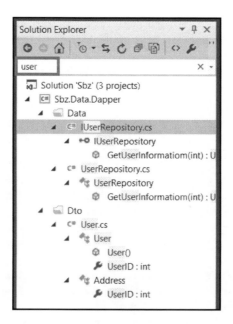

3. We can also search in the **Object Browser**, the **Toolbox,** or the **Class View** panel:

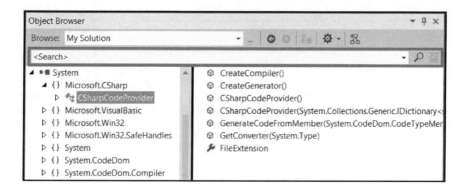

4. We can find the **Class View** panel by navigating to **View** | **Class View**.
5. We can find the **Object Browser** panel by navigating to **View** | **Object Browser**:

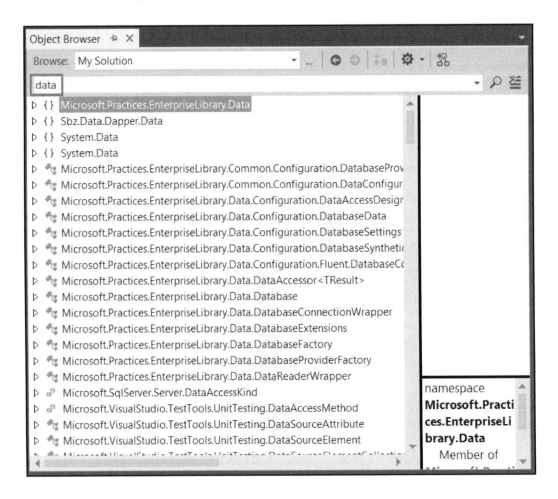

4. Code snippets:

   1. Snippets are a way to reuse code and improve productivity, and thus, they help you save time.
   2. There are many preregistered snippets in VS. For instance, open a C# code file and place the caret within a method definition.
   3. Type `try`, then press the *Tab* key once:

   VS generates a `try`/`catch` code block, as follows:

```
try
{

}
catch (System.Exception)
{

        throw;
}
```

   4. Type `if`, then press the *Tab* key once:

   VS generates an `if` code block, as follows:

```
if (true)
{

}
```

5. Type `foreach`, then press the *Tab* key once:

VS generates a `foreach` code block, as follows:

```
foreach (var item in collection)
{

}
```

We can replace all the elements of the `foreach` statement by pressing *Tab* to navigate between them, then we press *Enter* to validate.

6. When selecting code, we can surround it with an existing snippet by typing *Ctrl + K* and *Ctrl + S:*

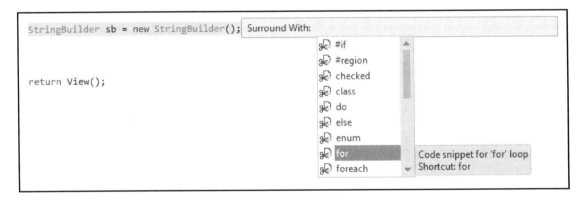

7. Let's select `for`, then press the *Tab* key once:

```
for (int i = 0; i < length; i++)
{
    StringBuilder sb = new StringBuilder();
}
```

8. We can use predefined snippets as well as our own snippets. Right-click and click on **Insert Snippet...** or press the *Ctrl + K / Ctrl + X* keys:

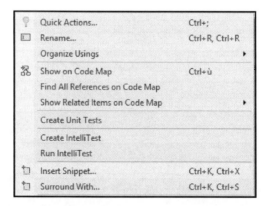

We can consult the default code snippets list on MSDN at `https://msdn.microsoft.com/en-us/library/z41h7fat.aspx`.

9. We can see the snippet categories as follows:

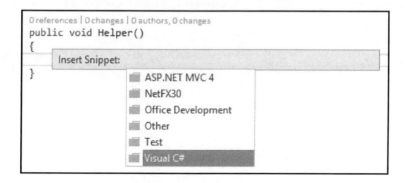

10. We can see the snippet list for each category:

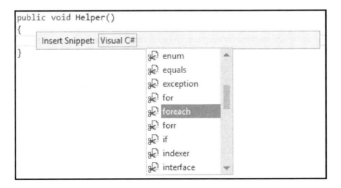

11. We can explore all the snippets from the menu **Tools | Code Snippets Manager**.

The **Code Snippets Manager** dialog box, with all the available snippets, is shown as follows:

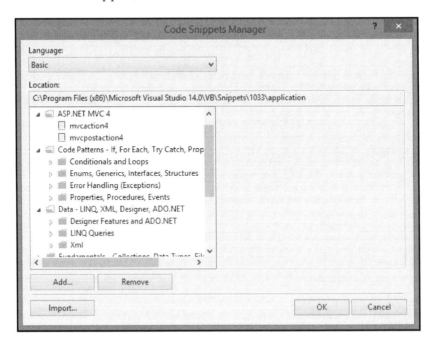

12. We can also select a list of snippets by language and, afterward, select a category:

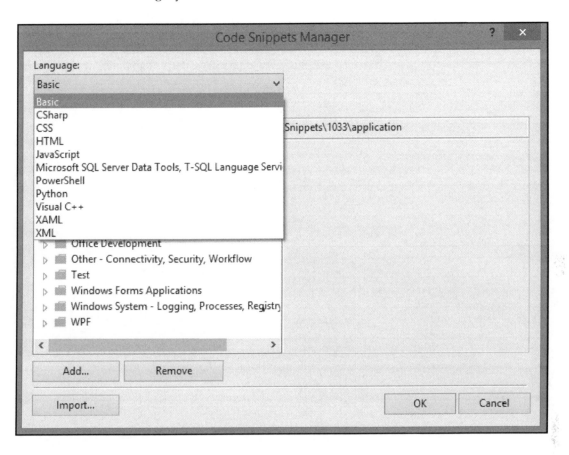

5. Code map:

This feature creates a diagram representing the hierarchy of your method calls, including their classes and DLL containers during debugging. This feature is available only in VS 2017 Enterprise Edition.

1. We can access it by right-clicking on the code and selecting one of these options on the contextual menu:

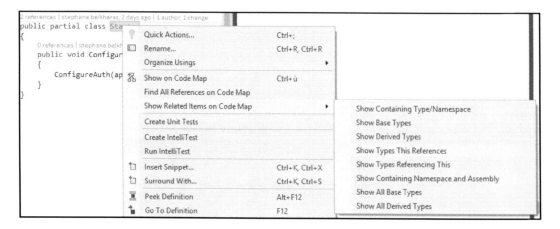

2. These diagrams can be saved as `.dgml` extensions, but also as images to be used in a document or to be sent by email.

Code map allows us to do the following things:

-   Navigate and examine code from the map
-   Understand relationships between pieces of code
-   Find and fix a problem by examining the map

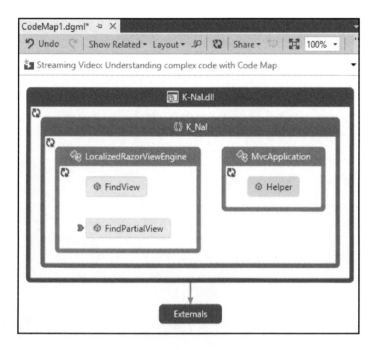

6. Analyzers:

There are many analyzers available in NuGet, including Tsql, Azure, and CSharp. Each of them increases the quality of your code, similar to FxCop (a code, analysis tool that gives you advice to correct the code).

Let's explore one of them—code cracker:

1. Right-click on a project; let's click on **Manage NuGet Package** and type analyzer in the search input.
2. We see all the available analyzers, then select and install the package, CodeCracker.CSharp.
3. We can also find it by going to **Menu | Tools | Extensions and Updates** and searching CodeCracker.CSharp.

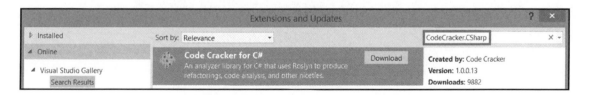

4. Now, when we write code and it doesn't respect one of the rules of the analyzer, we will have warnings on the code and suggestions to correct it.

5. **Code Analysis** can be enabled on build in our projects. Right-click on the **Solution Explorer**, root of the project, **Properties** | **Code Analysis** and check **Enable Code Analysis on Build**:

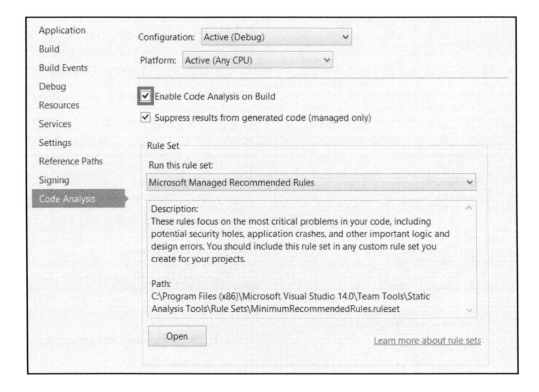

While building an application, if a rule is not respected, it will appear in the error list, and if documentation exists about this error, we will be able to consult the page by clicking on the error number.

7. Use LINQ and Lambdas in **Immediate Window**:

1. **Immediate Window** appears when selecting the VS menu **Debug |
Windows | Immediate**:

```
132          public void TestSnippet()
133          {
134              var listFloats = Enumerable.Range(0, 100);
135
136              Debugger.Break();
137
138          }
```

2. We can access object lists or specific variables using the LINQ or
Lambdas expression in this bottom window while debugging, by
typing LINQ or Lambdas expressions in it.

3. We can type a LINQ expression and see its result in the **Immediate
Window**:

```
Immediate Window
listFloats.Where(x => x < 10).ToList()
Count = 10
    [0]: 0
    [1]: 1
    [2]: 2
    [3]: 3
    [4]: 4
    [5]: 5
    [6]: 6
    [7]: 7
    [8]: 8
    [9]: 9
```

8. Perfprmance tips:

We can get performance information in a tooltip, for example:

1. Create one breakpoint at the beginning of a method
2. Create another breakpoint at the end of the method

3. When debugging, we will see, at the second breakpoint, the elapsed time in milliseconds between the first and the second breakpoint:

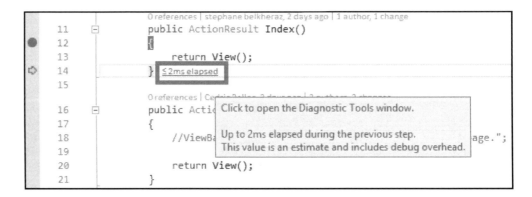

2. **Diagnostic Tools**:

- **Diagnostic Tools** displays some metrics when you are debugging your application.
- The timeline section indicates events and elapsed time during a debugging session.

- The memory section shows us real-time memory usage (the real one watching private bytes). We also have the ability to take a memory snapshot. The CPU section shows real-time CPU usage:

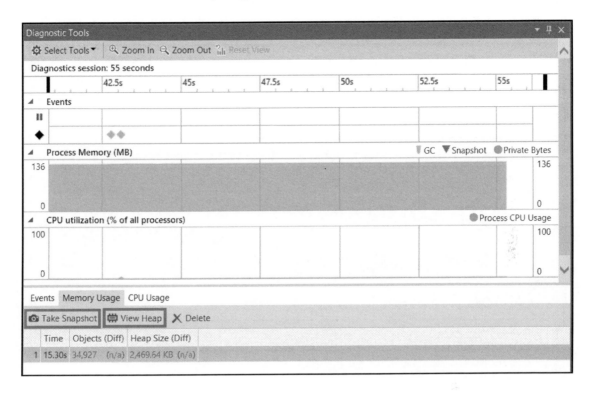

We can also view the content of the heap:

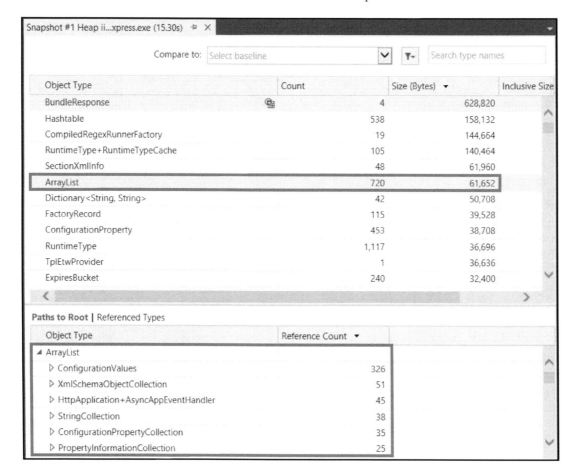

10. Code lens:

Code lens is a new VS 2017 feature which gives us real-time indications about our code in references, unit tests, and code changes. These pieces of information appear above the method names:

1. Passing the mouse over references, we can see information about where this method is called from:

```
◢ K-Nal\LocalizedRazorViewEngine.cs (2)
    ◉  40 : var result = base.FindView(controllerContext, localizedViewName, localizedMasterName, useCache);
    ◉  43 : result = base.FindView(controllerContext, viewName, masterName, useCache);
Show on Code Map | Collapse All

2 references | Cedric Bellec, 2 days ago | 1 author, 1 change
public override ViewEngineResult FindView(ControllerContext controllerContext, string viewName, string masterName, bool useCache)
{
```

2. The second item shows who the last developer that updated this class was:

```
namespace K_Na¹
{                    This type was last changed by Cedric Bellec on 12/01/2016 05:13. (Alt+5)
    0 references | Cedric Bellec, 1 day ago | 2 authors, 3 changes
    public class MvcApplication : System.Web.HttpApplication
    {
        0 references | Cedric      ✿ class K_Nal.MvcApplication
        protected void Application_Start()
        {
```

3. The third one shows code changes and collaboration information:

```
0 references | Cedric Bellec, 1 day ago | 2 authors, 3 changes
public class MvcApplication : System.Web.HttpApplication
{                                    This method was edited by 2 authors in 2 unique commits. (Alt+7)
    0 references | Cedric Bellec, 2 days ago | 2 authors, 2 changes
    protected void Application_Start()
    {
```

11. VS 2017 fixes errors for you:
    With Visual Studio 2017, we fix coding errors on the fly while writing code:

    1. We can right-click and select **Quick Actions...** if the little bulb doesn't appear on the left side of our code:

```
        1 reference | Cedric Bellec, 2 days ago | 1 author, 1 change
    public class LocalizedRazorViewEngine : RazorViewEn
    {                                          Quick Actions...              Ctrl+;
```

2. We right-click on the code highlighted in red:

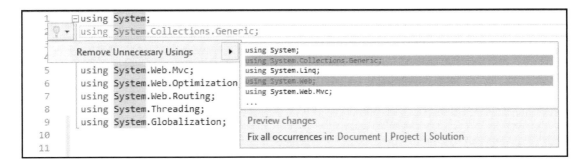

The **Quick Actions...** menu offers a number of possible actions, depending on the context.

3. It also offers some solutions to implement:

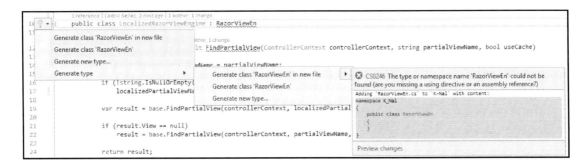

Working with Visual Studio Code

VS Code is a cross-platform, command-line, and file-folder editor. It can be installed on Windows, Linux, or macOS. We can see VS Code as a cross-platform, lightweight version of VS.

Getting ready

First of all, let's download VS Code from `https://code.visualstudio.com/`:

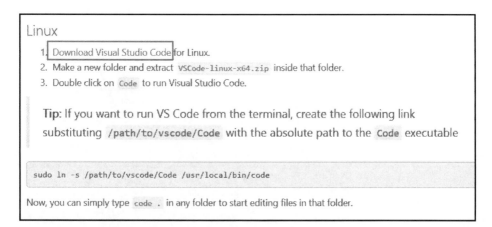

How to do it...

1. Let's launch VS Code by double-clicking on **Code** in the `VSCode-linux-x64` folder:

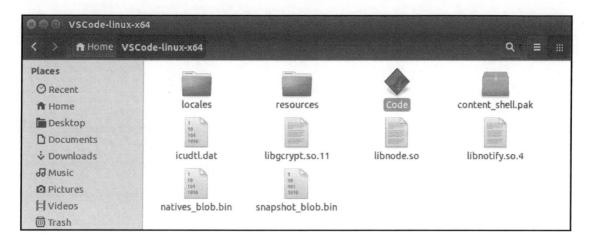

This will open VS Code:

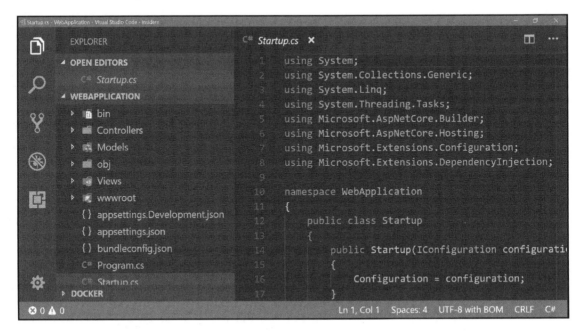

We can press *F1* to make the command palette appear, which gives you access to all the functionality of VS Code.

This way, you can also browse and install extensions by typing the extension.

 To install extensions, you can go to the VS Marketplace (`https://marketplace.visualstudio.com/#VSCode`).

Now, we will open the project we created with the Yeoman scaffolding generator (recipe three) into VS Code, and we will ensure that we have installed dotnet CLI.

2. Let's type *F1* to open the command-line tool in VS Code and type `.NET` to intellisense propose us the option to restore packages with dotnet CLI:

3. We select the `dotnet restore` command:

4. We can see the execution of the previous `dotnet restore` command in the Terminal:

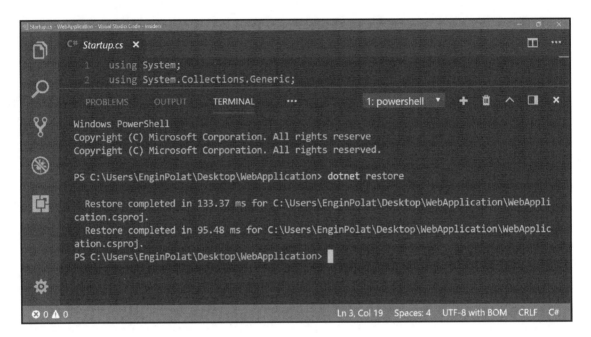

5. Let's run the web application by typing the following command:

```
dotnet run
```

 By default, Kestrel will use port 5004, and VS Code with Kestrel will use port 5000.

6. We see `dotnet run` executed on the Terminal:

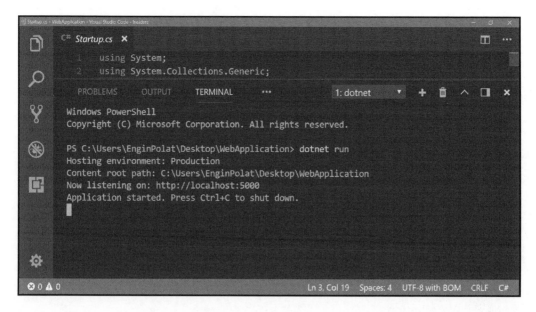

7. Now we can access the application at `http://localhost:5000/`:

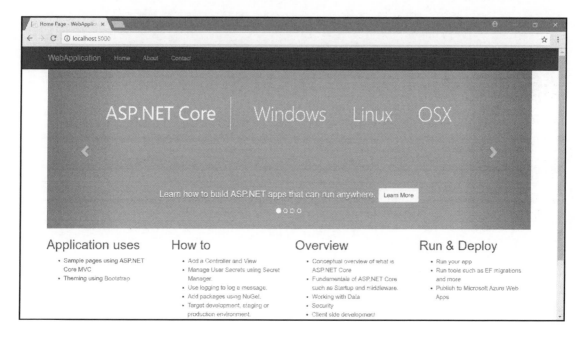

How it works...

VS Code supports many languages and technologies: C#, JS, TypeScript, AngularJS, Less, GIT, HTML, JSON, and SASS. We can associate VS Code with Node.js to get benefits from all task runners features such as gulp or grunt.

We will be able to use all Node.js features through **node package manager** (**npm**), which is a package manager like Maven or NuGet. It's possible to install Node.js using other package managers, such as Chocolatey on Windows or Homebrew on macOS. We can also download it from the official website (`https://nodejs.org/en/download/`).

VS Code has several features, some of which are listed as follows:

- Intellisense
- Debugging
- Version control using `GIT` features
- Snippets
- Warnings
- Code actions
- Go to definitions
- Refactoring

Debugging is available for C#, JavaScript, and TypeScript.

Installing and using OmniSharp on macOS

This recipe explains what OmniSharp is, how to install it, and how it is used on macOS.

How to do it...

In most of the previously mentioned text editors, a package manager is included and will be used to install the OmniSharp package:

1. Edit code on macOS with Atom:

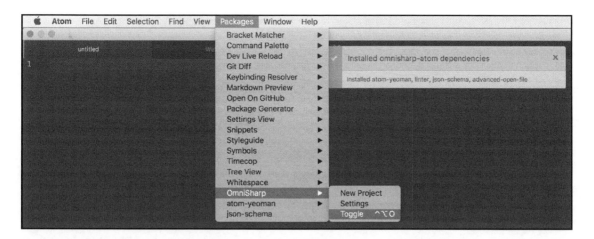

2. Let's install the OmniSharp package on Atom:

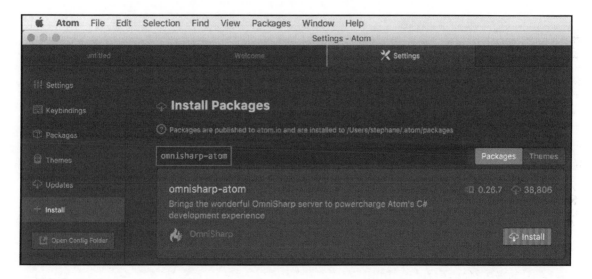

3. Next, let's create a new project:

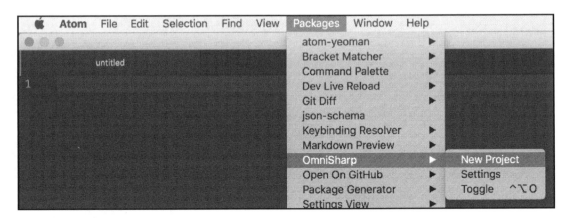

4. Now that OmniSharp is installed, we can use the project scaffolding for .NET projects:

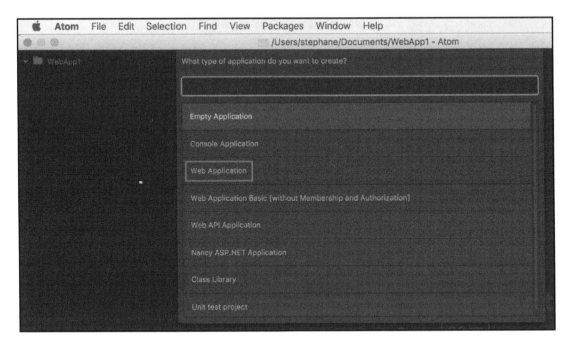

5. After choosing **Web Application**, the project and the associated files are generated.

6. We can see the `Startup.cs` class generated:

At the bottom of the picture, we can see the OmniSharp features on Atom, with the little green OmniSharp icon on the bottom-left, and two panels: the **Errors and Warnings** pane and the **Omnisharp output** pane. The little green icon on the bottom of the page is the OmniSharp icon:

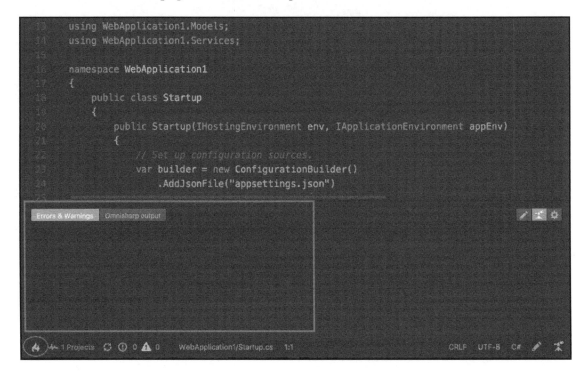

7. Let's type some code; we will see intellisense in action:

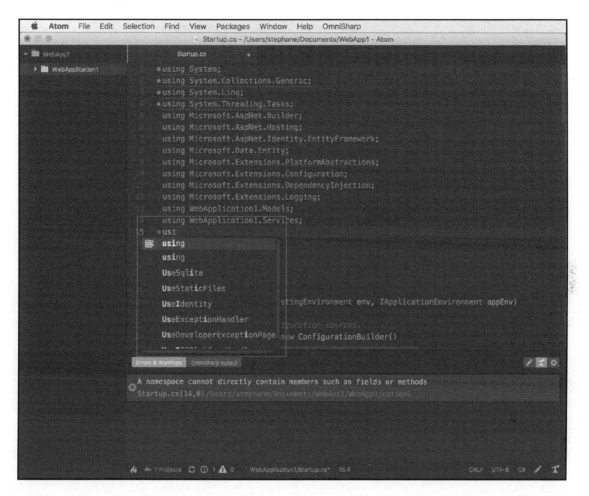

8. We can see what appears on the output window while typing:

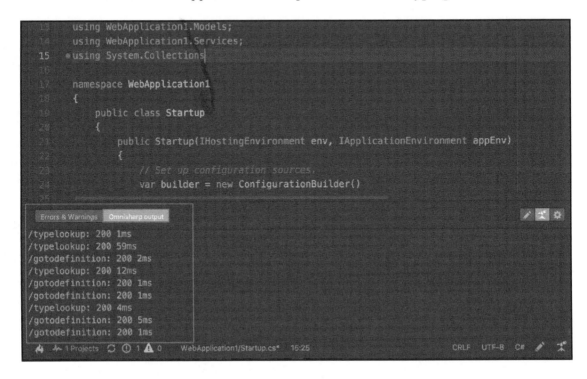

9. We can also see the errors and warnings in real time:

10. Opening the contextual menu by right-clicking, we can see the OmniSharp menu features:

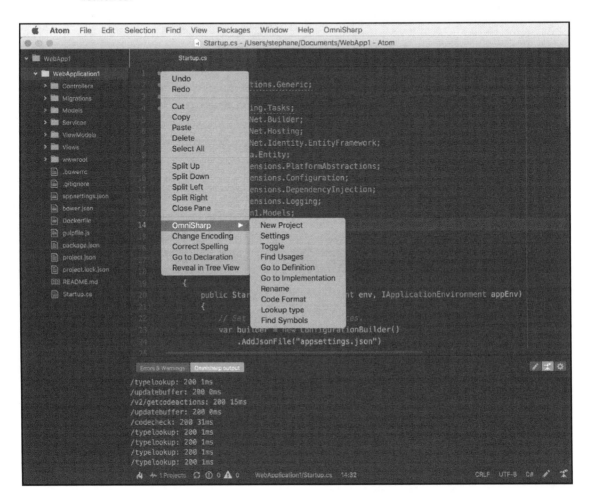

How it works...

OmniSharp is a set of open source tools and extensions used in order to analyze .NET code on macOS and Linux code editors in real time, wrapping the code analysis tools. It was initially a VIM plugin, and it is now a plugin available on Emacs, Brackets, Atom, Sublime Text, VS Code, and VIM. All these code editors are available on Windows, macOS, and Linux.

OmniSharp is linked to your current IDE and will watch the folders of the project you're currently working on, query NuGet, and provide error detection, but its main goal is to provide intellisense for C# and the .NET Framework library outside of VS.

See also

See the official website: `http://www.omnisharp.net/`

Installing and using OmniSharp on Linux

In this recipe, we will install and use OmniSharp with the Atom IDE on Linux.

Getting ready

For this recipe, we will use Ubuntu 14.04 VM. We have to make sure that we have followed recipe three to ensure Mono, DNVM, and the Kestrel web server are installed.

How to do it...

1. First, let's add a repository:

   ```
   sudo add-apt-get repository ppa:webudp8team/atom
   ```

2. Next, we update the repository:

   ```
   sudo apt-get update
   ```

3. After that, we install Atom:

   ```
   sudo apt-get install atom
   ```

4. Now we can launch Atom by typing `atom` in the command line:

   ```
   stef@stef-Virtual-Machine:~$ atom
   ```

We can see Atom opened as follows:

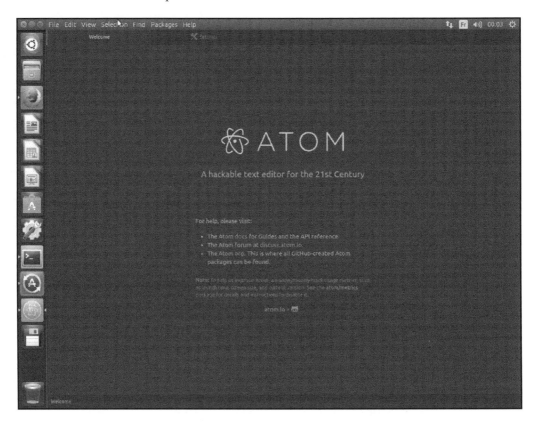

5. Let's install OmniSharp as a package by going to **Settings** | **Install**. We can see all the packages available according to keyword:

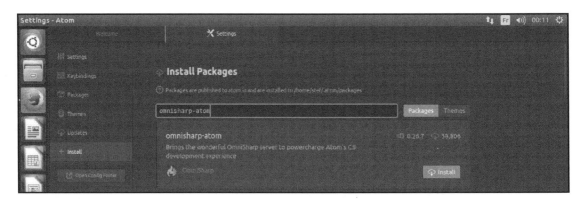

6. OmniSharp is installing the package:

7. OmniSharp has finished installing its dependencies:

8. We will be able to modify OmniSharp options:

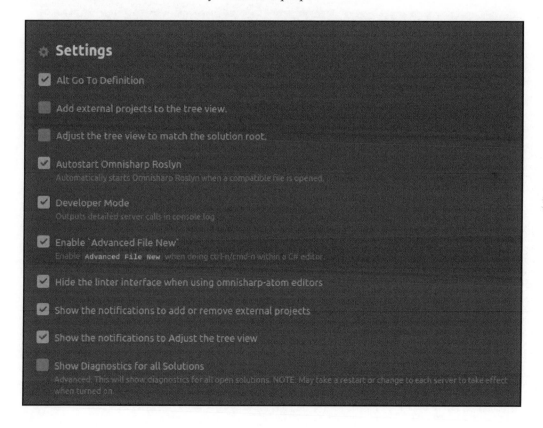

9. Now, let's open a new project by going to **Packages** | **Ominisharp** | **New Project**:

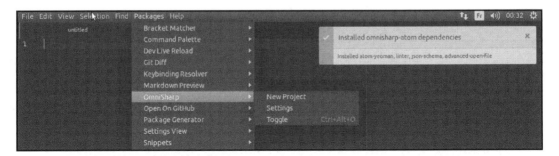

10. When creating a new project, OmniSharp automatically restores the missing packages needed for the application:

```csharp
using System;
using System.Collections.Generic;
using System.Linq;
using System.Threading.Tasks;
using Microsoft.AspNetCore.Builder;
using Microsoft.AspNetCore.Hosting;
using Microsoft.Extensions.Configuration;
using Microsoft.Extensions.DependencyInjection;

namespace WebApplication
{
    public class Startup
    {
        public Startup(IConfiguration configuration)
        {
            Configuration = configuration;
        }

        public IConfiguration Configuration { get; }
```

11. Let's now go into the application folder by the command line to run the application.

12. Run the application with the command `dnx web`:

```
stef@stef-Virtual-Machine: ~/new app/WebApplication2
stef@stef-Virtual-Machine:~/new app/WebApplication2$ dnx web
info: Microsoft.Data.Entity.Storage.Internal.RelationalCommandBuilderFactory[1]
      Executed DbCommand (13ms) [Parameters=[], CommandType='Text', CommandTimeo
ut='30']
      PRAGMA foreign_keys=ON;
info: Microsoft.Data.Entity.Storage.Internal.RelationalCommandBuilderFactory[1]
      Executed DbCommand (1ms) [Parameters=[], CommandType='Text', CommandTimeou
```

13. Earlier, we checked that the web command line was configured to run our Kestrel web server in the `project.json` file of our application:

```
34    "commands": {
35        "web": "Microsoft.AspNet.Server.Kestrel",
36        "ef": "EntityFramework.Commands"
37    },
```

14. We can see our web application running at `http://localhost:5000/`:

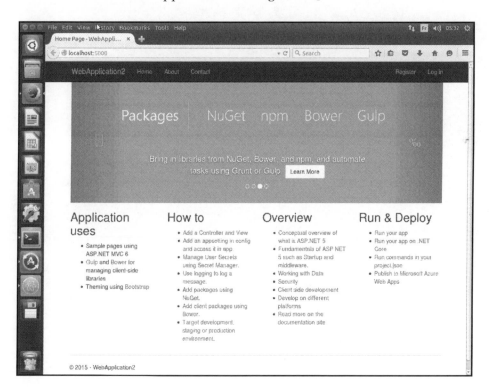

Working with Roslyn

We often think about a compiler as a black box which produces an output from an input. Compilers were generally written in C++ because of speed, custom memory, file, and thread management needs. For example, the C# compiler takes .cs files in input and generates .dll files in output.

Now the new Microsoft compiler written in C# and VB, Roslyn, is not just a compiler; it's a .NET compiler platform that we can extend.

Getting ready

Learning to use all Roslyn APIs could be the subject of an entire book. In this recipe, we will just manipulate one of these APIs: the Syntax Trees API. We will create a Syntax Tree and we will analyze it.

How to do it...

1. Let's download the SDK and extend the compiler, installing the VS extension, **.NET Compiler Platform SDK**, by going through the **Tools | Extensions and Updates** menu, searching for Roslyn SDK:

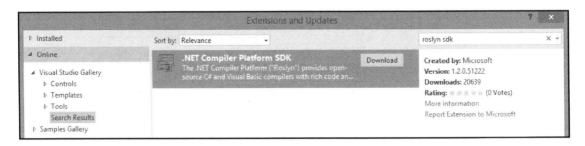

2. We can now download the .NET Compiler Platform SDK templates as a .vsix file, which gives us all the available project templates to create an analyzer:

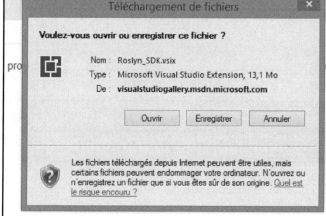

.NET Compiler Platform SDK Templates

Provides three Visual Studio project templates for both C# and Visual Basic that enable the creation of Analyzers, CodeFixes, and stand-alone analysis tools.

Download .NET Compiler Platform SDK Templates »

Téléchargement de fichiers ✕

Voulez-vous ouvrir ou enregistrer ce fichier ?

Nom : Roslyn_SDK.vsix
Type : Microsoft Visual Studio Extension, 13,1 Mo
De : **visualstudiogallery.msdn.microsoft.com**

Ouvrir | Enregistrer | Annuler

Les fichiers téléchargés depuis Internet peuvent être utiles, mais certains fichiers peuvent endommager votre ordinateur. N'ouvrez ou n'enregistrez un fichier que si vous êtes sûr de son origine. Quel est le risque encouru ?

pro ... equired templates.

3. We can now use the template projects in **New Project** | **Visual C#** | **Extensibility** | **Stand-Alone Code Analysis Tool**.

4. Let's open a new console application for an **Extensibility** project:

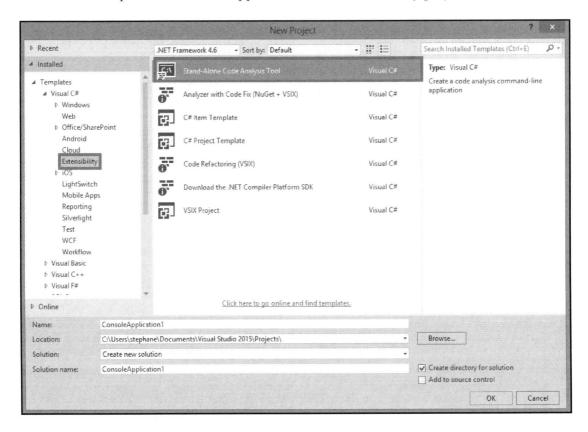

This console application will access the Roslyn API, with which we will be able to use the Syntax Tree API.

5. Let's now create a SyntaxTree, which is simply a class represented by a tree structure of elements using the SyntaxTree type:

```
using System;
using System.Collections.Generic;
using System.Linq;
using System.Text;
using Microsoft.CodeAnalysis;
using Microsoft.CodeAnalysis.CSharp;
using Microsoft.CodeAnalysis.CSharp.Symbols;
using Microsoft.CodeAnalysis.CSharp.Syntax;
using Microsoft.CodeAnalysis.Text;

namespace ConsoleApplication1
{
    0 references
    class Program
    {
        0 references
        static void Main(string[] args)
        {
            var tree = CSharpSynt.
        }
    }
}
```

CSharpSyntaxNode
CSharpSyntaxRewriter
CSharpSyntaxTree   class Microsoft.CodeAnalysis.CSharp.CSharpSyntaxTree
CSharpSyntaxVisitor   The parsed representation of a C# source document.
CSharpSyntaxVisitor<>
CSharpSyntaxWalker

This type has a method named `ParseText`, which will parse a string where a class is written:

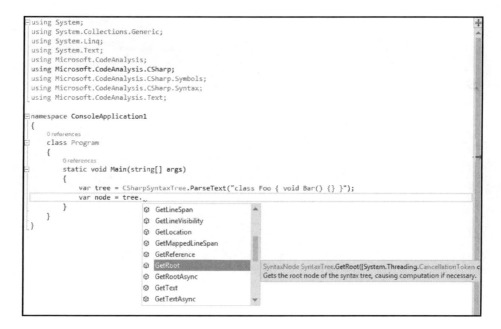

6. Let's write this piece of code:

```csharp
using System;
using System.Collections.Generic;
using System.Linq;
using System.Text;
using Microsoft.CodeAnalysis;
using Microsoft.CodeAnalysis.CSharp;
using Microsoft.CodeAnalysis.CSharp.Symbols;
using Microsoft.CodeAnalysis.CSharp.Syntax;
using Microsoft.CodeAnalysis.Text;

namespace ConsoleApplication1
{
    0 references
    class Program
    {
        0 references
        static void Main(string[] args)
        {
            var tree = CSharpSyntaxTree.ParseText("class Foo { void Bar() {} }");
            var node = tree.GetRoot();
            Console.WriteLine(node.ToString());
        }
    }
}
```

```
C:\WINDOWS\system32\cmd.exe                                    _  □  ✕

class Foo { void Bar() {} }
Appuyez sur une touche pour continuer... _
```

The GetRoot method will give us the root of the tree.

7. Using *Ctrl + F5*, we see the result.
8. Now, thanks to the `SyntaxFactory` type, let's create the same class by creating a `SyntaxTree` with the `Syntax` API:

```
namespace ConsoleApplication1
{
    0 references
    class Program
    {
        0 references
        static void Main(string[] args)
        {
            var tree = CSharpSyntaxTree.ParseText("class Foo { void Bar() {} }");
            var node = tree.GetRoot();
            Console.WriteLine(node.ToString());

            var res = SyntaxFact
        }                    SyntaxFactory    class Microsoft.CodeAnalysis.CSharp.SyntaxFactory
    }                       SyntaxFacts      A class containing factory methods for constructing syntax nodes, tokens and trivia.
}
```

9. With the `SyntaxFactory.ClassDeclaration` method, we create the class name:

```
    class Program
    {
        0 references
        static void Main(string[] args)
        {
            var tree = CSharpSyntaxTree.ParseText("class Foo { void Bar() {} }");
            var node = tree.GetRoot();
            Console.WriteLine(node.ToString());

            var res = SyntaxFactory.ClassDeclaration("Foo")
        }
    }
}
```

10. The `WithMembers` method allows us to create members of this class:

```
class Program
{
    0 references
    static void Main(string[] args)
    {
        var tree = CSharpSyntaxTree.ParseText("class Foo { void Bar() {} }");
        var node = tree.GetRoot();
        Console.WriteLine(node.ToString());

        var res = SyntaxFactory.ClassDeclaration("Foo")
            .WithMembers(SyntaxFactory.List<MemberDeclarationSyntax>(new[]
            {

            }))
    }
}
```

11. Now we create a method named `Bar` with `void` as the return type.

12. The `WithBody` method and its `SyntaxFactory.Block` parameter help us to add an empty block to the `Bar` method:

```csharp
using System;
using System.Collections.Generic;
using System.Linq;
using System.Text;
using Microsoft.CodeAnalysis;
using Microsoft.CodeAnalysis.CSharp;
using Microsoft.CodeAnalysis.CSharp.Symbols;
using Microsoft.CodeAnalysis.CSharp.Syntax;
using Microsoft.CodeAnalysis.Text;

namespace ConsoleApplication1
{
    0 references
    class Program
    {
        0 references
        static void Main(string[] args)
        {
            var tree = CSharpSyntaxTree.ParseText("class Foo { void Bar() {} }");
            var node = tree.GetRoot();
            Console.WriteLine(node.ToString());

            var res = SyntaxFactory.ClassDeclaration("Foo")
                .WithMembers(SyntaxFactory.List<MemberDeclarationSyntax>(new[]
                {
                    SyntaxFactory.MethodDeclaration(
                        SyntaxFactory.PredefinedType(
                            SyntaxFactory.Token(SyntaxKind.VoidKeyword)
                        ), "Bar"
                    )
                    .WithBody(SyntaxFactory.Block()
                    )
                }))~

        }
    }
}
```

13. The `NormalizeWithespace` method will add indentation and spaces to make this class more readable:

```
using System;
using System.Collections.Generic;
using System.Linq;
using System.Text;
using Microsoft.CodeAnalysis;
using Microsoft.CodeAnalysis.CSharp;
using Microsoft.CodeAnalysis.CSharp.Symbols;
using Microsoft.CodeAnalysis.CSharp.Syntax;
using Microsoft.CodeAnalysis.Text;

namespace ConsoleApplication1
{
    0 references
    class Program
    {
        0 references
        static void Main(string[] args)
        {
            var tree = CSharpSyntaxTree.ParseText("class Foo { void Bar() {} }");
            var node = tree.GetRoot();
            Console.WriteLine(node.ToString());

            var res = SyntaxFactory.ClassDeclaration("Foo")
                .WithMembers(SyntaxFactory.List<MemberDeclarationSyntax>(new[]
                {
                    SyntaxFactory.MethodDeclaration(
                        SyntaxFactory.PredefinedType(
                            SyntaxFactory.Token(SyntaxKind.VoidKeyword)
                        ), "Bar"
                    )
                    .WithBody(SyntaxFactory.Block()
                    )
                }))
                .NormalizeWhitespace();
        }
    }
}
```

14. Let's press *Ctrl + F5* to see the result of our code, putting the variable representing the Syntax Tree as the parameter of `Console.WriteLine`:

```csharp
using System;
using System.Collections.Generic;
using System.Linq;
using System.Text;
using Microsoft.CodeAnalysis;
using Microsoft.CodeAnalysis.CSharp;
using Microsoft.CodeAnalysis.CSharp.Symbols;
using Microsoft.CodeAnalysis.CSharp.Syntax;
using Microsoft.CodeAnalysis.Text;

namespace ConsoleApplication1
{
    0 references
    class Program
    {
        0 references
        static void Main(string[] args)
        {
            var tree = CSharpSyntaxTree.ParseText("class Foo { void Bar() {} }");
            var node = tree.GetRoot();
            Console.WriteLine(node.ToString());

            var res = SyntaxFactory.ClassDeclaration("Foo")
                .WithMembers(SyntaxFactory.List<MemberDeclarationSyntax>(new[]
                {
                    SyntaxFactory.MethodDeclaration(
                        SyntaxFactory.PredefinedType(
                            SyntaxFactory.Token(SyntaxKind.VoidKeyword)
                        ), "Bar"
                    )
                    .WithBody(SyntaxFactory.Block()
                    )
                }))
                .NormalizeWhitespace();

            Console.WriteLine(res.ToString());
        }
    }
}
```

```
class Foo
{
    void Bar()
    {
    }
}
appuyez sur une touche pour continuer...
```

How it works...

Roslyn is open source, like the TypeScript compiler. One of the reasons to have our compiler written in the same language we analyze and compile, to have the benefits of the .NET Framework; for example, using `lambdas` and `LINQ` in the immediate window. Another advantage is to see all the compiler code with a tool like ILSpy.

We will now have access to all stages of our compiler through an API, which allows us to manipulate an object model representing the source code we are analyzing as a Syntax Tree. Through these APIs, we will have access to a rich set of language services we can integrate to editors.

APIs

Inside a compiler, the components are the following:

- Parser
- Symbols and metadata import
- Binder
- IL emitter

For each component of the pipeline, we now have a set of compiler APIs we can use:

- For parser: the Syntax Tree API
- For symbols and metadata import: the Symbol API
- For binder: the Binding and Flow Analysis APIs
- For IL emitter: the Emit API

We also have the Workspace, the Diagnostic APIs, and the Scripting APIs.

Using C# 6 new features

In this recipe, we will discover some of the new features in C# 6.

How to do it...

1. Feature one—auto initializer for properties:

   Before C# 6, we should initialize a property with a value in the class constructor. There is no point in time before the class constructor, so we should use it. Thanks to C# 6 syntax, we can now initialize a property with a value right on the declaration line. No need to use constructor anymore:

   - Before:

     ```
     public class Person
     {
      Public class Name {get;set;}
      Public Person(){
      Name = "Stephane";
      }
     }
     ```

   - Now:

     ```
     Public string Name {get;set;} = "Stephane";
     ```

2. Feature two—auto initializer for static properties:

   Auto initializers can be applied to static properties, as well:

   - Before:

     ```
     Public static string Name {get;set;}
     ```

   - Now:

     ```
     Public static string Name {get;set;} = "Stephane";
     ```

3. Feature three—read-only properties:

Auto initializers can even be applied to read-only properties:

- Before:

```
public List SocialNetworks { get; }
```

- Now:

```
public List SocialNetworks { get; } =
new List { "Twitter", "Facebook", "Instagram" };
```

- Before:

```
Dictionary<string, User> Users = new Dictionary<string,
User>()
{
 { "root", new User("root") },
 { "baseUser", new User("baseUser")}
};
```

- Now:

```
Dictionary<string, User> Users = new Dictionary<string,
User>()
{
 ["root"] = new User("root"),
 ["baseUser"] = new User("baseUser")
};
```

4. Feature four—expression-bodied members:

Simple functions (functions with just a `return` statement) can now be written inline:

- Before:

```
public double GetVAT(int someValue)
{
 return someValue * 1.2;
}
```

- Now:

```
public double GetVAT(int someValue) => someValue * 1.2;
private DateTime timestamp;
```

- Before:

```
public DateTime TimeStampCreated
{
 get
 {
 return timestamp;
 }
}
```

- Now:

```
public DateTime TimeStampCreated => timestamp;
public static string ReadFile(string fileName) =>
Disposable.Using(
() => System.IO.File.OpenText(fileName),
r => r.ReadToEnd());
```

The previous piece of code highlights a potential problem that already exists in CSharp, since lambda expressions exist.

It is easy to make fun when writing lambda expressions by creating concise code. It is also easy to write unreadable code, especially for those who will have to use this code. Another problem is that this code is hard to debug.

5. Feature five—interpolated strings:

We can reference variables by their names directly in the code by using the dollar sign just before the string used to include the variable:

```
var name = "Stephane";
string.Format($"My name is {name}");
```

6. Feature six—null-conditional operators:

To return a `null` value, we can use a new syntax that allows us to not declare a `null` variable before returning it:

- Before:

```
var username = (User != null) ? User.Name :
string.empty;
```

- Now:

```
var username = User?.Name;
```

See also...

New features in C# 6: `http://blogs.msdn.com/b/csharpfaq/archive/2014/11/20/new-features-in-c-6.aspx`

New language reatures in C# 6: `https://github.com/dotnet/roslyn/wiki/New-Language-Features-in-C%23-6`

Interpolated strings: `https://msdn.microsoft.com/en-us/library/dn961160.aspx`

Null-conditional operators: `https://msdn.microsoft.com/en-us/library/dn986595.aspx`

3
Working with npm, Frontend Package Managers, and Task Runners

In this chapter, we will learn the following recipes:

- Using and creating npm modules
- Managing frontend dependencies with Bower
- Compiling LESS files to CSS files with Grunt
- Bundling and minifying JavaScript files with Gulp
- Using Yeoman code-generated templates
- Using JSPM

Introduction

In this chapter, we will learn about Node.js, Node modules, package managers, and task runners. With ASP.NET Core, we have different options to manage packages: NuGet, **node package manager** (**npm**), Bower, and JSPM. Most of the time, NuGet is used to manage .NET packages for server-side libraries, but it doesn't have to be used. We will cover NuGet in the next chapter. npm manages the JavaScript packages and modules for Node.js. Bower handles frontend dependencies (such as JavaScript, CSS, and other stuff, such as fonts). JSPM does the same as Bower, but also loads and compiles JavaScript files as AMD modules at runtime.

In this chapter, we will explore all these ways of managing client-side dependencies and how to use the two most famous task runners in the Node.js world, namely Grunt and Gulp.

Using and creating npm modules

Node.js (`https://nodejs.org/en/`) is an asynchronous, monothread web server built on Chrome's V8 JavaScript engine. It executes server-side, JavaScript-compiled code, and it is event based, like JavaScript.

The npm (`https://www.npmjs.com/`) manages the Node.js package ecosystem composed of open source JavaScript libraries. We will use npm using the command line and install all the node packages or modules in this way.

We can also use npm as a fast-build pipeline to develop, test, minify, and deploy our apps.

In this recipe, we will learn how to create and publish our own node package.

Getting ready

The installation of Visual Studio 2015 Community Edition includes the installation of Node.js, which is the IDE we will use during the processes described in this book. If, for some reason, Node.js is not installed with Visual Studio 2015, we can install it by going to the Node.js download page at `https://nodejs.org/en/download/`. The npm will be installed with Node.js:

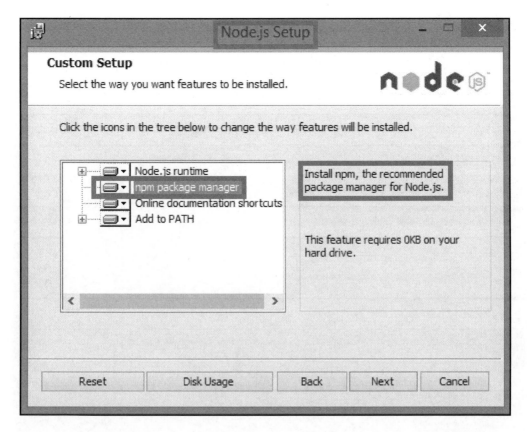

We can see from the preceding screenshot that installing Node.js also installs npm.

How to do it...

Here we will see how to create and publish a node package.

Creating a node package

1. Let's create a node package in the current folder that we are located in:

```
npm init
```

2. We answer a series of questions (regarding the **author**, **name**, **license**, and so on) that will fill the `package.json` file that will be created. Pressing *Enter* for each question will give the default answer to the question:

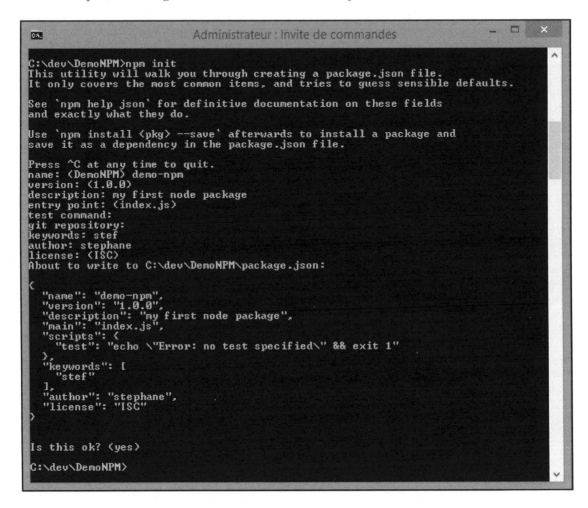

3. We could also enter the following command line to do the same, filling in all the questions with the default answers:

```
npm init -y
```

Publishing the package

1. First, let's create an account on the npm website:

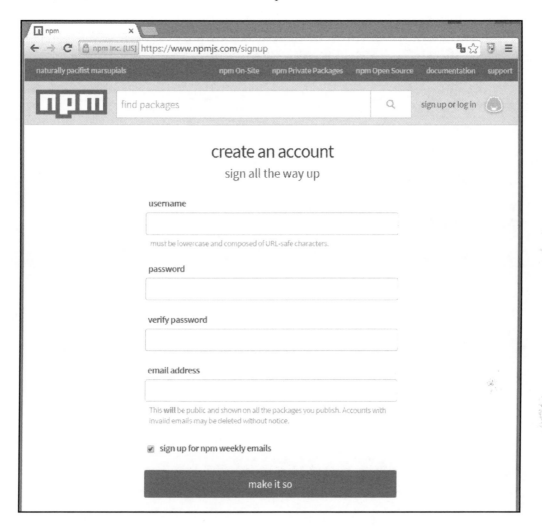

2. Now we can connect to the repository with our credentials by using the command line. The repository will be Git. Let's type the following:

```
npm adduser
```

3. We answer three questions about the username, password, and email:

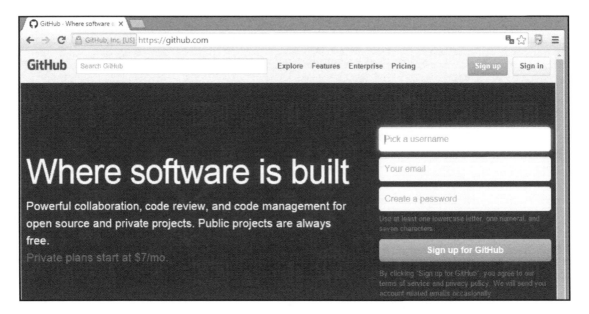

4. After that, we create the Git repository locally by typing the following:

```
git init
```

5. Let's now go to the GitHub website to create a remote repository. First, we need to create an account, if we don't have one yet.

6. To create an account we need to fill the form on the GitHub create-account page, which will provide `project.json`:

```
git remote add origin 'repo-url-adress'

npm init
```

Create a repository on your GitHub account:

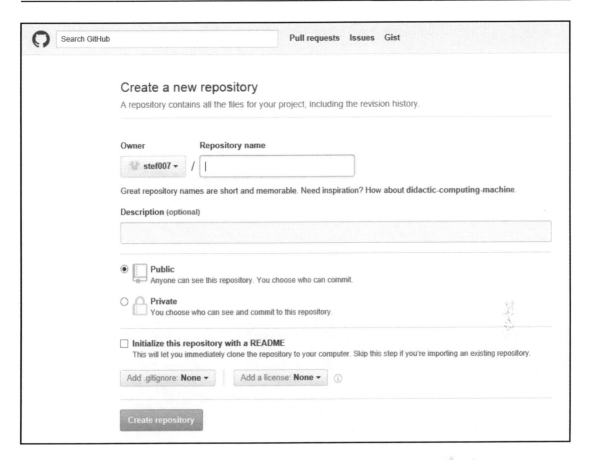

7. To push `package.json` on the GitHub online repository, enter the following:

```
git add .

git commit -m "my comment"

git push

git push origin master
```

8. Now let's type the following in our local project Git repository:

```
npm publish
```

If we excute the following command, we can see the `package.json`:

```
npm info [packagename]
```

Excute the following command:

```
npm repo [packagename]
```

A web page is launched on our GitHub repository website listing the existing files of our npm package.

If we type `http://npm.im/packagename` in the browser address bar, we will see our package homepage on the npm website.

We can find our node package on the npm website `https://www.npmjs.com/`, synchronized with our **GitHub** website `https://github.com/` repository.

How it works...

The difference between a package and a module is as follows: a module contains a single JavaScript file that has certain functionalities. A package is a directory that contains several modules with a metadata file for each package. This metadata file will be a `package.json` file that is used to create scripts and track dependencies.

We will find this file at the root of the ASP.NET Core projects. It will list the node packages used in our applications.

 Asynchronous module definition (**AMD**) is a concept or pattern that is used to provide a solution to create modular code in several JavaScript files and load them separately and asynchronously, even if they are interdependent.

There's more...

1. To run scripts, enter the following:

```
npm run [nameofthescriptwithextension]
```

2. To install packages, enter the following:

```
npm install [nameofthepackage]
```

3. To install packages and save the dependency in `package.json`, enter the following:

```
npm i [nameofthepackage] -S
```

4. To list all the node packages installed on your computer, enter the following:

```
npm list -global true

//Or

npm ls
```

5. To install a package for global use, add `-g` at the end:

```
npm install gulp -g
```

6. To upgrade npm, enter the following:

```
npm I npm@latest -g
```

Managing frontend dependencies with Bower

Bower is a frontend package manager. It is used in the web development world to install and uninstall JavaScript and CSS frameworks, including their fonts. The official documentation can be found here: `http://bower.io/`.

In this recipe, we will learn how to manage frontend dependencies with Bower.

Getting ready

We will assume that we have already installed Visual Studio 2015 Community Edition, which is a free version of Visual Studio for Windows.

How to do it...

1. To install a frontend dependency with Bower in ASP.NET Core project using Visual Studio, we just have to right-click the project name in **Solution Explorer** and select **Manage Bower Package** in the contextual menu:

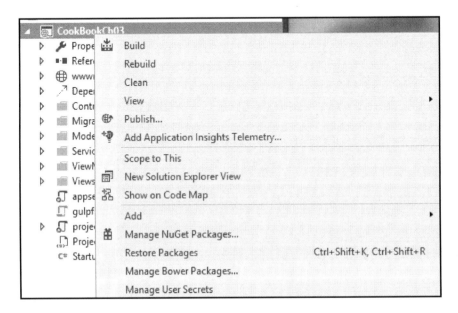

Using the **Manage Browser Packages** window, we can install, uninstall, or update packages such as Bootstrap, jQuery, AngularJS, and a lot more. The **Manage Bower Packages** dialog box is now open:

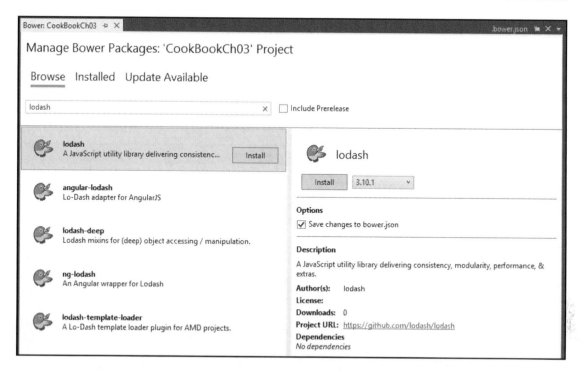

2. Let's install the `LoDash` library with Bower by clicking the **Install** button.

   We can see in the **Output** window that Visual Studio internally uses Bower's command lines, which we could use ourselves, without Visual Studio, to install packages from Bower. We can see the location from which the version dependency is downloaded (GitHub in this case) and the destination folder:

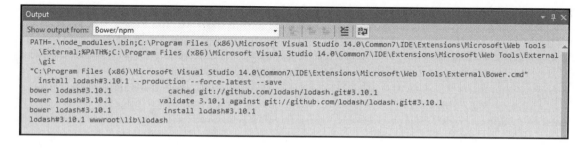

How it works...

Every newly installed package will be placed in the `lib` folder inside the `wwwroot` folder. This root folder exposes all the files accessed by HTTP requests. It contains all the static files of the application:

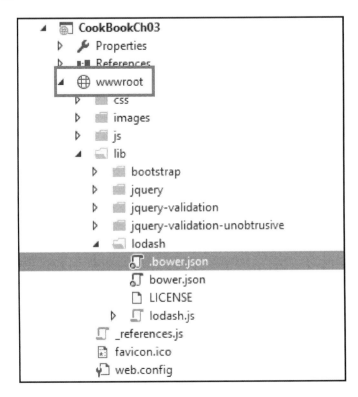

In the `wwwroot` folder, each dependency has its own folder and in this folder, each has its own `.bower.json` file. This JSON file describes all the information relevant to the client-side framework.

Opening the `.bower.json` file located in the `lodash` folder, we can see a JSON object that contains the `name`, the `main` files, `version`, license, and dependencies, if the package has any:

```
Schema: http://json.schemastore.org/bower
   1 💡  ⊟ {
   2          "name": "lodash",
   3          "main": "lodash.js",
   4      ⊞   "ignore": [...],
  19          "homepage": "https://github.com/lodash/lodash",
  20          "version": "3.10.1",
  21          "_release": "3.10.1",
  22      ⊞   "_resolution": [...],
  27          "_source": "git://github.com/lodash/lodash.git",
  28          "_target": "3.10.1",
  29          "_originalSource": "lodash",
  30          "_direct": true
  31      }
```

Global information about Bower packages will be visible in the bower.json file at the root of the application, especially the list of the installed dependencies in our application. We can see the details of this file in the following screenshot:

```
Schema: http://json.schemastore.org/bower
   1    ⊟ {
   2          "name": "ASP.NET",
   3          "private": true,
   4      ⊟   "dependencies": {
   5            "bootstrap": "3.3.5",
   6            "jquery": "2.1.4",
   7            "jquery-validation": "1.14.0",
   8            "jquery-validation-unobtrusive": "3.2.4",
   9            "lodash": "3.10.1"
  10          }
  11      }
```

In the project folder named `Dependencies`, just under `wwwrooot`, we can also see the list in the following screenshot:

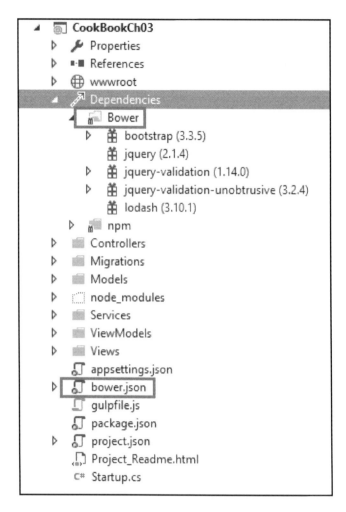

Before Bower, NuGet was the only package manager for all dependencies. We will now use NuGet for .NET external dependencies and Bower for frontend dependencies (JavaScript, CSS, fonts, and so on). Bower is installed when any version of Visual Studio is installed, and comes with the Node.js world-with npm, Gulp, and Grunt. We can also install it as a `Node` module by using this link `https://www.npmjs.com/package/bower` so that we can use it without Visual Studio with another IDE, after having installed Node.js, npm, and Git.

There's more...

With Bower, we could also create our own package, but that's not part of this recipe.

See also

To create the aforementioned package, please refer to the Pluralsight (`https://www.pluralsight.com/`) course *Bower Fundamentals* by Joe Eames at `https://www.pluralsight.com/courses/bower-fundamentals`.

Compiling LESS files to CSS files with Grunt

In this recipe, we will learn how to compile LESS files to CSS files with a task runner named Grunt.

Getting ready

For this recipe, we will assume that you've already installed Visual Studio 2015 Community and that the installer automatically installed Node.js and npm.

After that, we will have to install all the modules we need to execute all the tasks we want to run.

How to do it...

We can use Grunt in two ways:

Without using Visual Studio, through the command line, using Command Prompt, Node.js, npm, and installing and using all the modules you need to execute all the tasks we want to run.

Installing Visual Studio 2015 Community Edition and the Visual Studio extensions that allow us to run these tasks in the Visual Studio user interface.

In this recipe, we will use Grunt in the second of these two ways, using Visual Studio to compile LESS files to CSS files:

1. To install Grunt, let's open `package.json`, or if we begin from an empty project, just add a `package.json` file.

2. Let's type grunt in the `devDependencies` section. IntelliSense will help us to find the Grunt package:

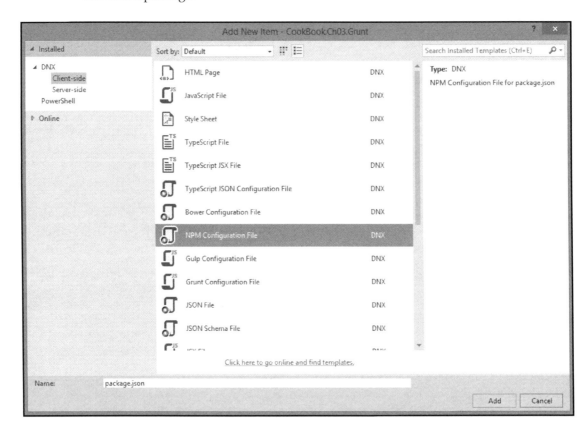

3. After that, we type the version. IntelliSense will also help us to find the right Grunt version among all of the available versions. The `grunt` package will be downloaded automatically:

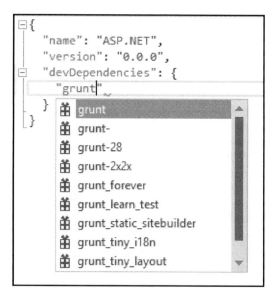

Select the version of the package you wish to use.

4. We can also observe the new `npm` folder inside `Dependencies`, which contains the new `Node` module just installed, as well as all of its dependencies:

```
Output                                                                    ─ □ ✕
Show output from: Bower/npm                          ▼   ⸝  ⸝ ⸝  ⤨  ⸝⸝
PATH=.\node_modules\.bin;C:\Program Files (x86)\Microsoft Visual Studio\Preview\Enterprise\Web\External; ▲
"C:\Program Files (x86)\Microsoft Visual Studio\Preview\Enterprise\Web\External\npm.CMD" install
npm WARN prefer global coffeescript@1.10.0 should be installed with -g
npm WARN prefer global coffeescript@1.10.0 should be installed with -g
webapplication@1.0.0 C:\Users\EnginPolat\Desktop\WebApplication
└─┬ grunt@1.0.2
  ├── coffeescript@1.10.0
  ├─ dateformat@1.0.12
  ├── get-stdin@4.0.1
  └─┬ meow@3.7.0
    ├─┬ camelcase-keys@2.1.0
    │ └── camelcase@2.1.1
    ├── decamelize@1.2.0
    ├─┬ loud-rejection@1.6.0
    │ ├─┬ currently-unhandled@0.4.1
    │ │ └── array-find-index@1.0.2
    │ └── signal-exit@3.0.2
    ├── map-obj@1.0.1
    ├── minimist@1.2.0
    ├─┬ normalize-package-data@2.4.0
    │ ├── hosted-git-info@2.5.0
    │ ├─┬ is-builtin-module@1.0.0
    │ │ └── builtin-modules@1.1.1
    │ ├── semver@5.5.0
    │ └─┬ validate-npm-package-license@3.0.1
    │   ├─┬ spdx-correct@1.0.2
    │   │ └── spdx-license-ids@1.2.2
    │   └── spdx-expression-parse@1.0.4
    ├── object-assign@4.1.1
    ├─┬ read-pkg-up@1.0.1
    │ ├─┬ find-up@1.1.2
    │ │ ├── path-exists@2.1.0
    │ │ └─┬ pinkie-promise@2.0.1                                          ▼
◄ ▒▒▒▒▒▒▒▒▒▒▒▒▒▒▒                                                    ►
```

5. Let's create a `.less` file named `site.less`, selecting **File** | **New** item in the `wwwroot/css` folder:

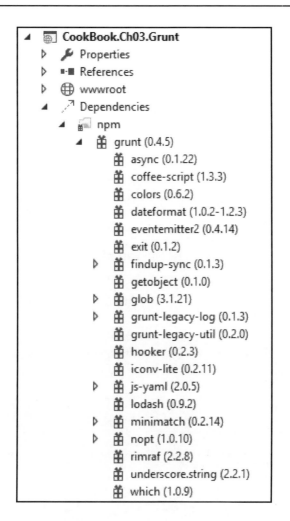

6. Let's add two grunt packages:
    - `grunt-contrib-less` to compile `.less` files to `.css` files.
    - `grunt-contrib-watch` to automate this task, watching the modifications being made to a `.less` file in real time:

7. Let's create the `Gruntfile.js` by right-clicking on the application and choosing **Add** | **New Item** | **DNX** | **client-side:**

```
"devDependencies": {
    "grunt": "0.4.5",
    "grunt-contrib-less": "1.1.0",
    "grunt-contrib-watch"
}
```

8. Let's add the following line of code to the `initConfig` method:

```
pkg: grunt.file.readJSON('package.json')
```

9. Let's create the less task, which will compile a `.less` file into a `.css` file.

10. We add the following code after `grunt.config` to be sure that our task uses the correct plugin:

```
grunt.loadNpmTasks('grunt-contrib-less');
```

11. We will then add the following code to register this task as the default `grunt` task:

```
grunt.registerTask('default', ['less']);
```

Let's refresh the `gruntfile.js`:

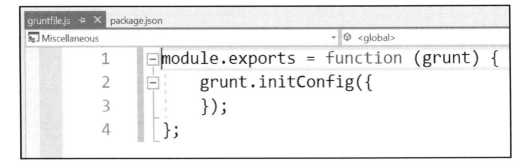

```
module.exports = function (grunt) {
    grunt.initConfig({
    });
};
```

12. After refreshing the `gruntfile.js`, we can see the `.less` task just created:

```
gruntfile.js  ↗  ×
{ } module                                              ▾  ⊕ exports(grunt)
  1  ⊟/*
  2   │  This file in the main entry point for defining grunt tasks and using grunt plugins.
  3   │  Click here to learn more. http://go.microsoft.com/fwlink/?LinkID=513275&clcid=0x409
  4   │ */
  5  ⊟module.exports = function (grunt) {
  6  ⊟     grunt.initConfig({
  7   │         pkg: grunt.file.readJSON('package.json'),
  8  ⊟         less: {
  9   │             // production config is also available
 10  ⊟             development: {
 11  ⊟                 options: {
 12  ⊟                     // Specifies directories to scan for @import directives when parsing.
 13   │                     // Default value is the directory of the source, which is probably what you want.
 14   │                     paths: ["wwwroot/css/"],
 15   │                 },
 16  ⊟                 files: {
 17   │                     // compilation.css  :  source.less
 18   │                     "wwwroot/css/site.css": "wwwroot/css/site.less"
 19   │                 }
 20   │             }
 21   │         },
 22   │     });
 23
 24   │     // Load the plugin that provides the "less" task.
 25   │     grunt.loadNpmTasks('grunt-contrib-less');
 26
 27   │     // Default task(s).
 28   │     grunt.registerTask('default', ['less']);
 29
 30  └};
```

13. Let's now run the task by right-clicking on the name of the task in **Task Runner Explorer**:

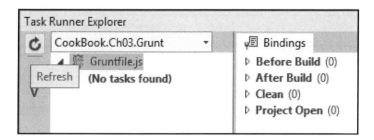

We can see the command line that is generated by Visual Studio:

Now we can also see that the `.css` file is generated:

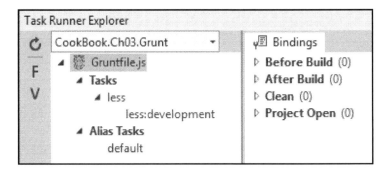

We can see the `.css` code has been generated as well:

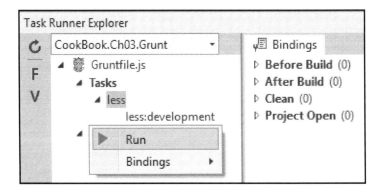

How it works...

During a web developer's day, a lot of repetitive tasks are executed: minification or compression (deleting whitespaces in the file), bundlisation (forming one file out of several files, so that there is only one file that uses only one HTTP request to send a few files to a client), validation of the CSS and JavaScript, compilation and code checking for TypeScript, CoffeScript, or CSS preprocessor, and minimizing and optimizing pictures so that you have different versions of your pictures according to the different platforms that your applications run on.

All these tasks can be done by a task runner. All task runners work with Node.js, and are composed of plugins written in JavaScript (like everything that works on Node.js). Grunt is the older task runner on Node.js, with more than 4,000 plugins, and is one of the most famous.

There's more...

There are other ways to install and use Grunt. When using Visual Studio 2015, we can install a Visual Studio extension named Grunt Launcher. This extension will launch Grunt, Gulp, and Bower commands in Visual Studio when you right-click the `gruntfile.js` of your application.

It can be installed in two ways:

- From the IDE menu go to **Tools** | **Extentions and Updates** | **Online** | **Search** | **Task runner explorer**
- Downloading the extension as a `.vsix` file from `https://visualstudiogallery.msdn.microsoft.com/dcbc5325-79ef-4b72-960e-0a51ee33a0ff`

See also

We can also download the Web Extension Pack (`https://visualstudiogallery.msdn.microsoft.com/f3b504c6-0095-42f1-a989-51d5fc2a8459`) from the same creator, Mads Kristensen. This pack installs some very useful extensions for web development to use inside Visual Studio, such as Web Essentials, Web Compiler (for compiling LESS, Scss, Stylus, JSX, and CoffeeScript files), Bundler and Minifier (for bundling and minifying JS, CSS, and HTML files), and Image Optimizer (for lossless optimization of PNGs, JPGs, and GIFs).

Bundling and minifying JavaScript files with Gulp

In this recipe, we will learn how to bundle and minify two JavaScript files with the Gulp task runner.

Getting ready

We will assume that you've already installed Visual Studio 2015 Community Edition, and that the installer automatically installed Node.js and npm. Here are the two JavaScript files to bundle and minify:

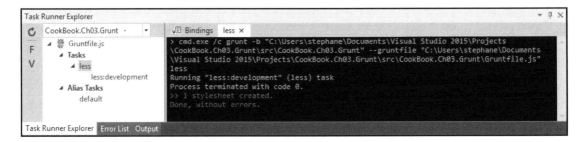

Let's see the code of the first of these two files:

Here is the code of the second:

```
site.css
1  body {
2      background-color: #2d5e8b;
3  }
```

How to do it...

1. First, we add Gulp to `package.json` and the `Gulp` plugins. Then we need to minify and bundle these two JavaScript files if this file doesn't exist in the web application:

2. We add the `gulp-concat` plugin, which concatenates the (bundle) files, and then we add `gulp-uglify`, which minifies the `.js` files, removing whitespaces and comments, and writes the name of the module we want to add to the `devDependencies` section:

```
script1.js
<global>
1    var Foobar = Foobar || {};
2    Foobar.Toto = (function (Toto) {
3        // Modification du namespace
4        return Toto;
5    })(Foobar.Toto || {});
6
```

3. Let's create a `gulpfile.js` (a gulp configuration file):

4. The generated file contains the following code:

```
script2.js  ⇥  X
⠿ <global>
  1  ⊟var Foobar2 = (function () {
  2        var visible = function () { };
  3        var notVisible = function () { };
  4
  5  ⊟      return {
  6            visible: visible
  7        };
  8  })();
```

5. Let's add the following code in order to store the file paths for the files we will manipulate:

```
package.json*  ⇥  X
Schema: http://json.schemastore.org/package
  1  ⊟{
  2       "name": "ASP.NET",
  3       "version": "0.0.0",
  4  ⊟    "devDependencies": {
  5         "gulp": "|
  6       }              ⊞ 3.9.0        The latest stable version of the package
  7     }                ⊞ ^3.9.0
  8                      ⊞ ~3.9.0
```

The path variable represents the `wwwroot` folder.

The `path.js` file represents all the JavaScript files in the `wwwroot/js` folder. `path.minJs` represents all the minified JavaScript files in the `wwwroot/js` folder that have a `.min.js` extension. `path.concatJsDest` represents the JavaScript file named `site.min.js`, which is the minification result of the two previous JavaScript file folders.

6. Let's add the following code in order to create the task:

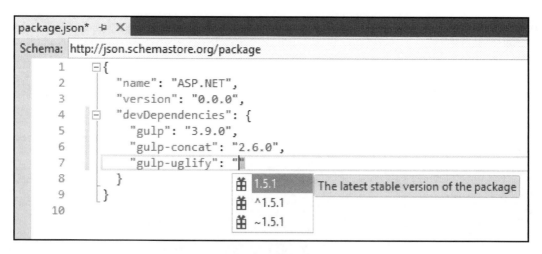

We require a Node.js function that will get the reference to a `Gulp` plugin or a `Node` module:

- `gulp.task` is a Gulp API that defines a task
- `gulp.src` is a Gulp API that reads a set of files

Inside `gulp.task`, we create all the tasks to be executed and rename default to `min:js`. We will chain the pipe functions to run these plugins in parallel:

1. First, we save `gulpfile.js`
2. Then, we refresh the task runner explorer
3. Lastly, we run the task by right-clicking on the name of the task

The `min:js` gulp task exists now in the gulpfile task list:

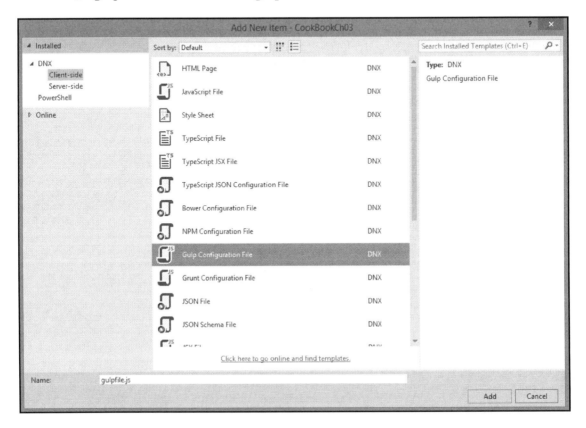

We can look at the command line that is executed in the **Output** window:

```
gulpfile.js

<global>

1
2   var gulp = require('gulp');
3
4   gulp.task('default', function () {
5       // place code for your default task here
6   });
```

The `site.min.js` file is now generated by the `min:js` task, which is the result of the minification and the concatenation of `script1.js` and `script2.js`:

```
gulpfile.js  ╪  ✕
▪ <global>                                                            ▾
    1    "use strict";
    2
    3  ⊟var paths = {
    4        webroot:  "./wwwroot/"
    5   };
    6
    7    paths.js = paths.webroot + "js/**/*.js";
    8    paths.minJs = paths.webroot + "js/**/*.min.js";
    9    paths.concatJsDest = paths.webroot + "js/site.min.js";
   10
```

How it works...

Like Grunt, Gulp is a Node.js module that helps us to run frequent tasks in web development. For a lot of common tasks in web development, we could use both Grunt and Gulp. Grunt is older, file based, and has more plugins than Gulp (around 4,500). Gulp is younger, stream based, has more than 100 plugins, and is more performant, because it uses Node.js stream-asynchronous features.

Minifying and bundling are two mandatory tasks in web development before sending an application in a production environment.

In the older versions of MVC, to execute these tasks, we used to create bundles programmatically in C# for JavaScript and CSS files in the `BundleConfig.cs` file, stored in the `App_Start` folder:

```
var gulp = require('gulp'),
    concat = require("gulp-concat"),
    uglify = require("gulp-uglify");


⊟gulp.task("min:js", function () {
    return gulp.src([paths.js, "!" + paths.minJs], { base: "." })
        .pipe(concat(paths.concatJsDest))
        .pipe(uglify())
        .pipe(gulp.dest("."));
});
```

This code creates two bundles, one for jQuery files and another one for CSS files:

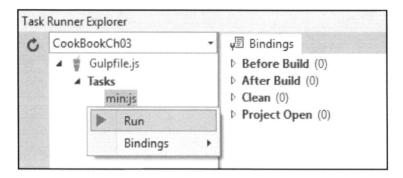

There's more...

For some Gulp recipes, please visit https://github.com/gulpjs/gulp/blob/master/docs/recipes/README.md

Using Yeoman code-generated templates

Yeoman (http://yeoman.io/) is a code-generator tool. It enables the generation of all the necessary files that you will need in a project template, according to a particular web technology. Yeoman allows us to generate full project templates but also pieces of code or optional features we could use in our projects. They are called **subgenerators**.

In this recipe, we will learn how to install Yeoman and use it in Windows. We will create Yeoman generators and subgenerators.

Getting ready

We will assume that you already have Node.js installed on your computer (Node.js and npm comes together). We will also assume that you've already installed Visual Studio Code. We have already talked about lightweight, cross-platform Visual Studio version in a previous recipe *Bundling and minifying JavaScript files with Gulp*.

Visual Studio Code will help us to realize the value of using Yeoman in an IDE that contains no project templates.

How to do it...

1. To install Yeoman, enter the following command:

   ```
   npm install -g yo
   ```

2. Let's go to the Yeoman generators web page (`http://yeoman.io/generators/`) to see all the available generators:

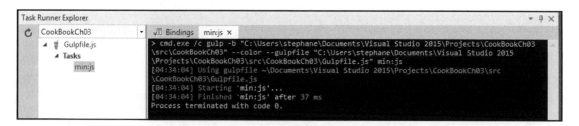

3. Let's install a Yeoman project template by choosing a `scaffolding` project for ASP.NET Core:

   ```
   npm install -g generator-aspnet
   ```

4. To install a Yeoman generator, enter the following:

   ```
   npm install -g generator-[NameOfTheGenerator]
   ```

5. Launch Yeoman by entering the following:

   ```
   yo
   ```

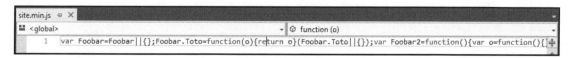

6. Choose `Install a generator`:

7. When Yeoman offers to find a generator for us, type `aspnet`. Yeoman should propose a list of generators corresponding to the research.

8. We can choose the one that we want to use by moving the cursor. In our case, the first one is `Yeoman generator for ASP.NET 5`:

```
public static void RegisterBundles(BundleCollection bundles)
{
    bundles.Add(new ScriptBundle("~/bundles/jquery").Include(
                "~/Scripts/jquery-{version}.js"));

    bundles.Add(new StyleBundle("~/Content/css").Include(
                "~/Content/bootstrap.css",
                "~/Content/site.css"));
```

9. Yeoman will install the ASP.NET 5 generator:

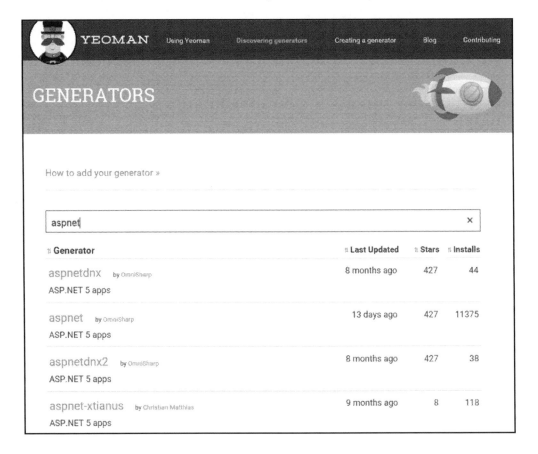

10. Now we can see the installed generator within the list of generators:

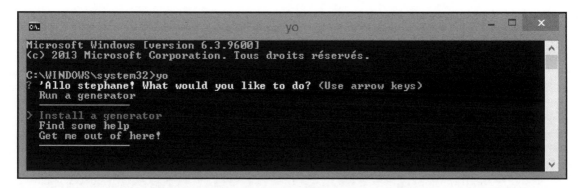

11. Let's create a folder where our application will be saved:

    ```
    mkdir AspnetYeomanWebapp
    ```

    ```
    cd AspnetYeomanWebapp
    ```

12. Let's launch VS Code in the folder that we just created by typing the following:

    ```
    code .
    ```

13. Let's also create an ASP.NET 5 project template with Yeoman by entering the following:

    ```
    yo aspnet
    ```

    The output of the preceding code is as follows:

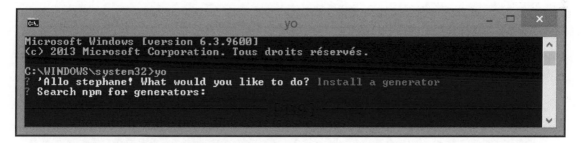

14. Now let's select **Web Application**.

15. Yeoman will ask us a name for the new application that will be generated. We can see all the files, generated for us:

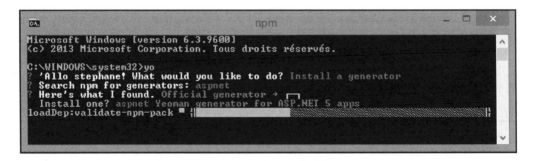

16. We can see also the `bower.json` that is generated, listing all, the frontend dependencies in our project:

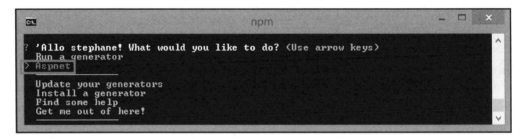

17. We can also see the `Gulpfile.js` generated and all the tasks that are automatically generated in this project template:

18. Now we restore the missing assemblies and build the generated application:

    dnu restore

19. Let's run the application:

    dnx web

    This command line will execute the command specified in project.json that corresponds to web in the commands section. This command will launch the **Kestrel** web server:

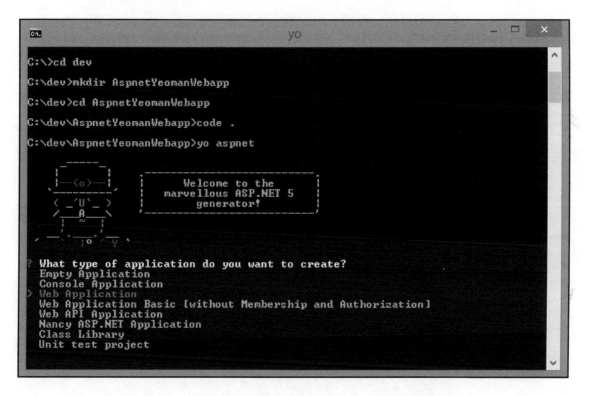

20. We can now see our application launched on `http://localhost:5000`:

21. Let's type *Ctrl + C* to close the Kestrel web server.
22. Let's see all the available subgenerators integrated into the current generator we just created by typing the following:

```
yo aspnet -help
```

Among all the given generators, we can see Angular, CoffeeScript, JavaScript, TypeScript, and CSS files. We can also see MvcController, MvcViews, Nuget packages, and many others:

23. To use a subgenerator to add an MVC controller to the project, we type one of the commands we saw previously, corresponding to an MVC controller creation, thanks to the `yo aspnet:MvcController` command, followed by the name we want for the MVC controller:

```
yo aspnet:MvcController ProductController
```

As we can see, a new MVC controller named `ProductController` has just been added to the `Controller` folder, with no need to be placed into the specific folder with the `cd` command:

To see all the available options for a subgenerator, we can type the command line that corresponds to the subgenerator, followed by `--help`.

24. To use a subgenerator to add an MVC view to the project, we create an MVC view using another subgenerator by typing `yo aspnet:MvcView`, followed by the name of the view (we know the view name has to be the same as the controller in ASP.NET MVC by convention), after it is placed in the `Views` folder by the `cd Views` command.

25. Let's create the specific `Views` subfolder corresponding to the controller that does not exist yet:

    mkdir Product

26. Let's place it into the folder we've just created:

    cd Product

27. Now we use the `MvcView` subgenerator to create a view named `Index`:

    yo aspnet:MvcView Index

    The view has just been created in the `Product` folder.

28. Let's add some HTML code to this view:

29. Now let's add a link to the `Layout.cshtml` page to access the view we just created:

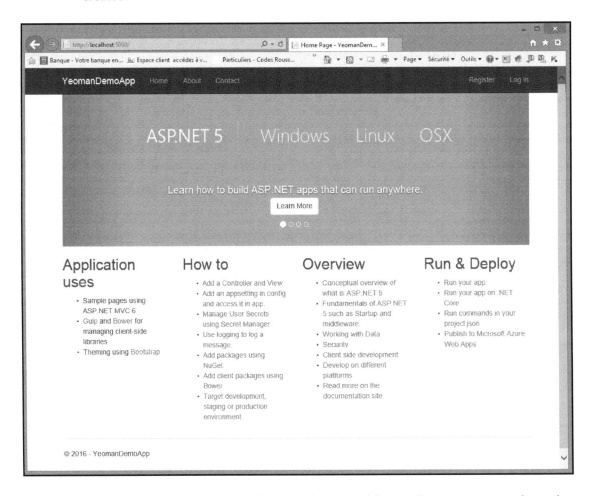

30. Now we save this file and go back to the root of the application to rerun the web server and refresh the website homepage:

```
cd ../..

dnx web
```

31. Let's click on this link to see the newly generated view, created by the Yeoman subgenerator.

We can see the new link named `Product` listed as the second item in the menu:

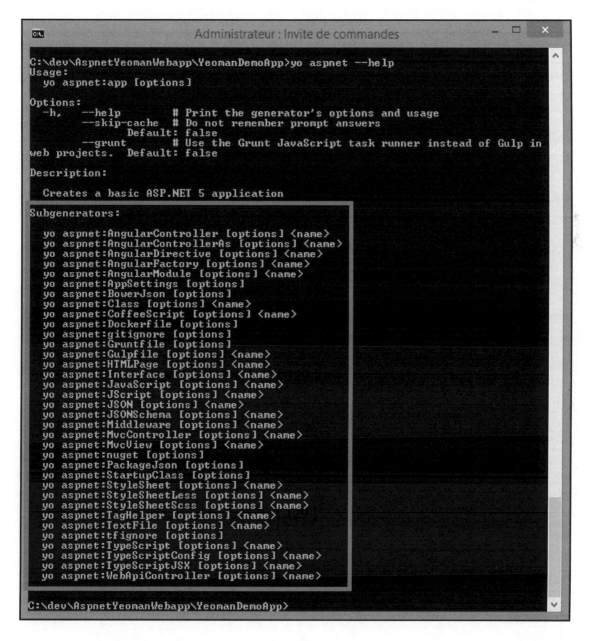

How it works...

Yeoman is open source, cross platform, and allows us productivity and efficiency while we develop the project. Many Yeoman generators (http://yeoman.io/generators/) already exist for almost all server-side and client-side frameworks, such as AngularJS, ReactJS, Ionic, Polymer, Bootstrap, CakePHP, ASP.NET 5, ASP.NET WEB API, and many others.

Yeoman is part of the Node.js world, where we use Node modules, package managers through npm or Bower, and task runners, such as Grunt or Gulp.

Note: The other Visual Studio versions already use their own scaffolding project system, and a lot of template projects can be installed by selecting **Tools** | **Extensions and Updates** | **Online** and choosing a project template in the displayed list.

Using JSPM

In this recipe, we will create a simple web page using ASP.NET for server-side code and Node.js for web tooling, but this time we will not use Bower as the package manager for client-side libraries, but JSPM.

Getting ready

We will use Visual Studio 2015 Community Edition as the IDE—although we could use any text editor—and Node.js for the client-side part of our development. When installing Visual Studio 2015 Community Edition, we know that Node.js and npm were also installed.

How to do it...

1. Let's install Git from https://git-scm.com/.
2. Choose Use Git from the Windows Command Prompt.
3. Let's create an ASP.NET empty application:
4. We install JSPM through the console/Command Prompt by typing the following:

```
npm install jspm -g
```

-g allows us install this module globally, which means we can open a Command Prompt from anywhere and typing jspm will be recognized and usable.

5. To configure JSPM, let's open a Command Prompt window, and place ourselves in the project directory using the cd command.

6. Now let's type the following:

```
jspm init
```

7. Now we have to answer a set of questions.

   The following question will be asked only if package.json doesn't exist:

   ```
   Package.json file does not exist, create it? [yes]
   ```

The JSPM configuration and the list of our client-side dependencies will be stored in package.json, as with Bower. Pressing *Enter* will choose the default answer (yes) for all the following questions. A package.json will be created at the root of our application:

```
Would you like jspm to prefix the jspm package.json properties
under jspm?[yes]
Enter server baseURL (public folder path)
The answer to this question is ./wwwroot.
Enter jspm packages folder [wwwrootjspm_packages]
Enter config file path [wwwrootconfig.js]
```

We accept the default value by pressing *Enter*. With JSPM, we need a JavaScript file as a .config file that our application will need to reference at runtime:

```
Configuration file wwwrootconfig.js doesn't exist, create it? [yes]
Enter client baseURL (public folder URL) [/]
Do you wish to use a transpiler? [yes]
Which ES6 transpiler would you like to use, Babel, Typescript, or
Traceur? [babel]
```

8. By pressing *Enter*, we accept the default value `Babel`. Now we can see all the generated files in our project:

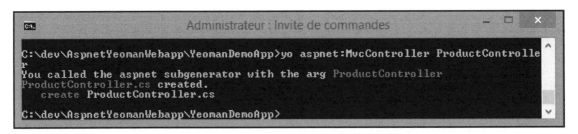

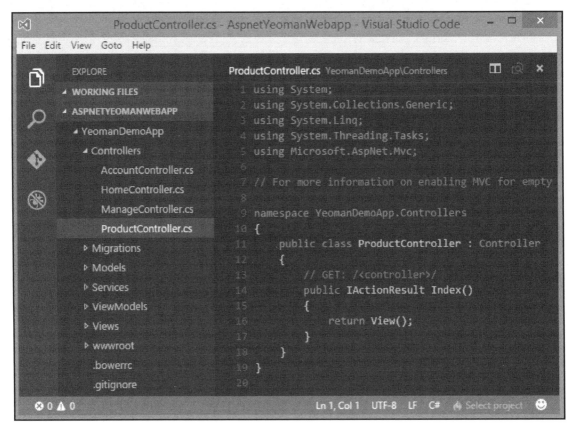

9. Create three files named `index.html`, `app.js`, and `appAction.js`:

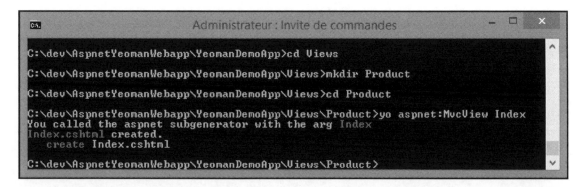

10. Let's add code to these files:

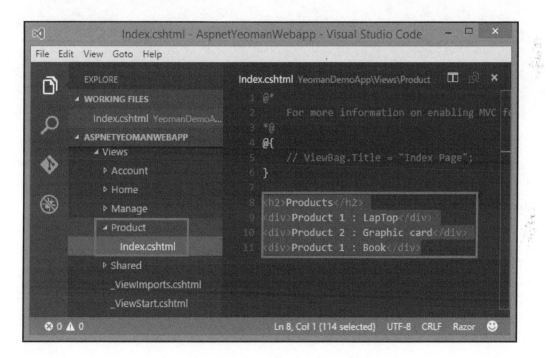

11. We create a welcome function to be exported:

Now we will use this welcome function from `appMessage.js` in `app.js`. The import keyword will use a JavaScript function or object as a module, and, like this, the dependency will be managed by a specific framework: `system.js`, a universal module loader. This gives us an API and a runtime to load and transpile JavaScript code for the browser:

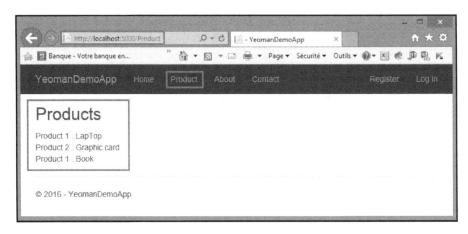

12. We import `app.js` from `system.js`, which will manage the JavaScript dependency, transpiling the code in the ECMAScript version used by the Browser JavaScript engine. `system.js` will also load `app.js` as a module. This will allow the ECMAScript code written in these files to work in any browser.

We can see the code working on `index.html`:

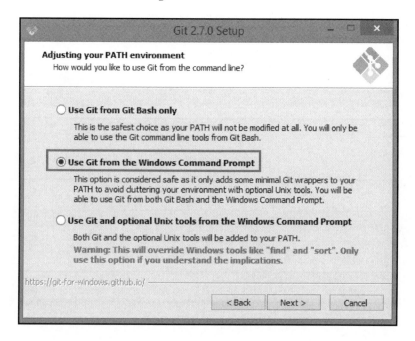

How it works...

JSPM (`http://jspm.io/`) is a package manager for JavaScript files, and it uses the SystemJS universal module loader. It will also load JavaScript code as modules in any module format, such as AMD, CommonJS, and ES6. Another interesting feature of JSPM is that it can compile on-the-fly JavaScript ECMAScript 6-compliant code into JavaScript ECMAScript 5-compliant code. In this way, our JavaScript will work even on old browsers that are not ECMAScript 5 compliant. To do this, JSPM will use Traceur (`https://github.com/google/traceur-compiler/wiki/Getting-Started`), Babel (`https://babeljs.io/`), or TypeScript, which are tracer ECMAScript transpilers.

4
Reusing Code with NuGet

In this chapter, we will cover the following topics:

- Managing NuGet packages
- Creating a NuGet package with the NuGet package class library
- Creating a local NuGet repository and consuming packages from it
- Creating a NuGet package with NuGet Package Explorer
- Sharing NuGet packages with the community
- Creating an Azure NuGet repository

Introduction

Building reusable components is one of the basic skills of the computer development world. The reuse of classes that are integrated in a .NET class library has been possible since the beginning of .NET. We are able to compile these classes in a .NET class library project as a **DLL (dynamic link library)**, the implementation of a shared library by Microsoft.

Since the creation of Visual Studio 2010 and ASP.NET MVC's arrival on the scene, the ASP.NET world became more and more open source-friendly, and the necessity to share open source libraries and components became unavoidable.

To share libraries, Microsoft uses **NuGet**, an open source package manager used to install, uninstall, or update .NET libraries and components on projects through Visual Studio. We can also search for packages from Microsoft or anyone else in the NuGet Online repository, resolve missing packages, manage package dependencies from other packages, and support multiple frameworks.

In this way, we no longer have to search libraries on different existing repositories, such as CodePlex, Github, or Microsoft websites.

In this chapter, we will learn how to manage and create our own NuGet package in several ways.

We will learn how to publish a NuGet package that we've just created in our private repository. This package could be published on Premise or Azure, but it could also be published on the public NuGet repository to be shared with the community.

Managing NuGet packages

In this recipe, we will learn how to manage NuGet packages.

Getting ready

Since Visual Studio 2012, NuGet has been totally integrated into Visual Studio, and we can install NuGet packages in several different ways after opening or creating a project in Visual Studio and selecting it in the Solution Explorer.

How to do it...

1. Select **Project | Manage NuGet Packages**. This action will open the **NuGet Package Manager** dialog box:

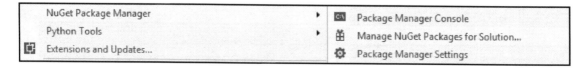

2. Open the menu by selecting **Tools | Manage Package Manager | Manage NuGet Package for Solution...**. This action will open the **NuGet Package Manager** dialog box:

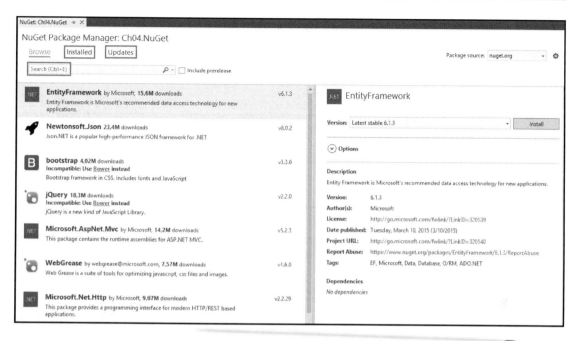

3. Open the menu by selecting **Tools | Manage Package Manager | Package Manager Console**. This action will open the **Package Manager Console** to allow us to install, uninstall, or update NuGet packages thanks to **PowerShell** command line:

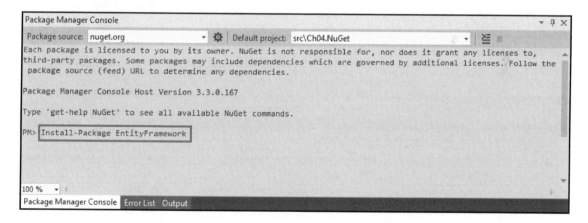

4. By typing `Install-Package` followed by the name of the package, we will install a Nuget package using PowerShell.

We can find which Powershell command line is used for each package by visiting the official NuGet website and searching for a specific package:

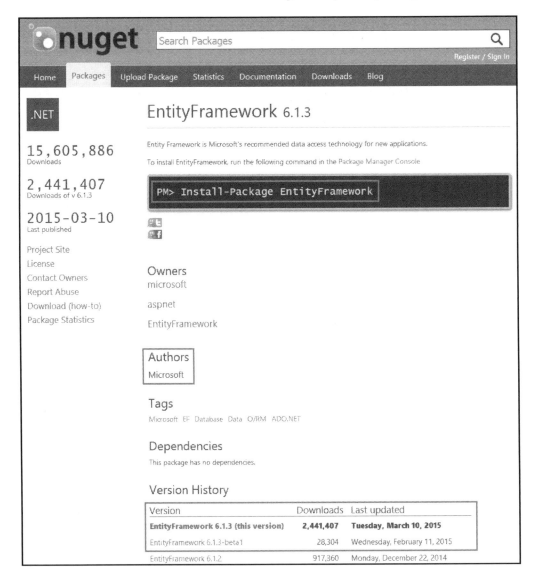

The link will lead us to the NuGet package homepage for this specific package, and we can see the command-line.

5. Right-click the project root folder in **Solution Explorer** and select **Manage NuGet Packages**.

6. By opening `project.json` and typing the name of our package in the dependencies section, we can see IntelliSense working and propositioning all the packages containing the name `EntityFramework`:

```
project.json*  ⊣  ✕

Schema:  http://json.schemastore.org/project

 1   ⊟{
 2        "version": "1.0.0-*",
 3   ⊟    "compilationOptions": {
 4            "emitEntryPoint": true
 5        },
 6
 7   ⊟    "dependencies": {
 8            "Microsoft.AspNet.IISPlatformHandler": "1.0.0-rc1-final",
 9            "Microsoft.AspNet.Server.Kestrel": "1.0.0-rc1-final",
10            "En|
11        },        ▣ Microsoft.AspNet.PageExecutionInstrumenta ▲
12                  ▣ Microsoft.AspNet.Identity.EntityFramework
13   ⊟    "c       ｛≣ Microsoft.Extensions.                        ▮
14                 ｛≣ Microsoft.AspNet.Authentication.
15        },｛≣ EntityFramework.
16               ｛≣ WCFRIA.EntityFramework
17   ⊟    "f      EntityFramework
18               🔌 Dino.EntityFramework
19               🔌 XAct.EntityLibrary5
20        },      🔌 EnumUtilities                                ▼
21
22   ⊟    "exclude": [
23            "wwwroot",
24            "node_modules"
25        ],
26   ⊟    "publishExclude": [
27            "**.user",
28            "**.vspscc"
29        ]
30    }
31
```

7. In saving the `project.json` file, the typed package will be automatically loaded from the NuGet online repository by the VS NuGet tool:

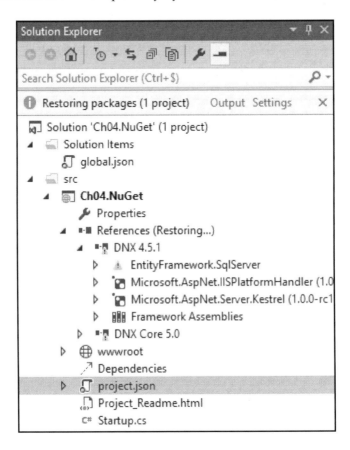

We can now see all the package dependencies:

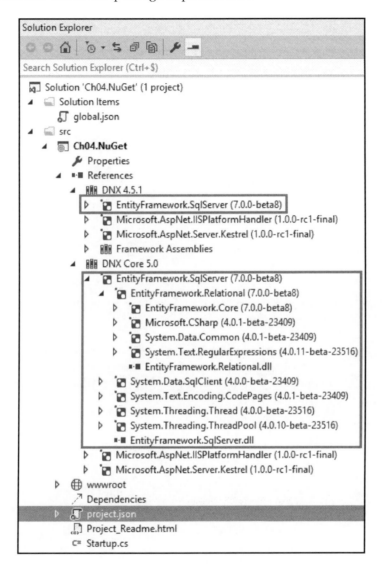

See also

We can consult the NuGet gallery online, at `http://www.nuget.org/`.

We can see news and info about NuGet packages, at `http://blog.nuget.org/`.

We can consult the NuGet source code repository, at `http://github.com/nuget/home`.

Creating a NuGet package with the NuGet package class library

In this recipe, we will learn how to create a NuGet package with the NuGet package class library.

Getting ready

When we build a .NET project, a DLL file, or an exe file is generated. Every compiled .NET EXE or .NET DLL is a reusable component as well.

A more modern and universal way to create and use reusable components is to create NuGet packages from our code. Thus, we will create these components for personal use in our private organization and share them with the community (thereby making them public) by publishing it in the public NuGet repository.

How to do it...

There's several ways to create a NuGet package.

The old way

1. First, we have to download NuGet.exe from the following URL:
   `https://dist.nuget.org/index.html`.
2. At this page we can choose the latest Windows x86 `Commandline.exe` file.
3. We can also choose the latest VS 2015 VSIX extension for Visual Studio.
4. To use `NuGet.exe` to create packages from an assembly, we have to place
   `NuGet.exe` in the same folder as our DLL. The goal is to create a `nuspec` file.

The new way

1. We can now use a new project template that comes with Visual Studio 2015 to
   create class libraries as NuGet packages by choosing **New Project** | **Visual C#** or
   Web | **Class library package**.
2. We create a new class that we will reuse in other projects:

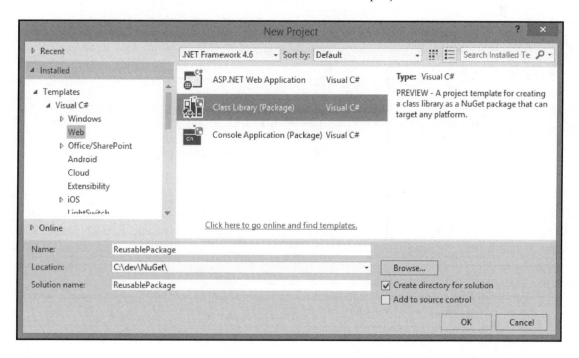

3. We create the code to be reused in the `Message` class:

```
Message.cs  ⊕  ✕
                                                                    ▾ | ⚙ ReusablePack
    1       using System;
    2       using System.Collections.Generic;
    3       using System.Linq;
    4       using System.Threading.Tasks;
    5
    6       namespace ReusablePackage
    7       {
    8           // This project can output the Class library as a NuGet Package.
    9           // To enable this option, right-click on the project and select the Properties menu item.
   10           // In the Build tab select "Produce outputs on build".
             1 reference
   11           public class Message
   12           {|
                 0 references
   13               public Message()
   14               {
   15               }
   16
                 0 references
   17               public string GetMessage()
   18               {
   19                   return "This is a message";
   20               }
   21           }
   22       }
```

4. We have to right-click on the name of the project and select **Properties**. On the **Build** menu, let's check **Produce outputs on build** before building the project:

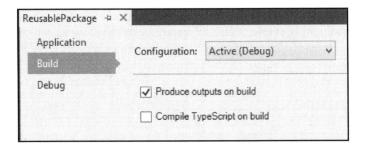

5. Right-click on the name of the project and select **Build**. We can see the `.nupkg` and `.symbols.nupkg` files that are generated.

We can see, in the output window, the compilation result:

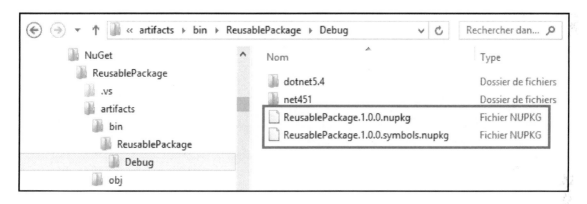

We can find these files that begin at the root of the project by navigating to `artifacts\bin\[ProjectName]\Debug`:

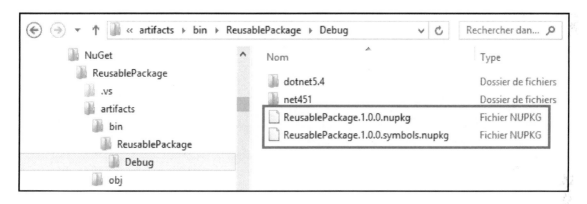

Creating a local NuGet repository and consuming packages from it

In this recipe, we will learn how to consume packages from a local repository. We will also learn how to create a local repository.

How to do it...

1. After having created a folder locally on our own computer, we will use it to be the local repository for our packages. In this case, this folder will be `C:\dev\NuGetPkg`:

2. Let's configure Visual Studio to configure this new repository. Navigate to **Tools | NuGet Package Manager | Package Manager Settings | Package Sources**:

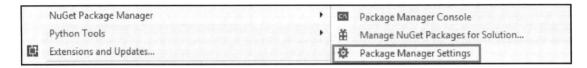

3. Let's click on the + button to add a new repository:

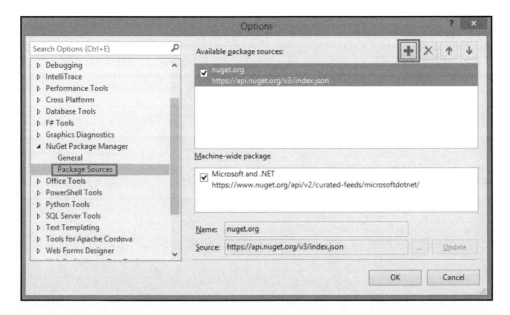

4. Let's add a name to this repository:

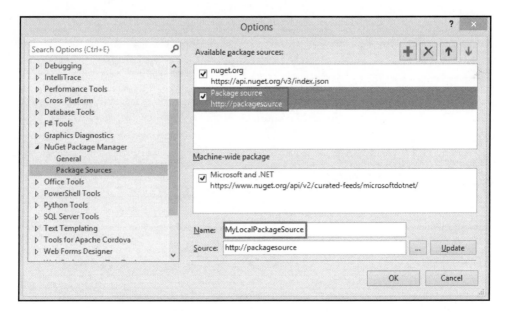

5. Select a local folder:

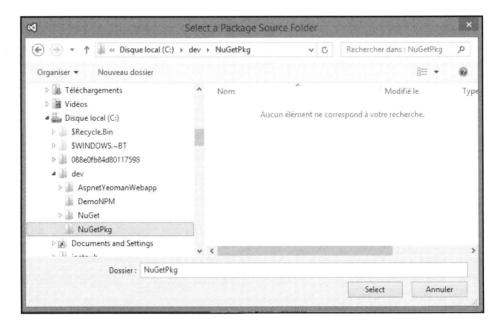

6. Let's click on the **Update** button to update the directory address:

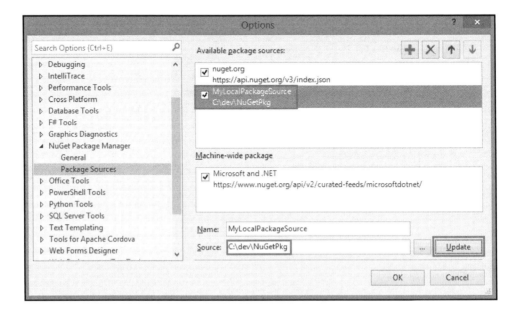

7. Let's place the NuGet package we just created in the previous recipe:

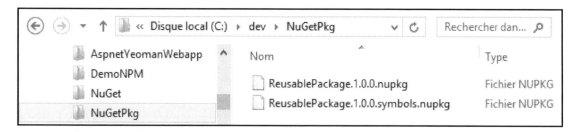

8. Right-click on the root project in **Solution Explorer** and select **Manage NuGet Packages** to open the **NuGet Package Manager**.

9. If we open the Package source drop-down list in the top-right corner, we can see our new package repository:

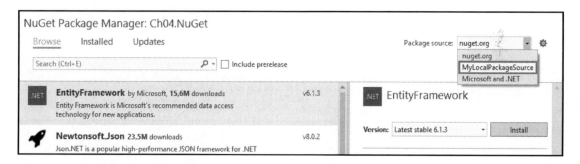

10. We can now see the package in the installed package list for the current project:

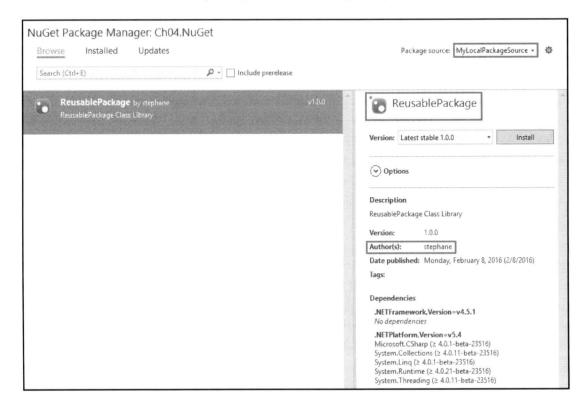

11. Now let's install this package in the current project by clicking on the **Install** button; the following dialog box will appear:

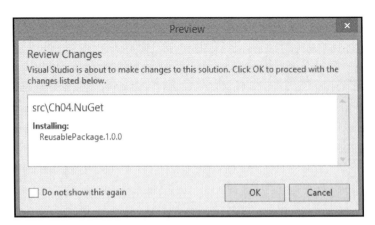

12. Let's click **OK** to install the package and close the dialog box.

13. Let's select the **Installed** button to verify whether we see the package in the installed package list for this project:

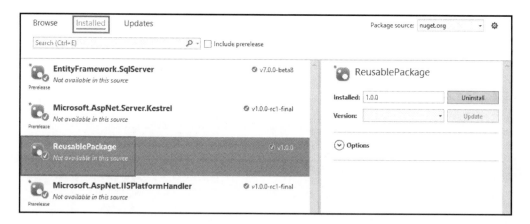

14. Clicking on the References folder in **Solution Explorer**, we can also see the installed package:

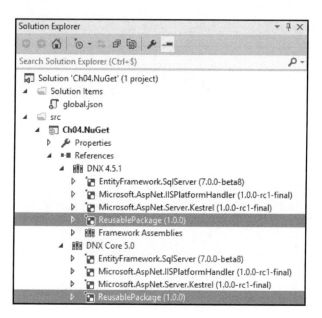

Creating a NuGet package with NuGet Package Explorer

In this recipe, we will create a NuGet package with .NET 4.5.1 in order to use it in an ASP.NET CORE application under DNX 4.5.1.

How to do it...

1. Let's open Visual Studio 2015 and create a class library:

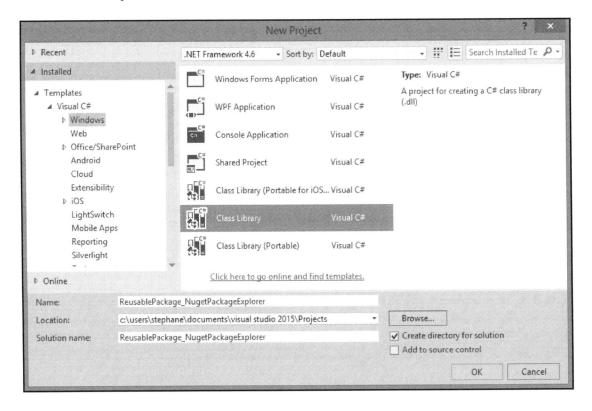

2. We will now create a class in this library:

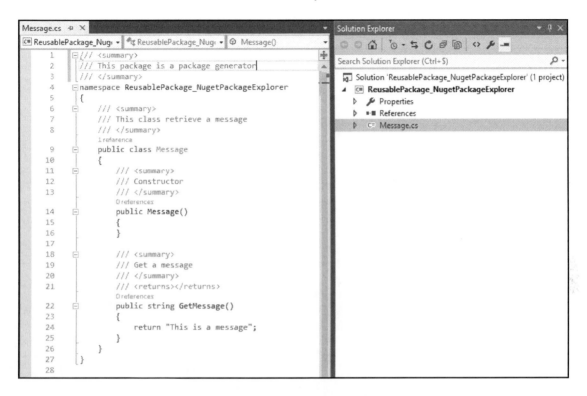

3. Right-click on the project name and then click on Properties.
4. We will set the project build option to Release Mode.
5. We will then check the **Generate XML** documentation.

6. To create a package, we will need the DLL and the associated XML documentation, which are the .xml comments in the code:

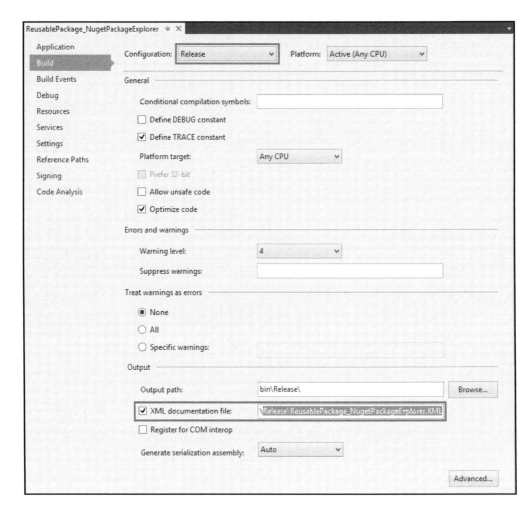

7. Let's build the library. We can see the output window result for this build.

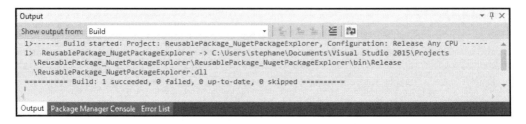

8. We can see the DLL and the XML files that are generated:

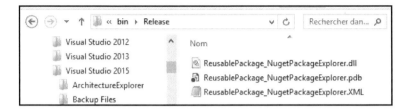

9. Let's download **NuGet Package Explorer** on the Codeplex website, at `https://npe.codeplex.com/`. This is a free tool to create and explore NuGet packages very easily:

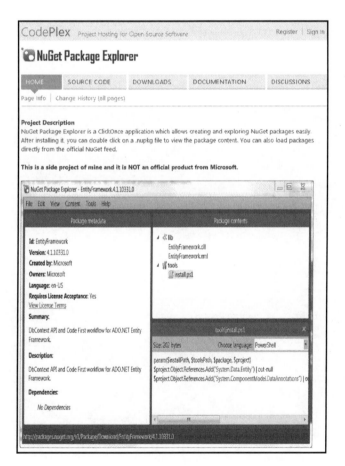

Here's a look at the installation screen:

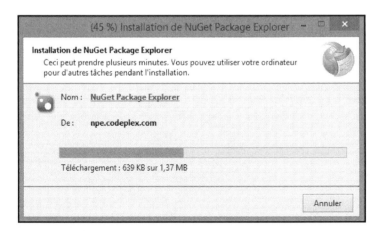

10. We will now launch `NuGetPackageExplorer.application.exe` and select **File | New | Create a new package**:

The **NuGet Package Explorer** will look something like this:

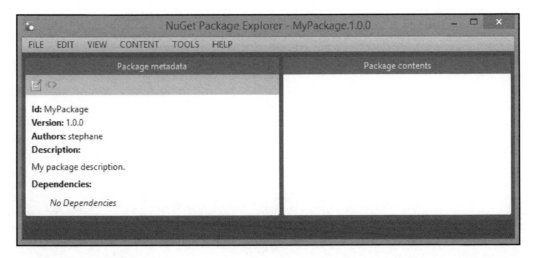

11. We will now create a `lib` folder by right-clicking on the **Package contents** pane on the right and selecting **Add Lib Folder**:

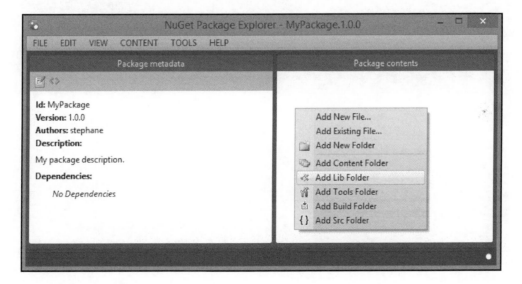

12. Next, we create a target framework folder by right-clicking on the `lib` folder we just created:

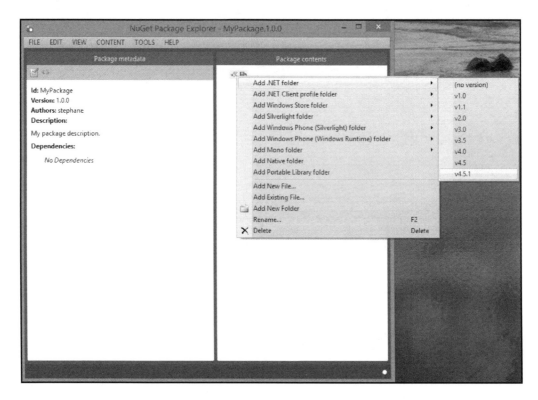

13. Add the **DLL** and **XML** files by right-clicking on the folder we just created:

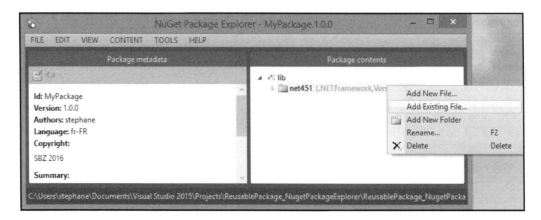

14. Select the **DLL** and **XML** files that we wish to use:

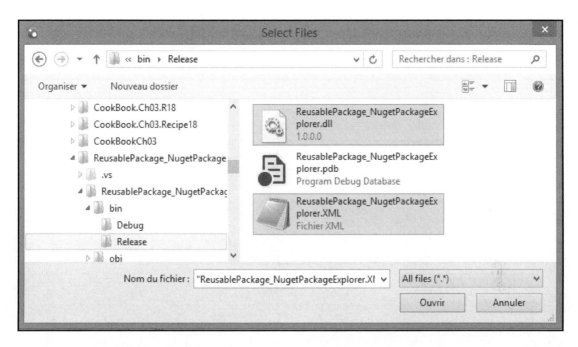

15. Next, select the **EDIT** menu and the **Edit Metadata** menu item to modify the package metadata:

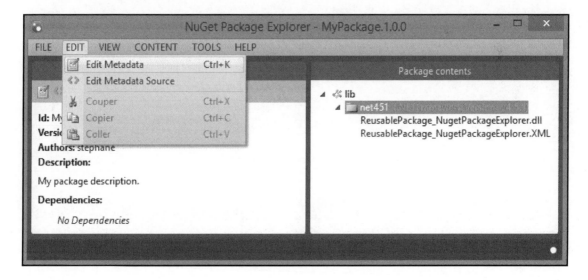

16. Let's click on the 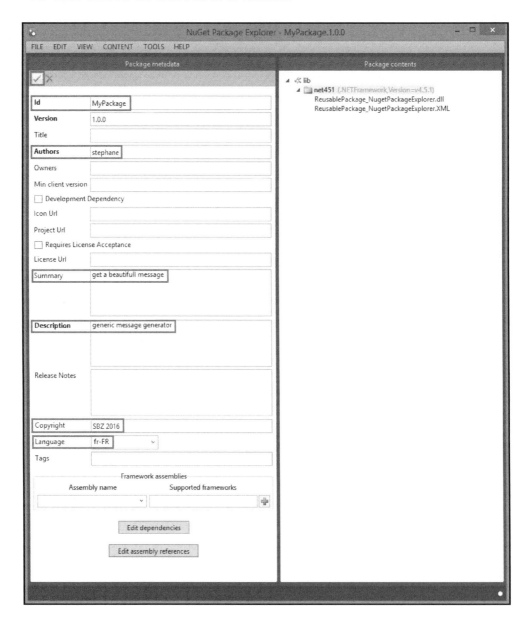 button to validate:

17. The package is ready to be published:

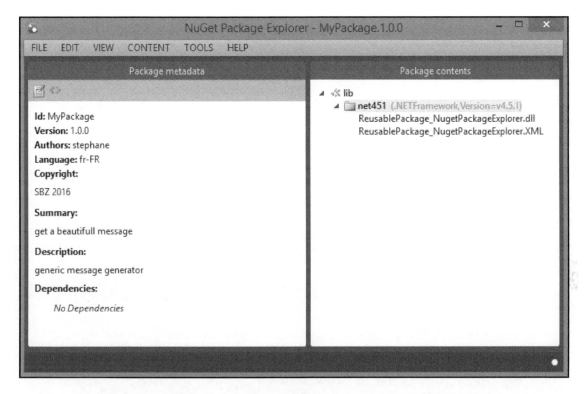

18. Select **File | Publish**. The **Publish Package** dialog box will open.

We can publish on the NuGet website or on any local or remote repository. We will need the publish key that was generated when we created our NuGet account on the NuGet website.

19. Let's click on the **Publish** button to publish the package:

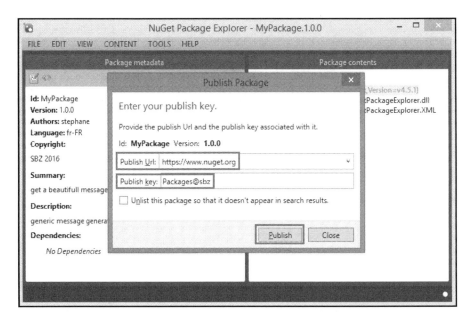

20. Finally, we can save the NuGet package locally as a `.nupkg` package:

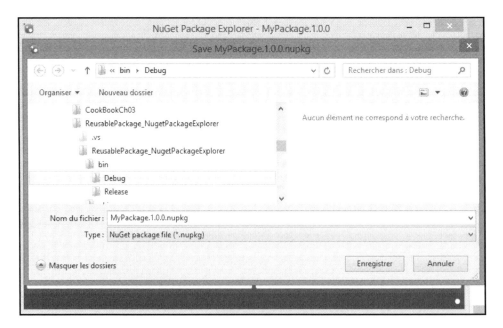

The packages are now stored in our local repository:

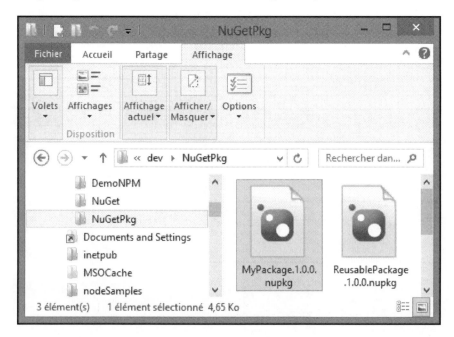

Sharing NuGet packages with the community

After having created our own NuGet package in the *Creating a NuGet package* recipe, we will publish it in the NuGet public repository.

How to do it...

1. First, we create an account on the NuGet website:

2. Next, we fill in the form on the NuGet website:

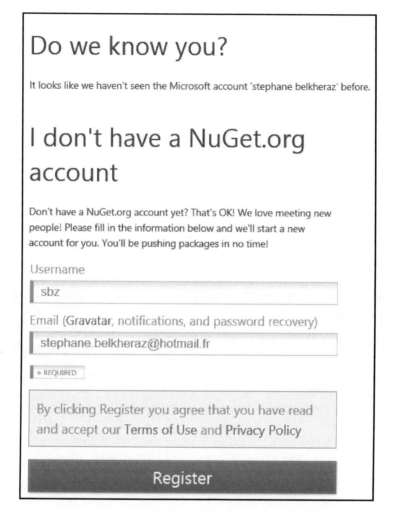

We are now registered:

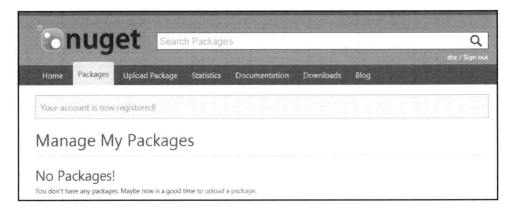

3. Let's click on the username of the account to see the page account (**sbz** in our case). On this page, we can see our API key that we can include in our Visual Studio projects to generate NuGet packages:

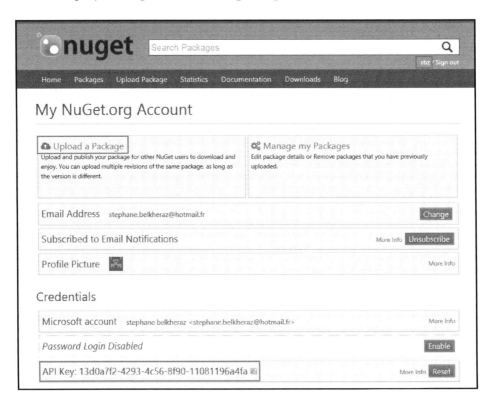

4. Next, we click on the **Upload a Package** button:

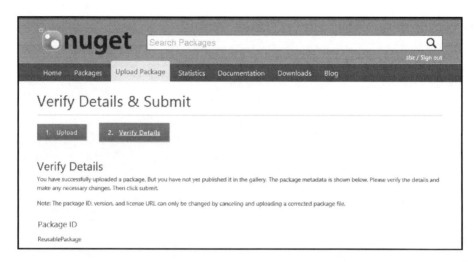

5. Let's go to the **Upload Package** page to upload a package. We can now see that our package was just uploaded to the NuGet public repository:

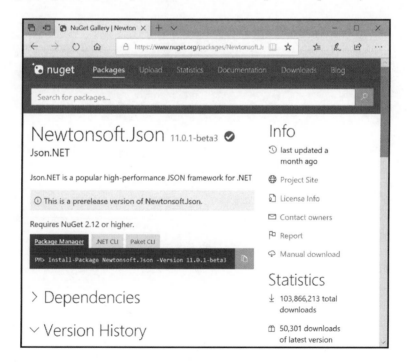

Creating an Azure NuGet repository

In this recipe, we will create a NuGet repository on Azure.

How to do it...

1. First, we create an empty **ASP.NET Web Application**:

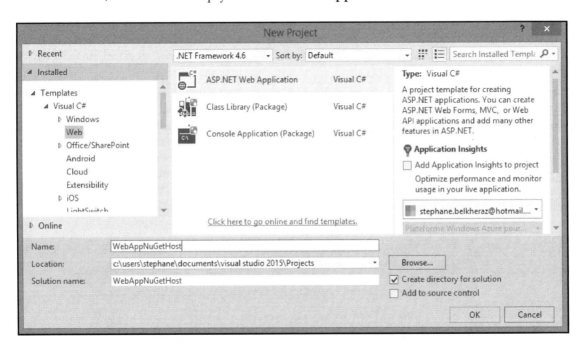

2. Next, let's check **Host in the cloud**:

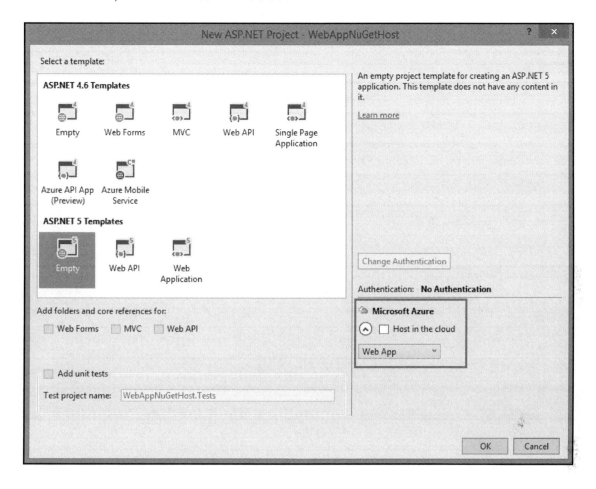

3. Now let's configure the Azure account for publishing:

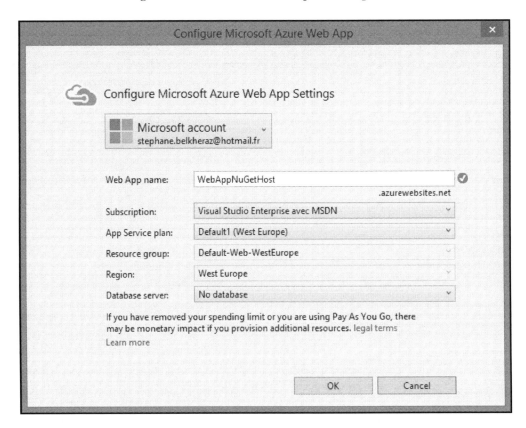

4. Right-click on the project name and select **Manage NuGet Packages:**

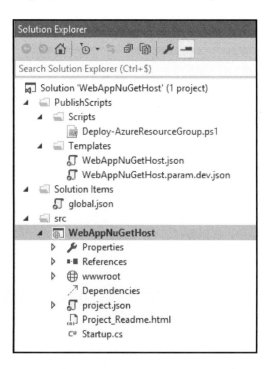

5. Search for the NuGet.Server NuGet package and install it. It will allow us to host NuGet feeds:

This package will be added to the DNX 4.5.1 references:

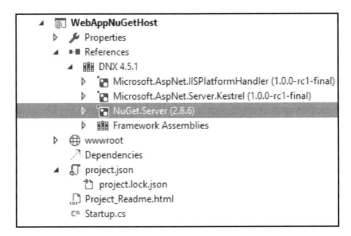

6. We will now publish the web application by clicking on the **Publish** button:

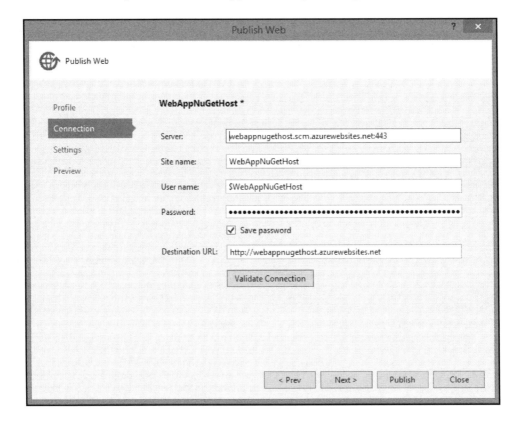

7. We can see the Azure NuGet feed online:

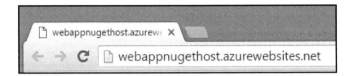

8. Next, we will add this repository to the NuGet repositories by first selecting **Tools | Options**.
9. Click the plus button, enter the Azure website feed, and click **Update**:

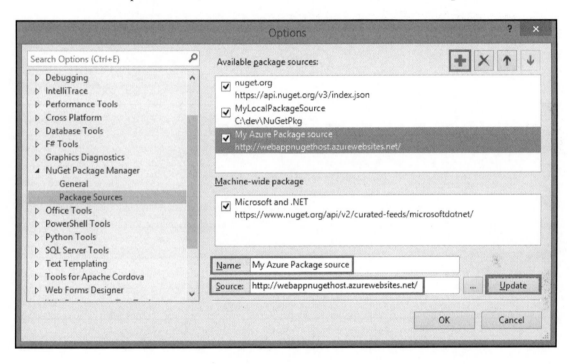

5

SOLID Principles, Inversion of Control, and Dependency Injection

In this chapter, we will talk about the following topics:

- Implementing DI with Native IOC in ASP.NET Core
- Using the life cycles available in ASP.NET Core
- Implementing DI with Autofac
- Implementing DI with StructureMap
- Implementing DI with DryIoc

Introduction

In this chapter, we will learn what SOLID principles are, what the IOC, DI, and service locator patterns are, why we should use these patterns, what problems they solve, what tools we can use to solve them, and how they are implemented natively in ASP.NET Core.

Those who know all the concepts surrounding IOC and DI can go directly to the first recipe of this chapter. For the rest, we will show you some of these concepts in this introduction.

First of all, we have to follow these common design principles when programming with object-oriented languages:

- **Keep It Simple, Stupid**: We have to keep our code simple and not over-complicate. Stupid does not mean silly.
- **Don't Repeat Yourself**: Every piece of knowledge must have a single, unambiguous, authoritative representation within a system. In other words, we try to use abstraction in our system, avoiding repetition and not duplicating logic.
- **Tell, Don't Ask**: We tell objects what to do instead of asking them what they should do. This practice promotes loose coupling and encapsulation.
- **You Ain't Gonna Need It**: We should code only the functionality we need and not the things we think we might need in the future.
- **Separation of Concerns**: We should divide our application into distinct features so that we can easily reuse and maintain these features or behaviors.

SOLID principles

Even if you're not an architect, or you don't intend to become one, as a serious developer, you should implement SOLID principles when you develop object-oriented software. In this introduction, we will just briefly look at each of the principles without developing them in detail.

The patterns we need should have the following properties:

- Loose coupling
- Testability
- Responsibility delegation
- Flexibility

According to Uncle Bob (Robert Martin), the SOLID design principles are as follows:

- **S - Single Responsibility Principle**: Objects should each have a single responsibility and a single reason to change.
- **O - Open-Closed principle**: Software entities should be open for responsibility, but closed for modification.
- **L - Liskov Substitution Principle**: You should be able to replace an interface implementation without having to break the actual implementation. This pattern forces us to use interfaces, making our code more testable.

- **I - Interface Segregation**: Clients should not be forced to depend upon interfaces that they do not use.
- **D - Dependency Injection**: You should code to an interface or abstract class rather than an implementation.

Inversion of control

The term inversion of control refers to a set of patterns that can help us when we have a lot of regression bugs or when it's hard to redeploy our code.

The inconvenience of these patterns becomes clear when we add more complexity to our applications; if they are not well used and understood, they can generate big performance issues and can be hard to debug.

When using inversion of control patterns, we want to invert the control that our classes have on their dependencies. The problem is that when we use classes inside other classes, modifying the low-level classes will impact the high-level classes.

That's why we would prefer to have a dependency on an abstraction rather than a concrete implementation.

IOC is a way of following the Hollywood principle: *Don't call us; we will call you.*

With IOC, the business-logic flow of our code depends on the object graph that is built during program execution, instead of being determined by objects that are statically bound to one another.

There are several design patterns that implement IOC:

- **Template method pattern**: One or more algorithm steps can be overridden by subclasses to allow differing behaviors while ensuring that the overarching algorithm is still followed.
- **Strategy pattern**: An algorithm varies independently from clients that use it, and has to be interchangeable.
- **Service locator pattern**: This pattern contains references to a set of services and encapsulates the logic that locates them. Use it to obtain service instances.
- **Factory pattern**: This pattern delegates the instantiation of a class to another class.
- **Dependency injection pattern**: High-level modules should not depend on low-level modules; both should depend on abstraction.

Dependency injection (DI)

Dependency injection is one of several ways to implement **IOC**.

When classes collaborate with each other-or, more precisely, when we use *composition* between two classes (when class *B* is the property of class *A*)-we say that we have strongly coupled objects, which is a bad practice in object-oriented programming. Class *A* is too dependent on class *B* and could be badly affected by modifications to class *B*.

To avoid this strong dependency, we could use an abstraction of class *B*. We could use an interface, called **IB**, to replace class *B* as a property and then delegate the resolution of the interface IB with this concrete class to a tier component, a DI container, for example.

You do not have to use a DI container to do that, but that would be called **the poor man's DI** if we use *new* in the constructor to instantiate objects:

```
public class ProductService
{
  private readonly IProductRepository productRepository;
  public ProductService () : this(new ProductRepository())
  {}
  public ProductService (ProductRepository
  productRepository)
  {
    this.productRepository = productRepository;
  }
}
```

Using DI to develop an application is a best practice, but if the performance cost is bigger than the benefits it brings, we should think about it and certainly test it using a performance test.

Let's now look at how to implement DI.

We have several ways to inject a dependency from an interface:

- By constructor (constructor injection)
- By class properties (setter injection)
- By interface (interesting for scalability, though we might need a different life cycle depending on the place where it instantiates)

IOC truly makes sense when using constructor injection.

The control over dependencies is inverted only in the constructor. That's why constructor injection is the best practice with which to implement DI.

DI containers

A DI container follows the **RRR (Register-Resolve-Release)** pattern.

A DI container is a framework or a library used in order to compose the object graph of an application, creating a *composition root* at the application entry point and managing their lifetime. This composition root registers the objects and their abstractions that are to be resolved.

There are a lot of free DI containers, such as the following:

- **Unity**
- **Ninject**
- **StructureMap**
- **Autofac**
- **Simple Injector**
- **DryIoc**
- **And many others**

When creating the composition root, we configure the DI container. We can do that by using code, but also by an XML configuration file if the DI container we chose has this functionality.

Configuring a DI container

Let's look at an example of configuration by code using the StructureMap DI container:

```
public static class IoC
{
  public static IContainer Initialize()
  {
    ObjectFactory.Initialize(x =>
    {
      x.For()
      .Use();
    });
    return ObjectFactory.Container;
  }
}
```

We call the `Initialize` method from the `IoC` static class in `global.asax`:

```
public class MvcApplication :      System.Web.HttpApplication
{
  protected void Application_Start()
  {
    IoC.Initialise();
    ...
  }
}
```

An example of the composition root in the `application_start` method of the `global.asax`, which is the entry point of an MVC 5 application.

We can see, in the fifth line, that we are using the `IDependencyResolver` instance to ask it to replace the current MVC `DependencyResolver` with the DI `DependencyResolver` container we chose.

If we used the ASP.NET Web API, we should have to use another `DependencyResolver`. The same is true for `SignalR`; this library also has its own mechanism for calling its own classes to call its `DependencyResolver`.

The `DependencyResolver` is used until MVC 5 to resolve many different types in the ASP.NET MVC framework internally. It is used by the controller factory to get controller instances.

Using an IOC/DI container, we create and use a custom dependency resolver.

Now, let's look at an example of XML configuration.

The advantage of the XML configuration file is that we are able to change the *composition root* of our application without recompiling.

The disadvantage of this is that we do not have an error at compile time if an abstraction we resolve or a concrete type doesn't exist (we could have made a mistake writing the name).

Some DI containers use an XML-oriented configuration, and some others use a more code-oriented configuration.

IOC versus service locator

Service locator is a design pattern used to locate other services. It is the opposite of DI. Depending on its usage, it can be an antipattern when we move the dependency to the service locator instead of the concrete class.

The other issue with using service locator is that it can often be difficult to change the implementation and to test the system.
Taking the opposite approach, IOC builds the dependencies once for each application when the application is launched for first time.

The goal of DI is to inject dependencies during the application initialization. If we call the dependencies later, this becomes a service location.

Life cycles

Depending on the DI container we choose, we will have a larger or smaller number of life cycles available.

The more common life cycles are as following:

- **Transient**: The object instance will exist in memory at the time it exists in the code block it is contained in

- **Singleton**: The object instance exists in memory until it is released explicitly

- **Per request**: The object instance exists in memory at the time of the HTTP request in which it is instantiated

There are lots of other life cycles avaliable, depending on the DI container we choose.

Implementing DI with Native IOC in ASP.NET Core

In this recipe, we will learn in a simple way how to register, resolve, and give a life cycle to an abstraction in ASP.NET Core.

Getting ready

Dependency injection is now native in ASP.NET Core.
Importing `Microsoft.Extensions.DependencyInjection`
in `project.json` (formerly `web.config`), and by a using statement in `Startup.cs`
(formerly `global.asax`), we can use this internal component to manage DI for our
application, represented by the `IServiceProvider` interface.

How to do it...

We will inject the `ServiceProducts` class by using a constructor in the `HomeController`
of an ASP.NET MVC 6 application:

1. First, we create a class called `Product`:

```csharp
5 references
public class Product
{
    2 references
    public int ID { get; set; }
    2 references
    public string Name { get; set; }
    2 references
    public double Price { get; set; }
}
```

2. We then create an interface called `IProductService`:

```csharp
1 reference
public interface IProductService
{
    1 reference
    List<Product> GetSomeProducts();
}
```

3. Next, we create a class called `ProductService`:

```csharp
0 references
public class ProductService : IProductService
{
    1 reference
    public List<Product> GetSomeProducts()
    {
        return new List<Product>
        {
            new Product
            {
                ID = 1,
                Name="Laptop",
                Price = 320.00
            },
            new Product
            {
                ID = 2,
                Name="Smartphone",
                Price = 206.00
            }
        };
    }
}
```

4. Let's use `ProductService` in our `HomeController`, creating an instance of `ProductService` by injecting the `ProductService` abstraction in the `HomeController` constructor. `ProductService` will be available for the whole `HomeController` class:

```csharp
4 references
public class HomeController : Controller
{
    private readonly IProductService _service;
    0 references
    public HomeController(IProductService service)
    {
        _service = service;
    }

    3 references
    public IActionResult Index()
    {
        var model = _service.GetSomeProducts();
        return View(model);
    }
}
```

5. Let's add the view:

```
Products.cshtml
 1    @model List<Mvc6.CookBook.Ch05.R1.Services.Product>
 2
 3    <h3>Products available</h3>
 4
 5    @foreach (var product in Model)
 6    {
 7        <p>ID : @product.ID</p>
 8        <p>Name : @product.Name</p>
 9        <p>Price : @product.Price</p>
10    }
```

6. Finally, we configure the `ProductService` life cycle in the `ConfigureServices` method:

```
services.AddTransient<IProductService, ProductService>();
```

We can see now the result in an HTML page:

The `IServiceCollection` interface already contains some helpers to manage dependencies for the most-used objects in the framework.

We can use these helpers, and can create others for the new libraries we want to resolve.

The life cycle of every object instantiated in our application can be managed by
`IServiceCollection`:

```
services.AddSingleton<ProductManager>();
```

How it works...

The life cycles available in ASPNET CORE are as follows:

- **Instance**: The instance is given all the time. We are responsible for its creation.
- **Transient**: The instance is created each time we use the object.
- **Scoped**: The instance is created once by the HTTP request.
- **Singleton**: The instance is created once by the application instance.

With ASP.NET Core, we can inject dependencies by property, but the best practice is to do this by using the constructor, and to create the composition root, we have to register, resolve, and add the life cycle of our object graph in the `ConfigureServices` method of the `Startup.cs` file.

In our example, we created the object graph of our dependencies for our application.

To do that, we used the `IServiceCollection` object passed in the parameter of the `ConfigureService` method.

We created a `ServiceProduct` class to use in our controller. We configured the behavior of this class in the `ConfigureService` method.

For the moment, there are a lot of limitations, such as resolving types with only one constructor, only supporting constructor injection, and having a limited number of life cycles.

To use more life cycles, we will have to use our favorite DI container, if it has ported in **ASP.NET Core**.

There's more...

For some very interesting reading, try Mark Seemann's book about dependency injection, at `http://amzn.to/12p90MG`.

We can also read Mark Seemann's blog, at `http://blog.ploeh.dk/`.

Using the life cycles available in ASP.NET Core

In this recipe, we will see an example with all the life cycles available and look at what it involves.

Getting ready

We will see what the differences between all these life cycles are.

How to do it...

1. First, let's create an interface named `IOperation` with a getter on a `Guid` type, and four interfaces that represent a task for each life cycle available:

```
5 references
public interface IOperation
{
    5 references
    Guid OperationId { get; }
}

6 references
public interface IOperationTransient : IOperation
{
}
6 references
public interface IOperationScoped : IOperation
{
}
6 references
public interface IOperationSingleton : IOperation
{
}
6 references
public interface IOperationInstance : IOperation
{
}
```

2. We will now implement these interfaces in an `Operation` class:

```
6 references
public class Operation : IOperationTransient,
    IOperationScoped, IOperationSingleton, IOperationInstance
{
    private Guid? empty;

    0 references
    public Operation()
    {
    }
    1 reference
    public Operation(Guid empty)
    {
        this.empty = empty;
    }

    5 references
    Guid IOperation.OperationId
    {
        get
        {
            if (!empty.HasValue)
                empty = Guid.NewGuid();

            return empty.Value;
        }
    }
}
```

3. In the `ConfigurationServices` method of the `Startup.cs` class, we manage the lifetime for each interface:

```
services.AddTransient<IOperationTransient, Operation>();
services.AddScoped<IOperationScoped, Operation>();
services.AddSingleton<IOperationSingleton, Operation>();
services.AddInstance<IOperationInstance>(new Operation(Guid.Empty));
```

4. Now, let's create an `OperationService` class that we will use in an MVC controller and execute in several HTTP requests:

```csharp
2 references
public class OperationService
{
    1 reference
    public IOperationTransient TransientOperation { get; private set; }
    1 reference
    public IOperationScoped ScopedOperation { get; private set; }
    1 reference
    public IOperationSingleton SingletonOperation { get; private set; }
    1 reference
    public IOperationInstance InstanceOperation { get; private set; }

    0 references
    public OperationService(IOperationTransient transientOperation,
        IOperationScoped scopedOperation,
        IOperationSingleton singletonOperation,
        IOperationInstance instanceOperation)
    {
        TransientOperation = transientOperation;
        ScopedOperation = scopedOperation;
        SingletonOperation = singletonOperation;
        InstanceOperation = instanceOperation;
    }
}
```

5. Now, we create the MVC controller and add an `Index` action to show the value of `Guid` for each implementation:

```
public class HomeController : Controller
{
    private readonly IOperationTransient _transientOperation;
    private readonly IOperationScoped _scopedOperation;
    private readonly IOperationSingleton _singletonOperation;
    private readonly IOperationInstance _instanceOperation;

    0 references
    public HomeController(
        IOperationTransient transientOperation,
        IOperationScoped scopedOperation,
        IOperationSingleton singletonOperation,
        IOperationInstance instanceOperation)
    {
        _transientOperation = transientOperation;
        _scopedOperation = scopedOperation;
        _singletonOperation = singletonOperation;
        _instanceOperation = instanceOperation;
    }

    3 references
    public IActionResult Index()
    {
        ViewBag.Transient = _transientOperation.OperationId;
        ViewBag.Scoped = _scopedOperation.OperationId;
        ViewBag.Singleton = _singletonOperation.OperationId;
        ViewBag.Instance = _instanceOperation.OperationId;
        return View();
    }
}
```

6. Finally, we create the view that shows the result:

```
<h2> Transient @ViewBag.Transient</h2>
<h2> Scoped @ViewBag.Scoped</h2>
<h2> Singleton @ViewBag.Singleton</h2>
<h2> Instance @ViewBag.Instance</h2>
```

How it works...

We can see the different values of `Guids`.

Request 1 :

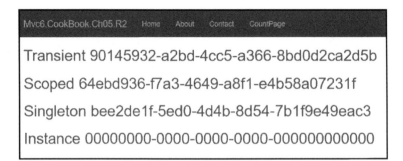

Request 2:

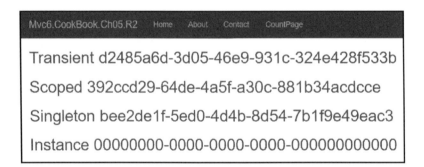

The conclusion is the following:

- **Transient**: Objects are always different; a new instance is provided to every controller and every service
- **Scoped**: Objects are the same within a request, but different across different requests
- **Singleton**: Objects are the same for every object and every request
- **Instance**: Objects are the same for every object and every request, and are the exact instance which were specified in the code

Implementing DI with Autofac

In this recipe, we will use Autofac as a DI container to compose our application's object graph. It is famous, performant, and has a lot of features.

ASP.NET Core has an out-of-the-box DI container. In this chapter, we'll use another DI container-Autofac. Autofac is very well-received by the community.

An inbuilt DI container is very lightweight and doesn't support every feature that full-fledged DI containers support.

Autofac is also very light, but it has almost every feature that you would expect from a complete DI container library.

Getting ready

In the two previous recipes, we resolved the dependency on `ServiceProduct` by using the native IOC component in ASP.NET Core. This time, that will be done by a third-party component called **Autofac**. Now, in ASP.NET applications, we will be able to manage MVC, WebAPI, and SignalR components with the same IOC container.

How to do it...

As in the first recipe, we do the following:

1. Inject the `ServiceProducts` class by using a constructor in the `HomeController` of an ASP.NET MVC 6 application.
2. Create a class called `Product`.
3. Create an interface called `IProductService`.
4. Create a class called `ProductService`.
5. Modify `HomeController` to add a constructor that will inject `IProductService`.
6. Create an action method called `Products` in `HomeController`.
7. Create a view called `Products.cshtml`.

8. Now, to use Autofac, we have to add the `Autofac` and `Autofac.Extensions.DependencyInjection` NuGet packages in the `project.json` file's **dependencies** section:

```
"Autofac": "4.0.0-rc1-177",
"Autofac.Extensions.DependencyInjection": "4.0.0-rc1-177"
```

9. We use a module to help us to configure dependencies:

```
1 reference
public class AutofacModule : Module
{
    0 references
    protected override void Load(ContainerBuilder builder)
    {
        builder.Register(c => new ProductService())
            .As<IProductService>()
            .InstancePerLifetimeScope();
    }
}
```

10. We configure the Autofac DI component in the `ConfigureService` method in `Startup.cs`:

```
0 references
public IServiceProvider ConfigureServices(IServiceCollection services)
{
    // We add MVC here instead of in ConfigureServices.
    services.AddMvc();

    // Create the Autofac container builder.
    var builder = new ContainerBuilder();

    // Add any Autofac modules or registrations.
    builder.RegisterModule(new AutofacModule());

    // Populate the services.
    builder.Populate(services);

    // Build the container.
    var container = builder.Build();

    // Resolve and return the service provider.
    return container.Resolve<IServiceProvider>();
}
```

Now, when returning the `IServiceProvider`, we don't explicitly use `DependencyResolver` anymore; ASP.NET Core does it for us internally.

ASP.NET Core has built-in functionalities in IServiceProvider that use `DependencyResolver` for us. With this support, we should not use `DependencyResolver` explicitly.

11. Finally, we test the application with this new configuration:

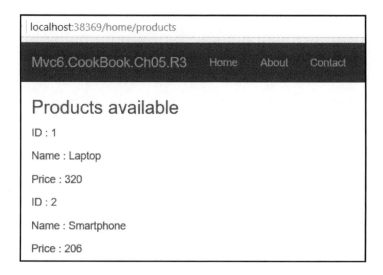

How it works...

Let's use `ProductService` in our `HomeController` to create an instance of `ProductService` by injecting the `ProductService` abstraction in the `HomeController` constructor.

`ProductService` will be available for the whole `HomeController` class.

We will use a **module** to help us to configure dependencies.

According to the Autofac documentation:

> *A module is a small class that can be used to bundle up a set of related components behind a 'facade' to simplify configuration and deployment. The module exposes a deliberate, restricted set of configuration parameters that can vary independently of the components used to implement the module.*

Implementing DI with StructureMap

Now we will use a DI container called StructureMap to be the external component to resolve our dependencies.

In this recipe, we'll use another DI container, StructureMap. StructureMap is very well received by the community.

StructureMap is also very light, but it has almost every feature that you would expect from a complete DI container library.

How to do it...

We will create the object graph of our dependencies for our application. To do that, we will create a `ConfigureService` method that returns an `IServiceProvider` type.

As in the first recipe, we will do the following:

1. Inject the `ServiceProducts` class by using a constructor in the `HomeController` of an ASP.NET MVC 6 application.
2. Create a class called **Product**.
3. Create an interface called `IProductService`.
4. Create a class called `ProductService`.
5. Modify `HomeController` to add a constructor that will inject `IProductService`.
6. Create an action method called Products in `HomeController`.
7. Create a view called `Products.cshtml`.
8. Now, to use StructureMap, we have to add the StructureMap and `structuremap.Dnx` NuGet packages in the `project.json` file's `dependencies` section. They will be downloaded automatically:

```
"structuremap": "4.1.1.372",
"structuremap.Dnx": "0.4.0-rc1-final"
```

9. In the `ConfigureServices` method, we create a StructureMap container:

```
0 references
public IServiceProvider ConfigureServices(IServiceCollection services)
{
    // Add framework services.

    services.AddMvc();

    services.AddTransient<IProductService, ProductService>();

    var container = new Container();

    // This will register all services from the collection
    // into the container with the appropriate lifetime.
    container.Populate(services);

    // Finally, make sure we return an IServiceProvider. This makes
    // DNX use the StructureMap container to resolve its services.
    return container.GetInstance<IServiceProvider>();
}
```

10. Finally, we test the application with this new configuration:

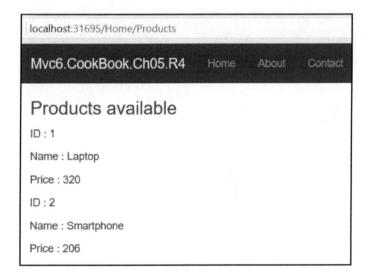

How it works...

We populated the container using the `ServiceCollection` passed in the parameter that registered our types.

Calling the populate method of the StructureMap container called the `Configure` method internally.

Implementing DI with DryIoc

Now we will use a DI container called DryIoc to be the external component to resolve our dependencies.

In this recipe, we'll use another DI container-DryIoc. DryIoc is very well received by the community.

DryIoc is also very light, but it has almost every feature that you would expect from a complete DI container library.

Getting ready

We want to compose the application's object graph.

To do that, we will create a `ConfigureService` method that returns an `IServiceProvider` type.

How to do it...

As in the first recipe, we will do the following:

1. Inject the `ServiceProducts` class by using a constructor in the `HomeController` of an ASP.NET MVC 6 application.
2. Create a class called `Product`.
3. Create an interface called `IProductService`.
4. Create a class called `ProductService`.
5. Modify `HomeController` to add a constructor that will inject `IProductService`.

6. Create an action method called `Products` in `HomeController`.

7. Create a view called `Products.cshtml`.

8. Now, to use DryIoc, we will add the `DryIoc` and `DryIoc.Dnx.DependencyInjection` NuGet packages in `project.json` file's `dependencies` section. They will be downloaded automatically:

```
"DryIoc": "2.2.2",
"DryIoc.Dnx.DependencyInjection": "1.4.0-rc1"
```

9. We will now create a bootstrap class to register and resolve `IProductService` with `ProductService`:

```
1 reference
public static class Bootstrap
{
    1 reference
    public static void RegisterServices(IRegistrator registrator)
    {
        registrator.Register<IProductService, ProductService>(Reuse.Singleton);
    }
}
```

10. This class will also resolve the `ServiceProvider` for us before returning it:

```
0 references
public static class IocDiExtensions
{
    1 reference
    public static IServiceProvider ConfigureDI(
        this IServiceCollection services,
        Action<IRegistrator> configureServices)
    {
        var container = new Container()
            .WithDependencyInjectionAdapter(services);

        configureServices(container);

        return container.Resolve<IServiceProvider>();
    }
}
```

11. In the `ConfigureServices` method, we call the `extension` method that calls the `Bootstrap` class:

```
0 references
public IServiceProvider ConfigureServices(IServiceCollection services)
{
    // Add framework services.

    services.AddMvc();
    return services.ConfigureDI(Bootstrap.RegisterServices);
}
```

12. Now, let's test the application with this new configuration:

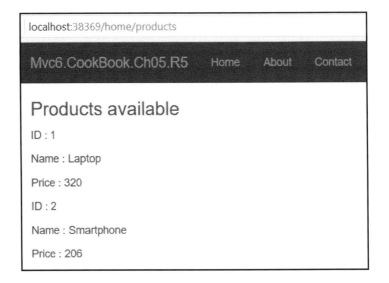

How it works...

We created an extension method named `ConfigureDI` in a static class named `IocDiExtensions` to create a wrapper for `IServiceProvider`.

6

Data Access - EF7 with Repository, SQL Server, and Stored Procedures

In this chapter, we will cover the following:

- Configuring the IOC life cycle for repository pattern
- Using EF with an existing database
- Using an InMemory provider
- Managing a long request batch
- Using a stored procedure with EF
- Writing an EF provider

Introduction

In this chapter, we will learn how to create a data access layer with the object relational mapper called Entity Framework. We will configure its IOC life cycle, create a CRUD with and without stored procedures, and log and manage exceptions.

We will first explain some concepts used internally by Entity Framework that are recurrent in ORMs, and then we will see which of the EF features no longer exist in EF.

ORM is a library that maps data classes with datatables in a database, such as `Customer` class maps with a Customer table in a database, `BankTransaction` class maps with a `BankTransaction` table in a database, and so on.

ORM libraries help developers build data access layers without the hassle of table query complexities. For example, they can help you set the `IsDeleted` field in the next 20 rows of a table to `False`. It's so easy to write these kinds of queries with ORM libraries.

DbContext

An ORM uses the code representation of a SQL schema to request databases. Originally, they mapped a relational database. Now there's a lot of wrapper to map an ORM, with a lot of different data sources, such as noSQL databases, key-value pairs or documents, redis, document DB, CSV files, and so on.

With Entity Framework, a class that inherits the `DbContext` class maps the SQL schema.

This `DbContext` contains DbSet objects that map with DB tables.

Entity Framework (EF) approach

To work with EF, we need a class that inherits from the `DbContext` class and the `DbSet` object as the `DbContext` class properties.

Before EF, we had several approaches to working with EF:

- The empty code first model (from C# classes used to generate a new database)
- Code first from an existing database (generating EF entities' classes and the `DbContext` class, but the goal was to keep on using EF with the code first model features)
- The empty EF designer model (in an `.edmx` model file via a graphic interface, we created object-oriented entities that generated a new database (schema, tables, relations, constraints) and the associated C# code.
- The EF designer from the database (this generated an `.edmx` file model from an existing database)

We can use EF 7 in three ways:

- Code first
- Database first
- Both (we can begin using EF with an existing database and extend this database with the code first approach)
- The EF Designer model has been removed, and so there are no more EDMX files
- The ObjectContext API has been removed
- The Entity SQL has been removed

 The unique ability of an ORM is that it can store the object representation of the database in memory. The design pattern used internally in ORMs to do this is the repository pattern that we will talk about later in this chapter in another recipe.

Configuring the IOC life cycle for the repository pattern

In this recipe, we will learn a simple way of registering, resolving, and giving a life cycle to EF in ASP.NET Core.

Getting ready

We will inject EF in the `ConfigureServices` method of `Statup.cs`. The `IServiceCollection` interface parameter of `ConfigureServices` already has some helpers for the most common libraries used in ASP.NET MVC.

This code does not exist by default in the empty project in Visual Studio's ASP.NET Core templates, but it already exists if we use a Web Application ASP.NET Core template.

After that, we will add a class that inherits from DbContext to our application to perform database operations that throw an ORM. Finally, we will create a repository layer between the application and the database persistence layer (even if all the code is physically in the same application) before configuring its life cycle.

But, first of all, let's create a database on SQL Server (from 2008 to 2014) named CookBook.

After that, we will create two tables, Book and Recipe:

```
CREATE TABLE [dbo].[Book](
 [Id] [int] IDENTITY(1,1) NOT NULL,
 [Name] [varchar](50) NOT NULL,
CONSTRAINT [PK_Book] PRIMARY KEY CLUSTERED
(
 [Id] ASC
)WITH (PAD_INDEX = OFF, STATISTICS_NORECOMPUTE = OFF, IGNORE_DUP_KEY = OFF,
ALLOW_ROW_LOCKS = ON, ALLOW_PAGE_LOCKS = ON) ON [PRIMARY]
) ON [PRIMARY]

GO
CREATE TABLE [dbo].[Recipe](
 [Id] [int] IDENTITY(1,1) NOT NULL,
 [Name] [varchar](50) NOT NULL,
 [IdBook] [int] NOT NULL,
 CONSTRAINT [PK_Recipes] PRIMARY KEY CLUSTERED
(
 [Id] ASC
)WITH (PAD_INDEX = OFF, STATISTICS_NORECOMPUTE = OFF, IGNORE_DUP_KEY = OFF,
ALLOW_ROW_LOCKS = ON, ALLOW_PAGE_LOCKS = ON) ON [PRIMARY]
) ON [PRIMARY]

ALTER TABLE [dbo].[Recipe] WITH CHECK ADD CONSTRAINT [FK_Recipes_Book]
FOREIGN KEY([IdBook])
REFERENCES [dbo].[Book] ([Id])
GO
ALTER TABLE [dbo].[Recipe] CHECK CONSTRAINT [FK_Recipes_Book]
GO
```

Finally, let's insert some items in the Book table and the Recipe table:

```
USE [CookBook]

INSERT INTO [dbo].[Book]([Name]) VALUES ('ASP.NET MVC 6')
INSERT INTO [dbo].[Book]([Name]) VALUES ('EF 7')

INSERT INTO [dbo].[Recipe]([Name],[IdBook]) VALUES('Tasks runners',1)
INSERT INTO [dbo].[Recipe]([Name],[IdBook]) VALUES('IoC',1)
INSERT INTO [dbo].[Recipe]([Name],[IdBook]) VALUES('DbContext',2)
INSERT INTO [dbo].[Recipe]([Name],[IdBook]) VALUES('In-Memory Provider',2)
GO
```

How to do it...

1. First, we add EF as an injected service:

   ```
   public void ConfigureServices(IServiceCollection services)
   {
   services.AddEntityFramework()
   }
   ```

   IntelliSense can help us to find this method, which already exists as an extension method helper.

2. Next, we associate EF with a database. EF doesn't know anything about the data store we will use (any relational database, any nonrelational database, and so on):

```
public void ConfigureServices(IServiceCollection services)
{
services.AddEntityFramework()
.AddSqlServer()
}
```

3. Now we add the `DbContext` named `ApplicationDbContext` associated with the connection in the parameter stored in `appsettings.json`.

In doing this, we configure a database provider when setting up the services for our application:

```
public void ConfigureServices(IServiceCollection services)
{
services.AddEntityFramework()
.AddSqlServer()
.AddDbContext(
options => options.UseSqlServer(
 Configuration["Data:DefaultConnection:ConnectionString"]
 ));
}
```

We access the hierarchy of the `appsettings.json` file JSON object with the following syntax:

```
"Data": {
"DefaultConnection": {
"ConnectionString": "Server=(localdb)...."
}
}
```

4. Next, we create our own `DbContext` to communicate with a database by overriding the `OnConfiguring` method of the `CookBookContext` class:

```
public class CookBookContext : DbContext
{
 public CookBookContext()
 {
 var config = new ConfigurationBuilder()
 .AddJsonFile("appsettings.json")
 .AddEnvironmentVariables();
 Configuration = config.Build();
 }
 public IConfiguration Configuration { get; set; }
 public DbSet Books { get; set; }
 public DbSet Recipes { get; set; }
 protected override void OnConfiguring
 (DbContextOptionsBuilder options)
 {
 var connectionString =
 Configuration["Data:DefaultConnection:ConnectionString"];
 options.UseSqlServer(connectionString);
```

```
  }
}
```

We will now create a service layer to isolate the controller code to the database code:

```
public class RecipeRepository : IRecipeRepository
{
 private readonly CookBookContext _context;

 public RecipeRepository(CookBookContext context)
 {
 _context = context;
 }

 public IEnumerable GetAllRecipes()
 {
 return _context.Recipes.AsEnumerable();
 }
}
```

5. Finally, we will configure the repository life cycle, configuring all the object graphs that depend on it at the same time. In this case, `CookBookContext` will have the same life cycle as `RecipeRepository`. We will choose the ASP.NET Core scoped life cycle, which corresponds to a per request life cycle; this means that this class instance will be available during the time of an HTTP request without having to re-instantiate it (as a singleton per request).

Let's add the following line of code to the `ConfigureService` method of the `Startup.cs` class:

```
services.AddScoped<IRecipeRepository, RecipeRepository>();
```

Using EF with an existing database

In this recipe, we will learn how to create a `DbContext` file from an existing database.

There are methods to create the `DbContext` and `DbSet` classes in EF.

One is the database first approach. With this method, EF tooling support covers database tables and the fields in them to create the `DbContext` and `DbSet` classes.

Another is the code first approach. With this method, developers create the `DbContext` and `DbSet` classes by hand, and the EF library can use these classes to reach database tables.

When they released EF Core 1.0, Microsoft declared that EF tooling has no more support for covering and creating the `DbContext` and `DbSet` classes from existing databases.

Getting ready

Using Visual Studio 2015, we will create an ASP.NET MVC 6 project.

How to do it...

We will create a repository:

1. First, we have to be sure that we have imported the following dependencies in `project.json`:

```
"dependencies": {
  "EntityFramework.Commands": "7.0.0-rc1-final",
  "EntityFramework.MicrosoftSqlServer": "7.0.0-rc1-final",
  "EntityFramework.Core": "7.0.0-rc1-final",
  "EntityFramework.MicrosoftSqlServer.Design": "7.0.0-rc1-final",
```

2. Let's open a **Developer Command Prompt** for Visual Studio 2015. We will type the following command after it has been placed in the project folder:

```
dnx ef
```

The output of the preceding command is as follows:

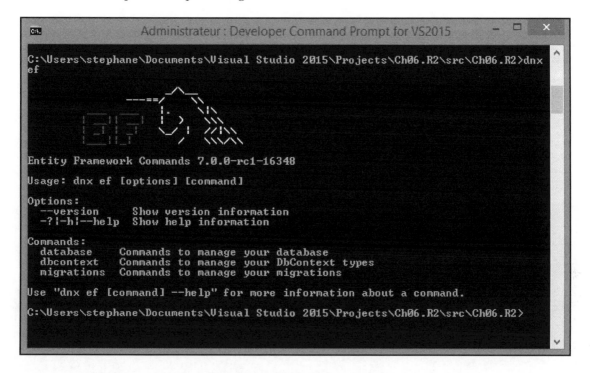

3. After that, we type the following command:

```
dnx ef scaffold "DatabaseConnectionString"
EntityFramework.MicrosoftSqlServer --outputDir Models
```

The output of the preceding command is as follows:

We can see now all the files that are generated:

▷   C# Book.cs
▷   C# CookBookContext.cs
▷   C# Recipe.cs

4. Let's open `CookBookContext` to see what is generated:

```
0 references
public partial class CookBookContext : DbContext
{
    1 reference
    protected override void OnConfiguring(DbContextOptionsBuilder options)
    {
        options.UseSqlServer(@"Data Source=PC-HOME\SQLEXPRESS;
                        Initial Catalog=CookBook;Integrated Security=True");
    }

    3 references
    protected override void OnModelCreating(ModelBuilder modelBuilder)
    {
        modelBuilder.Entity<Book>(entity =>
        {
            entity.Property(e => e.Name)
                .IsRequired()
                .HasMaxLength(50)
                .HasColumnType("varchar");
        });

        modelBuilder.Entity<Recipe>(entity =>
        {
            entity.Property(e => e.Name)
                .IsRequired()
                .HasMaxLength(50)
                .HasColumnType("varchar");

            entity.HasOne(d => d.IdBookNavigation)
                .WithMany(p => p.Recipe)
                .HasForeignKey(d => d.IdBook)
                .OnDelete(DeleteBehavior.Restrict);
        });
    }

    0 references
    public virtual DbSet<Book> Book { get; set; }
    0 references
    public virtual DbSet<Recipe> Recipe { get; set; }
}
```

5. Let's now open `Book.cs` and `Recipe.cs`:

```
7 references
public partial class Book
{
    2 references | 1/1 passing
    public Book()
    {
        Recipes = new HashSet<Recipe>();
    }

    2 references | 1/1 passing
    public int Id { get; set; }
    3 references | 1/1 passing
    public string Name { get; set; }

    4 references | 1/1 passing
    public virtual ICollection<Recipe> Recipes { get; set; }
}
```

6. Let's also open `Revipe.cs`

```
6 references
public partial class Recipe
{
    0 references
    public int Id { get; set; }
    1 reference
    public int IdBook { get; set; }
    1 reference
    public string Name { get; set; }

    1 reference
    public virtual Book IdBookNavigation { get; set; }
}
```

Using an InMemory provider

In this recipe, we will learn how to use the InMemory provider option in EF DbContext.

Getting ready

We will create an ASP.NET Core project in Visual Studio 2015.

How to do it...

1. First, let's see the rows contained in our Book table in the Cookbook database on SQL Server:

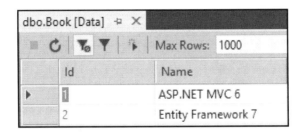

2. We can see in the OnConfiguring method of CookbookContext that we use SQL Server as the provider:

```
1 reference
public class CookbookContext : DbContext
{
    2 references
    public DbSet<Book> Book { get; set; }
    0 references
    public DbSet<Recipe> Recipe { get; set; }

    0 references
    protected override void OnConfiguring(DbContextOptionsBuilder options)
    {
        options.UseSqlServer(@"Data Source=PC-HOME\SQLEXPRESS;Initial Catalog=CookBook;Integrated Security=True;");
    }
}
```

3. Let's create an MVC `Cookbook` controller and a `Books` view to see all the rows of the `Book` table:

```
0 references
public class CookbookController : Controller
{
    0 references
    public IActionResult Books()
    {
        List<Book> books = new List<Book>();
        using (var context = new CookbookContext())
        {
            books = context.Book.ToList();
        }
        return View(books);
    }
}
```

The `Books` view should look as follows:

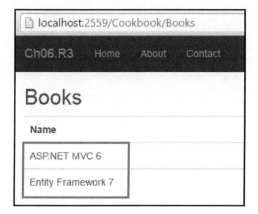

4. Now we will install the necessary packages to use the new `InMemory` provider for EF Core. We can do that in one of three ways:

   1. One is by the NuGet Package Manager:

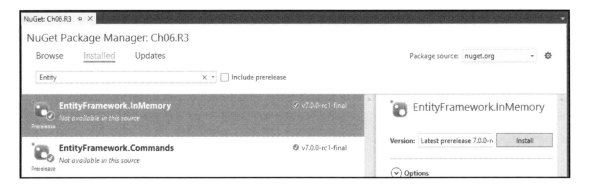

   2. The second method involves using the **Package Manager Console** by typing the following command:

```
Install-Package EntityFramework.InMemory -pre
```

   The output of the preceding command is as follows:

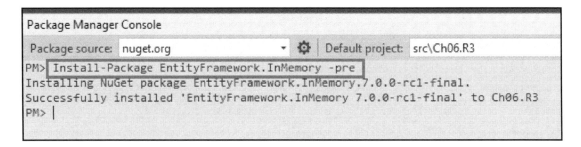

We can see the `EntityFramework.InMemory` is installed:

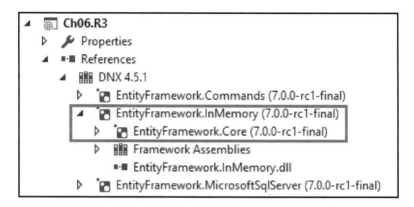

3. The third way involves directly typing the name of the package in the `project.json` file:

```
"dependencies": {
  "EntityFramework.Commands": "7.0.0-rc1-final",
  "EntityFramework.MicrosoftSqlServer": "7.0.0-rc1-final",
  "EntityFramework.Core":
  "Microsoft.AspNet.Authen    7.0.0-rc1-final      .0.0-rc1-final",
  "Microsoft.AspNet.Diagno    7.0.0-beta8          -rc1-final",
  "Microsoft.AspNet.Identi    7.0.0-beta5          3.0.0-rc1-final",
  "Microsoft.AspNet.IISPla    7.0.0-beta4          -rc1-final",
  "Microsoft.AspNet.Mvc":                          -final",
  "Microsoft.AspNet.Mvc.Ta    " "                  -final",
  "Microsoft.AspNet.Server    {}                   nal",
  "Microsoft.AspNet.Static                         final",
  "Microsoft.AspNet.Toolin    7.0.0-beta8          final",
  "Microsoft.Extensions.Co    7.0.0-beta7          .0.0-rc1-final",
  "Microsoft.Extensions.Co    7.0.0-beta6          derExtensions" : "1.0.0-rc1
  "Microsoft.Extensions.Configuration.Json": "1.0.0-rc1-final",
  "Microsoft.Extensions.Configuration.UserSecrets": "1.0.0-rc1-final",
  "Microsoft.Extensions.Logging": "1.0.0-rc1-final",
  "Microsoft.Extensions.Logging.Console": "1.0.0-rc1-final",
  "Microsoft.Extensions.Logging.Debug": "1.0.0-rc1-final",
  "Microsoft.VisualStudio.Web.BrowserLink.Loader": "14.0.0-rc1-final"
},
```

IntelliSense asks us which version we want to use for `EntityFramework.Core`

5. Now, let's test the `InMemory` provider, changing the provider option in the `OnConfiguring` method:

```
0 references
protected override void OnConfiguring(DbContextOptionsBuilder options)
{
    options.UseInMemoryDatabase();
}
```

6. Let's change the code in the MVC controller by adding an item to the books collection:

```
0 references
public IActionResult Books()
{
    Book EF7_book = new Book() { Id = 3, Name = "EF Core" };
    List<Book> books = new List<Book>();
    using (var context = new CookbookContext())
    {
        context.Book.Add(EF7_book);
        context.SaveChanges();
        books = context.Book.ToList();
    }
    return View(books);
}
```

7. Finally, we will display only the item we've just added, because we work in memory and not on the database:

8. Because the `InMemory` provider is very important for testing, we will also test it in a `test` method using `xUnit` (we will talk about `xUnit` in the next recipe).

To do that let's install the `xUnit` libraries that we need:

```
"dependencies": {
    "EntityFramework.Core": "7.0.0-rc1-final",
    "EntityFramework.Commands": "7.0.0-rc1-final",
    "EntityFramework.InMemory": "7.0.0-rc1-final",
    "EntityFramework.MicrosoftSqlServer": "7.0.0-rc1-final",
    "EntityFramework.MicrosoftSqlServer.Design": "7.0.0-rc1-final",
    "xunit": "2.1.0",
    "xunit.runner.dnx": "2.1.0-rc1-build204"
},

"commands": {
    "ef": "EntityFramework.Commands",
    "test": "xunit.runner.dnx"
}
```

We've also created the test command to run unit tests by the command line if needed.

9. Next, let's create the `test` method and specify to the `DbContextOptionsBuilder` that we are using `InMemory` provider:

```
[Fact]
0 references
public void TestInMemoryProvider()
{
    var contextBuilderInMemory = new DbContextOptionsBuilder<CookBookContext>();
    contextBuilderInMemory.UseInMemoryDatabase();
    var optionsInMemory = contextBuilderInMemory.Options;

    using (var context = new CookBookContext(optionsInMemory))
    {
        var books = new List<Book>
        {
            new Book { Id = 3, Name = "EF Core InMemory", Recipes = new List<Recipe>() },
            new Book { Id = 4, Name = "EF Core Tests", Recipes = new List<Recipe>() },
        };
        context.Book.AddRange(books);
        context.SaveChanges();
        Assert.Equal(2, context.Book.ToList().Count()); ≤31ms elapsed
    }
}
```

10. We can see the following result by right-clicking on the `test` method name and selecting **Debug test** or launching the test command created just before in the `project.json` file:

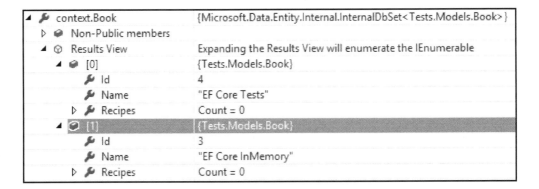

How it works...

The `InMemory` provider is very useful for unit testing without having to mock the database.

Managing a long request batch

In this recipe, we will learn the new EF 7 long request batch features.

Getting ready

We will use Visual Studio 2015 with EF 7, using the SQL Server provider.
In the previous recipe, we installed `xUnit` to run the unit test. In this recipe, we will create another unit test to run batches with EF.

We will see the generated SQL in the SQL profiler, a tool used to capture the database traffic on our SQL server. In this way, we will be able to watch the SQL code generated by EF.

How to do it...

1. First, we will configure the `DbContext` to indicate what the maximum number of requests we will allow for this `DbContext` should be, and, optionally, the timeout duration in the new unit test method we've just created:

```csharp
[Fact]
0 references
public void TestBatchSQLProvider()
{
    var contextBuilderSqlServer = new DbContextOptionsBuilder<CookBookContext>();
    contextBuilderSqlServer
        .UseSqlServer(@"Data Source=PC-HOME\SQLEXPRESS;Initial Catalog=CookBook;Integrated Security=True")
        .MaxBatchSize(10)
        .CommandTimeout(CommandTimeout);

    var options = contextBuilderSqlServer.Options;

    using (var context = new CookBookContext(options))
    {
```

2. Next, let's add some requests to insert some items in the `Book` table:

```csharp
using (var context = new CookBookContext(options))
{
    var bookAzureSQL = new Book { Name = "Azure SQL", Recipes = new List<Recipe>() };
    var bookAzureRedis = new Book { Name = "Azure Redis", Recipes = new List<Recipe>() };
    var bookSqlBatch = new Book { Name = "SQL Batch", Recipes = new List<Recipe>() };
    var bookSqlBatch2 = new Book { Name = "SQL Batch", Recipes = new List<Recipe>() };
    var bookSqlBatch3 = new Book { Name = "SQL Batch", Recipes = new List<Recipe>() };
    var bookSqlBatch4 = new Book { Name = "SQL Batch", Recipes = new List<Recipe>() };

    context.Book.AddRange(bookAzureSQL, bookAzureRedis,
        bookSqlBatch, bookSqlBatch2, bookSqlBatch3, bookSqlBatch4);

    context.SaveChanges();
```

We can see the generated SQL in the SQL Profiler now:

```
exec sp_executesql N'SET NOCOUNT OFF;
INSERT INTO [Book] ([Name])
OUTPUT INSERTED.[Id]
VALUES (@p0),
(@p1),
(@p2),
(@p3),
(@p4),
(@p5);
',N'@p0 varchar(8000),@p1 varchar(8000),@p2 varchar(8000),@p3 varchar(8000),@p4 varchar(8000),@p5 varchar(8000)',@p0='Azure
SQL',@p1='Azure Redis',@p2='SQL Batch',@p3='SQL Batch',@p4='SQL Batch',@p5='SQL Batch'
```

3. Next, let's add some requests to update some items in the Book table

```
using (var context = new CookBookContext(options))
{
    var bookAzureSQLToUpdate = context.Book.Where(b => b.Name == "Azure SQL").FirstOrDefault();
    bookAzureSQLToUpdate.Name = "Azure SQL to update";
    var bookAzureRedisToUpdate = context.Book.Where(b => b.Name == "Azure Redis").FirstOrDefault();
    bookAzureRedisToUpdate.Name = "Azure Redis to update";

    context.Update(bookAzureSQLToUpdate);
    context.Update(bookAzureRedisToUpdate);
    context.SaveChanges();
}
```

We can see the generated SQL in the SQL Profiler:

```
exec sp_executesql N'SET NOCOUNT OFF;
UPDATE [Book] SET [Name] = @p1
WHERE [Id] = @p0;
SELECT @@ROWCOUNT;
UPDATE [Book] SET [Name] = @p3
WHERE [Id] = @p2;
SELECT @@ROWCOUNT;
',N'@p0 int,@p1 varchar(8000),@p2 int,@p3 varchar(8000)',@p0=15,@p1='Azure SQL to update',@p2=16,@p3='Azure Redis to update'
```

4. Let's see the item in the `Book` table:

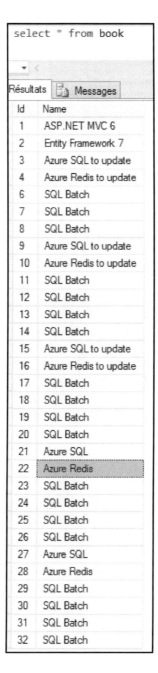

5. Next, let's add some requests to delete some items from the Book table:

```
using (var context = new CookBookContext(options))
{
    var books = context.Book.ToList();
    context.RemoveRange(books.Where(b => b.Name == "SQL Batch").ToArray());
    context.SaveChanges();
}
```

We can see the generated SQL in the SQL Profiler:

Remember, we configure the MaxBatchRequest value to 10, so the EF will generate a second SQL batch for a request that is over 10:

We can see the deleted items in the Book table:

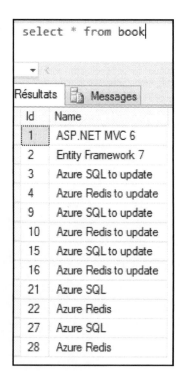

There's more...

There's a library named EntityFramework.Extended that is used to create batches in the older versions of EF. We can also use it in ASP.NET Core with Framework .NET 4.6.

The syntax would be the following:

```
//update all book with id of 1 to id of 2
context.Books.Where(b => b.Id == 1)
 .Update(t => new Book { Id = 2 });
//delete all books where Name matches
context.Books.Where(u => u.Name == "SQL").Delete();
```

Using a stored procedure with EF

In this recipe, we will learn how to use stored procedures in EF.

Getting ready

As in the previous recipes, we will continue to use the same CookBook database and to use xUnit to create unit test methods.

How to do it...

We will create a repository:

1. First, we create two stored procedures in the CookBook database:

    ```
    CREATE PROCEDURE [dbo].[GetBooks]
    AS
    BEGIN
     SET NOCOUNT ON;
     SELECT [Id],[Name] FROM [dbo].[Book]
    END
    GO

    CREATE PROCEDURE [dbo].[InsertBook]
     @name varchar(50)
    AS
    BEGIN
     SET NOCOUNT ON;
     INSERT INTO [dbo].[Book] ([Name]) VALUES (@name)
    END
    GO
    ```

2. After that, we add two methods corresponding to the two stored procedures just created to `DbContext`:

- First, we add `GetBooks`:

```
1 reference | 1/1 passing
public virtual IQueryable<Book> GetBooks()
{
    return Set<Book>().FromSql("dbo.GetBooks");
}
```

- Then, we add `InsertBook`:

```
1 reference | 1/1 passing
public virtual void InsertBook(string name)
{
    string sqlRequest = string.Format("InsertBook @name = '{0}'", name);
    Database.ExecuteSqlCommand(sqlRequest);
}
```

3. Next, let's consume these methods:

```
using (var context = new CookBookContext(options))
{
    List<Book> booksFromStoredProcedure = new List<Book>();
    booksFromStoredProcedure = context.GetBooks().ToList();
```

Writing an EF provider

In this recipe, we will learn how to create a new EF provider. It can be used to create a relational or a nonrelational provider.

Getting ready

We will import the `Microsoft.EntityFrameworkCore.Relational` library in `project.json` or NuGet.

How to do it...

1. First, let's get some sample code to override, and which allows us to create a new EF provider. We can find the template at `https://github.com/aspnet/ EntityFramework.Docs/tree/master/docs/internals/sample`.

2. Next, we can add this new provider by creating an extension method on `DbContextOptionBuilder` as follows:

```
public static class MyProviderDbContextOptionsExtensions
{
 public static DbContextOptionsBuilder UseMyProvider(
 this DbContextOptionsBuilder optionsBuilder, string
connectionString)
 {
 ((IDbContextOptionsBuilderInfrastructure)optionsBuilder)
 .AddOrUpdateExtension(
 new MyProviderOptionsExtension
 {
 ConnectionString = connectionString
 });
 return optionsBuilder;
 }
}
```

The `UseMyProvider()` method can also be used to return a special wrapper around `DbContextOptionsBuilder` that allows users to configure multiple options with chained calls.

3. Let's implement the `Add` method:

```
public static class EntityFrameworkServicesBuilderExtensions
{
public static EntityFrameworkServicesBuilder
 AddMyProvider(this EntityFrameworkServicesBuilder
 builder)
{
var serviceCollection = builder.GetInfrastructure();
 serviceCollection.TryAddEnumerable(ServiceDescriptor
.Singleton<IDatabaseProvider,
DatabaseProvider<MyDatabaseProviderServices,
 MyProviderOptionsExtension>>());
serviceCollection.TryAdd(new ServiceCollection()
// singleton services
.AddSingleton()
.AddSingleton()
```

```
// scoped services
.AddScoped()
.AddScoped()
.AddScoped()
.AddScoped
 ()
.AddScoped()
.AddScoped()
.AddScoped());
return builder;
}
}
```

We can use this new provider with its UseX method in our
OnConfiguring DbContext method.

See also

https://github.com/aspnet/EntityFramework/wiki/Writing-an-EF-Provider

7
Accessing data with Micro ORMs, NoSQL, and Azure

In this chapter, we will learn the following recipes:

- Accessing data with Dapper
- Accessing data with OrmLite
- Accessing data with MongoDb
- Accessing data with Azure storage tables
- Accessing data with storage Blobs
- Accessing data with SQL Azure

Introduction

In this chapter, we will learn how to access data in other ways different to Entity Framework in ASP.NET Core. We will do that with micro ORMs, such as Dapper and OrmLite (but we could use also Massive, SimpleData, or PetaPoco); with NoSQL Databases, such as MongoDB and ElasticSearch (but we could also use Redis, RavenDB, DocumentDB, and so many others); and with the database capabilities of Azure.

Micro ORMs

A micro ORM is a lightweight and performant ORM.

That does not mean that the other ORMs, such as Entity Framework, NHibernate, and others, cannot be performant, but it does mean they need some configuration (no entity tracking, use of stored procedures). They are faster, and they have fewer features because they don't want to cover all the possible scenarios.

These Micro ORMs will often allow us to map the result of a SQL request to a CLR object directly, as `AutoMappers` do. However, they will not track the state of our entities, have an object relational representation in memory of our database, or allow us to manage our object relational mapping graphically via a visual designer.

Using a Micro ORM makes it more difficult to create a domain model and use Domain Driven Development for our application, but it's a philosophical and/or architectural discussion we will not enter into in this book.

NoSQL

NoSQL databases are very popular now. Document-Oriented or Graph-Oriented, they allow us to store data as a key-value pair and retrieve it very quickly.

Accessing data with Dapper

In this recipe, we will learn how to get data from a database with the Dapper Micro ORM in ASP.NET Core.

Getting ready

Dapper was created by Sam Saffron and can be found in his GitHub repository at: `https://github.com/SamSaffron/dapper-dot-net`.

Let's create a new empty web application with Visual Studio 2017.

How to do it...

We will query the Book table in our SQL Express database:

1. First, we will create three folders: `Controllers`, `Models`, and `Views`.

2. Next, we add the following NuGet packages to the dependencies to the project:

```
"Microsoft.AspNetCore.Server.IISIntegration",
"Microsoft.AspNetCore.Server.Kestrel",
"Microsoft.AspNetCore.Mvc",
"Microsoft.AspNetCore.Razor.Tools",
"Microsoft.Extensions.Configuration.EnvironmentVariables",
"Microsoft.Extensions.Configuration.Json",
"System.Data.Common",
"System.Data.SqlClient",
"Dapper"
```

3. Next, let's create an `appsettings.config` file to add our database connection string and add the following code:

```
{
  "ConnectionStrings": {
    "CookBookConnection":
  "Data Source=PC-HOME\\SQLEXPRESS;Initial
Catalog=CookBook;Integrated
Security=True;MultipleActiveResultSets=true;"
  }
}
```

4. Next, we will configure dependency injection in the `ConfigureServices` method of `Startup.cs` to inject `IDbConnection` we need in the controller we will create:

```
services.AddScoped<IDbConnection>
(connection => new SqlConnection(
Configuration.GetConnectionString(
"CookBookConnection")));
```

The `Startup.cs` class will be as follows:

```
using System.Data;
using System.Data.SqlClient;
using Microsoft.AspNetCore.Builder;
using Microsoft.AspNetCore.Hosting;
using Microsoft.Extensions.DependencyInjection;
using Microsoft.Extensions.Configuration;
```

```
public class Startup
{
  public Startup(IHostingEnvironment env)
  {
    // Set up configuration sources.
    var builder = new ConfigurationBuilder()
    .SetBasePath(env.ContentRootPath)
    .AddJsonFile("appsettings.json",
  optional: true, reloadOnChange: true);

    builder.AddEnvironmentVariables();
    Configuration = builder.Build();
  }
  public IConfigurationRoot Configuration { get; set; }
  // This method gets called by the runtime. Use this method to add
services to the container.
  // For more information on how to configure your application,
visit http://go.microsoft.com/fwlink/?LinkID=398940
  public void ConfigureServices(IServiceCollection services)
  {
    services.AddScoped<IDbConnection>
    (connection => new SqlConnection(
    Configuration.GetConnectionString(
    "CookBookConnection")));

    services.AddMvc();
  }

  // This method gets called by the runtime. Use this method to
configure the HTTP request pipeline.
  public void Configure(IApplicationBuilder app)
  {
    app.UseMvc(routes =>
    {
      routes.MapRoute(
      name: "default",
      template: "{controller=Home}/{action=Index}/{id?}");
    });
  }
}
```

We can see that the routing is configured to launch the application directly with the `Book` controller.

5. Next, we create a class called `Book` inside the `Model` folder.
   This class corresponds to the `Book` table in our SQL Server Express database:

```
public class Book
{
  public int Id { get; set; }
   public string Name { get; set; }
}
```

6. Next, we create a controller called `BookController`:

```
public class BookController : Controller
{
  private readonly IDbConnection _db;
  public BookController(IDbConnection db)
  {
     _db = db;
  }

  public IActionResult Index()
  {
    List<Book> books = _db.Query<Book>("GetAllCookbooks",
    commandType: CommandType.StoredProcedure)
    .ToList();
    return View(books);
  }
}
```

As we can see, we have injected `IDbConnection` into the `BookController` constructor.

7. In the `Views` folder, we will add a `Book` and a `Shared` folder.

8. In the `Views` folder, we will also add a `ViewStart` file:

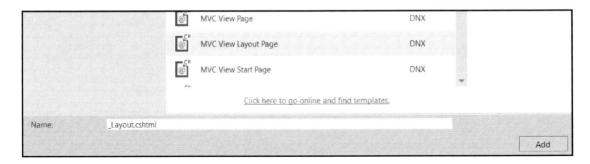

9. In the `Shared` folder, we add a `Layout` file:

10. In the `Book` folder, we add the `index.cshtml` file corresponding to the `Index` action method in the `Book` controller:

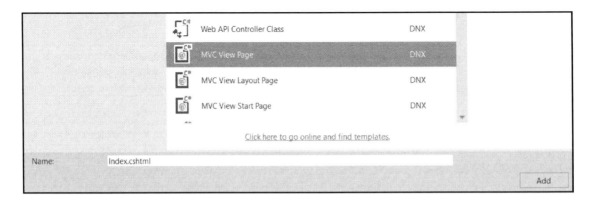

This file contains the following code:

```
@model List<Ch07.Book>
<h2>Books</h2>
<ul>
  @foreach(var book in Model)
  {
    <li>@book.Name</li>
  }
</ul>
```

Finally, we can see the application working by pressing *F5* or the launch application button:

There's more...

A very interesting reading is Mark Seemann's book about dependency injection `http://amzn.to/12p90MG`.

We can also read Mark Seemann's blog (`http://blog.ploeh.dk/`).

Accessing data with OrmLite

In this recipe, we will learn how to get data from a database with the OrmLite Micro ORM in ASP.NET Core.

Getting ready

The code is almost the same as the previous recipe; there are only a few changes.

How to do it...

1. First, we will create three folders: `Controllers`, `Models`, and `Views`.
2. Next, we add the following NuGet packages to the dependencies in the project:

   ```
   "Microsoft.AspNetCore.Server.IISIntegration",
   "Microsoft.AspNetCore.Server.Kestrel",
   "Microsoft.AspNetCore.Mvc",
   "Microsoft.AspNetCore.Razor.Tools",
   "Microsoft.Extensions.Configuration.EnvironmentVariables","Microsof
   t.Extensions.Configuration.Json",
   "System.Data.Common",
   "System.Data.SqlClient",
   "ServiceStack.OrmLite.SqlServer"
   ```

3. Next, let's create an `appsettings.config` file to add our database connection string and add the following code:

   ```
   {
     "ConnectionStrings":
     {
       "CookBookConnection":
       "Data Source=PC-HOME\SQLEXPRESS;Initial
       Catalog=CookBook;Integrated
       Security=True;MultipleActiveResultSets=true;"
     }
   }
   ```

4. Next, we will configure dependency injection in the `ConfigureServices`
   method of `Startup.cs` to inject `IDbConnection` we need in the controller we
   will create:

```
services.AddScoped<IDbConnection>
(connectionFactory => new OrmLiteConnectionFactory(
Configuration.GetConnectionString("CookBookConnection"),
SqlServer2012Dialect.Provider).OpenDbConnection());
```

The `Startup.cs` class will be as follows:

```
using Microsoft.AspNetCore.Builder;
using Microsoft.AspNetCore.Hosting;
using Microsoft.Extensions.DependencyInjection;
using Microsoft.Extensions.Configuration;
using System.Data;
using ServiceStack.OrmLite;

public class Startup
{
  public Startup(IHostingEnvironment env)
  {
    // Set up configuration sources.
    var builder = new ConfigurationBuilder()
    .SetBasePath(env.ContentRootPath)
    .AddJsonFile("appsettings.json", optional: true,
    reloadOnChange: true);
    builder.AddEnvironmentVariables();
    Configuration = builder.Build();
  }
  public IConfigurationRoot Configuration { get; set; }
  // This method gets called by the runtime. Use this
  method to add services to the container.
  // For more information on how to configure your
  application, visit http://go.microsoft.com/fwlink/?
  LinkID=398940
  public void ConfigureServices(IServiceCollection
  services)
  {
    services.AddScoped<IDbConnection>
    (connectionFactory => new OrmLiteConnectionFactory(
    Configuration.GetConnectionString
    ("CookBookConnection"), SqlServer2012Dialect.Provider)
    .OpenDbConnection());
    services.AddMvc();
  }
```

```
// This method gets called by the runtime. Use this
method to configure the HTTP request pipeline.
public void Configure(IApplicationBuilder app)
{
  app.UseMvc(routes =>
  {
    routes.MapRoute(
    name: "default",
    template: "{controller=Home}/{action=Index}/{id?}");
  });
}
}
```

We can see that the routing is configured to launch the application directly with the Book controller.

5. Next, we create a class called Book inside the Model folder. This class corresponds to the Book table in our SQL Server Express database:

```
public class Book
{
  public int Id { get; set; }
  public string Name { get; set; }
}
```

6. Next, we create a controller called BookController:

```
using System.Collections.Generic;
using Ch07R2.NetFrmk.Models;
using Microsoft.AspNetCore.Mvc;
using System.Data;
using ServiceStack.OrmLite;

public class HomeController : Controller
{
  private IDbConnection _db;
  public HomeController(IDbConnection db)
  {
    _db = db;
  }
  public IActionResult Index()
  {
    List<Book> books = new List<Book>();
    books = _db.SqlList<Book>("GetBooks");
    return View(books);
  }
}
```

As we can see, we have injected the `OrmLiteConnectionFactory` in the `BookController` constructor.

7. In the `Views` folder, we will add a `Book` and `Shared` folder.

8. In the `Views` folder, we will also add a `ViewStart` file:

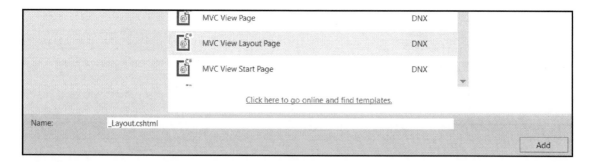

9. In the `Shared` folder, we add a `Layout` file:

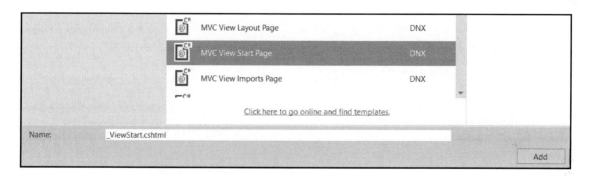

10. In the `Book` folder, we add the `index.cshtml` file corresponding to the index action method in the `Book` controller:

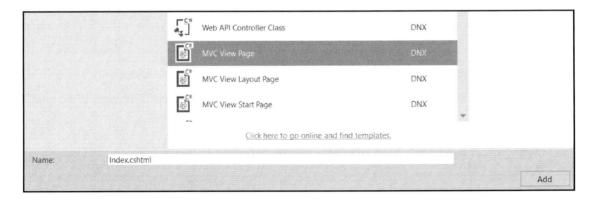

This file contains the following code:

```
@model List<Ch07.Book>
<h2>Books</h2>
<ul>
  @foreach(var book in Model)
  {
    <li>@book.Name</li>
  }
</ul>
```

Finally, we can see the application working by pressing *F5* or the launch application button:

Accessing data with MongoDb

In this recipe, we access data with MongoDB, a NoSQL database.

Getting ready

We will use VS 2017 with ASP.NET Core.

To access the data, we will first install MongoDB locally. After that, we will install a Node.js module called AdminMongo to provide us with an interface to see and manage mongo data via a graphic interface and then, after creating some data, we will consume it in an ASP.NET Core application.

How to do it...

1. First, we download the MongoDB Community version from the official website at `https://www.mongodb.com/download-center#community` and double-click on the `.msi` file:

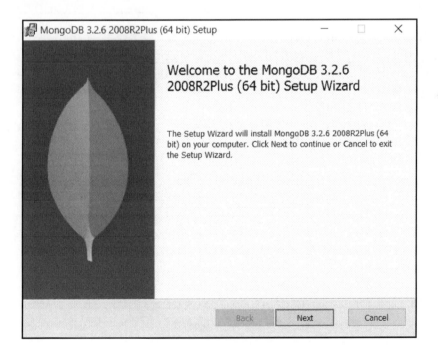

2. Let's specify an installation directory and choose the custom installation option:

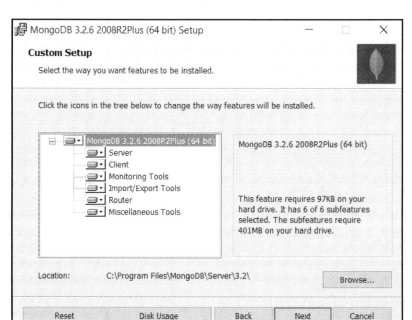

3. Next, we create the directory where we will store the data. By default, we have to create the /data/db folder inside the MongoDB directory we choose when we install it. We also have to create /log/mongo-server.log in the MongoDB directory.

4. After that, we will create our MongoDB configuration file. Let's create mongod.cfg in the MongoDB directory root. This file will contain the following data:

```
bind_ip = 127.0.0.1
dbpath = C:mongodbdatadb
logpath = C:mongodblogmongo-server.log
verbose=v
```

5. Now MongoDB is installed on our computer. Let's tell MongoDB to use this file as the configuration file:

```
C:\mongodb\bin\mongod.exe -config C:\mongodb\
mongod.cfg -install
```

```
C:\WINDOWS\system32>C:\mongodb\bin\mongod.exe --config c:\mongodb\mongod.cfg --
nstall
2016-06-13T13:37:58.706+0200 I CONTROL  [main] log file "C:\mongodb\log\mongo-s
rver.log" exists; moved to "C:\mongodb\log\mongo-server.log.2016-06-13T11-37-58
.
```

6. Let's start the MongoDB Windows service by typing the following command in a Command Prompt with admin privileges:

```
net start MongoDB
```

```
C:\WINDOWS\system32>net start mongodb
Le service MongoDB a démarré.
```

 The default port for Mongo is 27001

We can see the **MongoDB** service started in services.msc:

```
MongoDB          MongoDB Server     En cours d'exécution     Automatique     Système local
```

7. Now we will install the opensource free tool AdminMongo to manage MongoDB data. To do that, let's go to the Node.js modules directory through the Command Prompt by typing the following:

```
cd C:\Program Files (x86)\nodejs\node_modules\npm\node_modules
```

8. Next, let's clone the `AdminMongo` GitHub repository to our local machine by typing the following:

```
git clone https://github.com/mrvautin/adminMongo.git
&& cd adminMongo
```

```
C:\WINDOWS\system32>cd C:\Program Files (x86)\nodejs\node_modules\npm\node_modu
es

C:\Program Files (x86)\nodejs\node_modules\npm\node_modules>git clone https://g
thub.com/mrvautin/adminMongo.git && cd adminMongo
Cloning into 'adminMongo'...
remote: Counting objects: 688, done.
remote: Compressing objects: 100% (48/48), done.
remote: Total 688 (delta 20), reused 0 (delta 0), pack-reused 638R
Receiving objects: 100% (688/688), 1.20 MiB | 872.00 KiB/s, done.
Resolving deltas: 100% (345/345), done.
Checking connectivity... done.

C:\Program Files (x86)\nodejs\node_modules\npm\node_modules\adminMongo>
```

8. Next, we install dependencies:

```
npm install
```

```
C:\Program Files (x86)\nodejs\node_modules\npm\node_modules\adminMongo>npm insta
ll
loadDep:statuses → reques █ ║
```

9. We can now start the application by typing:

```
npm start
```

10. Finally, we launch http://127.0.0.1:1234:

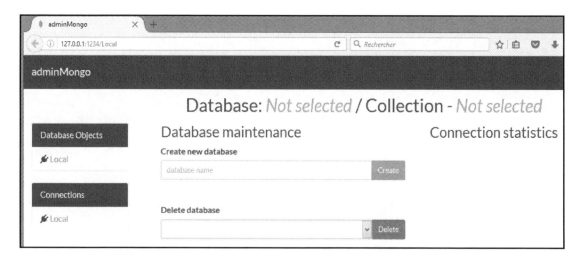

11. Let's create the `Cookbook` database by inserting the following name in **Create new database** and clicking **Create**:

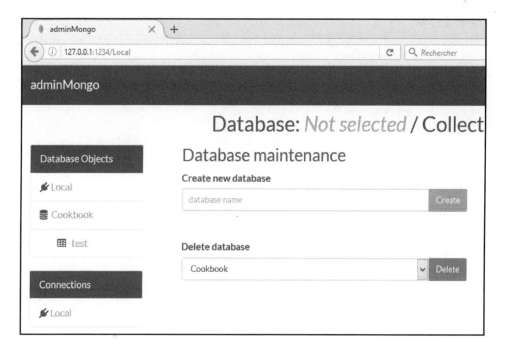

The `Cookbook` database now appears in the **Database Object** menu.

12. Now the `Cookbook` database is created, let's add a collection named `Book` in order to request data by selecting the database name on the left:

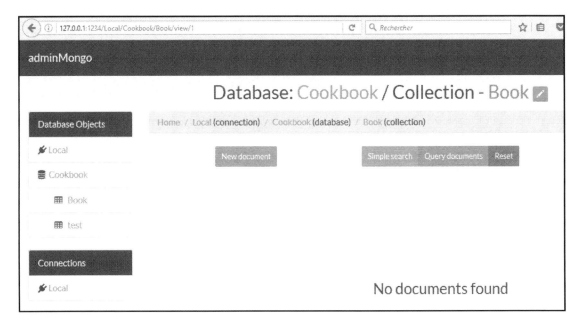

A collection in MongoDB is the equivalent of a table, and a document is the equivalent of a row in a SGBDR.

The document in MongoDB is a BSON object.

13. We add a JSON object, Book, as a document by clicking **New document**. The following screen will appear:

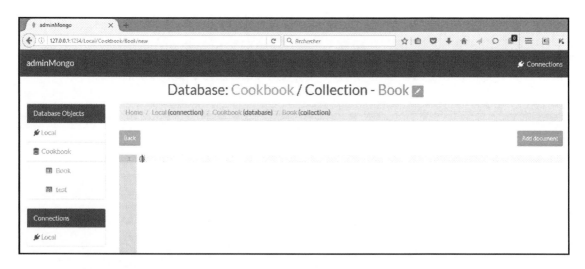

14. Let's create the new document and select **Add document**:

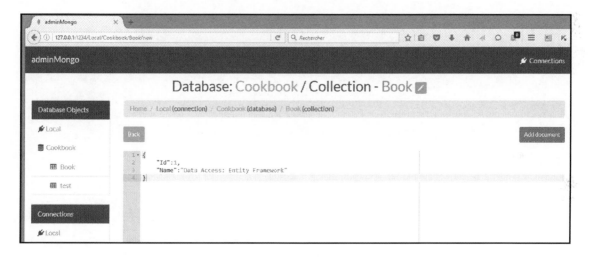

15. We will create another document and watch the result selection on the left of the Book table:

The two BSON objects created are the following:

```
{
  "_id": "575eaac5f8e681b00fc607f7",
  "Id": 1,
  "Name": "Data Access: Entity Framework"
}
{
  "_id": "575eab2af8e681b00fc607f8",
  "Id": 2,
  "Name": "Data Access : Azure"
}
```

The _id is generated by MongoDB.

We now have two documents in our Book table; let's create a web page to display this data.

16. Let's open Visual Studio and create a new empty **ASP.NET Core application (.NET Framework)**:

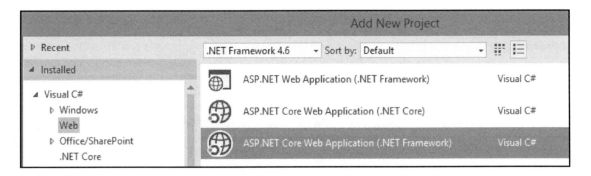

17. We will create the folder structure for our web application. To do that, we add the following directories at the root of the application: `Controllers`, `Data`, `Models`, and `Views`:

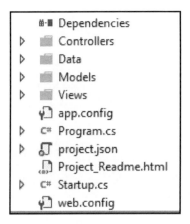

18. Next, we manually add the following libraries to the dependencies in the project:

- For ASP.NET MVC usage:

```
"Microsoft.AspNetCore.Server.IISIntegration",
"Microsoft.AspNetCore.Server.Kestrel",
"Microsoft.AspNetCore.Mvc",
"Microsoft.AspNetCore.Razor.Tools"
```

- For MongoDB usage:

```
"mongocsharpdriver": "2.2.4",
"MongoDB.Bson": "2.2.4",
"MongoDB.Driver": "2.2.4",
"MongoDB.Driver.Core": "2.2.4"
```

The corresponding NuGet packages will be downloaded automatically.

19. Now, we create a model in the `Models` folder corresponding to the `Book` table structure in the `MongoDB` database:

```
using MongoDB.Bson;
using MongoDB.Bson.Serialization.Attributes;
public class Book
{
   [BsonRepresentation(BsonType.ObjectId)]
   public string Id { get; set; }
   public string Name { get; set; }
}
```

20. Next, we create the `CookbookContext` class to communicate with MongoDB thanks to the `MongoDB.Driver` library in the `Data` folder.

Let's add the following code:

```
using MongoDB.Driver;
public class CookbookContext
{
   private readonly string connectionString = "mongodb://localhost";
   private readonly string databaseName = "CookBook";
   public IMongoDatabase Database;
   public CookbookContext()
   {
     var settings = MongoClientSettings.FromUrl(
     new MongoUrl(connectionString));
     var client = new MongoClient(settings);
     Database = client.GetDatabase(databaseName);
   }
   public IMongoCollection<Book> Books =>
Database.GetCollection<Book>("Book");
}
```

21. Next, we create a `ViewModel` class in the `Models` folder:

```
public class BookViewModel
{
  public string Id { get; set; }
  public string Name { get; set; }
}
```

22. Then, we create a controller in the `Controllers` folder:

```
using Microsoft.AspNetCore.Mvc;
using System.Threading.Tasks;
using MongoDB.Driver;
using MongoDB.Driver.Linq;
public class HomeController : Controller
{
  private readonly CookbookContext _context;

  public HomeController(CookbookContext context)
  {
    _context = context;
  }
  public async Task<ActionResult> Index()
  {
    var books = await _context.Books.AsQueryable()
    .Select(b => new BookViewModel
    {
      Id = b.Id,
      Name = b.Name
    })
    .OrderByDescending(b => b.Id)
    .ToListAsync();
    return View(books);
  }
}
```

23. Let's add the following code to the `Startup.cs` file:

```
public class Startup
{
  public void ConfigureServices(IServiceCollection
  services)
  {
    services.AddScoped(repository => new
    CookbookContext());
    services.AddMvc();
  }
```

```
public void Configure(IApplicationBuilder app)
{
  app.UseMvc(routes =>
  {
    routes.MapRoute(
    name: "default",
    template: "{controller=Home}/{action=Index}/{id?}");
  });
}
}
```

24. Next, we create a `View` file in a `Home` folder in the `Views` folder we created earlier:

```
@model List<Ch07R3.NetFrmk.Models.BookViewModel>
<h2>Books</h2>
<ul>
    @foreach (var b in Model)
    {
        <li>@b.Name</li>
    }
</ul>
```

25. Let's see the result in the browser when launching the application:

How it works...

With MongoDB, we work with a NoSQL document database. MongoDB stores JSON objects as binary JSON (a document), and each document (each JSON object) is a row in a table.

JSON (JavaScript Object Notation) is simply a JavaScript literal object used as a data interchange format. It is represented like this: { }, a pair of braces with key-value pairs inside.

MongoDB uses BSON format, which is just binary JSON to store, receive, and send JSON data. Mongo extends the JSON with BSON to provide additional data types, and to encode and decode between different languages more efficiently.

We can use MongoDB on-premises, but we can also use it as a cloud service with all cloud providers and, of course, in the Azure platform.

There's more...

To Learn about MongoDB documentation and white papers, go to:

- https://docs.mongodb.com/
- https://www.mongodb.com/nosql-explained
- https://www.mongodb.com/white-papers

For JSON documentation, go to:

- http://www.json.org/

And for BSON documentation, go to:

- http://bsonspec.org/
- https://www.mongodb.com/json-and-bson

Accessing data with Windows Azure storage tables

In this recipe, we will use Windows Azure Table storage to retrieve data from a NoSQL database in Azure.

Getting ready

To communicate with Azure storage, we have to:

- Install Azure SDK for .NET
- Create an Azure Storage account
- Install two NuGet packages: `WindowsAzure.ConfigurationManager` and `WindowsAzure.Storage`

After doing that, we will be able to use all the services in Azure storage: blobs, files, queues, and tables.

How to do it...

As in the previous recipe (Data access with MongoDb), we'll dive right into coding:

1. First, we open **Server Explorer** in Visual Studio to consult the Azure services available for our Azure subscription:

2. Next, let's install Azure SDK for .NET:

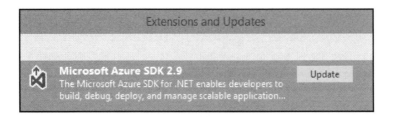

3. Save and run this file:

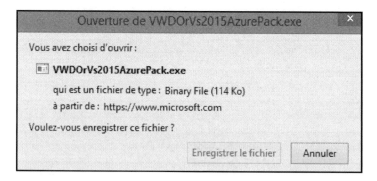

This will open the Microsoft Platform Installer and download the Azure SDK for .NET:

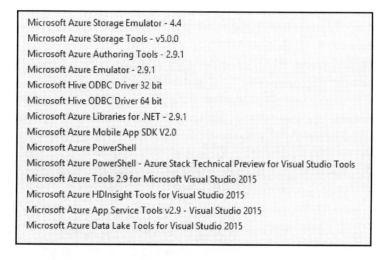

Here are all the installed libraries and components with Azure SDK:

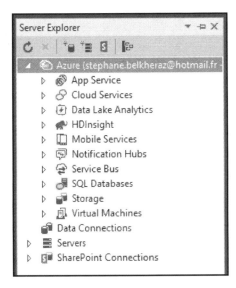

We can see a lot more items in the Azure menu.

4. Now we will use our Azure subscription to create an Azure storage account.
5. After connecting to our Azure account, we click on the **New button** | **Data + Storage** | **Storage Account**:

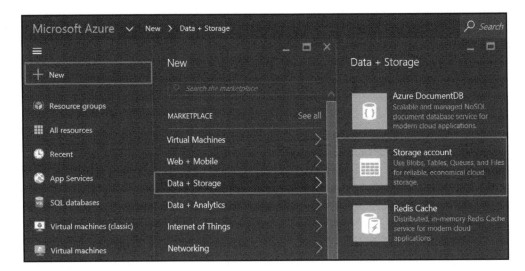

6. To create a storage account, we have to add a name, a subscription, and a resource group:

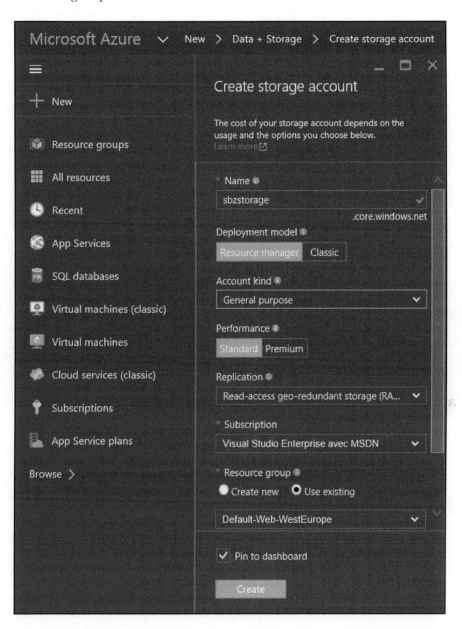

7. After clicking on the **Create** button, the storage account is now available, and we can use the blob, file, table, and queue storage services:

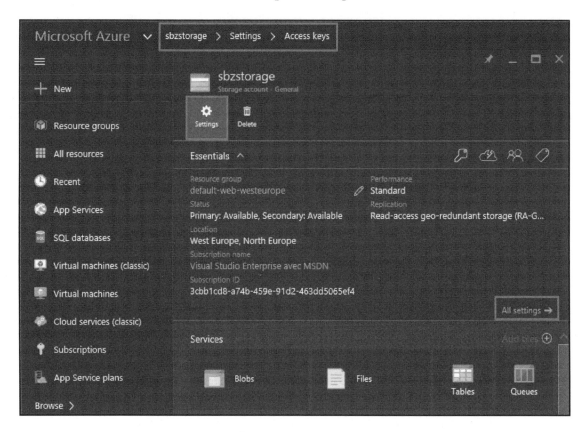

8. We will copy the storage key for use in the application as a credential in **Settings | Account Keys | Key 1**:

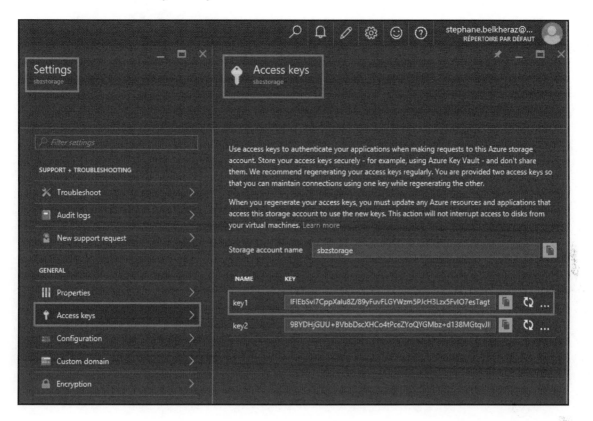

9. Now let's go back to the Visual Studio Cloud Explorer and create some data to retrieve:

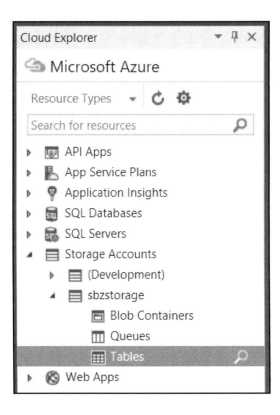

10. Right-click on **Tables**, and select **Create Table**:

11. Now the Book table is created, let's create some rows:

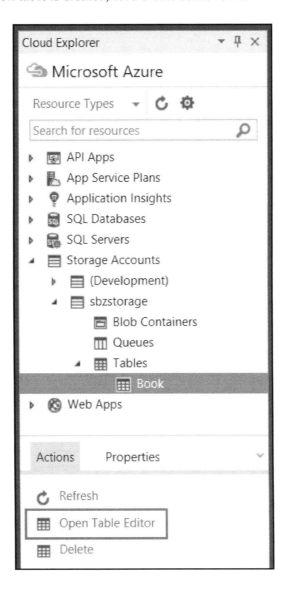

12. Let's open the table editor for the `Book` table, and click on the **Add Entity** button. The following dialog box will open:

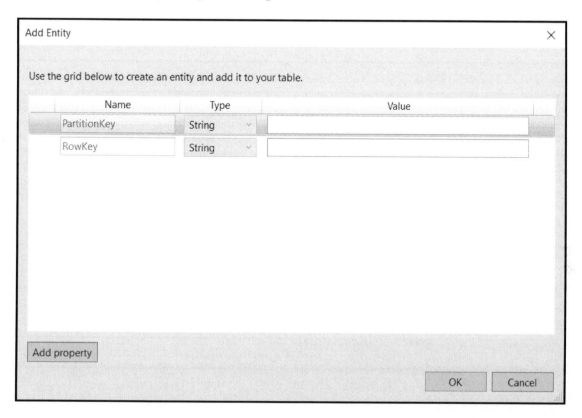

13. We add a first row:

 The primary key in a storage table is the concatenation of the partition key and the row key. The **Timestamp** field is automatically created by the system to manage concurrency of updates.

14. We add a second row:

15. To call the Azure storage service, we have to add the following libraries to the project:

- To run ASP.NET Mvc:

```
"Microsoft.AspNetCore.Server.IISIntegration",
"Microsoft.AspNetCore.Server.Kestrel",
"Microsoft.AspNetCore.Mvc",
"Microsoft.AspNetCore.Razor.Tools"
```

- To run Azure Storage:

```
"Microsoft.WindowsAzure.ConfigurationManager",
"WindowsAzure.Storage"
```

16. Now we have data to retrieve from our Azure storage, let's create an empty ASP.NET Core Application with .NET Framework. We create inside the folder the structure we need: `Models`, `Repository`, `Controllers`, and `Views`.

    In the `Models` directory, we will create the `BookViewModel` class. This class will be mapped with the entities stored in the Azure storage table:

```
public class BookViewModel
{
  public string Id { get; set; }
   public string Name { get; set; }
}
```

17. Next, we create a repository to retrieve Azure Tables:

```
public class AzureStorageRepository
{
  private const string _name = "sbzstorage";
  private const string _key =
```

```
"1FlEbSvI7CppXalu8Z/89yFuvFLGYWzm5PJcH3Lzx5FvIO7esTagtRB
dZ5m1Xv...";

private readonly CloudStorageAccount _account;

public AzureStorageRepository()
{
  StorageCredentials creds =
  new StorageCredentials(_name, _key);

  _account = new CloudStorageAccount(creds, false);
}

public List<DynamicTableEntity>
GetBooksFromAzureStorage()
{
  // Create a table client.
  CloudTableClient tableClient =
  _account.CreateCloudTableClient();

  // Get a reference to the Book table
  // in Azure Storage Table
  CloudTable bookStorageTable =
  tableClient.GetTableReference("Book");

  // Create a query for all entities.
  List<DynamicTableEntity> query =
  bookStorageTable
  .CreateQuery<DynamicTableEntity>()
  .ToList();
  return query;
}
}
```

18. Next, let's create a `Controller`:

```
public class HomeController : Controller
{
  private readonly AzureStorageRepository _repository;
  public HomeController(AzureStorageRepository repository)
  {
    _repository = repository;
  }
  public ActionResult Index()
  {
    var books = _repository.GetBooksFromAzureStorage()
    .AsQueryable()
```

```
    .Select(
    b => new BookViewModel
    {
      Id = b.PartitionKey,
      Name = b.RowKey
    })
    .OrderByDescending(b => b.Id)
    .ToList();
    return View(books);
  }
}
```

19. We also have to modify `Startup.cs` to add the necessary middleware and to manage the repository life cycle:

```
public class Startup
{
  public void ConfigureServices(IServiceCollection
  services)
  {
    services.AddScoped(repository =>
    new AzureStorageRepository());
    services.AddMvc();
  }

  public void Configure(IApplicationBuilder app)
  {
    app.UseMvc(routes =>
    {
      routes.MapRoute(
      name: "default",
      template: "{controller=Home}/{action=Index}/{id?}");
    });
  }
}
```

20. Finally, we create a view to display the result of the Azure storage request:

```
@model List<Ch07R4.NetFrmk.Models.BookViewModel>

<h2>Books</h2>
<ul>
    @foreach (var b in Model)
    {
        <li>@b.Name</li>
    }
</ul>
```

21. We can see the entities from the Azure table displayed in the browser:

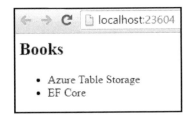

How it works...

Azure table storage allows our applications to store schema-less data persistently. Azure table storage has tables and rows inside tables. We can store a class' instance in Azure table storage if that class, inherits from the `TableEntity` class.

The `TableEntity` class comes with the Azure table storage .NET library; we just create a class that inherits from `TableEntity`, instantiate it, and use Azure table storage .NET library to store that instance in the cloud.

Azure table storage has enormous programming language support, such as, .NET, Java, PHP, C++, Node.js, Python, Ruby, and so on.

Accessing data with Azure storage Blobs

In this recipe, we will display a picture stored in a Blob thanks to the storage account previously created in the last recipe.

Getting ready

We will use VS 2017 and a storage account with our Azure subscription.

How to do it...

1. First, let's connect to our Azure portal:

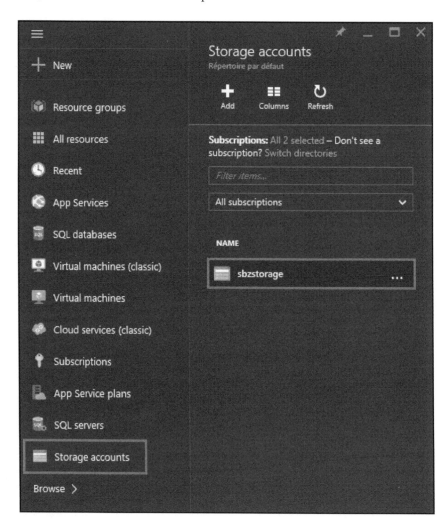

2. Next, we select the Azure storage created in the last recipe, and we select the **Blob service**:

3. Next, we click on the plus container button, and the new container panel appears. We add a name to the container and an access type (Blob or Container):

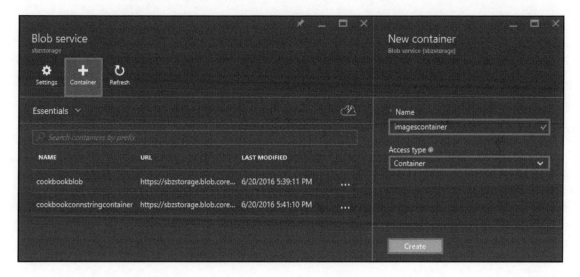

4. Now let's open Visual Studio, create an empty ASP.NET Core application with .NET Framework, and add the following directories: `Controllers`, `Images`, `Models`, `Repository`, and `Views`.

We also add the `Home` directory into the `Views` directory and a picture to upload and download from the Blob storage just created:

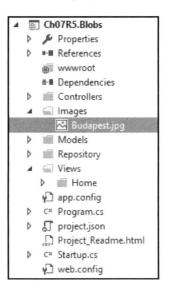

5. Next, we add the two NuGet packages manually in the `project.json` file, `Microsoft.Azure.ConfigurationManager` and `WindowsAzure.Storage`, to use the Azure storage APIs:

```
{
    "dependencies": {
        "Microsoft.AspNetCore.Server.IISIntegration": "1.0.0-rc2-final",
        "Microsoft.AspNetCore.Server.Kestrel": "1.0.0-rc2-final",
        "Microsoft.WindowsAzure.ConfigurationManager": "3.1.0",
        "WindowsAzure.Storage": "7.0.0"
    },
```

6. Next, we add the `ImageViewModel` class to the `Models` folder:

```
5 references
public class ImageViewModel
{
    2 references
    public string Url { get; set; }
}
```

7. Now we create the `IAzureStorageRepository` interface in the `Repository` folder:

```
4 references
public interface IAzureStorageRepository
{
    2 references
    string GetImageFromAzureBlobStorage();
}
```

8. Next, we create the `AzureStorageRepository` class, which inherits from `IAzureStorageRepository` to communicate with the Azure storage APIs:

```
2 references
public class AzureStorageRepository : IAzureStorageRepository
{
    private const string _name = "sbzstorage";
    private const string _key = "lFlEbSvI7CppXalu8Z/89yFuvFLGYWzm5PJcH3Lzx5FvIO
```

9. We retrieve the key account from the Azure storage panel in our Azure portal:

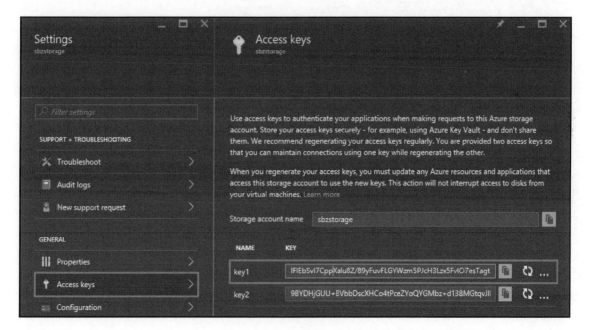

10. Next, we add the `CloudStorageAccount` and `StorageCredentials` classes to authenticate:

```
1 reference
public class AzureStorageRepository
{
    private const string _name = "sbzstorage";
    private const string _key = "1FlEbSvI7CppXalu8Z/89yFuvFLGYWzm5PJcH3Lz
    private readonly CloudStorageAccount _account;

    0 references
    public AzureStorageRepository()
    {
        StorageCredentials creds = new StorageCredentials(_name, _key);
        _account = new CloudStorageAccount(creds, false);
    }
}
```

11. By right-clicking on the class, `CodeLens` asks us to resolve `CloudStorageAccount`:

```
public class AzureStorageRepository
{
    private const string _name = "sbzstorage";
    private const string _key = "1FlEbSvI7CppXalu8Z/89yFuvFLGYWzm5PJ
    private readonly CloudStorageAccount _account;

    0 references
    public AzureStor    using Microsoft.WindowsAzure.Storage;          ▶
    {
        StorageCrede    Microsoft.WindowsAzure.Storage.CloudStorageAccount
        _account = n    Generate class 'CloudStorageAccount' in new file
    }
                        Generate class 'CloudStorageAccount'

    0 references        Generate nested class 'CloudStorageAccount'
    public List<Dyna    Generate new type...
```

12. The same thing happens for the `StorageCredentials` class:

```
                1 reference
                public class AzureStorageRepository
                {
                    private string _key;
                    private string _name;
                    private CloudStorageAccount account;

                    0 references
                    public AzureStorageRepository()
                    {
                        StorageCredentials creds = new StorageCredentials(_name, _key);
```

using Microsoft.WindowsAzure.Storage.Auth;   ▸   ❌ CS0246 The type or namespace name 'StorageCredentials' could not
Microsoft.WindowsAzure.Storage.Auth.StorageCredentials   be found (are you missing a using directive or an assembly reference?)
Generate type 'StorageCredentials'   ▸   using Microsoft.WindowsAzure.Storage;
                                              using Microsoft.WindowsAzure.Storage.Auth;
                                              using System;
                                              ...

                                              Preview changes

13. Let's add this code to upload the `Budapest.jpg` in the `Images` folder and retrieve the URL of this picture now stored in the Microsoft Cloud:

```
2 references
public string GetImageFromAzureBlobStorage()
{
    // Create a blob client.
    CloudBlobClient blobClient = _account.CreateCloudBlobClient();

    // Get a reference to a blob container.
    CloudBlobContainer imageContainer = blobClient.GetContainerReference("imagescontainer");

    // Create a blob and upload a file.
    CloudBlockBlob blob = imageContainer.GetBlockBlobReference("Budapest.jpg");
    blob.UploadFromFile(@"C:\Users\stephane\Documents\Visual Studio 2015\Projects\Ch07RC2\src\Ch07

    string urlBudapestImage = null;
    foreach (IListBlobItem blobItem in imageContainer.ListBlobs())
    {
        urlBudapestImage = blobItem.Uri.AbsoluteUri;
    }

    return urlBudapestImage;
}
```

14. Next, we create a controller to get the URL image from the
    `AzureStorageRepository`:

```csharp
1 reference
public class HomeController : Controller
{
    private readonly IAzureStorageRepository _repository;

    0 references
    public HomeController(IAzureStorageRepository repository)
    {
        _repository = repository;
    }

    0 references
    public IActionResult Index()
    {
        ImageViewModel model = new ImageViewModel();
        model.Url = _repository.GetImageFromAzureBlobStorage();
        return View(model);
    }
}
```

15. Let's modify the `Startup.cs` file to configure the repository injected into the
    controller constructor, to add the MVC middleware to the HTTP pipeline, and
    also configure the MVC routing:

```csharp
1 reference
public class Startup
{
    0 references
    public void ConfigureServices(IServiceCollection services)
    {
        services.AddScoped<IAzureStorageRepository, AzureStorageRepository>();
        services.AddMvc();
    }

    0 references
    public void Configure(IApplicationBuilder app)
    {
        app.UseMvc(routes =>
        {
            routes.MapRoute(
                name: "default",
                template: "{controller=Home}/{action=Index}/{id?}");
        });
    }
}
```

16. Next, we add a view in the `Views/Home` folder to display `Budapest.jpg` from the Blob container in Azure:

```
Index.cshtml ⊣ ✕
     1      @model Ch07R5.Blobs.Models.ImageViewModel
     2
     3      <h2>Budapest</h2>
     4
     5 💡    <img src="@Model.Url" alt="budapest" />
     6
```

17. Let's launch the web application:

18. Finally, we check the uploaded and displayed picture stored in our imagescontainer Blob:

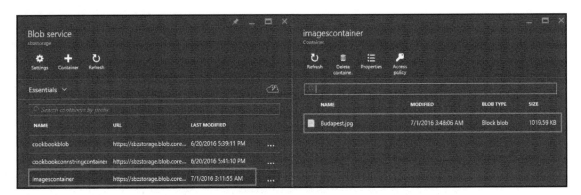

Accessing data with SQL Azure

In this recipe, we will access data from a SQL Server hosted on Azure. We talk about a SQL Server Service on Azure, not a virtual machine.

Getting ready

We will connect to our Azure subscription to subscribe to a SQL Azure database.

After creating a SQL Server, we will create a database on this SQL Server.
We will create a table and add data to it from Visual Studio 2017.
Finally, we will create a web page that consumes our data from our newly created Azure database that we created using SQL.

To do that, we need Visual Studio 2017, with SQL Data Tools installed, and an Azure subscription.

How to do it...

1. First, we will connect to our Azure subscription.
2. Next, we will create a SQL Server named `dbcookbook`:

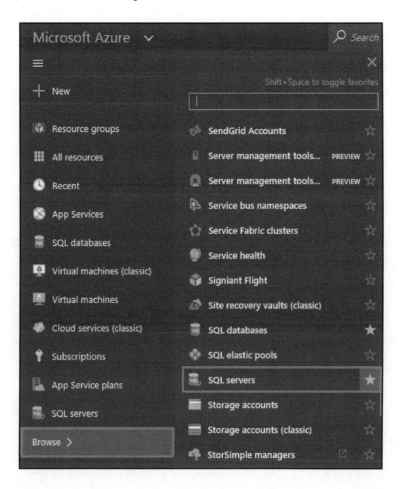

3. We select **Browse** | **SQL Servers**:

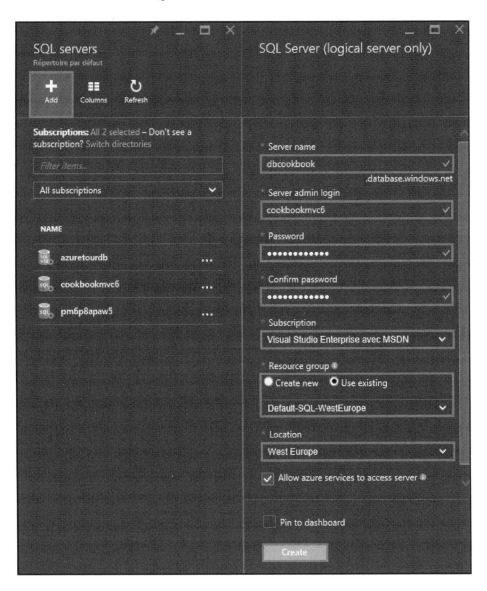

4. We click on **Add**, and we fill the **SQL Server** form to give the server name, admin login, password, subscription, resource group, and location.

5. To create the server, we click on the **Create** button at the bottom:

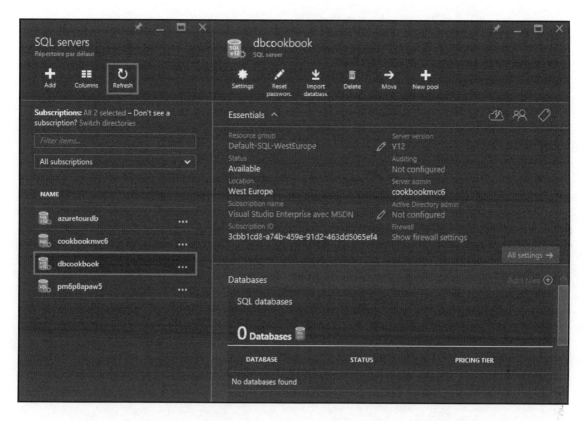

Clicking on the **Refresh** button, we can see the SQL Server newly created.

6. Next, we create an Azure SQL database named `CookbookCh07` on the SQL Server `dbcookbook` previously created:

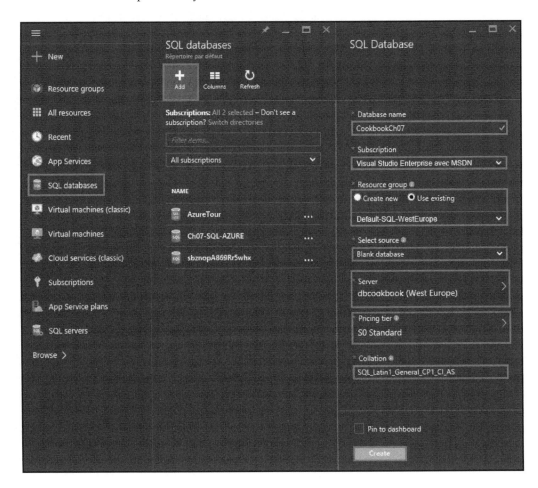

We can click on **Browse** or click directly on SQL databases, if we have it in the main menu on the left. The SQL databases panel will open, and, after clicking on the **Add** button, we will have to fill in the SQL databases form.

7. We fill in the database name, subscription, resource group, source (blank, sample, or backup), server (we will add the SQL Server previously created), pricing tier (which will determine the database price and capabilities), and collation:

By clicking on Pricing tier, we can see all the available price and configuration options for a database.

8. We click on the **Refresh** button to see the new `CookbookCh07` SQL Server database newly created:

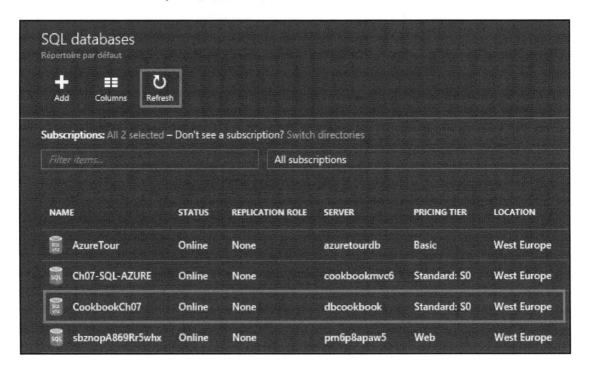

9. Now we select the `CookbookCh07` SQL Server database and click on the **Tools** button:

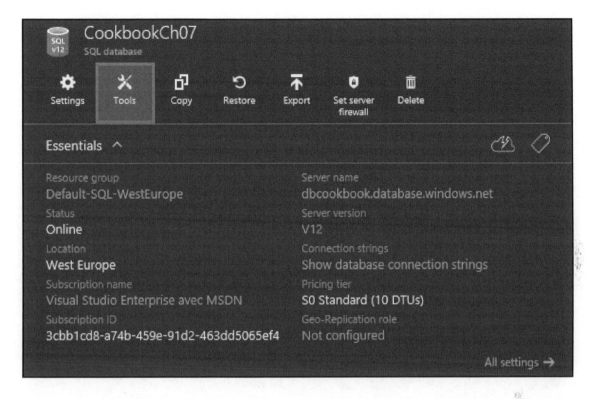

10. Next, we select the **Open in Visual Studio** button to open the database with Visual Studio 2017 via the VS 2017 SQL Data Tools:

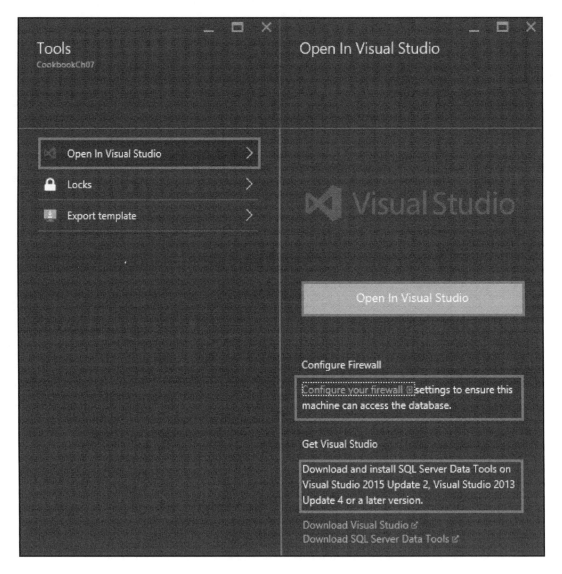

We can see that before opening VS 2017 we can configure a firewall rule and/or download SQL Server Data Tools if they are not installed.

11. The following dialog box asks to create a remote connection with Visual Studio:

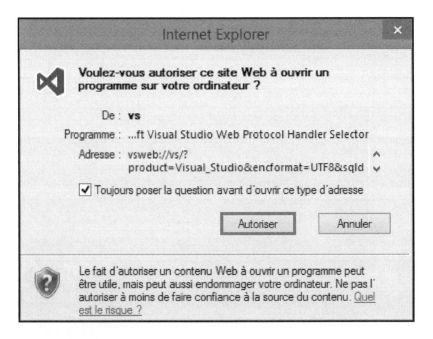

We authorize this connection:

Visual Studio is launched.

12. The following dialog box asks us for a database information connection:

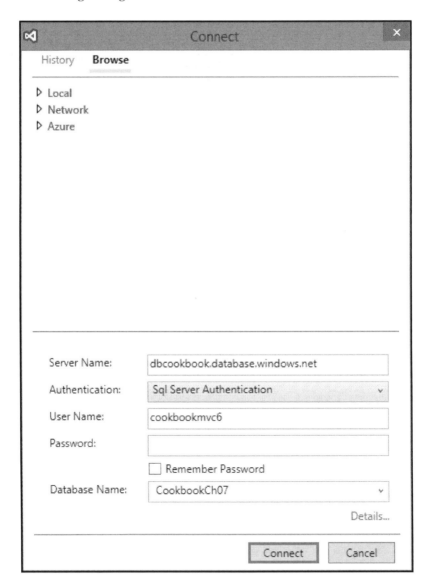

We click on the **Connect** button, after filling in the correct information.

13. The following dialog box opens if a firewall rule is not created for our computer on the Azure portal:

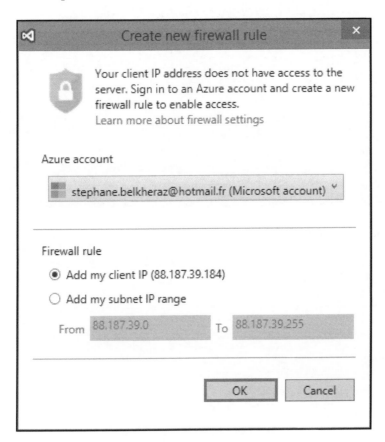

We can add an authorized IP address or a range of IP addresses:

We can set a firewall rule in the Azure portal via the SQL database options.

14. We can see that Visual Studio opens, and the SQL Server, and the database created in the SQL Server object explorer:

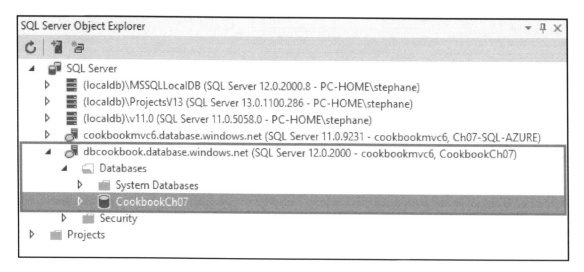

15. Next, we create a `Book` table by right-clicking on the `Tables` folder:

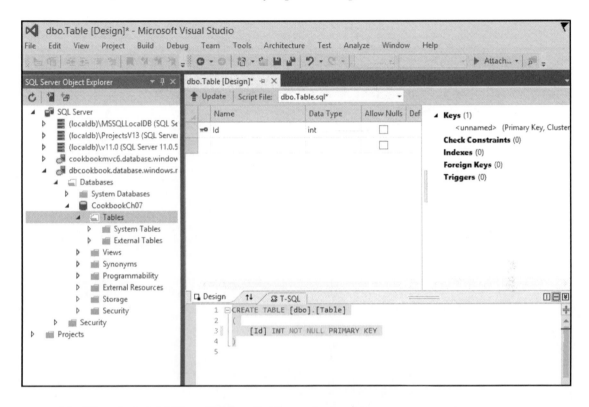

16. We select **Add New Table...** in the contextual menu:

17. Next, we modify the SQL script in the T-SQL panel, adding the code framed in red:

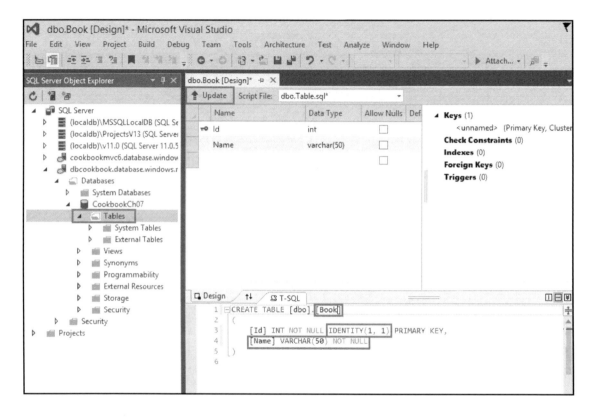

18. In the first box, we add the **T-SQL** code to make the primary key automatically increment, and in the second box we add the varchar **Name** field to the Book table. We also modify the table name with Book. To apply these modifications, we click on the **Update** button:

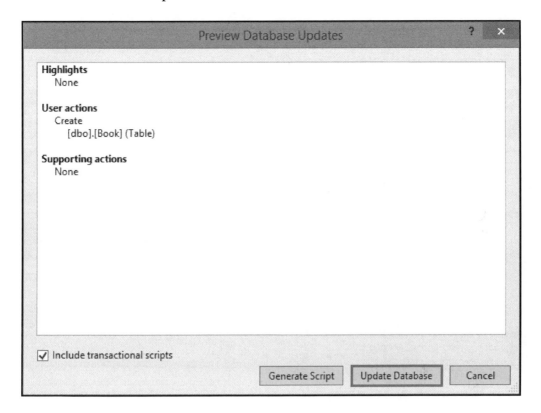

The dialog box appears and asks us whether we want to generate a SQL script, update the database, or cancel. We click on the **Update Database** button.

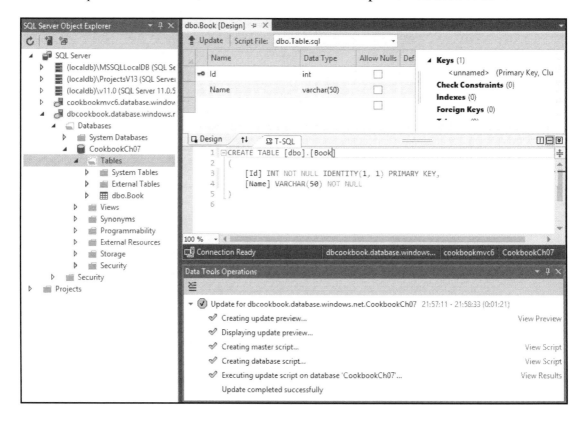

We can see whether the tasks have been correctly executed in the **Data Tools Operations** panel.

19. Next, let's add data to the Book table just created:

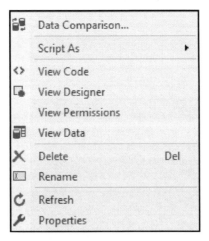

To do that, we right-click on the Book table:

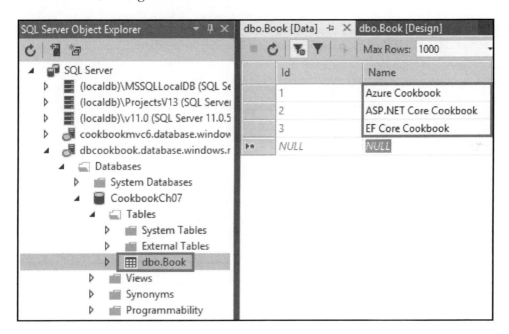

Now let's add three items in the Book table.

20. Next, we will create a web application to display data from the Azure SQL database:

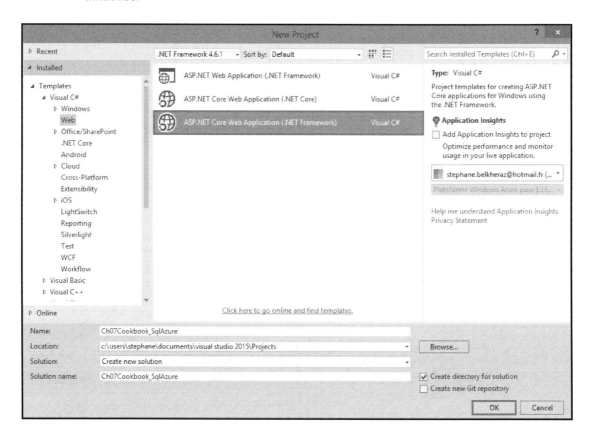

We create an ASP.NET Core application running with the .NET Framework.

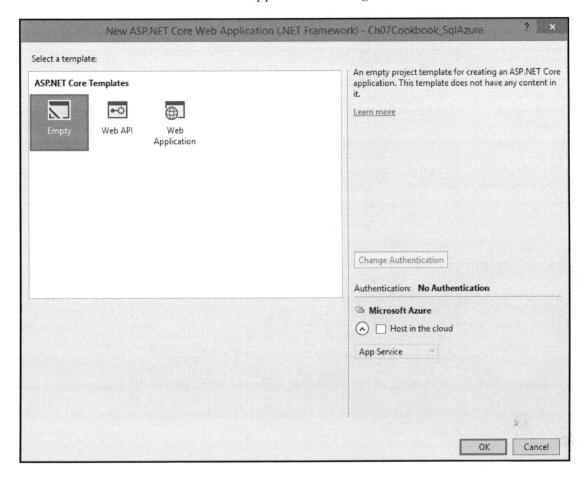

We select an empty web application.

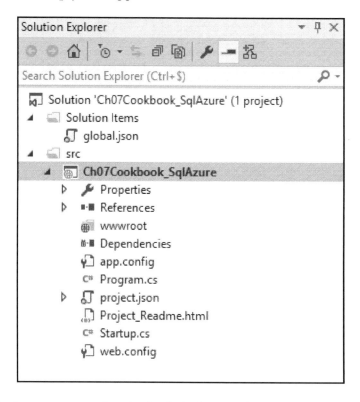

Here is the empty template in the **Solution Explorer**.

21. We add the following folders in the application: Controllers, Data, Models, Views, and Home inside Views:

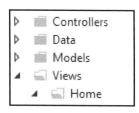

22. Now we create a `Book` class in the `Models` directory corresponding to the `Book` table in the SQL Azure database:

```csharp
namespace Ch07Cookbook_SqlAzure.Models
{
    0 references
    public class Book
    {
        0 references
        public int Id { get; set; }
        0 references
        public string Name { get; set; }
    }
}
```

23. Next, we create the `CookBookContext` class to manage the data. Let's add the following code to this class:

```csharp
namespace Ch07Cookbook_SqlAzure.Data
{
    1 reference
    public class CookbookContext : DbContext
    {
        0 references
        public CookbookContext(DbContextOptions<CookBookContext> options)
            : base(options)
        {
        }

        0 references
        public DbSet<Book> Book { get; set; }
    }
}
```

24. Next, we resolve the dependencies by right-clicking on the `DbContext`. `CodeLens` proposes several options:

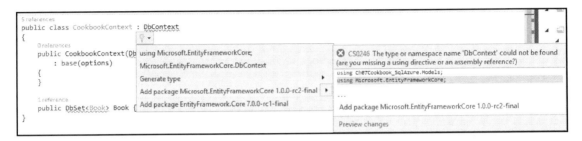

We choose to add the Entity Framework Core package.

The dependency will be added automatically to the project.

25. We resolve the other dependencies in the same way with `CodeLens`:

```
CookbookContext.cs ⊕ X

C# Ch07Cookbook_SqlAzure..NET Framewo ▾   ⁺ꞁ Ch07Cookbook_SqlAzure.Data.Cookboo ▾   ⊕ CookbookCont

     1    ⊟using Ch07Cookbook_SqlAzure.Models;
     2      using Microsoft.EntityFrameworkCore;
     3
     4    ⊟namespace Ch07Cookbook_SqlAzure.Data
     5      {
               2 references
     6    ⊟    public class CookbookContext : DbContext
     7         {
                   0 references
     8    ⊟        public CookbookContext(DbContextOptions<CookbookContext> options)
     9                : base(options)
    10             {
    11             }
    12
                   0 references
    13             public DbSet<Book> Book { get; set; }
    14         }
    15      }
```

26. Next, we add a `Controller` file in the `Controllers` directory by right-clicking on the `Controllers` directory and selecting **Add New Item** in the contextual menu:

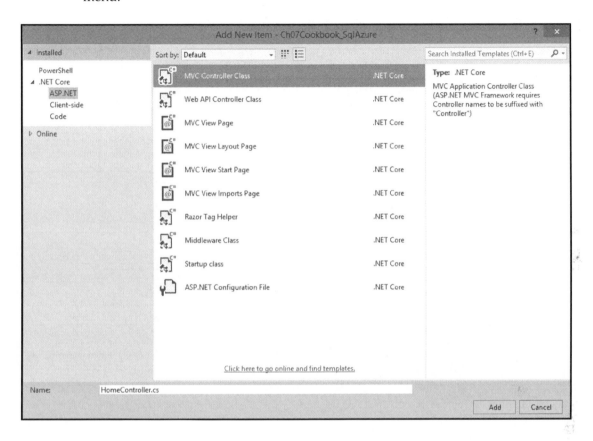

Now we select MVC `Controller` Class.

```
1        using Microsoft.AspNetCore.Mvc;
2
3      namespace Ch07Cookbook_SqlAzure.Controllers
4        {
            0 references
5            public class HomeController : Controller
6            {
7                //GET: /<controller>/
                 0 references
8                public IActionResult Index()
9                {
10                   return View();
11               }
12           }
13       }
14
```

Next, we add the preceding code.

Let's manually add the `Microsoft.AspNetCore.Mvc` to resolve the `Controller` dependency in the `HomeController` file. We can also see the `Microsoft.EntityFrameworkCore` added previously by resolving the `DbContext` class:

```
HomeController.cs ╬ ✕
C# Ch07Cookbook_SqlAzure..NET Framewo ▾   ⁂ Ch07Cookbook_SqlAzure.Controllers.Ho ▾
   1       using Ch07Cookbook_SqlAzure.Data;
   2       using Ch07Cookbook_SqlAzure.Models;
   3       using Microsoft.AspNetCore.Mvc;
   4       using System.Collections.Generic;
   5       using System.Linq;
   6
   7       // For more information on enabling MVC for empty projects,
   8
   9       namespace Ch07Cookbook_SqlAzure.Controllers
  10       {
             1 reference
  11           public class HomeController : Controller
  12           {
  13               private readonly CookbookContext _context;
                 0 references
  14               public HomeController(CookbookContext context)
  15               {
  16                   _context = context;
  17               }
  18
                 0 references
  19               public IActionResult Index()
  20               {
  21                   List<Book> listBook = _context.Book.ToList();
  22
  23                   return View(listBook);
  24               }
  25           }
  26       }
  27
```

After having added the preceding code, we can see the resolved dependencies in the HomeController class. We added code that injects the CookbookContext class we use in the Index action method with a constructor, to retrieve the list of Book items.

27. Next, we add the MVC View page in the `Views/Home` directory corresponding to the previous `Index` method just created:

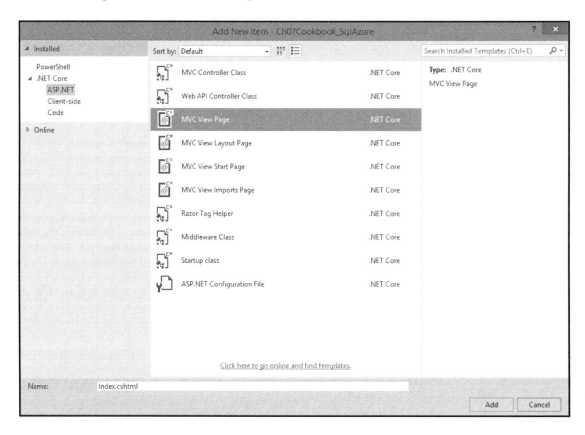

28. Let's add the following code to the `Index` file:

```
Index.cshtml

1   @model List<Ch07Cookbook_SqlAzure.Models.Book>
2
3   <h2>Books</h2>
4   <ul>
5       @foreach (var b in Model)
6       {
7           <li>@b.Name</li>
8       }
9   </ul>
10
```

29. Now, we add a JSON configuration file to add the connection string to connect to the database:

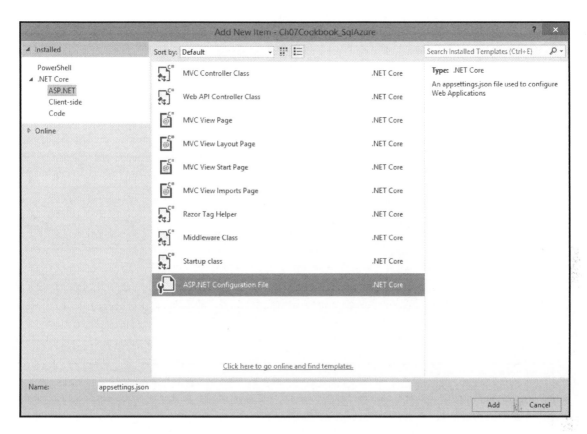

30. Let's add the following code to the `appsetting.json` file:

```
appsettings.json ↵ ×
Schema: <No Schema Selected>
    1   {
    2       "ConnectionStrings": {
    3           "CookBookConnection": "Data Source=dbcookbook.database.windows.net;Initial Catalog=CookbookCh07;User ID=cookbookmvc6;Password=$tefidoo007S"
    4       }
    5   }
```

31. Now let's open the `Startup.cs` to modify the code inside:

```
1
2    namespace Ch07Cookbook_SqlAzure
3    {
         0 references
4        public class Startup
5        {
             0 references
6            public void ConfigureServices(IServiceCollection services)
7            {
8            }
9
             0 references
10           public void Configure(IApplicationBuilder app)
11           {
12               app.Run(async (context) => {
13                   await context.Response.WriteAsync("Hello World!");
14               });
15           }
16       }
17   }
```

32. Let's add the following code to the `Startup.cs` file:

```
0 references
public Startup(IHostingEnvironment env)
{
    var builder = new ConfigurationBuilder()
        .SetBasePath(env.ContentRootPath)
        .AddJsonFile("appsettings.json", optional: true, reloadOnChange: true);

    Configuration = builder.Build();
}

1 reference
public IConfigurationRoot Configuration { get; }
```

33. Next, we resolve the `ConfigurationBuilder` dependency:

```
0 references
public Startup(IHostingEnvironment env)
{
    var builder = new ConfigurationBuilder()
        .SetBasePath(en ☼ ▾ ntentRootPath)
        .AddJsonFile("a
                                using Microsoft.Extensions.Configuration;
    Configuration = bui        Microsoft.Extensions.Configuration.ConfigurationBuilder
}
                                Generate type                                        ▶
1 reference                     Add package Microsoft.Extensions.Configuration 1.0.0-rc2-final ▶
public IConfigurationRo         Add package Microsoft.Framework.Configuration 1.0.0-beta8
```

34. We also resolve the `SetBasePath` method dependency:

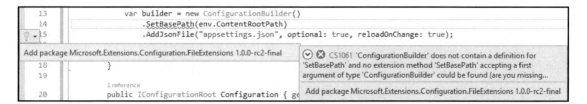

35. We also resolve the `AddJsonFile` method dependency:

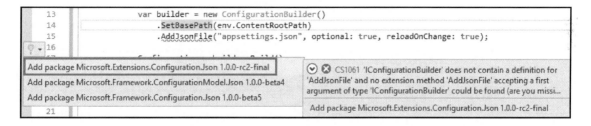

36. We can see the dependencies automatically added to the project with the corresponding NuGet packages automatically downloaded when resolved:

```
"dependencies": {
    "Microsoft.AspNetCore.Mvc": "1.0.0-rc2-final",
    "Microsoft.AspNetCore.Server.IISIntegration": "1.0.0-rc2-final",
    "Microsoft.AspNetCore.Server.Kestrel": "1.0.0-rc2-final",
    "Microsoft.EntityFrameworkCore": "1.0.0-rc2-final",
    "Microsoft.Extensions.Configuration": "1.0.0-rc2-final",
    "Microsoft.Extensions.Configuration.FileExtensions": "1.0.0-rc2-final",
    "Microsoft.Extensions.Configuration.Json": "1.0.0-rc2-final"
},
```

37. Next, we replace the following code:

```
0 references
public void ConfigureServices(IServiceCollection services)
{
}

// This method gets called by the runtime. Use this method
0 references
public void Configure(IApplicationBuilder app)
{
    app.Run(async (context) =>
    {
        await context.Response.WriteAsync("Hello World!");
    });
}
```

38. We replace it with the following, which injects the dependencies, configuring DbContext to be injected into the Controller constructor in the ConfigureServices method. This code also adds the MVC middleware to the Configure method configuring the routing rules:

```
0 references
public void ConfigureServices(IServiceCollection services)
{
    services.AddDbContext<CookBookContext>(options =>
            options.UseSqlServer(Configuration.GetConnectionString("CookBookConnection")));

    services.AddMvc();
}

// This method gets called by the runtime. Use this method to configure the HTTP request pipeline.
0 references
public void Configure(IApplicationBuilder app)
{
    app.UseMvc(routes =>
    {
        routes.MapRoute(
            name: "default",
            template: "{controller=Home}/{action=Index}/{id?}");
    });
}
```

39. The `UseSqlServer` method is resolved by adding the
    `Microsoft.EntityFrameworkCore.SqlServer` package to add the SQL
    provider to the Entity Framework:

```
                          0 references
23                        public void ConfigureServices(IServiceCollection services)
24                        {
25                            services.AddDbContext<CookbookContext>(options =>
26                                    options.UseSqlServer(Configuration.GetConnectionString("CookBookConnection")));
27
```

Add package Microsoft.EntityFrameworkCore.SqlServer 1.0.0-rc2-final ▶

Add package EntityFramework.MicrosoftSqlServer 7.0.0-rc1-final

Add package EntityFramework.SqlServer 7.0.0-beta8

⊙ ⊗ CS1061 'DbContextOptionsBuilder' does not contain a definition for
'UseSqlServer' and no extension method 'UseSqlServer' accepting a first
argument of type 'DbContextOptionsBuilder' could be found (are you mis...   pipeline.

...
using Microsoft.AspNetCore.Http;
using Microsoft.EntityFrameworkCore;
using Microsoft.Extensions.Configuration;
...

Add package Microsoft.EntityFrameworkCore.SqlServer 1.0.0-rc2-final

Preview changes

```
32                        public void Configure(IApplica
33                        {
34                            app.UseMvc(routes =>
35                            {
36                                routes.MapRoute(
37                                    name: "default",
38                                    template: "{contro
39                            });
```

40. Finally, we launch the application to be sure that the code works, and it retrieves the Book data from SQL Azure correctly:

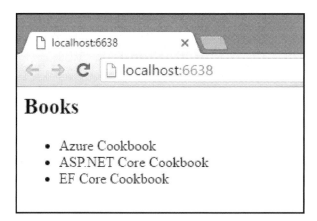

8

Cache and Session - Distributed, Server, and Client

In this chapter, we will cover:

- Using .NET Cache with MemoryCache
- Caching HTML with Cache TagHelpers
- Using ResponseCache attribute
- Using Session
- Using Redis as Cache on-Premises
- Using Redis as a cache on Azure
- Caching with HTML5 cache manifest
- Caching with HTML5 localStorage and sessionStorage

Introduction

In this chapter, we will learn the different mechanisms we can use to store data in our application development. We will learn about the server-side features in .NET, but not with IIS, because now with ASP.NET Core, we try to be server-agnostic and design the application with middlewares. This is why we will not cover IIS cache mechanisms we already know, such as *output* caching.

We will also learn about some HTML5 features to cache files or data on the client. This data can be either simple or complex data in JavaScript. If it is complex, we will store it as JSON.

To store this data, we will use JavaScript global variables named `localStorage` and `sessionStorage`. To cache files, we will prefer to use a manifest file.

Finally, we will learn how to store data as NoSQL data (or non-relational data as key-value pairs) in some client-side mechanism with IndexedDB, or using a distributed cache mechanism with Redis on Azure.

For the client-side cache features we will be talking about in this chapter, we will have to consult www.caniuse.com to be sure the browser we use has these HTML5 capabilities. To avoid JavaScript errors, which could block the other client scripts of our application, we can use a library such as Modernizr to allow us to check programmatically the HTML5 capabilities of our browser.

Using .NET Cache with MemoryCache

In this recipe, we will learn how to use the default Cache object in ASP.NET Core to cache CLR objects.

Getting ready

We will create an empty ASP.NET Core web application running on .NET Framework with VS 2017.

How to do it...

1. First, we import the following dependency to be able to use caching in ASP.NET Core applications:

    ```
    "Microsoft.Extensions.Caching.Memory": "2.0.0"
    ```

2. Next, we import the MVC dependency:

    ```
    "Microsoft.AspNetCore.Mvc": "2.0.0"
    ```

3. We can now add the cache middleware:

    ```
    public void ConfigureServices(IServiceCollection services)
    {
        services.AddMemoryCache();
        services.AddMvc();
    }
    public void Configure(IApplicationBuilder app)
    ```

```
{
    app.UseMvc(routes =>
    {
        routes.MapRoute(
        name: "default",
        template: "{controller=Home}/{action=Index}/{id?}");
    });
}
```

4. Next, we create two folders at the project root, Controllers and Views.

5. We then create HomeController.cs by right-clicking on the Controllers directory and selecting **Add | New item | MVC Controller class.**

6. Next, we inject the IMemoryCache interface in the Controller's constructor:

```
public class HomeController : Controller
{
    private readonly IMemoryCache cache;
    public HomeController(IMemoryCache cache)
    {
        this.cache = cache;
    }
    ...
}
```

7. Now let's add some data to cache:

```
public IActionResult Index()
{
    var strToCache = "Hello from cache";
    DateTime absoluteExpiration = DateTime.Now.AddDays(1);
    DateTimeOffset expirationFromNow = DateTime.UtcNow.AddDays(1);
    cache.Set<string>("str1", strToCache);
    cache.Set<string>("str1", strToCache, absoluteExpiration);
    cache.Set<string>("str1", strToCache, expirationFromNow);

    List<string> listColors = new List<string>
    {
        "green", "white", "black"
    };
    cache.Set<List<string>>("listColors", listColors);

    return View();
}
```

We have to set the key, the value, and optionally the expiration date.

Note that with the following syntax, we don't have to cast the object to the cache, or to retrieve from the cache:

```
cache.Set<string>
cache.Set<List<string>>
```

8. Next, we will retrieve some data from the cache. To do that, we have several options:

```
cache.Get
cache.TryGetValue
cache.GetOrCreate
cache.GetOrCreateAsync
public IActionResult TryShowCachedData()
{
    var str1 = cache.Get<string>("str1");

    List<string> listColors =
cache.Get<List<string>>("listColors");

    List<string> listStrings = null;
    bool dataExist = cache.TryGetValue<List<string>>("lstStr", out
listStrings);
    if (!dataExist)
        listStrings = new List<string>();
        return View(listStrings);
}
```

Caching HTML with Cache TagHelpers

In this recipe, we will learn how to use Cache TagHelpers.

Getting ready

TagHelpers let developers use their C# classes and methods in CSHTML files. With TagHelpers, developers can reuse most of the C# codes and logics in CSHTML files.

We will now create a view where we will use Cache TagHelper to cache elements in a view.

How to do it...

1. First, we use the TagHelper expires-after:

```
<!-- expires-after -->
<cache expires-after="@TimeSpan.FromMinutes(10)">
    @Html.Partial("_MyPartialView")
</cache>
```

2. Next, we use the TagHelper expires-on:

```
<!-- expires-on -->
<cache expires-on="@DateTime.Today.AddDays(1).AddTicks(-1)">
    @Html.Partial("_MyPartialView")
</cache>
```

3. Next, we use the TagHelper expires-sliding:

```
<!-- expires-sliding -->
<cache expires-sliding="@TimeSpan.FromMinutes(5)">
    @Html.Partial("_MyPartialView")
</cache>
```

4. Next, we use the TagHelper vary-by-user:

```
<!-- vary-by-query -->
<cache vary-by-user="true">
    @Html.Partial("_MyPartialView")
</cache>
```

5. Next, we use the TagHelper vary-by-route:

```
<!-- vary-by-user -->
<cache vary-by-route="id">
    @Html.Partial("_MyPartialView")
</cache>
```

6. Next, we use the TagHelper vary-by-query:

```
<!-- vary-by-route -->
<cache vary-by-query="search">
    @Html.Partial("_MyPartialView")
</cache>
```

7. Next, we use the TagHelper `vary-by-header`:

```
<!-- vary-by-header -->
<cache vary-by-header="User-Agent">
    @Html.Partial("_MyPartialView")
</cache>
```

8. Next, we use the TagHelper `vary-by-cookie`:

```
<!-- vary-by-cookie -->
<cache vary-by-cookie="MyAppCookie">
    @Html.Partial("_MyPartialView")
</cache>
```

9. Next, we use the TagHelper `vary-by`:

```
<!-- vary-by -->
<cache vary-by="@ViewBag.ProductId">
    @Html.Partial("_MyPartialView")
</cache>
```

How it works...

Caching can improve our application's load time significantly. Mostly, we cache the output of a request, such as HTML and Json.

 Do not cache frequently-changed data, it's more problematic to invalidate cache before it's time-to-live duration.

The `cache` TagHelper basically cache the output of inner blocks output. Caching mechanism by default, cache the inner blocks output in single instance.

We can increment the instance count by several parameters, such as `vary-by-header`, `vary-by-cookie`, and so on.

Those parameters create new cache instances for every different values for corresponding parameter keys, such as, `vary-by-query` parameter can create new cache instances for *q=aspnetcore, u=polatengin, fruit=orange* querystrings in url.

Also, we can control the *time-to-live* duration by adding one of the expiration policies into the `cache` TagHelper, such as `expires-after`, `expires-on`, or `expires-sliding`.

The `expires-after` parameter determines the lifetime duration of a cached item in memory. Later on the cached item will be deleted automatically.

The `expires-on` parameter determines the exact time of a cached item in memory; after that time, the cached item will be deleted automatically.

The `expires-sliding` parameter determines the lifetime duration of a cached item in memory. It's different to `expires-after` by, each read operation on cached item, slides the expiration time by this parameters value. No read for expiration duration will delete the cached item automatically.

Using ResponseCache attribute

In this recipe, we will learn how to use the `ResponseCache` attribute in ASP.NET Core.

Getting ready

We will be using VS 2017, and will create a controller to manipulate the `ResponseCache` attribute.

How to do it...

1. First, we add the `Microsoft.AspNetCore.Mvc` dependency to the project:

```
"dependencies": {
 "Microsoft.AspNetCore.Mvc": "2.0.0",
```

2. Next, we configure the ASP.NET routing in the `Configure` method in `Startup.cs`:

```
public void Configure(IApplicationBuilder app)
  {
        app.UseMvc(routes =>
        {
            routes.MapRoute(
                name: "default",
                template: "{controller=Home}/{action=Index}/{id?}");
        });
  }
```

3. Now, we configure `Startup.cs` to create some cache profiles, adding some code in the `ConfigureServices` method:

```
public void ConfigureServices(IServiceCollection services)
{
    services.AddMvc(options =>
    {
        options.CacheProfiles.Add("Default",
            new CacheProfile()
            {
                Duration = 60
            });
        options.CacheProfiles.Add("Never",
            new CacheProfile()
            {
                Location = ResponseCacheLocation.None,
                NoStore = true
            });
    });
}
```

4. Next, let's create a controller and some views. We will add caching attributes to action methods to parametrize the caching options for each corresponding view:

```
[ResponseCache(Duration = 30)]
public class HomeController : Controller
{
    [ResponseCache(CacheProfileName = "Default")]
    public IActionResult Index()
    {
        return View();
    }

    [ResponseCache(CacheProfileName = " Never")]
    public IActionResult NeverCachedView()
    {
        return View();
    }

    [ResponseCache(Duration = 10, Location =
            ResponseCacheLocation.Any, NoStore = false)]
    public IActionResult About()
    {
        ViewData["Message"] =
                    "Your application description page.";
        return View();
    }
```

```
[ResponseCache(Duration = 60, Location =
                        ResponseCacheLocation.Client)]
public IActionResult Contact()
{
    ViewData["Message"] = "Your contact page.";
    return View();
}
}
```

How it works...

When we use the ReponseCache attribute, we generate HTTP headers and their values when we create the `Response` to the `Request`. The HTTP headers generated are **Cache-Control**, **Pragma**, and **Vary**, and their values depend on the values we add to our ResponseCache attributes.

ResponseCache attributes can be added at controller level, or at action method level. At action method level, the ResponseCache attribute will override the controller attribute in the decorated method. For the moment, ResponseCache doesn't cache on the server memory; this feature will come soon.

The properties of the ResponseCache attribute are the following:

- Duration (in seconds)
- Location (Any, None, or Client)
- NoStore (true or false)
- VaryByHeader (the name of the header)
- CacheProfileName (a profile created in the `ConfigureServices` method of `Startup.cs`)
- Order

```
For this decoration:
[ResponseCache(CacheProfileName = "Default")]
The generated header will be the following:
Cache-Control: public,max-age=60
For this decoration:
[ResponseCache(CacheProfileName = " Never")]
The generated headers will be the following:
Cache-Control :"no-store,no-cache"
Pragma :"no-cache"
```

```
For this decoration:
[ResponseCache(Duration = 10, Location =
                 ResponseCacheLocation.Any, NoStore = false)]
The generated header will be the following:
Cache-Control :"public,max-age=10"

For this decoration:
[ResponseCache(Duration = 60, Location =
                           ResponseCacheLocation.Client)]
The generated header will be the following:
Cache-Control :"private,max-age=60"
```

Using Session

In this recipe, we will learn how to use **Session** in ASP.NET Core.

Getting ready

We will be using VS 2017, and creating a controller to manipulate Session.

How to do it......

1. First, we add the following library to the project:

    ```
    "Microsoft.AspNetCore.Session": "2.0.0"
    ```

2. Next, let's configure Session in `Startup.cs`. We also add the MVC services to use the ASP.NET MVC pipeline:

    ```
    public void ConfigureServices(IServiceCollection services)
      {
          services.AddSession(options =>
          {
              options.IdleTimeout = TimeSpan.FromMinutes(30);
              options.CookieName = ".Session";
          });

          services.AddMvc();
      }
    ```

```
public void Configure(IApplicationBuilder app)
{
    app.UseSession();

    app.UseMvc(routes =>
    {
        routes.MapRoute(
            name: "default",
            template: "{controller=Home}/{action=Index}/{id?}");
    });
}
```

3. Next, we create some helper methods to serialize objects, to get and store objects in Session:

```
// Convert an object to a byte array
public byte[] ObjectToByteArray(Object obj)
{
    BinaryFormatter bf = new BinaryFormatter();
    using (var ms = new MemoryStream())
    {
        bf.Serialize(ms, obj);
        return ms.ToArray();
    }
}

// Convert a byte array to an Object
public Object ByteArrayToObject(byte[] arrBytes)
{
    using (var memStream = new MemoryStream())
    {
        var binForm = new BinaryFormatter();
        memStream.Write(arrBytes, 0, arrBytes.Length);
        memStream.Seek(0, SeekOrigin.Begin);
        var obj = binForm.Deserialize(memStream);
        return obj;
    }
}
```

4. Next, let's store a list of strings in the HttpContext.Session object:

```
public IActionResult Index()
{
    List<string> listColors = new List<string>
    {
        "green", "white", "black"
    };
```

```
    var listColorsBytes = ObjectToByteArray(listColors);
    HttpContext.Session.Set("listColors", listColorsBytes);
    return View();
}
```

5. We can see the cookie created launching **F12** tools in the browser previously configured in the `ConfigureServices` method in `Startup.cs`:

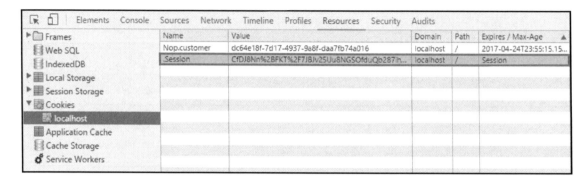

6. Now, we retrieve this list of strings from the `Session` object:

```
public IActionResult Colors()
{
    List<string> listColors = new List<string>();
    var listBytesColors = new Byte[1000];

    bool hasValue =
      HttpContext.Session.TryGetValue("listColors",
                                        out listBytesColors);
    if(hasValue)
        listColors =
            (List<string>)ByteArrayToObject(listBytesColors);


    return View(listColors);
}
```

7. Finally, let's see the result in the browser view:

How it works...

With the `HttpContext.Session` object, clients have a corresponding memory space in the server's RAM. By using a `Session` object, we can develop applications that enable a user's entire activity to be remembered in the server. For example, if the user hasn't yet logged in, we can redirect the user to the login page; after successful login, the application can remember all properties of the logged-in user, and let the user navigate through the application. We can clear the `Session` object, and let the application forget the user. Logout functionality usually clears the `Session` object.

Using Redis as Cache on-Premises

In this recipe, we will learn how to install Redis on Windows, and use it as a cache in-memory system with ASP.NET Core MVC applications.

Getting ready

We will download Redis for Windows, and launch VS 2017 to create an empty web application.

How to do it...

1. First, let's launch `http://redis.io`:

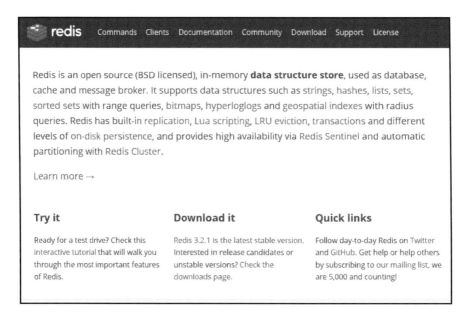

2. Next, we go to the **Download | Windows** section:

Windows

The Redis project does not officially support Windows. However, the Microsoft Open Tech group develops and maintains this Windows port targeting Win64. Learn more

3. We are automatically redirected to a GitHub project named **MSOpenTech/redis**:

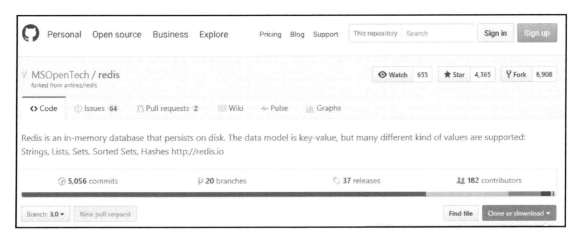

4. In the following **Redis on Windows** section, we will find a link for an **MSI installer**:

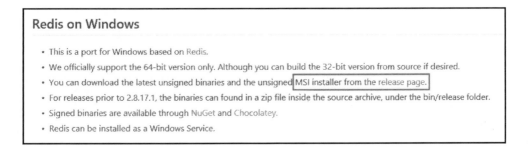

5. Here is the download page for the MSI, but we can also download the binaries for Linux or macOS:

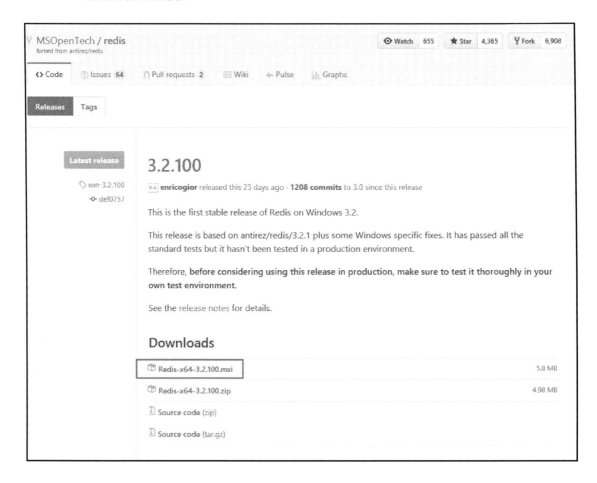

6. After downloading, we click on the installer:

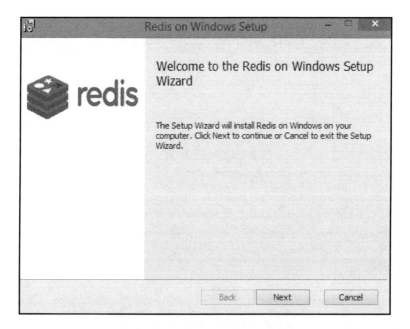

7. Let's select the destination folder for the Redis server:

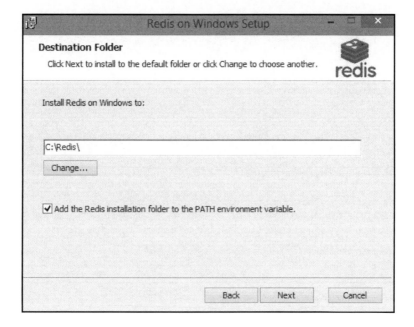

8. Next, we select the port number, where we will request Redis and add an exception to the Windows Firewall:

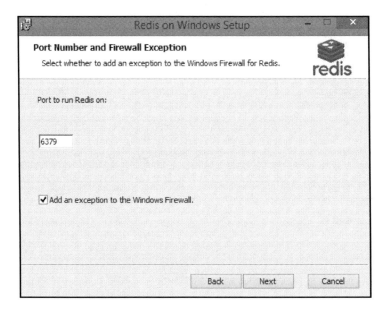

9. Next, we add the memory limit:

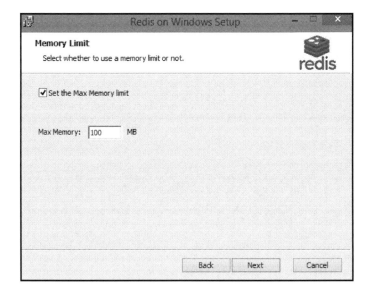

10. Redis is finally installing:

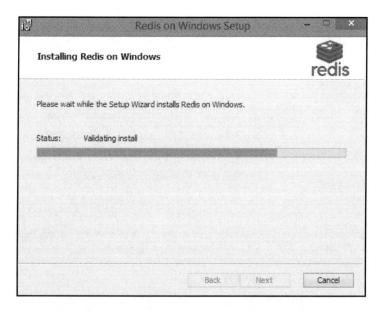

11. Now we will run Redis as a service. To do that, let's launch the **Services** console on Windows by typing `services.msc` in an execution prompt:

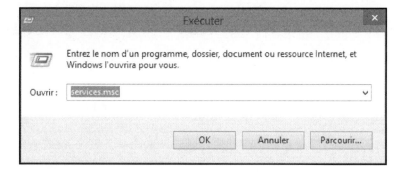

12. Then, we right-click on the **Redis** line, and select **Run** if the service is not running. We will also select the **Start** mode:

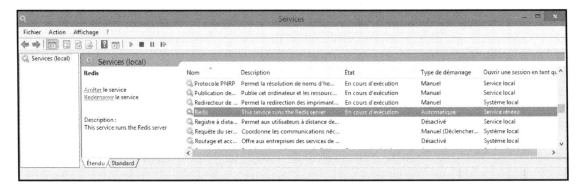

13. Now Redis is installed, we launch VS 2017 and create an empty web application.

14. First, we have to import the `StackExchange.Redis` dependency in the project to manipulate the Redis API:

```
"StackExchange.Redis": "1.2.6"
```

15. Next, we create a few extension methods to use Redis more efficiently, because we have to serialize and deserialize the `clr` object to store them as binary tables in Redis:

```csharp
using StackExchange.Redis;
using System.IO;
using System.Runtime.Serialization.Formatters.Binary;
public static class RedisCacheExtensions
{

    public static T Get<T>(this IDatabase cache, string key)
    {
        return Deserialize<T>(cache.StringGet(key));
    }

    public static void Set(this IDatabase cache, string key,
                                            object value)
    {
        cache.StringSet(key, Serialize(value));
    }

    static byte[] Serialize(object o)
    {
```

```
        if (o == null)
        {
                return null;
        }

        BinaryFormatter binaryFormatter = new BinaryFormatter();
        using (MemoryStream memoryStream = new MemoryStream())
        {
                binaryFormatter.Serialize(memoryStream, o);
                byte[] objectDataAsStream = memoryStream.ToArray();
                return objectDataAsStream;
        }
    }

    static T Deserialize<T>(byte[] stream)
    {
        if (stream == null)
        {
                return default(T);
        }

        BinaryFormatter binaryFormatter = new BinaryFormatter();
        using (MemoryStream memoryStream =
                                    new MemoryStream(stream))
        {
                T result =
                        (T)binaryFormatter.Deserialize(memoryStream);
                return result;
        }
    }
}
```

16. Next, we create an `ICacheRedis` interface and its implementation to encapsulate Redis configuration and features, as well as inject this implementation into our MVC controller:

```
public interface ICacheRedis
{
    T Get<T>(string key);
    void Set<T>(string key, T obj);
}
public class CacheRedis : ICacheRedis
{
    private static IDatabase redis;

    public T Get<T>(string key)
    {
```

```
        redis = Connection.GetDatabase();
        var obj = redis.Get<T>(key);
        if (obj == null)
                return default(T);

        return obj;
    }

    public void Set<T>(string key, T obj)
    {
        redis = Connection.GetDatabase();
        if (obj != null)
                redis.Set(key, obj);
    }

    public void InvalidateCache(string key)
    {
        IDatabase cache = Connection.GetDatabase();
        cache.KeyDelete(key);
    }

    private static Lazy<ConnectionMultiplexer>
    lazyConnection = new Lazy<ConnectionMultiplexer>
    (() =>
    {
        return ConnectionMultiplexer.Connect(
        "localhost:6379,abortConnect=False");
    });

    public static ConnectionMultiplexer Connection
    {
        get
        {
                return lazyConnection.Value;
        }
    }
}
```

17. We then add the Redis local connection string in the private `lazyConnection` field.

18. Next, we configure `Startup.cs` to inject `ICacheRedis` into our controller:

```
    public void ConfigureServices(IServiceCollection services)
    {
services.AddSingleton<ICacheRedis, CacheRedis>();
    ...
}
```

19. We can inject and use Redis now in the controller. After creating a controller, let's add the following code:

```
public class HomeController : Controller
{
    private ICacheRedis redisCache;
    public HomeController(ICacheRedis redisCache)
    {
        this.redisCache = redisCache;
    }

    public IActionResult Index()
    {
        List<string> listColors = new List<string>
        {
            "green", "white", "black"

         redisCache.Set<List<string>>("listColors", listColors);

        return View();
    }

    public IActionResult ShowCacheData()
    {
        List<string> listColors =
                redisCache.Get<List<string>>("listColors");

        return View(listColors);
    }
}
```

20. We then create an `index` method, where we will store data on Redis, and a `ShowCacheData` method, where we retrieve and display this data from the Redis cache.

21. Finally, we can see the result displaying the **ShowCacheData** view:

How it works...

Redis is a very performant in-memory object store with configurable cache expiration policy.

Lots of web applications rely heavily on Redis, such as Twitter, StackOverflow, GitHub, Pinterest, Snapchat, and so on.

We can use Redis to store and retrieve in-memory data in a distributed fashion.

Using Redis as a cache on Azure

In this recipe, we will learn how to use Redis on Azure as a cache in-memory system with ASP.NET Core MVC applications.

Getting ready

First, we will connect to our Azure subscription, create a Redis cache provider, launch VS 2017, and create an empty web application.

How to do it...

1. First, let's launch `http://portal.azure.com`, connect with our subscription, and select **Redis Caches**:

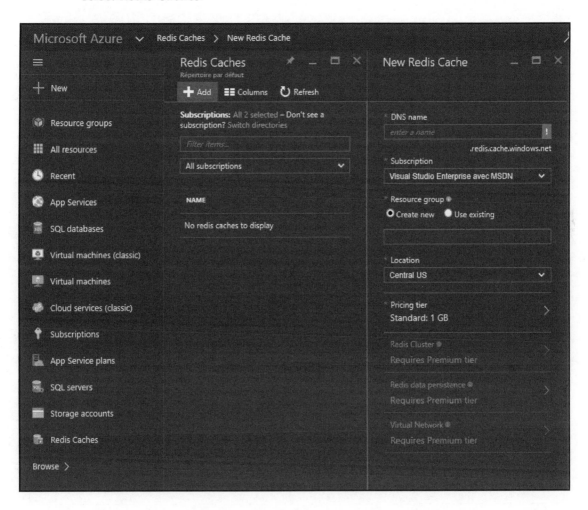

2. Then we will create a Redis cache. To do that, we configure it, adding a **DNS name**, a **Subscription**, a **Resource group**, a **Location**, and a **Pricing tier**:

3. Refreshing the **Redis Caches** section, we can see the new Redis cache just created:

4. Now Redis is created on Azure, we launch VS 2017 and create an empty web application.

5. First, we have to import the `StackExchange.Redis` dependency in the project to manipulate the Redis API:

```
"StackExchange.Redis": "1.2.6"
```

6. Next, we create some extension methods to use Redis more efficiently, because we have to serialize and deserialize the `clr` object to store them as binary tables in Redis:

```
using StackExchange.Redis;
using System.IO;
using System.Runtime.Serialization.Formatters.Binary;
public static class RedisCacheExtensions
{

    public static T Get<T>(this IDatabase cache, string key)
    {
        return Deserialize<T>(cache.StringGet(key));
    }

    public static void Set(this IDatabase cache, string key,
                                            object value)
    {
        cache.StringSet(key, Serialize(value));
```

```
    }

    static byte[] Serialize(object o)
    {
        if (o == null)
        {
            return null;
        }

        BinaryFormatter binaryFormatter = new BinaryFormatter();
        using (MemoryStream memoryStream = new MemoryStream())
        {
            binaryFormatter.Serialize(memoryStream, o);
            byte[] objectDataAsStream = memoryStream.ToArray();
            return objectDataAsStream;
        }
    }

    static T Deserialize<T>(byte[] stream)
    {
        if (stream == null)
        {
            return default(T);
        }

        BinaryFormatter binaryFormatter = new BinaryFormatter();
        using (MemoryStream memoryStream =
                                new MemoryStream(stream))
        {
            T result =
                    (T)binaryFormatter.Deserialize(memoryStream);
            return result;
        }
    }
}
```

7. Next, we create an `ICacheRedis` interface and its implementation to encapsulate Redis configuration and features, and inject this implementation into our MVC controller:

```
public interface ICacheRedis
{
    T Get<T>(string key);
    void Set<T>(string key, T obj);
}

public class CacheRedis : ICacheRedis
{
```

```csharp
private static IDatabase redis;

public T Get<T>(string key)
{
    redis = Connection.GetDatabase();
    var obj = redis.Get<T>(key);
    if (obj == null)
            return default(T);

    return obj;
}

public void Set<T>(string key, T obj)
{
    redis = Connection.GetDatabase();
    if (obj != null)
            redis.Set(key, obj);
}

public void InvalidateCache(string key)
{
    IDatabase cache = Connection.GetDatabase();
    cache.KeyDelete(key);
}

private static Lazy<ConnectionMultiplexer> lazyConnection =
                new Lazy<ConnectionMultiplexer>(() =>
{
    return ConnectionMultiplexer.Connect(
"CookbookMvc6.redis.cache.windows.net:6380,
        password=IhwUE/oo4QNkBgEUpZ0AnM4pT81uL6/+mM5piGCJdGs=,
        ssl=True,abortConnect=False");
});

public static ConnectionMultiplexer Connection
{
    get
    {
            return lazyConnection.Value;
    }
}
}
```

8. We then add the Redis local connection string in the private `lazyConnection` field.

   The only difference in the ASP.NET code compared with the previous recipe is the connection string.

9. To get this Azure Redis connection string, we have to go to our Azure portal, select the Redis Cache we just created, select **Settings** | **Access keys**, and copy the **Primary connection string** as follows:

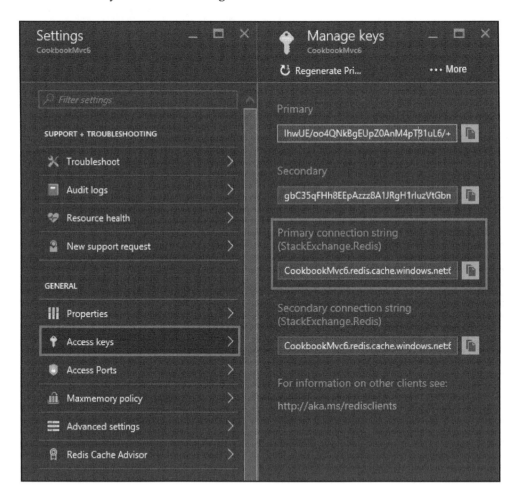

10. Next, we configure `Startup.cs` to inject `ICacheRedis` into our controller:

```
public void ConfigureServices(IServiceCollection services)
    {
services.AddSingleton<ICacheRedis, CacheRedis>();
 ...
}
```

11. We can now inject and use Redis in the controller. After creating a controller, let's add the following code:

```
public class HomeController : Controller
{
    private ICacheRedis redisCache;
    public HomeController(ICacheRedis redisCache)
    {
        this.redisCache = redisCache;
    }

    public IActionResult Index()
    {
        List<string> listColors = new List<string>
        {
            "green", "white", "black"

         redisCache.Set<List<string>>("listColors", listColors);

        return View();
    }

    public IActionResult ShowCacheData()
    {
        List<string> listColors =
                redisCache.Get<List<string>>("listColors");

        return View(listColors);
    }
}
```

12. We then create an `index` method, where we will store data on Redis, and a `ShowCacheData` method, where we retrieve and display this data from the Redis cache.

13. Finally, we can see the result displaying the **ShowCacheData** view:

Caching with HTML5 cache manifest

In this recipe, we will learn how to use the HTML5 manifest file in order to store JavaScript and CSS files in the cache browser, along with images.

Getting ready

To test the HTML5 cache manifest file, we just need to create an empty web application. To add it a manifest file at the root of the application, some static files to put in cache and a HTML5 compliant browser.

How to do it...

We'll add the manifest file to enable the cache on the client side, and configure which files will be cached and which files will not.

Let's start by including the manifest file with the relative path as follows:

```
<!DOCTYPE html>
<html manifest="mySite.appcache">
```

Or with an absolute path:

```
<html manifest="http://www.mywebsite.com/mySite.appcache"
```

First of all, let's analyze the anatomy of a cache manifest file:

```
CACHE MANIFEST
# version 1.0
```

- CACHE:

```
/Content/Styles/Site.css
/Content/Scripts/Site.js
http://ajax.aspnetcdn.com/ajax/jQuery/jquery-2.2.0.js
```

- NETWORK:

```
/Login/
Network.html
```

- FALLBACK:

```
/Content/Images/Products/
```

The **CACHE MANIFEST** section is only here to add comments (about the version, for example).

The three sections of a cache manifest are **CACHE**, **NETWORK**, and **FALLBACK**:

- CACHE: Files to be cached. The URLs can be relative or absolute.
- NETWORK: Files not to be cached, that have to come from a network. The URLs can be relative or absolute.
- FALLBACK: Fallback pages the browser should use if the browser is not available.

Now that we have seen how to create a manifest file manually, let's manage a manifest file by using our preferred task runner (gulp or grunt).

How it works......

The HTML5 cache manifest is a file stored at the root of our application. This file describes all the files we want to be in the browser cache, with their expiration date.

This is a mechanism often used to cache resources as localStorage in order to load them faster, to reduce server load, and for offline applications.

The W3C recommend that we use the .appcache file extension to create a cache manifest file.

 The HTML5 File API could be a good alternative to store images, videos, or text files, but it's only available on Firefox, Chrome, Safari, and Opera on Desktop.

Caching with HTML5 localStorage and sessionStorage

In this recipe, we will learn how to use the **HTML5 Storage API** (it's also called **Web Storage**, or **DOM Storage**) with `localStorage` and `sessionStorage` objects, in order to store non-sensitive data on the client.

Getting ready

First, we create an empty project with VS 2017, and use JavaScript code to store data.

We need as a minimum browser requirement IE8, Firefox 3.5, or Chrome 4.0 to benefit from HTML5 capabilities in the browser.

All the following methods and properties are available for both `localStorage` and `seesionStorage`:

- `getItem(key)`: Store a key/value pair
- `setItem(key, value)`: Return a value associated with a key
- `removeItem(key)`: Delete a key/value pair with a key
- `clear()`: Delete all key/value pairs
- `length`: Return the number of stored pairs

How to do it...

1. To test if `localStorage` or `sessionStorage` is available on our browser, we can use the following code:

```
(function () {
    if (typeof sessionStorage != 'undefined')
    // or
    if (window['localStorage'] !== null)
    // or using the ModernizR library
    if (Modernizr.localstorage)
})();
```

2. Let's use the `getItem(key)` method:

```
var color = localStorage.getItem('white');
var color = localStorage['white'];
var color = localStorage.white;
```

3. Now let's use the `setItem(key, value)` method to store data in the `localStorage` object:

```
localStorage.setItem('name', $('#name').val());
localStorage['name'] = $('#name').val();
localStorage.name = $('#name').val();
```

4. Next, we will store a complex object in the `localStorage`:

```
var colors = { white: '#000', black: '#fff' };
localStorage.setItem('htmlColors', JSON.stringify(colors));
```

5. To remove an item, let's use the `removeItem(key)` method:

```
localStorage.removeItem('lastName');
```

6. Next, to clear the `localStorage` object, we use the `clear()` method:

```
localStorage.clear();
```

7. Finally, to know the number of items stored in the `localStorage` object, we will use the `length` property:

```
var storageCount = localStorage.length;
```

How it works......

HTML5 Storage can be very useful to increase performance in applications. Why do a round trip to the web server, when we can store this data in a browser cache object?

HTML5 Storage is available in all modern browsers with a capacity limited to 5MB of data, but Internet Explorer supports a limit of 10MB.

`localStorage` and `sessionStorage` are two JavaScript object-storing key-value pairs. If the value is a complex JavaScript object, it has to be stored as a JSON string, using `JSON.stringify()`.

The differences between them both are:

- The `sessionStorage` shares data in the same tab or window during a navigation session
- The `localStorage` shares data between all tabs and windows, with no time limitation

 If we work with old browsers, we can check programmatically with a library like ModernizR if the HTML Storage feature is available in the browser. ModernizR can do that for all HTML5 objects or APIs.

We could also use persistent storage to store data on the client as cookies, but this way is limited in capacity; we can only store text on it, and it is sent to the server for each request on the server.
`localStorage` and `sessionStorage` objects are not shared between different browsers.

See also

`http://caniuse.com` allows us to check HTML5 API availability for all browsers.

9
Routing

In this chapter, we will cover:

- Creating a route using convention routing
- Creating a route using attribute routing
- Creating a custom route using IRouter
- Creating a route constraint
- Creating a domain route
- Creating SEO-friendly routes

Before ASP.NET Core

Before MVC, a URL represented a physical `.ASPX` file, but MVC added an abstraction layer to map URLs with controllers and actions. The goal was to call methods calling resources in a REST way, rather than calling pages.

In an MVC framework, regardless of the technology used, a routing system maps an incoming URL with a URL route pattern corresponding to an action's controller. A routing system doesn't work with physical files.

All the URL patterns are stored in an object called `routecollection`.

If there's no match, a HTTP 404 error is returned.

The routing system was linked with IIS.

`HTTP.sys`, the listener process in IIS, redirects to the `UrlRouting` module, which redirects to the ASP.NET and the ASP.NET MVC pipeline.

Since ASP.NET Core

Now, it's different. No default route is created by default and no 404 error is returned by default when a route is not matched. The routing system is added on the HTTP pipeline as a middleware.

On Windows, IIS will only redirect to `kestrel` or any other web server using the `aspnetcore` module on the IIS mapping handlers.

If a URL requested by a client matches an existing route in the route collection, the `RouteAsync` method of its handler is called, and if there's an exception handling the request, the next route pattern is tried instead of directly returning a 404 error.

MVC and Web API routing

Originally, MVC and Web API didn't share the same routing framework. Web API routing was RESTful by default.

Since ASP.NET Core, MVC and the Web API have been unified into a single framework. Both MVC and the Web API inherit from the same controller base class, and their routing systems have also been unified to be used in many situations:

- Self-hosting
- In-memory local requests (to unit testing)
- WebServer host (IIS, NGinx, Azure, and so on)

The route order

The order in which the routes are added to the routes table is important.

The best practice is to add the routes in the following order:

1. Ignore routes
2. Specific routes
3. General routes

Routing with ASP.NET Core

To use the routing middleware in our applications, we add
`Microsoft.AspNetCore.Routing` to `project.json` and also add
`services.AddRouting()` to the `ConfigureServices` method of `Startup.cs`.

Creating a route using convention routing

In this recipe, we will learn how to create a route using convention routing.

How to do it...

We can do it in two ways. The first way to create a route using convention routing is as
follows:

1. We add `services.AddMvc()` to `ConfigureServices`:

   ```
   app.AddMvc();
   ```

2. We add `app.UseMvc()` to configure the route definitions:

   ```
   app.UseMvc(routes =>
                   {
                   routes.MapRoute(
                       name: "default",
                       template:
   "{controller=Home}/{action=Index}/{id?}");
   });
   ```

The second way to create a route using convention routing is as follows:

1. We add `services.AddMvc()` to `ConfigureServices`:

   ```
   app.AddMvc();
   ```

2. Now, it's time to add `app.UseMvc()` method call inside `Configure()` method:

   ```
   app.UseMvc();
   ```

3. We add attribute routing to the controller and/or action:

```
[Route("api/[controller]")]
 public class ValuesController : Controller
```

How it works...

We can mix the first way with the second way by adding routes to `routescollection` in the `configure` method and completing or overriding the route definition with attribute routing at the action level.

Creating a route using attribute routing

In this recipe, we will learn how to create a route using attribute routing.

Getting ready

We create a controller with an `action` method to decorate it with routing attributes.

How to do it...

Attribute routing is the ability to define a route by adding an attribute defining a route above an `action` method in a controller.

1. First, let's add a routing attribute to an `action` method specifying an `id` parameter:

```
//Route: /Laptop/10
[Route("Products/{id}")]
public ActionResult Details(int id)
```

2. Next, let's add an optional parameter:

```
//Route: /Products/10/Computers or /Products/10
 [Route("Products/{id}/{category?}")]
public ActionResult Details(int id, string category)
We can see how to do that for a RESTfull Web API method :
 // GET api/values/5
        [HttpGet("{id?}")]
public string Get(int? id)
```

3. Now, let's add `RoutePrefix`. This attribute will be applied to every action of this controller:

```
[Route("Products")]
        public class HomeController : Controller
        {
        //Route: /Products/10
        [Route("{id?}")]
        public ActionResult Details(int? id)
        {
                return View();
        }
}
```

4. Finally, we add an `Order` attribute. The `Order` parameter in attribute routing corresponds to the order in which it would be inserted in the `routecollection` if the routes are added conventionally. The `Name` parameter allows us to override the `ActionMethod` name:

```
[Route("Products")]
    public class HomeController : Controller
    {
        [Route("Index", Name = "ProductList", Order = 2)]
        public ActionResult Index() { return View(); }

        [Route("{id?}", Name = "ProductDetail", Order = 1)]
        public ActionResult Details(int? id) { return View(); }
}
```

Creating a custom route using IRouter

In this recipe, we will learn how to create a custom route.

Getting ready

In MVC 6, we will use IRouter instead of IRouteHandler and IHttpHandler to define routes. ASP.NET Core works with recursive implementations of IRouter. At higher level, it can write an HTTP response, and at lower level it add my routing table to the routing middleware.

How to do it...

1. First, the class we create has to implement IRouter and the RouteAsync method:

```
public class ProductsRouter : IRouter
{
        private readonly Route _innerRoute;
        public VirtualPathData GetVirtualPath
(VirtualPathContext context)
        { return null; }

        public Task RouteAsync(RouteContext context)
        {
            // Test QueryStrings
            var qs = context.HttpContext.Request.Query;
            var price = qs["price"];

            if(string.IsNullOrEmpty(price))
            { return Task.FromResult(0); }

            var routeData = new RouteData();
            routeData.Values["controller"] = "Products";
            routeData.Values["action"] = "Details";
            routeData.DataTokens["price"] = price;
            context.RouteData = routeData;

            return _innerRoute.RouteAsync(context);
        }
}
```

2. Next, let's create an `extension` method to add this route to the `routeBuilder`:

```
public static class Extensions {
public static IRouteBuilder AddProductsRoute(
this IRouteBuilder routeBuilder, IApplicationBuilder app)
    {
        routeBuilder.Routes.Add(
            new Route(new ProductsRouter(),
"products/{lang:regex(^([a-z]{{2}})-([A-Z]{{2}})$)}/
{category:alpha}/{subcategory:alpha}/{id:guid}",
app.ApplicationServices.GetService(
typeof(IInlineConstraintResolver))
as IInlineConstraintResolver
                ));
            return routeBuilder;
        }
}
```

 Regex makes it relatively simple to check whether a string value matches certain rules. Also, we can get certain parts of a string value after some rules have been applied to it. With Regex, we can create a rule to be applied to a route URL. You can learn more at `https://regexr.com/`.

3. Finally, let's add this route to the route collection in the `Configure` method in `Startup.cs`:

```
public void Configure(IApplicationBuilder app)
{
  var routeBuilder = new RouteBuilder(app);
  routeBuilder.AddProductsRoute(app);
  app.UseRouter(routeBuilder.Build());
}
```

4. We have to match with this action method signature:

```
public IActionResult Details
  (string lang, string category, string subcategory, Guid id)
```

Creating a route constraint

In this recipe, we will learn how to create a route constraint using convention routing.

Getting ready

A route constraint is inserted with an inline syntax, called inline constraints, in the following form: {parameter:constraint}.

There are several ways to create a route constraint:

- Inserting a constraint when creating a route conventionally
- Inserting a constraint when creating an attribute routing
- Creating a class that implements IRouteConstraint

How to do it...

1. Here is the first way, inserting a constraint when creating a route conventionally:

```
app.UseMvc(routes =>
        {
            routes.MapRoute(
                name: "default",
                template:
"{controller=Home}/{action=Index}/{id?}"
            );

            routes.MapRoute(
                name: "products",
                template: "Products/{id=1}",
                defaults: new { controller = "Product", action
= "Details" }
            );
        });
```

2. This is the second way, inserting a constraint by attribute routing:

```
// for an api controller
  [Route("api/[controller]")]
    public class ProductValuesController : Controller
    {
        // GET api/productvalues/5
        [HttpGet("{id}")]
        public string Get(int id)
        {
            return "value";
        }


        // PUT api/productvalues/laptop
        [HttpPut("{name:alpha:length(3)}")]
        public void UpdateProductName(string name) { }
}
// for a MVC controller
  [Route("[controller]")]
    public class HomeController : Controller
    {
        // GET home/index/5
        [Route("{id?}")]
        public IActionResult Index(int? id) { return View(); }


        [Route("{name:alpha:length(3)}")]
        public IActionResult UpdateProductName(string name)
  { return View(); }
    }
```

3. And this is the third way, creating a class that implements `IRouteConstrains`:

```
public class ValuesConstraint : IRouteConstraint
{
        private readonly string[] validOptions;
        public ValuesConstraint(string options)
        {
            validOptions = options.Split('|');
        }

        public bool Match(HttpContext httpContext, IRouter route,
string routeKey, RouteValueDictionary values, RouteDirection
routeDirection)
        {
            object value;
            if (values.TryGetValue(routeKey, out value) && value !=
```

```
        null)
                {
                        return validOptions.Contains(value.ToString(),
        StringComparer.OrdinalIgnoreCase);
                }
                return false;
            }
        }
```

Here's an example of creating a route constraint based on a regular expression:

```
public class RegexLangConstraint : RegexRouteConstraint
{
        public RegexLangConstraint() : base(@"^([a-z]{2})-([A-Z]{2})$")
        {
        }
}
```

This constraint will check the language parameter using the following pattern:
[fr-FR] or [en-US].

Let's see how to apply this constraint to a route definition:

```
routes.MapRoute(
name: "fr_products",
template: "products/{lang}/{category:alpha}/{id:guid}",
defaults: new { controller = "Products", action = "Details" },
constraints: new { lang = new RegexLangConstrain() });
```

How it works...

Here is a non-exhaustive list of constraints used with convention routing or attribute routing:

- int :{id:int}
- bool :{isActive:bool}
- datetime :{dateBirth:datetime}
- decimal :{price:decimal}
- guid :{id:guid}
- required :{userName:required}
- alpha :{userName:alpha}

- `minlength(value)` : `{userName:minlength(8)}`
- `maxlength(value)` : `{userName:maxlength(20)}`
- `length(min,max)` :`{userName:length(8,20)}`
- `min(value)` :`{age:min(18)}`
- `max(value)` :`{age:max(100)}`
- `range(min,max)` :`{age:range(18,100)}`
- `regex(expression)` :`{ssn:regex(^d{3}-d{3}-d{4}$)}`

Creating a domain route

In this recipe, we will learn how to create a domain route.

Getting ready

There are some scenarios where domain routing could be very useful and interesting:

- URLs can be as follows when using multi-lingual web applications:

  ```
  route like "www.{language}-{culture}.domain.com" or
  "www.{language}.domain.com"
  ```

- URLs can be as follows when using multi-tenant web applications:

  ```
  route like "www.{controller}.domain.com", "www.{area}.domain.com",
  "www.{subentity}.domain.com"
  ```

How to do it...

Let's just add new routes to `Startup.cs`:

```
public void Configure(IApplicationBuilder app)
{
app.UseMvc(routes =>
{
  routes.MapRoute(
 name: "DomainRoute",
 template: "home.domain.com/{action=Index}/{id?}");

  routes.MapRoute(
```

```
name: "DomainRoute2",
template: "{controller=Home}.domain.com/{id?}");

  routes.MapRoute(
name: "DomainRoute3",
template: "{controller=Home}-{action=Index}.domain.com/{id?}");
 }
}
```

Creating SEO-friendly routes

In this recipe, we will learn how to create SEO-friendly routes. To do this, we can use the MVC routing system, the IIS `UrlRewriting` module, or both.

Getting ready

There are some scenarios where thinking about SEO is mandatory.

We are creating a new version of our website with MVC. But we have a lot of legacy URLs that are already used, or were recorded before the MVC version of our application. We also spent a lot of money for buying keyword to motorsearch as Google to throw all these URLs.

To manage this problem, we will use the IIS `UrlRewriting` module to redirect the legacy URLs to corresponding controller as an action.

How to do it...

1. First, we have to install the `UrlRewriting` module using **Web Plateform Installer**:

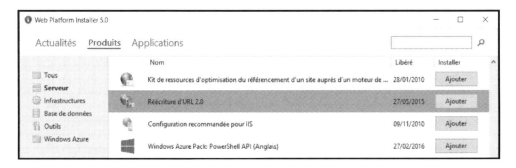

2. Next, we add a rule to redirect a legacy URL such as
    ```
    http://localhost:1962/products.ASPX?lang=fr-FR&category=smartph
    one&subcategory=samsung&id=cadc5808-75a7-4428-b491-3cacfe37d9ce
    ```
    to this existing MUV
    route: ```;http://localhost:1962/fr-FR/products/smartphone/samsung/c
    adc5808-75a7-4428-b491-3cacfe37d9ce```.

    The MVC route has the following template pattern:
    ```
    http://localhost:1962/products/{lang}/{category}/{subcategory}/
    {id}.
    ```

10
ASP.NET Core MVC

In this chapter, we will cover the following topics:

- Injecting dependencies and configuring IoC for a controller
- Using ActionResults
- Creating and working with areas
- Creating and using POCO controllers
- Creating and using controllers with MediatR
- Managing exceptions

Injecting dependencies and configuring IoC for a controller

In this recipe, you will learn how to inject a dependency with a constructor in a controller, and how to configure its lifetime.

Getting ready

We created an empty web application with VS 2017, and then added an empty controller to it.
Let's create a repository with hardcoded values to be injected into the controller.

How to do it...

We've already talked about injecting dependencies with ASP.NET Core in Chapter 5, *SOLID Principles, Inversion of Control, and Dependency Injection*. We learned that the IoC mechanism is internal to ASP.NET Core. It's done by a constructor, and its life cycle has to be configured in the Configure method in Startup.cs. We'll make some adjustments, and everything will work automatically.

1. First, let's see the repository to inject in the controller:

```
public interface IProductRepository
{
  int GetCountProducts();
}
public class ProductRepository : IProductRepository
{
  public int GetCountProducts()
  {
    return 10;
  }
}
```

As we can see, this repository has only one method that retrieves a list of strings.

2. Next, let's inject this repository in the controller constructor. In ProductController.cs, we'll develop the following code:

```
public class ProductController : Controller
{
private readonly IProductRepository repo;
  public ProductController(IProductRepository repo)
  {
    this.repo = repo;
  }
  public IActionResult Index()
  {
    var count = repo.GetCountProducts();
    return View(new ValueViewModel(count));
  }
}
```

3. We will now create a ViewModel class and the View file:

```
public class ValueViewModel
{
  public ValueViewModel(object val)
```

```
    {
      Value = val.ToString();
    }
    public string Value { get; set; }
  }
```

The code for `Index.cshtml` is as follows:

```
@model Ch10.R1.ValueViewModel
<h1>Products count @Model.Value</h1>
```

4. Next, we will configure the lifetime repository in the `ConfigureServices` method of `Startup.cs`:

```
public void ConfigureServices(IServiceCollection services)
{
  services.AddMvc();
  services.AddTransient<IProductRepository, ProductRepository>();
}
```

5. Finally, we can see the view that shows the data we retrieve from the repository in the action method without errors. This is because the IoC internal mechanism of ASP.NET Core automatically instantiates the repo for us without using any new keywords, or applying loose coupling principles.

6. We can also inject this repository by inserting the `FromServices` attribute above the repository used as a parameter of an action method in `ProductController`, after having configured it in `ConfigureServices`.
   We should make changes in `Startup.cs` as follows:

```
public void ConfigureServices(IServiceCollection services)
{
  services.AddMvc();
  services.AddScoped<IProductRepository, ProductRepository>();
}
```

Let's change the `ProductController.cs` file as follows:

```
public class ProductController : Controller
{
  public IActionResult Index([FromServices]IProductRepository repo)
  {
    var count = repo.GetCountProducts();
    return View();
  }
}
```

7. We can read the following code and see that the same repo has been injected in the same controller with a third-party IoC container as Autofac, instead of the internal ASP.NET Core IoC default container.

We will create an `IoConfig` class to configure the new IoC container. Of course, the IoC container could be any of the existing IoC containers that ASP.NET Core is compatible with, such as Unity, Ninject, Castle Windsor, StructureMap, SimpleInjector, or many others. In this example, we will use an `Autofac` module that is, according to the Autofac documentation:

> *A small class that can be used to bundle up a set of related components behind a facade to simplify configuration and deployment.*

Let's create the `AutofacModule.cs` file as follows:

```
public class AutofacModule : Module
{
  protected override void Load(ContainerBuilder builder)
  {
    builder.Register(c => new ProductRepository())
    .As<IProductRepository>()
    .InstancePerLifetimeScope();
  }
}
```

We should change the `Startup.cs` file and register the `Autofac` module:

```
using Autofac;
using Autofac.Extensions.DependencyInjection;
using Microsoft.AspNetCore.Builder;
using Microsoft.Extensions.DependencyInjection;
using System;
public class Startup
{
  public IServiceProvider ConfigureServices
  (IServiceCollection services)
  {
    services.AddMvc();
    // Add Autofac
    var containerBuilder = new ContainerBuilder();
    containerBuilder.RegisterModule<AutofacModule>();
    containerBuilder.Populate(services);
    var container = containerBuilder.Build();
    return new AutofacServiceProvider(container);
  }
}
```

Also, we should change the `ProductController.cs` file:

```
public class ProductController : Controller
{
  private readonly IProductRepository repo;
  public ProductController(IProductRepository repo)
  {
    this.repo = repo;
  }
  public IActionResult Index()
  {
    var count = repo.GetCountProducts();
    return View();
  }
}
```

In any class where we use IoC, we have to use only the constructor where we inject dependencies. Adding a default empty constructor will generate an exception, because the IoC container will wait for only one construction with the dependencies to inject.

8. Let's now see the `ConfigureServices` method code in `Startup.cs` that is still with `Autofac`, but without a module:

```
public class Startup
{
  public IServiceProvider ConfigureServices
  (IServiceCollection services)
  {
    services.AddMvc();
    // Add Autofac
    var containerBuilder = new ContainerBuilder();
    containerBuilder
    .RegisterType<ProductRepository>()
    .As<IProductRepository>();
    containerBuilder.Populate(services);
    var container = containerBuilder.Build();
    return new AutofacServiceProvider(container);
  }
}
```

9. ASP.NET Core goes about registering and resolving our controllers as services automatically; however, if we substitute the ASP.NET Core DI container with `Autofac` (or another DI container), the code in `ConfigureServices` should change as follows:

```
public class Startup
{
  public IContainer AppContainer { get; private set; }
  public IServiceProvider ConfigureServices
  (IServiceCollection services)
  {
    services
    .AddMvc()
    .AddApplicationPart(typeof(ProductController).Assembly)
    .AddControllersAsServices();
    // Add Autofac
    var containerBuilder = new ContainerBuilder();
    containerBuilder
    .RegisterType<ProductRepository>()
    .As<IProductRepository>();
    containerBuilder.Populate(services);
    this.AppContainer = containerBuilder.Build();
    return new AutofacServiceProvider(this.AppContainer);
  }
}
```

10. We may want to dispose of resources that have been resolved in the application container. To be able to do this, we have to register for the `ApplicationStopped` event by adding the following code to the `Configure` method:

```
public void Configure(IApplicationBuilder app,
IApplicationLifetime appLifetime)
{
  app.UseMvc(routes =>
  {
    routes.MapRoute(
    name: "default",
    template: "{controller=Home}/{action=Index}/{id?}");
  });
  appLifetime.ApplicationStopped.Register(() =>
  this.ApplicationContainer.Dispose());
}
```

Using ActionResults

In this recipe, you will learn what `ActionResults` we will use in an MVC-compliant application.

Getting ready

We created an empty web application with VS 2017 and added to it an empty controller. We'll create a repository with hardcoded values to be injected into the controller.

How to do it...

Here are all the types, the specific `ActionResults` we can return from a controller action:

```
public virtual JsonResult Json(object data)

public virtual ViewResult View()

public virtual ViewComponentResult ViewComponent(string componentName)

public virtual PartialViewResult PartialView()

public virtual ChallengeResult Challenge()

public virtual ForbidResult Forbid()

public virtual SignInResult SignIn(ClaimsPrincipal principal, string
authenticationScheme)

public virtual SignOutResult SignOut(params string[] authenticationSchemes)

public virtual ContentResult Content(string content)

public virtual FileContentResult File(byte[] fileContents, string
contentType)

public virtual FileStreamResult File(Stream fileStream, string contentType)

public virtual VirtualFileResult File(string virtualPath, string
contentType)

public virtual FileStreamResult File(Stream fileStream, string contentType,
string fileDownloadName)
```

```
public virtual LocalRedirectResult LocalRedirect(string localUrl);

public virtual PhysicalFileResult PhysicalFile(string physicalPath, string
contentType)

public virtual RedirectResult Redirect(string url)

public virtual RedirectToActionResult RedirectToAction(string actionName)

public virtual RedirectToRouteResult RedirectToRoute(object routeValues)
```

Creating and working with areas

In this recipe, you will learn how to manage areas in ASP.NET Core. To do this, we will:

- Create areas
- Create area routes
- Avoid area route conflict
- Change the default views location
- Create links for an area's action controllers

Getting ready

We created an empty web application with VS 2017.

How to do it...

When structuring an MVC application, sometimes, we need functional separation. The application we develop could be larger than it seems, such that we have several applications in an application. Areas give us the capability to create a lot of MVC structures in function of our needs, and give us a way to manage complex applications more easily. For example, in an e-commerce application, we could need different areas for the administration part of the website, which correspond to different roles (user managing, marketing, motor search reference, orders tracking, stock management), plus the website itself, of course.

Each area has its own controller, model, and view folders, and we will have to configure the area's routes in `Startup.cs` to match the physical file path of an area structure with an incoming URL.

There is no scaffolding to create areas like in the previous versions of MVC. So, we have to create areas from scratch:

1. Let's create an empty ASP.NET Core Web Application in VS 2017.
2. Next, we will right-click on the application root, and create the area's structures with an MVC structure folder inside, as shown in the following screenshot. We can also add a classic MVC structure to talk about a potential routing conflict with areas:

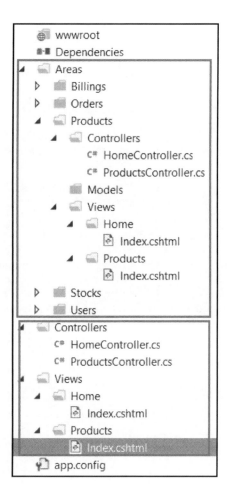

3. Next, let's create routes for areas and controllers, adding the following code in the `Configure` method of `Startup.cs`:

```
app.UseMvc(routes =>
{
  routes.MapRoute(
  name: "area",
  template: "{area=Products}/{controller=Home}/{action=Index}");
  routes.MapRoute(
  name: "default",
  template: "{controller=Home}/{action=Index}/{id?}");
});
```

4. If we launch the application using *Ctrl + F5*, we will get the following page:

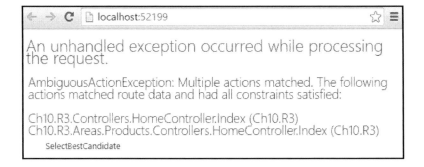

5. For older versions of ASP.NET MVC, we would add `namespaces` to each route definition in the `MapRoute` method to avoid conflict between controllers that have the same name. With ASP.NET Core MVC, we would rather use the routing attribute above each controller to specify that the controller comes from an area, such as:

```
public class HomeController : Controller
{
  [Area("Products")]
  [Route("[area]/[controller]/[action]")]
  public IActionResult Index()
  {
    return View();
  }
}
```

6. To access the `Home` controller in the `Product` area, we have to explicitly type the area route in the address toolbar of our browser:

This is Index Home Controller for Products Area

7. If we want to change the `AreaViewLocation`, we have to add the following code to `ConfiguresServices` of `Startup.cs`:

```
services.Configure<RazorViewEngineOptions>(options =>
{
  options.AreaViewLocationFormats.Clear();
  options.AreaViewLocationFormats.Add(
  "/Products/{2}/Views/{1}/{0}.cshtml");
  options.AreaViewLocationFormats.Add(
  "/Products/{2}/Views/Shared/{0}.cshtml");
  options.AreaViewLocationFormats.Add("/Views/Shared/{0}.cshtml");
});
```

We could also recreate the area's location by overriding `RazorViewEngine`.

8. To generate links based on areas, we can use the `HtmlHelper` or `TagHelper` syntax:

- `HtmlHelper`:

```
@Html.ActionLink("Products Area Home Page",
"Index", "Home", new { area = "Products" })
```

- `TagHelper`:

```
<a asp-area="Products" asp-controller="Home" asp-
action="Index">Products Area Home Page</a>
```

Creating and using POCO controllers

In this recipe, you will learn what POCO controllers are, and why we will use them.

Getting ready

We created an empty web application with VS 2017.

How to do it...

POCO controllers are simple classes decorated with two attributes:

- The [Controller] attribute, for the class itself, or its base class
- A routing attribute, defining its route in the application

They don't inherit from the Controller class, so they will not be able to return any MVC or WebAPI result as a view, an HttpStatus code, or any type inheriting from IActionResult.

We can place them anywhere in the application, at the root of the project, or in a folder named POCOController. In this exercise, we'll create a class and make it a controller by adding the Controller attribute on top of it, by following the given steps:

1. We'll add Microsoft.AspNetCore.Mvc Nuget package to project:

   ```
   "Microsoft.AspNetCore.Mvc": "2.0.0"
   ```

2. We will add the MVC service, and use it in Startup.cs:

   ```
   public class Startup
   {
     public void ConfigureServices(IServiceCollection services)
     {
       services.AddMvc();
     }
     public void Configure(IApplicationBuilder app)
     {
       app.UseMvc();
     }
   }
   ```

3. Now, let's add a POCO controller:

```
[Controller]
[Route("api/[controller]")]
public class PocoCtrl
{
    [HttpGet]
    public string Get()
    {
        return "This is a POCO Controller";
    }
}
```

4. Let's see if this controller works:

5. Now, let's create another POCO controller by creating one base class decorated by the controller and the routing attribute as a simple class not decorated, but inheriting from the base class:

```
[Controller]
public class PocoCtrlBase { }
[Route("api/[controller]")]
public class PocoCtrlInherits : PocoCtrlBase
{
    [HttpGet]
    public string Get()
    {
        return "This is a POCO Controller inherited";
    }
}
```

6. Let's see if the controller works:

The goal of the POCO controller is to create a lightweight controller which includes only action methods.

Creating and using controllers with MediatR

In this recipe, you will learn another way to work with MVC controllers without services and repositories.

This recipe could be applied to the WebAPI controller. We could add that it's logical to mix MVC and WebAPI practices in the same controller. Now, there's no difference between them.

Getting ready

We created an empty web application with VS 2017.

How to do it...

1. First, let's add the **MediatR Dependency Injection** package in project.json. It will include the MediatR 4.0.0 package:

   ```
   "MediatR.Extensions.Microsoft.DependencyInjection": "4.0.0"
   ```

   We will also need the AutoMapper package to map Business models to ViewModels. We will talk about AutoMapper in more detail in Chapter 13, *Views, Models, and ViewModels*:

   ```
   "AutoMapper.Extensions.Microsoft.DependencyInjection": "3.2.0"
   ```

2. Next, let's add some configuration in Startup.cs:

   ```
   public class Startup
   {
     public void ConfigureServices(IServiceCollection services)
     {
       var connection = @"Data Source=MyServer;Initial
   ```

```
      Catalog=CookBook;Integrated Security=True";
      services.AddDbContext<CookBookContext>(
      options => options.UseSqlServer(connection));
      services.AddMvc();
      services.AddAutoMapper(StartupAssembly());
      services.AddMediatR(StartupAssembly());
    }
    public void Configure(IApplicationBuilder app)
    {
      app.UseDeveloperExceptionPage();
      app.UseMvc(routes =>
      {
        routes.MapRoute(
        name: "default",
        template: "{controller=Book}/{action=Index}/{id?}");
      });
    }
    private static Assembly StartupAssembly()
    {
      return typeof(Startup).GetTypeInfo().Assembly;
    }
  }
```

We added MVC, Entity Framework, Automapper, and MediatR as services to the ASP.NET Core application. We can now use them.

3. The DbContext and the Business object will be next:

```
  public class CookBookContext : DbContext
  {
    public CookBookContext(DbContextOptions<CookBookContext> options)
    : base(options) { }
    public DbSet<Book> Book { get; set; }
  }
  public class Book
  {
    public int Id { get; set; }
    public string Name { get; set; }
    public decimal Price { get; set; }
  }
```

4. Now, let's create the `Query` objects, which are used to read data. We will use two classes from MediatR to do that: one is the `Query` class that inherits from `IAsyncRequest`, and the other is the `Handler` class that inherits from `IAsyncRequestQueryHandler`. This `Handler` class implements the `Handle` method from `IAsyncRequestQueryHandler`, which accepts as a parameter the `Query` class, and returns `ViewModel` to display. Here is the code for these classes:

- `ViewModels`:

```
public class BookIndexViewModel
{
  public int Id { get; set; }
  public string Name { get; set; }
  public decimal Price { get; set; }
}
public class BookListIndexViewModel
{
  public List<BookIndexViewModel> BookList { get; set; }
  public string Message { get; set; }
}
```

- The `Query` class:

```
public class BookListIndexQuery :
IAsyncRequest<BookListIndexViewModel>{ }
```

- The `QueryHandler` class:

```
public class BookListIndexQueryHandler :
IAsyncRequestHandler<BookListIndexQuery,
BookListIndexViewModel>
{
  private readonly CookBookContext _context;
  public BookListIndexQueryHandler(CookBookContext context)
  {
    _context = context;
  }
  public async Task<BookListIndexViewModel>
  Handle(BookListIndexQuery query)
  {
    var books = await _context.Book.ToListAsync();
    var model = new BookListIndexViewModel
    {
      BookList = await _context.Book
      .ProjectTo<BookIndexViewModel>()
      .ToListAsync()
```

```
        };
        return model;
    }
}
```

5. Now, let's look at the controller's code:

```
public class BookController : Controller
{
    private readonly IMediator _mediator;
    public BookController(IMediator mediator)
    {
        _mediator = mediator;
    }
    public async Task<IActionResult> Index(BookListIndexQuery query)
    {
        var model = await _mediator.SendAsync(query);
        return View(model);
    }
}
```

6. Next, we will create the view in the Views | Book | Index.cshtml file:

```
@model Ch10.R5.MediatR.BookListIndexViewModel
@if (Model.BookList.Any())
{
    <div>Books available</div>
    foreach (var book in Model.BookList)
    {
        <div>Id : @book.Id</div>
        <div>Name : @book.Name</div>
        <div>Price : @book.Price</div>
    }
}
```

7. Let's see the result:

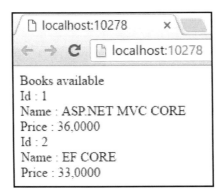

8. Now, lets create `ViewModel`, `Command` and `CommandHandler` classes to do insert operations on database.

- `ViewModel`:

```
public class BookAddViewModel
{
    [Required(ErrorMessage = "A name is required for the
book")]
    [StringLength(50, ErrorMessage =
    "The name of the book must not exceed 50 characters")]
    public string Name { get; set; }
    [Required(ErrorMessage = "A price is required for this
book")]
    [RegularExpression(@"^\d+(.\d{1,2})?$")]
    [Range(0.1, 100)]
    public decimal Price { get; set; }
}
```

- `Command`:

```
public class BookAddCommand : IAsyncRequest<Result>
{
    public string Name { get; }
    public decimal Price { get; }
}
```

- CommandHandler:

```
public class BookAddCommandHandler :
IAsyncRequestHandler<BookAddCommand, Result>
{
  private readonly CookBookContext _context;
  public BookAddCommandHandler(CookBookContext context)
  {
    _context = context;
  }
  public async Task<Result> Handle(BookAddCommand command)
  {
    var book = new Book
    {
      Name = command.Name,
      Price = command.Price
    };
    _context.Book.Add(book);
    await _context.SaveChangesAsync();
    var result = new Result { Success = true };
    return result;
  }
}
```

- The `Result` returns the type of `CommandHandler`:

```
public class Result
{
  public bool Success { get; set; }
  public string ErrorMessage { get; set; }
}
```

9. Let's see the new controller's code:

```
public class BookController : Controller
{
  private readonly IMediator _mediator;
  private readonly IMapper _mapper;
  public BookController(IMediator mediator, IMapper mapper)
  {
    _mediator = mediator;\
    _mapper = mapper;
  }
  public async Task<IActionResult> Index(BookListIndexQuery query)
  {
    var model = await _mediator.SendAsync(query);
    return View(model);
```

```
    }
    [HttpPost]
    [ValidateAntiForgeryToken]
    public async Task<IActionResult> Add(BookAddViewModel model)
    {
      if (ModelState.IsValid)
      {
        var command = new BookAddCommand();
        command = _mapper
        .Map<BookAddViewModel, BookAddCommand>(model);
        var result = await _mediator.SendAsync(command);
        if (result.Success)
        {
          return RedirectToAction("Index");
        }
        ModelState.AddModelError(string.Empty, result.ErrorMessage);
      }
      return View(model);
    }
  }
```

10. Finally, we can add this code to `View` after having created a
    `_ViewImports.cshtml` file:

    - `_ViewImports.cshtml`:

    ```
    @addTagHelper *, Microsoft.AspNetCore.Mvc.TagHelpers
    ```

    - `Index.cshtml`:

    ```
    <div>
      <form asp-controller="Book" asp-action="Add"
    method="post" role="form">
        <label>Book Name</label><input type="text" name="Name"
    /><br />
        <label>Book Price</label><input type="text"
    name="Price" /><br />
        <input type="submit" value="Add Book" />
      </form>
    </div>
    ```

11. We could structure the project this way:

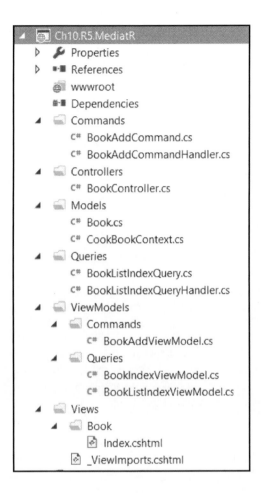

How it works...

MediatR is an implementation of a mediator pattern that you get by applying some **Command Query Responsibility Segregation** (or **Separation**) concepts. This NuGet package was created by Jimmy Bogard, who also created AutoMapper.

CQRS separates our code into two distinct parts: commands, and queries (the code that reads, and the code that writes persistently).

Here's a recap about CQRS pattern advantages:

- Separating reads and writes: We can propagate this concept to our database configuration to have a faster read-only (maybe denormalized) database for reads, and another one for writes. The issue will be to synchronize both, but there are several ways to do that.
- With Azure, it's very easy to incorporate a service bus with a message system in our software architecture. In function of your requirements, the more you add responsibility, the more you increase its maintainability; however, if you decide to not have any responsibility, the more you have a lightweight microservice architecture with decreased maintainability.
- CQRS pattern makes our code more readable, more testable, and more maintainable.
- In contrast, it can decrease productivity and readability, and increase complexity.

 There is no good or bad design pattern (except anti-pattern). They have to resolve a problem, and match with our project requirements. So, we don't have to follow a pattern or an architectural style by mode, but analyze seriously the pros and the cons of the pattern we apply, and ask ourselves the question: *Are they really relevant for my project?*

In MediatR, classes called **handlers** manage query and command messages. We don't use Event Sourcing or Domain-Driven Design concepts used in CQRS. Queries classes are used for reads, and commands classes are used for inserting, updating, and deleting operations. Commands and queries have their own ViewModels, and also have their handler class in order to communicate with a database, service, third-party services, and so on.

MediatR pattern brings us the following:

- We apply the Single Responsibility Principle, letting our controller focus on managing HTTP calls instead of having a lot of other responsibilities, such as querying databases, inserting a row in a table, and so on.
- No more need to have a repository to abstract data store or a service layer to put into a controller's logic. The separation of concern is better.

Managing exceptions

In this recipe, you will learn how to manage exceptions in an original way.

Getting ready

We created an empty web application with VS 2017.

How to do it...

1. First, we will create a `Result` class. This class will be returned by the `Service`
   layer. It allows us to manage the error messages to log and to display to the
   views:

```
public class Result
{
  public bool IsSuccess { get; }
  public string SuccessMessageToLog { get; set; }
  public string ErrorToLog { get; }
  public string ErrorToDisplay { get; set; }
  public ErrorType? ErrorType { get; }
  public bool IsFailure => !IsSuccess;
  protected Result(bool isSuccess, string error, ErrorType?
errorType)
  {
    if ((isSuccess && error != string.Empty) ||
    (isSuccess && !errorType.HasValue))
    throw new InvalidOperationException();
    if ((!isSuccess && error == string.Empty) ||
    (isSuccess && errorType.HasValue))
    throw new InvalidOperationException();
    IsSuccess = isSuccess;
    ErrorToLog = error;
  }
  public static Result Fail(string message)
  {
    return new Result(false, message, null);
  }
  public static Result Fail(ErrorType? errorType)
  {
    return new Result(false, string.Empty, errorType);
  }
  public static Result Fail(string message, ErrorType? errorType)
  {
    return new Result(false, message, errorType);
  }
  public static Result Ok()
  {
```

```
      return new Result(true, string.Empty, null);
   }
}
public enum ErrorType
{
  DatabaseIsOffline,
  CustomerAlreadyExists
}
```

2. Next, let's create `Product`, `ProductContext`, and `ProductInputViewModel`, which we will use later:

   - Product:

   ```
   public class Product
   {
     public int Id { get; set; }
     public string Name { get; set; }
     public decimal Price { get; set; }
   }
   ```

   - ProductContext:

   ```
   public class ProductContext : DbContext
   {
     public ProductContext(DbContextOptions<ProductContext>
   options) : base(options){ }
     public DbSet<Product> Product { get; set; }
   }
   ```

   - ProductInputViewModel:

   ```
   public class ProductInputViewModel
   {
     public string Name { get; set; }
     public decimal Price { get; set; }
   }
   ```

3. Next, we will add the `ProductService` class, where we will use the `Result` class to manage the exceptions that would occur, and the messages to log and display to the user interface:

```
public class ProductService : IProductService
{
  private readonly ILogger _logger;
  private readonly ProductContext _context;
  public ProductService(ILogger logger, ProductContext context)
  {
    _logger = logger;
    _context = context;
  }
  public Result CreateProduct(ProductInputViewModel
productViewModel)
  {
    var product = new Product()
    {
      Name = productViewModel.Name,
      Price = productViewModel.Price
    };
    Result result = SaveProduct(product);
    if (result.IsFailure && result.ErrorType.HasValue)
    {
      switch (result.ErrorType.Value)
      {
        case ErrorType.DatabaseIsOffline:
        Log(result);
        result.ErrorToDisplay = "Unable to connect to the
        database. Please try again later";
        break;
        case ErrorType.CustomerAlreadyExists:
        Log(result);
        result.ErrorToDisplay = "A product with the name " +
        productViewModel.Name + " already exists";
        break;
        default:
        throw new ArgumentException();
      }
    }
    return result;
  }
  private Result SaveProduct(Product product)
  {
    try
    {
      _context.Product.Add(product);
      _context.SaveChanges();
      return Result.Ok();
    }
    catch (DbUpdateException ex)
    {
```

```
      if (ex.Message == "Unable to open the DB connection")
      return Result.Fail(ex.Message,
      ErrorType.DatabaseIsOffline);
      if (ex.Message.Contains("IX_Customer_Name"))
      return Result.Fail(ex.Message,
      ErrorType.CustomerAlreadyExists);
      throw;
    }
  }
  private void Log(Result result)
  {
    if (result.IsFailure)
    _logger.LogError(result.ErrorToLog);
    else
    _logger.LogInformation(result.SuccessMessageToLog);
  }
}
```

4. Finally, we will add the `ProductController`:

```
public class ProductController : Controller
{
  private readonly IProductService _service;
  public ProductController(IProductService service)
  {
    _service = service;
  }
  [HttpGet]
  public ActionResult Index()
  {
    return View();
  }
  [HttpPost]
  public ActionResult CreateProduct(ProductInputViewModel product)
  {
    Result productResult = _service.CreateProduct(product);
    if (productResult.IsFailure)
    {
      ModelState.AddModelError(string.Empty,
      productResult.ErrorToDisplay);
      return View();
    }
    return RedirectToAction("Index");
  }
}
```

11
Web API

In this chapter, we will cover the following topics:

- Using ActionResults
- Configuring content negotiation
- Configuring cross-domain origin requests
- Using Swagger
- Testing Web APIs
- Managing exceptions

Using ActionResult

In this recipe, you will learn how to use `ActionResult` to return with a Web API. `ActionResult` is a core type of MVC for returning a result from server to client. `ActionResult` is a base class and its abstract, so we can use one of the derived classes of it, such as `JsonResult`, `ViewResult`, `RedirectResult`, or `FileResult`.

Getting ready

We will create a Web API controller with the `CRUD` method to understand what `ActionResult` we have to return for each HTTP verb.

How to do it...

With ASP.NET Core MVC and Web API-merging, the base class is now the same.
`ActionResults` now returns the HTTP status code result, as the `ApiController` base class returned before ASP.NET Core.

We will use `ActionResults` to return the HTTP status code with a CRUD Web API controller:

1. First, let's create the Web API application by creating an empty web application.

2. Next, we will add the ASP.NET Core MVC dependency to the project:

   ```
   "Microsoft.AspNetCore.MVC": "2.0.0",
   ```

3. Next, let's add the following code to `Startup.cs`. This code will allow us to use the Web API's controllers:

   ```
   public void ConfigureServices(IServiceCollection services)
   {
     services.AddMVC();
   }
   public void Configure(IApplicationBuilder app)
   {
     app.UseMVC();
   }
   ```

4. Next, we will create a repository to use in this Web API controller:

   ```
   public interface IProductRepository
   {
     IEnumerable<Product> GetAllProducts();
     void Add(Product product);
     Product Find(int id);
     void Update(Product product);
     void Remove(int id);
   }
   ```

5. Next, let's register and configure the repository lifecycle in `Startup.cs`:

   ```
   services.AddScoped<IProductRepository, ProductRepository>();
   ```

6. Next, let's create the Web API controller:

```
[Route("api/[controller]")]
public class ProductApiController : Controller
{
  private readonly IProductRepository _productRepository;
  public ProductApiController(IProductRepository repository)
  {
    _productRepository = repository;
  }
}
```

7. Now we will add the GET method. Its route will be api/productapi:

```
[HttpGet]
public IActionResult Get()
{
  var productsFromRepo = _productRepository.GetAllProducts();
  if (productsFromRepo == null)
  return NotFound();
  // return HTTP response status code 404
  return Ok(productsFromRepo);
  // return HTTP status code 200
}
```

8. Now we will add the GET method with a different route, api/productapi/{id}:

```
[HttpGet("{id:int}")]
public IActionResult Get(int id)
{
  var productFromRepo = _productRepository.Find(id);
  if (productFromRepo == null)
  return NotFound();
  // return HTTP response status code 404
  return Ok(productFromRepo);
  // return HTTP response status code 200
}
```

9. Next, we will add the POST method. Its route will be api/productapi, with a Product object in the request body:

```
[HttpPost]
public IActionResult Post([FromBody]Product product)
{
  if (product == null)
  return BadRequest();
  // return HTTP response status code 400
```

```
    _productRepository.Add(product);
    return CreatedAtRoute("GetProduct",
    new { id = product.Id }, product);
    // return HTTP response status code 201
}
```

10. Next, we will add the PUT method. Its route will be api/productapi/{id}, with a Product object in the request body:

```
[HttpPut("{id}")]
public IActionResult Put(int id, [FromBody]Product product)
{
    if (product == null || product.Id != id)
    return BadRequest();
    // return HTTP response status code 401
    var productFromRepo = _productRepository.Find(id);
    if (productFromRepo == null)
    return NotFound();
    // return HTTP response status code 404
    _productRepository.Update(product);
    return new NoContentResult();
    // return HTTP response status code 204
}
```

11. Next, we will add the PATCH method. Its route will be api/productapi/{id}, with a Product object in the request body. The PATCH verb is used when we do a partial update:

```
[HttpPut("{id}")]
public IActionResult Patch(int id, [FromBody]Product product)
{
    if (product == null)
    return BadRequest();
    // return HTTP response status code 400
    var productFromRepo = _productRepository.Find(id);
    if (productFromRepo == null)
    return NotFound();
    // return HTTP response status code 404
    productFromRepo.Id = product.Id;
    _productRepository.Update(product);
    return new NoContentResult();
    // return HTTP response status code 204
}
```

12. Next, we will add the DELETE method. Its route will be `api/productapi/{id}`:

```
[HttpDelete("{id}")]
public IActionResult Delete(int id)
{
  var productFromRepo = _productRepository.Find(id);
  if (productFromRepo == null)
  return NotFound();
  // return HTTP response status code 404
  _productRepository.Remove(id);
  return new NoContentResult();
  // return HTTP response status code 204
}
```

How it works...

`IActionResult` is implemented by the `ActionResult` abstract class. The `ActionResult` abstract class is used to create several classes to return predefined HTTP status codes to the caller client, such as the following:

- `OkResult`: returns the 200 HTTP status code
- `CreatedResult`: returns the 201 HTTP status code
- `CreatedAtActionResult`: returns the 201 HTTP status code
- `CreatedAtRouteResult`: returns the 201 HTTP status code
- `NoContentResult`: returns the 204 HTTP status code
- `BadRequestResult`: returns the 400 HTTP status code
- `UnauthorizedResult`: returns the 401 HTTP status code
- `NotFoundResult`: returns the 404 HTTP status code

The `ControllerBase` class has several methods for each of these result types. We can call one of them to return the desired status code from Web API, such as the following code:

```
return Ok(); // returns OkResult

return Created(); // returns CreatedResult

return NotFound(); // returns NotFoundResult
```

Configuring content negotiation

In this recipe, you will learn how to manage content negotiation in ASP.NET Core. ASP.NET Core can return data in any format (such as JSON, XML, PLIST, and SOAP), thanks to `ContentFormatters`. More information can be found at `https://docs.microsoft.com/en-us/aspnet/core/mvc/advanced/custom-formatters`.

Any client can make a request with a header to tell the server in what format it wants the response. The server application can read a header value, and use it when creating a response to a request. **Content negotiation** is the name of whole process.

Getting ready

By default, ASP.NET Core will return JSON from action methods.

Let's get the code from the previous recipe, and let's see the result from `GetAllProducts`:

We get JSON values, because by default, ASP.NET Core doesn't take into account the `Accept` header the browser sent.

How to do it...

1. First, let's add the following dependency in the project:

   ```
   "Microsoft.AspNetCore.MVC.Formatters.Xml": "2.0.0"
   ```

2. Next, let's add the following code to the `ConfigureServices` method of `Startup.cs`:

   ```
   services.AddMVC(options =>
   {
     options.RespectBrowserAcceptHeader = true;
     options.InputFormatters.Add(
     new XmlDataContractSerializerInputFormatter());
   ```

```
        options.OutputFormatters.Add(
        new XmlDataContractSerializerOutputFormatter());
    });
```

3. Finally, we can see the list of products in the XML format:

```
←  →  C    localhost:5901/api/productapi

This XML file does not appear to have any style information associated with it. The document tree is shown below.

▼<ArrayOfProduct xmlns:i="http://www.w3.org/2001/XMLSchema-instance" xmlns="http://schemas.datacontract.org/2004/07/Ch11.R1">
    <Product/>
    <Product/>
    <Product/>
    <Product/>
    <Product/>
</ArrayOfProduct>
```

Configuring cross-domain origin requests

In this recipe, you will learn how to configure and use **Cross-Origin Resource Sharing (CORS)** in ASP.NET Core applications.

Getting ready

To configure and use CORS, we will create two applications: one Web API application to expose a service configured with CORS constraints, and a client application that tries to consume the Web API service from a jQuery AJAX call.

How to do it...

We'll create two separate application projects, and from one of them we'll make a request to other. The other project is an ASP.NET Core project, and we'll enable/configure CORS in it:

1. First, let's create the Web API application, by creating an empty web application:

   ```
   dotnet new mvc -n Chapter11.R3.Server
   ```

2. Next, we will add the ASP.NET Core MVC dependency to the project:

   ```
   "Microsoft.AspNetCore.MVC": "2.0.0"
   ```

3. Next, let's add the following code to `Startup.cs`. This code allows us to use Web API's controllers:

```
public void ConfigureServices(IServiceCollection services)
{
  services.AddMVC();
}
public void Configure(IApplicationBuilder app)
{
  app.UseMVC();
}
```

4. Next, let's add the CORS middleware to the ASP.NET Core pipeline, and let's configure it by adding the following code to `Startup.cs`:

```
public void ConfigureServices(IServiceCollection services)
{
  services.AddMVC();
  services.AddCors(options =>
  {
    options.AddPolicy("AllowMyClientOrigin", builder =>
    builder.WithOrigins("http://localhost:63125")
    .WithMethods("GET", "HEAD")
    .WithHeaders("accept", "content-type", "origin"));
  });
}
public void Configure(IApplicationBuilder app)
{
  app.UseMVC();
  app.UseCors("AllowMyClientOrigin");
}
```

To use the new CORS policy created in the `ConfigureServices` method, we call this policy in the `Configure` method. The current CORS policy has three methods:

- `WithOrigins`, which accepts as parameters the domain URL, to allow the Web API to consume
- `WithMethods`, which accepts as parameters the HTTP verbs, to allow them in the request
- `WithHeaders`, which accepts as parameters the different HTTP headers allowed in the request

If we would like to allow all client domain URLs to the Web API, we should change the CORS policy with this code in the `ConfigureServices` method:

```
services.AddCors(options =>options.AddPolicy("AllowMyClientOrigin",
p => p.AllowAnyOrigin()));
```

5. Next, we will create an API controller with a `GET` method:

```
[Route("api/[controller]")]
public class TestAPIController : Controller
{
    [HttpGet]
    public IActionResult Get()
    {
        var result = new { Success = "True", Message = "API Message" };
        return Ok(result);
    }
}
```

6. Finally, to allow applications from other domains to consume the `GET` method, we will also add the following attribute above the Web API methods that we want to expose to the domain. The `EnableCors` attribute accepts a string parameter, which is the CORS policy created previously in `Startup.cs`:

```
[HttpGet]
[EnableCors("AllowMyClientOrigin")]
public IActionResult Get()
{
    var result = new { Success = "True", Message = "API Message" };
    return Ok(result);
}
```

7. To allow CORS configuration at controller level to be available for all methods in this controller, we could add the `EnableCors` attribute above `controller` instead of the `Action` method:

```
[Route("api/[controller]")]
[EnableCors("AllowMyClientOrigin")]
public class TestAPIController : Controller
{
    [HttpGet]
    public IActionResult Get()
    {
        var result = new { Success = "True", Message = "API Message" };
        return Ok(result);
    }
```

}

8. To allow the CORS configuration at the application level to be available for all the controllers in this application, we could add the `CorsAuthorizationFilterFactory` filter to the global filter collection. The code should finally be as follows:

```
public void ConfigureServices(IServiceCollection services)
{
  services.AddMVC();
  services.AddCors(options =>
  {
    options.AddPolicy("AllowMyClientOrigin", builder =>
    builder.WithOrigins("http://localhost:63125")
    .WithMethods("GET", "HEAD")
    .WithHeaders("accept", "content-type", "origin"));
  });
  services.Configure<MVCOptions>(options =>
  {
    options.Filters.Add(new
    CorsAuthorizationFilterFactory("AllowMyClientOrigin"));
  });
}
[Route("api/[controller]")]
public class TestAPIController : Controller
{
  [HttpGet]
  public IActionResult Get()
  {
    var result = new { Success = "True", Message = "API Message" };
    return Ok(result);
  }
}
```

9. Next, let's create a new empty web application to test the Web API, and let's add a `bower.js` file to add front-end dependencies, by right-clicking on the root of the project. Then, go to **Add** | **New item** | **.NET Core** | **Client-side** | **Bower Configuration File**:

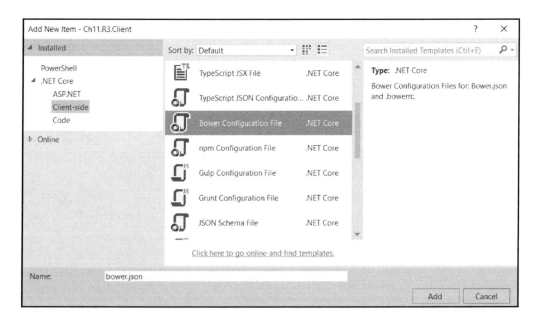

10. Next, let's add jQuery to our client application with **Bower Package Manager**, by right-clicking on the root of the project. Then, select **Manage Bower Packages** and install jQuery:

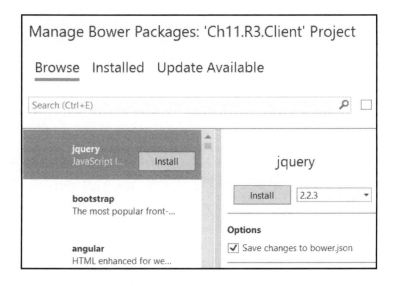

11. Next, let's add an HTML page in the `wwwroot` folder to add the JavaScript code, which will call the API service. The `wwwroot` folder is the folder where we add all static files (`.html`, `.css`, `.js`, `.font`, images, and so on). We could also add this `.js` code to a view:

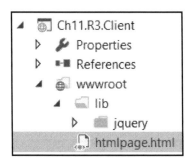

12. To allow static files in the ASP.NET Core application, we have to add the following code to the `Configure` method:

```
public void Configure(IApplicationBuilder app)
{
  app.UseStaticFiles();
}
```

13. Next, we will add the following code to the HTML page we just created:

```
<!DOCTYPE html>
<html>
  <head>
    <meta charset="utf-8" />
    <title></title>
  </head>
  <body>
    <button id="bt1">Call API</button>
    <script src="lib/jquery/dist/jquery.js"></script>
      <script type="text/javascript">
      $(document).ready(function () {
        jQuery.support.cors = true;
        $('#bt1').click(function () {
          console.log('Clicked');
          $.ajax({
            url: 'http://localhost:64112/api/TestAPI',
            type: 'GET',
            dataType: 'json',
            success: function (data) {
```

```
              console.log(data.success);
              console.log(data.message);
          },
          error: function (jqXHR, textStatus, errorThrown) {
            console.log(textStatus, errorThrown);
          }
        });
      });
    });
  </script>
  </body>
</html>
```

14. Finally, we will launch the HTML page and call the `TestAPI` controller with the
    `GET` HTTP method, by clicking on the **Call API** button. To ensure that no error
    has occurred, we will launch through *F12* button in the browser we are using to
    test the application. Let's open the console and see the result:

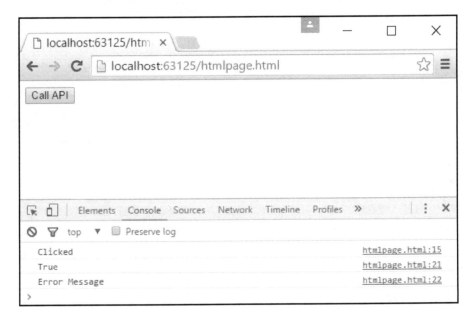

15. If any error occurred, the console message would have been the one shown in this screenshot:

Using Swagger

In this recipe, you will learn how to use **Swagger** to create help pages and documentation for our REST APIs.

Getting ready

Let's create an empty project with VS 2017.

How to do it...

1. First, let's add the Swashbuckle reference to the project:

   ```
   "Swashbuckle": "5.6.0"
   ```

2. Next, let's add **Swagger** as a middleware in Startup.cs:

   ```
   public void ConfigureServices(IServiceCollection services)
   {
     services.AddMVC();
     services.AddSwaggerGen();
   }
   public void Configure(IApplicationBuilder app)
   {
     app.UseMVC();
     app.UseSwagger();
     app.UseSwaggerUi();
   }
   ```

3. Now, let's launch our API documentation by going to http://{UrlAPI}/ swagger/ui. We can now see the generated API documentation:

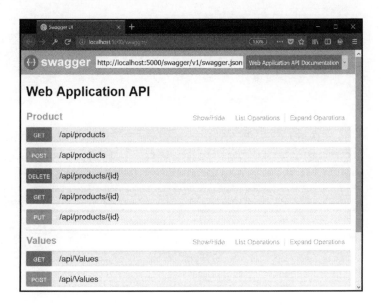

4. When we click on each HTTP method, we can see all the options Swagger offers to us, such as testing the API, easily:

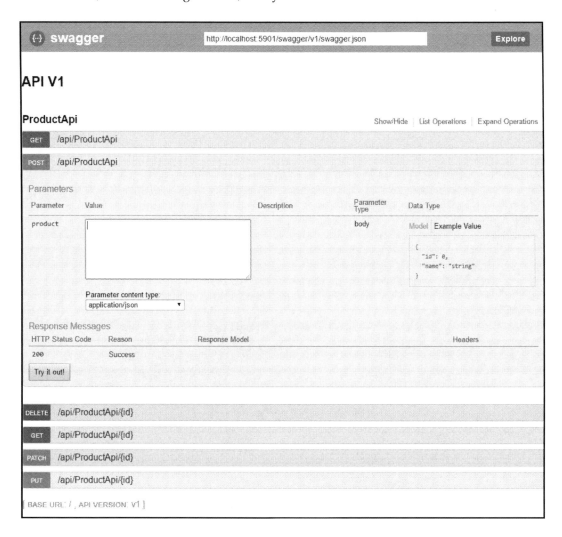

5. Next, let's use another feature: adding information about the API. To do this, let's add this code to `Startup.cs`:

```
public class Startup
{
  public Startup(IHostingEnvironment env)
  {
    var builder = new ConfigurationBuilder()
    .SetBasePath(env.ContentRootPath);
    Configuration = builder.Build();
  }
  public IConfigurationRoot Configuration
  {
    get;
  }
  public void ConfigureServices(IServiceCollection services)
  {
    services.AddMVC();
    services.AddSwaggerGen();
    services.ConfigureSwaggerGen(options =>
    {
      options.SingleApiVersion(new Info
      {
        Version = "v1",
        Title = "ECommerce API",
        Description = "The Api to get all data from the SB Store",
        TermsOfService = "None"
      });
        options.IncludeXmlComments(
        Path.ChangeExtension(Assembly.GetEntryAssembly().Location,
"xml")
        );
        options.DescribeAllEnumsAsStrings();
    });
  }
  public void Configure(IApplicationBuilder app)
  {
    app.UseMVC();
    app.UseSwagger();
    app.UseSwaggerUi();
  }
}
```

The `options.IncludeXmlComments()` method implies that we allow to take into account XML comments above the API method to generate Swagger documentation:

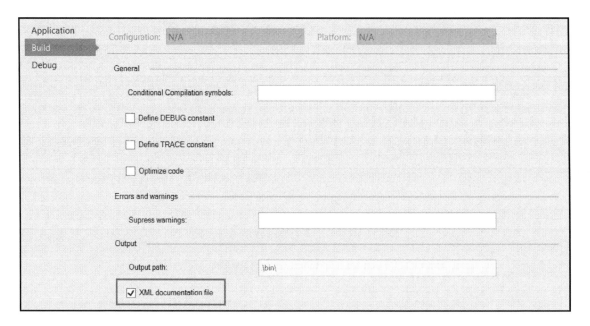

6. Let's add some comments into the C# code and see all these changes:

```csharp
/// <summary>
/// This method insert a product in the database
/// </summary>
/// <param name="product"></param>
/// <returns>CreatedAtRouteResult</returns>
[HttpPost]
public IActionResult Post([FromBody]Product product)
```

7. Let's see the changes now in the Swagger UI:

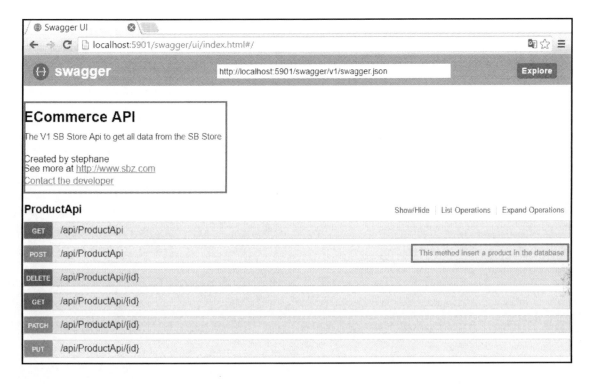

8. Finally, let's see Swagger's more interesting feature: the **Try it Out!** button tests the HTTP method, and allows us to watch the more relevant information of the response and the **Request URL**: the **Response Body**, the **Response Code**, and the **Response Headers**:

| GET | /api/ProductApi/{id} |

Parameters

Parameter	Value	Description	Parameter Type	Data Type
id	1		path	integer

Response Messages

HTTP Status Code	Reason	Response Model	Headers
200	Success		

| Try it out! | Hide Response |

Curl

```
curl -X GET --header 'Accept: application/json' 'http://localhost:5901/api/ProductApi/1'
```

Request URL

```
http://localhost:5901/api/ProductApi/1
```

Response Body

```
{
  "id": 1,
  "name": "Phone"
}
```

Response Code

```
200
```

Response Headers

```
{
  "date": "Fri, 09 Sep 2016 21:03:16 GMT",
  "x-sourcefiles": "=?UTF-8?B?QzpcVXNlcnNcc2JlGtoZXJlxkb2N1bWVudHNcdmlzdWFsIHN0dWRpbyAyMDE1XFByb2plY3RzXENoMTFFcc3JjXENoMTEuU..
  "server": "Kestrel",
  "x-powered-by": "ASP.NET",
  "transfer-encoding": "chunked",
  "content-type": "application/json; charset=utf-8"
}
```

| PATCH | /api/ProductApi/{id} |

How it works...

Swagger provides us with a nice and simple way to generate a complete UI documentation. This documentation will be generated by the existing API source code, and can be completed by the XML comments in the application. It also allows us to test each HTTP method (such as **Postman**), sends values via the generated UI, and selects different content-type headers, such as `application/json`, or `application/xml`.

It also provides some client APIs, allowing communication between the endpoints generated by Swagger, and client technologies such as JavaScript, AngularJS, or Xamarin, among others.

Testing Web API

In this recipe, you will learn how to test Web API controllers with Moq and xUnit.

Getting ready

Let's create a class library project with VS 2017, and use the `ProductAPIController` methods created in the *Using ActionResults* recipe of this chapter. We will create some test cases for this API.

How to do it...

1. First, let's create a class library project in the solution:

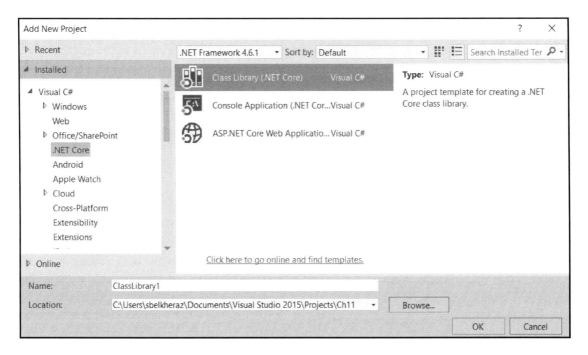

2. Next, we will change the generated code in the project to import `xunit`, `dotnet-test-xunit`, and `moq`. We will also have to add the reference on the Web API project.

3. Here are some of the test methods:

```
public class ProductApiControllerTests
{
  #region Tests for GET : api/productapi
  [Fact]
  public void GET
  _Returns404NotFoundResultIfProductListHaveNoItemsInRepo()
  {
    // Arrange
    var mockRepo = new Mock<IProductRepository>();
    var emptyProductList = GetEmptyProductsList();
    mockRepo.Setup(repo => repo.GetAllProducts())
    .Returns(emptyProductList);
```

```
    var controller = new ProductApiController(mockRepo.Object);
    // Act
    var result = controller.Get();
    // Assert
    Assert.IsType<NotFoundObjectResult>(result);
}
[Fact]
public void GET
_Returns200OkResultIfProductListHaveAtLeastOneItemInRepo()
{
    // Arrange
    var mockRepo = new Mock<IProductRepository>();
    var productList = GetProductsList();
    mockRepo.Setup(repo => repo.GetAllProducts())
    .Returns(productList);
    var controller = new ProductApiController(mockRepo.Object);
    // Act
    var result = controller.Get();
    // Assert
    Assert.IsType<OkObjectResult>(result);
}
#endregion
#region Tests for POST : api/productapi
public void POST
_Returns400BadRequestResultIfProductFromRequestParameterIsNull()
{
    // Arrange
    var mockRepo = new Mock<IProductRepository>();
    var product = GetProduct();
    var nullProduct = GetNullProduct();
    mockRepo.Setup(repo => repo.Add(product));
    var controller = new ProductApiController(mockRepo.Object);
    // Act
    var result = controller.Post(nullProduct);
    // Assert
    Assert.IsType<BadRequestObjectResult>(result);
}
public void POST
_Returns201CreatedAtRouteResultIfProductIsInsertedSuccesfully
InRepo()
{
    // Arrange
    var mockRepo = new Mock<IProductRepository>();
    var product = GetProduct();
    mockRepo.Setup(repo => repo.Add(product));
    var controller = new ProductApiController(mockRepo.Object);
    // Act
    var result = controller.Post(product);
```

```
      // Assert}
      Assert.IsType<CreatedAtRouteResult>(result);
    }
    #endregion
    #region private methods
    private IEnumerable<Product> GetEmptyProductsList()
    {
      return new List<Product>();
    }
    private IEnumerable<Product> GetProductsList()
    {
      return new List<Product>
      {
        new Product { Id = 1, Name = "Phone" },
        new Product { Id = 2, Name = "Laptop" },
        new Product { Id = 3, Name = "Computer" },
        new Product { Id = 4, Name = "Screen" },
        new Product { Id = 5, Name = "Mouse" }
      };
    }
    private Product GetEmptyProduct()
    {
      return new Product();
    }
    private Product GetNullProduct()
    {
      return null;
    }
    private Product GetProduct()
    {
      return new Product
      {
        Id = 6, Name = "Tablet"
      };
    }
    private Product GetProductById(int id)
    {
      return GetProductsList().Where(p => p.Id ==
id).SingleOrDefault();
    }
    private Product GetProductAleadyExist()
    {
      return GetProductsList()
      .Where(p => p.Id == 1).SingleOrDefault();
    }
    #endregion
}
```

Most of the test methods have been removed for brevity. The test project can be found on the GitHub repository, at `https://github.com/polatengin/B05277`.

There's more...

We could use several tools to test our APIs, such as:

- **WireShark** (`https://www.wireshark.org/`) is a great tool for monitoring a network, and listening to all the packets received and sent from a network adapter.
- **Postman** (`https://www.getpostman.com/`) and **Fiddler** (`https://www.telerik.com/fiddler`) are also very useful tools for testing APIs to creating HTTP calls to communicate with. They install themselves as some kind of proxy to the computer. They can send and display request and response pairs to a particular URL.

Managing exceptions

In this recipe, you will learn how to manage exceptions with Web API.

Usually, we don't want to lose the cause of an exception. So, we should persist and maintain all the exception's logs. Exception logs can be huge in terms of storage capacity needed to persist them.

We can log all the exceptions in files, or a database table (such as MSSQL, Oracle, or MySql), or document stores (such as MongoDb (`https://www.mongodb.com/`), or Azure CosmosDb (`https://azure.microsoft.com/en-us/services/cosmos-db/`)).

The logged exception would contain at least:

- A descriptive message
- The exception message
- The exception .NET type
- The stack trace

We generally send only the descriptive message to the client, and log other information about the exception.

With Web API 2, before ASP.NET Core, the `HttpError` class sent a structured error to the client.

`HttpError` was traditionally used by Web API to serve up error information to the client in a (kind of) standardized way. It had some interesting properties:

- `ExceptionMessage`
- `ExceptionType`
- `InnerException`
- `Message`
- `ModelState`
- `MessageDetail`
- `StackTrace`

Getting ready

Let's open the ASP.NET Core Web API project we created in the *Using ActionResults* recipe.

How to do it...

1. First, let's add the `WebApiCompatShim` library to `project.json`:

   ```
   "Microsoft.AspNetCore.MVC.WebApiCompatShim": "1.0.0"
   ```

2. To use `WebApiCompatShim`, we have to change a little bit of code in `ConfigureServices` in order to add a service:

   ```
   services.AddMVC().AddWebApiConventions();
   ```

3. Next, we will change the existing code for `api/productapi/{id}`:

   ```
   [HttpGet("{id:int}")]
   public IActionResult Get(int id)
   {
     var productFromRepo = _productRepository.Find(id);
     if (productFromRepo == null)
     return NotFound();
     return Ok(productFromRepo);
   }
   ```

We can add one more `Get()` method with different parameters, as follows:

```
[Route("{id:int}")]
public HttpResponseMessage Get(int id, HttpRequestMessage request)
{
  var product = _productRepository.Find(id);
  if (product == null)
  {
    Return request.CreateErrorResponse(HttpStatusCode.NotFound,
    new HttpError
    {
      Message = "This product does not exist",
      MessageDetail = string.Format("The product requested with
      ID {0} does not exist in the repository", id)
    });
  }
  return request.CreateResponse(product);
}
```

4. Finally, we will receive the following message if we send a product ID (that does not exist in the repository) as a parameter:

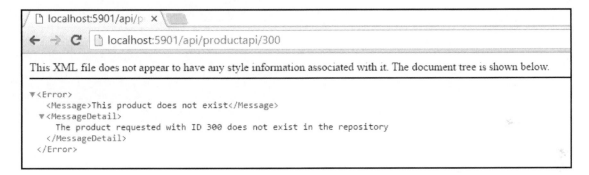

There's more...

We could manage exceptions globally by creating an `Exception` middleware.

Since Web API 2.1, we use `IExceptionHandler` to handle exceptions globally. It helps catch exceptions in controllers, actions, filters, routes, and sometimes, `MessageHandlers` and `MediaTypeFormatters`.

We can also think about creating a custom global `Exception` filter to log the exception, but we will talk about that in `Chapter 12`, *Filters*.

12
Filters

In this chapter, we will cover the following topics:

- Managing authentication and authorization with policies, requirements, and filters
- Managing dependency injection with filters
- Creating and using an action filter
- Creating and using a result filter
- Creating and using a resource filter
- Creating and using an exception filter
- Using a filter globally versus using a middleware

Introduction

Filters are code injected into request processing. There can be many categories of filters: authorization, caching, logging, exception, and more. The filters are executed after ActionInvocation, and after the middleware is executed on the ASP.NET Core pipeline.

Here is the filter pipeline from the official ASP.NET Core documentation:

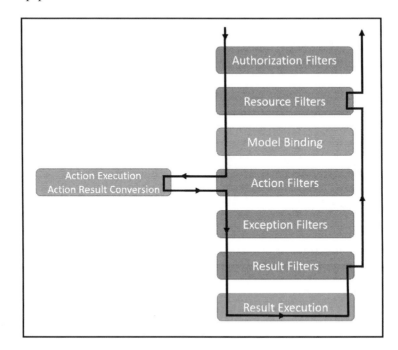

They can be applied at action or controller level as attributes, or at application level as global filters added in the global filter list in Startup.cs.

We can also control the order in which filters are executed on the same action.

We can create synchronous and asynchronous filters, but we should never mix both to avoid side effects.

There are predefined filters, and there are filters we create:

- Predefined filters (they are used at action and controller levels):
    - [AllowAnonymous]
    - [Authorize]
    - [FormatFilter]
    - [TypeFilter(typeof(MyFilterAttribute))]
    - [ServiceFilter(typeof(MyFilterAttribute))]

- Filters we create (global or not):
    - **Action filters** (deriving from `IActionFilter`, `IAsyncActionFilter`, or `IActionFilterAttribute`)
    - **Result filters** (deriving from `IResultFilter`, `IAsyncResultFilter`, or `IResultFilterAttribute`)
    - **Resource filters** (deriving from `IResourceFilter`, `IAsyncResourceFilter`, or `IResourceFilterAttribute`)
    - **Exception filters** (deriving from `IExceptionFilter`, `IAsyncExceptionFilter`, or `IExceptionFilterAttribute`)

However, the global filters will be executed first; after that, the filters at the controller level, and finally, the filters at action level.

For exception filters, the order is reversed:

1. Global.
2. Controller.
3. Action.

Managing authentication and authorization with policies, requirements, and filters

In this recipe, you will learn how to apply authorization and authentication at global, controller, and action levels.

Getting ready

Let's create an empty web application with VS 2017.

How to do it...

The authorization filter goal is to restrict action methods individually, or by controller to specific users, roles, or claims. It always runs before the action is executed:

1. A classic way to use the `Authorization` filter is to add this filter at the controller level, and override with the `AllowAnonymous` attribute at `Action` level, as shown in the following code:

```
[Authorize]
public class AccountController : Controller
{
  [HttpGet]
  [AllowAnonymous]
  public IActionResult Login(string returnUrl = null)
  {
    ViewData["ReturnUrl"] = returnUrl;
    return View();
  }
  [HttpGet]
  [AllowAnonymous]
  public IActionResult Register(string returnUrl = null)
  {
    ViewData["ReturnUrl"] = returnUrl;
    return View();
  }
  [HttpPost]
  [ValidateAntiForgeryToken]
  public async Task<IActionResult> LogOff()
  {
    await _signInManager.SignOutAsync();
    _logger.LogInformation(4, "User logged out.");
    return RedirectToAction(nameof(HomeController.Index), "Home");
  }
  [HttpGet]
  [AllowAnonymous]
  public IActionResult ForgotPassword()
  {
    return View();
  }
}
```

The `Authorization` filter automatically returns a `401` status code if an unauthorized user tries to access a `resource` or `action` method.

Before ASP.NET Core, it was possible to create our own `Authorization` attribute by inheriting from `IAuthorizationFilter` or `AuthorizeAttribute`. With Core, you can't write your own `Authorization` filter; however, it's possible to customize an `Authorization` filter through a policy and the `AuthorizationPolicyBuilder` object.

2. Let's override the `Authorize` attribute configuration, and let's add it as a global filter:

```
var authorizationPolicy = new AuthorizationPolicyBuilder()
.RequireAuthenticatedUser()
.Build();
config.Filters.Add(new AuthorizeFilter(authorizationPolicy));
```

3. We could also add some policies to apply to the `Authorize` filter, like this:

```
services.AddAuthorization(auth =>
auth.AddPolicy("AuthPolicyAdminRole", policy =>
policy.RequireRole("AdminRole")));
services.AddAuthorization(auth =>
auth.AddPolicy("AuthPolicyReviewerRole", policy =>
policy.RequireRole("ReviewerRole")));
services.AddAuthorization(auth =>
auth.AddPolicy("AuthPolicySpecificClaim", policy =>
policy.RequireClaim("SpecificClaim")));
```

4. That's the way we apply these policies at the controller or action level:

```
[Authorize(Policy = "AuthPolicyAdminRole")]
[Authorize(Policy = "AuthPolicyOtherRole")]
[Authorize(Policy = "AuthPolicySpecificClaim")]
public IActionResult AuthorizedRoleView()
```

Another great thing with policies is that they are testable. We can develop a Unit Test project, and test all the policies autonomously.

Authentication

It is common practice to use an `Authentication` and an `Authorization` filter simultaneously. With `WebForms`, we could add custom `Authentication` programmatically per page, but it is laborious.

MVC brought to `WebApplications` more granularity for authentication. Now, we can add `Authentication` at action, controller, or global level, according to the needs of our actions in a website. It was first executed before all the MVC filters.

The `Authentication` filter doesn't exist anymore in ASP.NET MVC 6 (maybe it's not ported yet).

Before ASP.NET Core, it was possible to create our own `Authorization` attribute by inheriting from `FilterAttribute` and `IAuthenticationFilter`.

For example, we use it to return a specific HTTP status code, action result, or route result, in the case of a non-authenticated user trying to access a method, or an action method in a controller. There are ways to check for authentication:

1. We can always run authentication by programmatically using the following code:

```
public IActionResult About()
{
  if (User.Identity.IsAuthenticated)
  RedirectToAction("Index");
  return View();
}
```

2. We could merge `Authentication` and `Authorization` by adding the previous authentication check through a policy applied to the `Authorization` filter, as follows:

```
services.AddAuthorization(auth =>
auth.AddPolicy("AuthPolicyAuthentication", policy =>
policy.RequireAuthenticatedUser()));
```

3. With this policy, we will be able to replace this code:

```
if (User.Identity.IsAuthenticated)
```

We can use the `Authorize` attribute to apply an authentication policy into an action, like this:

```
[Authorize(Policy = "AuthPolicyAuthentication")]
 public IActionResult About()
{
  if (User.Identity.IsAuthenticated)
  RedirectToAction("Index");
  return View();
}
```

Barry Dorran has one of the nicest implementation of basic authentication middleware on his GitHub repository at `https://github.com/blowdart/idunno.Authentication`.

There's more...

We can follow Barry Dorrans' works on the security aspects of ASP.NET Core. He created a very nice workshop on which this recipe is largely based. You can access it at `https://github.com/blowdart/AspNetAuthorizationWorkshop`.

Managing dependency injection with filters

In this recipe, you will learn how and when to use dependency injection with filters.

Getting ready

Let's create an empty web project with VS 2017.

How to do it...

We'll understand the `IActionFilter` interface, `TypeFilter`, and `ServiceFilter` attributes by applying a dependency injection into a controller.

1. First, let's create an `ActionFilter` class only by deriving from `IActionFilter`:

```
public class MyActionFilter : IActionFilter
{
  public void OnActionExecuting(ActionExecutingContext context)
  {
    // do something before the action executes
  }
  public void OnActionExecuted(ActionExecutedContext context)
  {
    // do something after the action executes
  }
}
```

2. To use this class as an attribute, we have to use a `TypeFilter` attribute, and give it this class as a parameter. We can't use `MyActionFilter` directly as an attribute, because it doesn't inherit from `ActionFilterAttribute`:

```
[TypeFilter(typeof(MyActionFilter))]
public IActionResult Index()
{
   return View();
}
```

3. If we test, this page works fine:

4. Let's now try with the `ServiceFilter` attribute:

```
[ServiceFilter(typeof(MyActionFilter))]
public IActionResult Index()
```

5. If we test again, we will get an HTTP error 500, with a message telling us that the filter is not registered:

6. Let's register the filter in the `ConfigureServices` method of `Startup.cs`:

```
services.AddScoped<MyActionFilter>();
```

7. We can now see that it works fine:

When we use the `TypeFilter` attribute, our filter is not resolved by the DI container, but instantiated by `ObjectFactory`, so it doesn't need have a life cycle.

8. An alternative could be to add `MyActionFilter` as a subclass to a class inheriting from `TypeFilterAttribute` if we have dependencies resolved by the ASP.NET Core DI container or another DI container used in the filter constructor (even if the `TypeFilter` attribute isn't resolved by DI):

```
public class MyActionTypeFilterAttribute : TypeFilterAttribute
{
  Public MyActionTypeFilterAttribute():
  base(typeof(MyActionTypeFilterAttributeImpl))
  { }
  private class MyActionTypeFilterAttributeImpl : IActionFilter
  {
    private readonly IRepository _repository;
    public MyActionTypeFilterAttributeImpl(IRepository repository)
    {
      _repository = repository;
    }
    public void OnActionExecuting(ActionExecutingContext context)
    {
      // do something before the action executes
      var id = context.ActionArguments["id"] as int?;
      if (id.HasValue)
      {
        var product = _repository.GetProduct(id.Value);
        if (product != null)
        {
          context.Result = new NotFoundObjectResult(id.Value);
        }
      }
    }
    public void OnActionExecuted(ActionExecutedContext context)
    {
      // do something after the action executes
    }
  }
}
```

9. We can also use `MyActionTypeFilterAttribute` by adding it on top of an action, as follows:

```
[MyActionTypeFilterAttribute]
public IActionResult Index()
instead of using the following code:
[TypeFilter(typeof(MyActionTypeFilterAttribute))]
public IActionResult Index()
```

10. Another great thing is to have the capability to inject some services by the constructor in the filter like a repository:

```
public class MyActionFilter : IActionFilter
{
  private readonly IAppRepository _repository;
  public MyActionFilter(IAppRepository repository)
  {
    _repository = repository ;
  }
  public void OnActionExecuting(ActionExecutingContext context)
  {
    // do something before the action executes
    if (context.ActionArguments.ContainsKey("id"))
    {
      var id = context.ActionArguments["id"] as int?;
      if (id.HasValue)
      {
        var product = _repository.GetProduct(id.Value);
        if (product != null)
        {
          context.Result = new NotFoundObjectResult(id.Value);
          return;
        }
      }
    }
  }
  public void OnActionExecuted(ActionExecutedContext context)
  {
    // do something after the action executes
  }
}
```

11. We can use a logging layer instead of a repository layer in an action filter:

```
public class MyActionFilterLogger : IActionFilter
{
  private readonly ILogger _logger;
```

```
public MyActionFilterLogger(ILoggerFactory loggerFactory)
{
  _logger = loggerFactory.CreateLogger<MyActionFilterLogger>();
}
public void OnActionExecuted(ActionExecutedContext context)
{
  _logger.LogInformation(
  "OnActionExecuted" + DateTime.Now.ToLongDateString());
}
public void OnActionExecuting(ActionExecutingContext context)
{
  _logger.LogInformation(
  "OnActionExecuting" + DateTime.Now.ToLongDateString());
}
}
```

12. We will now register these two filters in the ASP.NET Core IoC container:

```
services.AddScoped<MyActionFilter>();
services.AddScoped<MyActionFilterLogger>();
```

13. We can use them as global filters:

```
config.Filters.Add(typeof(MyActionFilter));
config.Filters.Add(typeof(MyActionFilterLogger));
```

14. We can also use them as controller filters:

```
[ServiceFilter(typeof(MyActionFilter))]
[ServiceFilter(typeof(MyActionFilterLogger))]
public class HomeController : Controller
```

15. Alternatively, we can use them as action filters:

```
[ServiceFilter(typeof(MyActionFilter))]
[ServiceFilter(typeof(MyActionFilterLogger))]
public IActionResult Index()
```

How it works...

ServiceFilterAttribute is the way with ASP.NET Core to inject filters that have dependencies in the constructor. If we do not use ServiceFilterAttribute to use filter attributes, they will be managed automatically by ASP.NET Core.

There are differences between the `TypeFilter` attribute and the `ServiceFilter` attribute. With `TypeFilter`, the filter type in the parameter will be resolved by the `ObjectFactory` class. With `ServiceFilter`, the filter type in the parameter will be resolved by the internal DI container.

Creating and using an action filter

In this recipe, you will learn how to create and use action filters.

Getting ready

Let's create an empty web project with VS 2017.

How to do it...

An **action filter** injects business logic before and/or after the action filter is executed. It usually checks and/or modifies elements of the request; for example, parameters and headers. Action filters can also check model bindings. A model binding sets values of UI elements (such as `textbox`, `combobox`, `checkbox`, and so on) by an instance of a class, and gets values of UI elements to the instance of a class. If a class is used to get/set values of UI elements, that class is called a `ViewModel`. The model binding mechanism binds the `ViewModel` and UI layer automatically.

To create our own action filter, we have to create a class that derives from any of the following base classes or interfaces:

- `IActionFilter` or `IAsyncActionFilter`, depending on whether we want to create a synchronous or an asynchronous filter
- `ActionFilterAttribute`

`IActionFilter` and `IAsyncActionFilter` inherit from the `IFilterMetadata` interface. All the classes implementing those interfaces can't be used as an attribute above a controller or action method. A class should implement `IActionFilter`, or `IAsyncActionFilter`, `TypeFilter`, or `ServiceFilter` attributes, to be added above a controller or action method. But they can be used as a global filter.

`ActionFilterAttribute` inherits from `Attribute`, `IActionFilter`, `IFilterMetadata`, `IAsyncActionFilter`, `IResultFilter`, `IAsyncResultFilter`, and `IOrderedFilter`.

1. Let's create an implementation of `ActionFilterAttribute`:

```
public class MyActionAttributeFilter : ActionFilterAttribute
{
  public override void OnActionExecuting(
  ActionExecutingContext context) {}
  public override void OnActionExecuted(
  ActionExecutedContext context) {}
  public override void OnResultExecuting(
  ResultExecutingContext context) {}
  public override void OnResultExecuted(
  ResultExecutedContext context) {}
}
```

We can use this class as a filter at the global, controller, or action level.

Note: We can be notified by `ActionExecutedResult.Canceled` property when another filter as a resource filter short circuits the current action filter.

2. At the global level, add the filter to the configuration in `Startup.cs`:

```
services.AddMVC(
config =>
{
  config.Filters.Add(new MyActionAttributeFilter());
});
```

3. At the controller or action level, it could be used by adding it above the action or the controller:

```
[MyActionAttributeFilter]
public IActionResult Index()
```

4. Alternatively, we can add it with a `TypeFilter` attribute:

```
[TypeFilter(typeof(MyActionAttributeFilter))]
public IActionResult Index()
```

5. Another alternative is to add with a `ServiceFilter` attribute, but in this case, its life cycle will be managed by the ASP.NET Core DI container. We should give it a life cycle:

```
services.AddScoped<MyActionAttributeFilter>();
```

And we can use it in a controller:

```
[ServiceFilter(typeof(MyActionAttributeFilter))]
public IActionResult Index()
```

6. Next, let's implement an `IActionFilter`:

```
public class MyValidateModelStateActionFilter : IActionFilter
{
  public void OnActionExecuting(ActionExecutingContext context)
  {
    // do something before the action executes
    if (!context.ModelState.IsValid)
    {
      context.Result =
      new BadRequestObjectResult(context.ModelState);
    }
  }
  public void OnActionExecuted(ActionExecutedContext context)
  {
    // do something after the action executes
  }
}
```

7. Now, we will implement an `IAsyncActionFilter`:

```
public class myAsyncActionFilter : IAsyncActionFilter
{
  public async Task OnActionExecutionAsync(
  ActionExecutingContext context,
  ActionExecutionDelegate next)
  {
    // do something before the action executes
    await next();
    // do something after the action executes
  }
}
```

8. To use it with `TypeFilter` (so it will not be managed by the ASP.NET Core DI container), we just have to add it above the action or the controller:

```
[TypeFilter(typeof(MyActionAttributeFilter))]
public IEnumerable<string> Get()
```

9. To use it with `ServiceFilter`, and manage it with the ASP.NET Core DI container, we have to give it a life cycle:

```
services.AddScoped<MyActionAttributeFilter>();
```

We will use it in a controller:

```
[ServiceFilter(typeof(MyActionAttributeFilter))]
public IEnumerable<string> Get()
```

We can also set the order for the filters:

```
[ServiceFilter(typeof(MyActionFilter))]
[ServiceFilter(typeof(MyActionAttributeFilter))]
public IEnumerable<string> Get()
```

`MyActionAttributeFilter` will be executed first, and `MyActionFilter` after that.

But we can change the order:

```
[ServiceFilter(typeof(MyActionFilter), Order = 2)]
[ServiceFilter(typeof(MyActionAttributeFilter), Order = 1)]
public IEnumerable<string> Get()
```

The filter with the highest `Order` property value is executed first. In this example, `MyActionFilter` will be executed first, and `MyActionAttributeFilter` second.

Creating and using a result filter

In this recipe, you will learn how to create and use a result filter.

Getting ready

Let's create an empty web application with VS 2017.

How to do it...

A result filter injects treatment before or after the result is executed. It could check and modify the result generated by action methods.

Some common result filter implementations could be adding or checking headers, and many others.

To create our own result filter, we have to create a class that derives from any of the following base classes or interfaces:

- IResultFilter or IAsyncResultFilter, depending on whether we want to create a synchronous or an asynchronous filter
- ResultFilterAttribute

As with IActionResult/IAsyncActionResult interfaces, IResultFilter and IResultActionFilter inherit from IFilterMetadata. All the classes implemented in those interfaces can't use an attribute above a controller or action method. A class should implement IResultFilter, or IResultActionFilter and TypeFilter, or ServiceFilter attributes to be added above a controller or action method; however, they can be used as a global filter.

ResultFilterAttribute inherits from Attribute, IFilterMetadata, IResultFilter, IAsyncResultFilter, and IOrderedFilter, and its implementation is as follows:

1. Let's create an empty synchronous resource filter:

```
public class MyResultFilter : IResultFilter
{
  public void OnResultExecuted(ResultExecutedContext context)
  {
    // code executed before the filter executes
  }
  public void OnResultExecuting(ResultExecutingContext context)
  {
    // code executed after the filter executes
  }
}
```

2. Let's create an empty asynchronous resource filter:

```
public class MyAsyncResultFilter : IAsyncResultFilter
{
  public async Task OnResultExecutionAsync(
  ResultExecutingContext context, ResultExecutionDelegate next)
  {
    // code executed before the filter executes
    await next();
    // code executed after the filter executes
  }
}
```

3. Now, we will implement a result filter by manipulating `ViewResult` and adding an item to the `ViewData` dictionary:

```
public class MyAsyncResultFilter : IAsyncResultFilter
{
  public async Task OnResultExecutionAsync(
  ResultExecutingContext context, ResultExecutionDelegate next)
  {
    // do something before the filter executes
    ViewResult result = context.Result as ViewResult; }
    if (result != null) }
    {
      result.ViewData["messageOnResult"] =
      "This message comes from MyAsyncResultFilter" +
      DateTime.Now.ToLongTimeString();
    }
    await next();
    // do something after the filter executes
  }
}
```

4. We can use it with `ServiceFilter`. Before calling it, we have to register it:

```
services.AddScoped<MyAsyncResultFilter>();
```

We will use it in a controller:

```
[ServiceFilter(typeof(MyAsyncResultFilter))]
 public IActionResult Index()
```

5. We can see the result displayed as follows:

The result filter will be executed only if the action filter is executed without exception.

A good practice is to use only asynchronous filters or synchronous filters, but mixing both can generate side effects.

Creating and using a resource filter

In this recipe, you will learn how to create a resource filter and when to use it.

Getting ready

Let's create an empty web application with VS 2017.

How to do it...

After authorization filters, resource filters are the first filters executed on the filter pipeline. This filter is executed after the `ActionFilter` if no exception occurs. It's also the last filter eventually executed, leaving the filter pipeline.

A common `resource` filter implementation is cache managing. The `OutputCache` attribute in MVC is an example of a resource filter.

To create our own resource filter, we have to create a class that derives from IResourceFilter or IAsyncResourceFilter, depending on whether we want to create a synchronous or asynchronous filter.

1. First, let's create an empty synchronous resource filter:

```
public class MyResourceFilter : IResourceFilter
{
  public void OnResourceExecuted(ResourceExecutedContext context)
  {
    // code executed before the filter executes
  }
  public void OnResourceExecuting(ResourceExecutingContext context)
  {
    // code executed after the filter executes
  }
}
```

2. Let's create an empty asynchronous resource filter:

```
public class MyAsyncResourceFilter : IAsyncResourceFilter
{
  public async Task OnResourceExecutionAsync(
  ResourceExecutingContext context, ResourceExecutionDelegate next)
  {
    // code executed before the filter executes
    await next();
    // code executed after the filter executes
  }
}
```

3. To use it without DI, we will call it with the TypeFilter attribute:

```
[TypeFilter(typeof(MyResourceFilter))]
public IEnumerable<string> Get()
```

4. Now, let's create a resource cache filter to see how we could implement a resource filter:

```
public class MyResourceCacheFilter : IResourceFilter
{
  private int _cacheDuration = 0;
  private bool _cacheEnabled = true;
  private readonly IConfigurationRoot _configuration;
  private readonly IMemoryCache _cache;
  private readonly ILogger _logger;
  public MyResourceCacheFilter(IConfigurationRoot configuration,
```

```
    IMemoryCache cache, ILoggerFactory loggerFactory)
    {
      _configuration = configuration;
      _cache = cache;
      _logger = loggerFactory.CreateLogger("MyResourceFilter");
      InitFilter();
    }
    public void OnResourceExecuted(ResourceExecutedContext context)
    {
      if (_cacheEnabled)
      {
        string _cachekey = string.Join(":", new string[]
        {
          context.RouteData.Values["controller"].ToString(),
          context.RouteData.Values["action"].ToString()
        });
        string cachedContent = string.Empty;
        if (_cache.TryGetValue(_cachekey, out cachedContent))
        {
          if (!String.IsNullOrEmpty(cachedContent))
          {
            context.Result = new ContentResult()
            {
              Content = cachedContent
            };
          }
        }
      }
    }
    public void OnResourceExecuting(ResourceExecutingContext context)
    {
      try
      {
        if (_cacheEnabled)
        {
          if (_cache != null)
          {
            string _cachekey = string.Join(":", new string[]
            {
              context.RouteData.Values["controller"].ToString(),
              context.RouteData.Values["action"].ToString()
            });
            var result = context.Result as ContentResult;
            if (result != null)
            {
              string cachedContent = string.Empty;
              _cache.Set(_cachekey, result.Content,
              DateTime.Now.AddSeconds(_cacheDuration));
```

```
                }
              }
            }
          }
        catch (Exception ex)
        {
          _logger.LogError("Error caching in MyResourceFilter", ex);
        }
      }
      private void InitFilter()
      {
        if (!Boolean.TryParse(
        _configuration.GetSection("CacheEnabled").Value,
        out _cacheEnabled))
        {
          _cacheEnabled = false;
        }
        if (!Int32.TryParse(
        _configuration.GetSection("CacheDuration").Value,
        out _cacheDuration))
        {
          _cacheDuration = 21600; // 6 hours cache by default
        }
      }
    }
}
```

5. We can use it with `ServiceFilter`. Before calling it, we have to register it:

```
services.AddScoped<MyResourceCacheFilter>();
```

We will use it in a controller:

```
[ServiceFilter(typeof(MyResourceCacheFilter))]
public IEnumerable<string> Get()
```

Creating and using an exception filter

In this recipe, you will learn how to create and use exception filters at global, controller, and action levels.

Getting ready

Let's create an empty web application with VS 2017.

How to do it...

ASP.NET Core MVC has a lot of advantages over earlier versions of ASP.NET MVC, such as ASP.NET MVC 5:

- No more `HandleError` attribute usable at global, controller, or action level (so, no more `customErrors` attribute to parametrize in `web.config`)
- No more `Application_Error` event in `global.asax`
- No more `OnException` method from the base `Controller` class to override

Of course, we could still use `try/catch` blocks, but it's considered a solution that is *not developer-friendly*. We can avoid this solution and get a cleaner code without it.

The solutions now are:

- Using an `Exception` filter (to handle exceptions in action methods)
- Using an `Exception` middleware (to handle more generic errors at the application level)

An exception filter will handle exceptions from any action or filter that throws an exception. To be an exception filter, a class has to implement one of the following classes or interfaces:

- `ExceptionFilterAttribute`
- `IExceptionFilter` or `IAsyncExceptionFilter` for asynchronous filter

An exception filter could be used to catch a specific exception type (and apply a specific treatment, or redirect to a specific error page).

Now, in ASP.NET Core, by default, no error message is displayed if an exception occurs. So, the need to redirect to an error page is not so relevant, but it's more elegant; however, we always need to catch all exceptions, at least to log the exception globally:

1. Let's create an `ExceptionFilterAttribute`. We'll have to use it with the `ServiceFilter` or `TypeFilter` attribute at the controller or action level:

```
public class MyExceptionAttributeFilter : ExceptionFilterAttribute
{
  public override void OnException(ExceptionContext context)
  {
    if (context.Exception is InvalidOperationException)
    {
      // Log the exception informations by ASP.NET Core
      // or custom logger
```

```
        context.Exception = null;
      }
    }
  }
```

We have to set null to `context.Exception` to stop executing the other exception filters. If we set true to `context.Exception`, we assume that the exception is handled.

2. To use it with `ServiceFilter` and manage it with the ASP.NET Core DI container, we have to give it a life cycle:

```
services.AddScoped<MyExceptionAttributeFilter>();
```

3. We will use it in a controller:

```
[ServiceFilter(typeof(MyExceptionAttributeFilter))]
public IEnumerable<string> Get() {  }
```

4. Next, let's create some global exception filter:

```
public class MyGlobalExceptionFilter : IExceptionFilter
{
  public void OnException(ExceptionContext context)
  {
    //throw new NotImplementedException();
  }
}

public class MyGlobalAsyncExceptionFilter : IAsyncExceptionFilter
{
  public Task OnExceptionAsync(ExceptionContext context)
  {
    return Task.FromResult(0);
    //throw new NotImplementedException();
  }
}
```

5. To use it as a global filter, we have to add it to the configuration:

```
services.AddMVC(
config =>
{
  config.Filters.Add(new MyGlobalExceptionFilter());
});
```

This filter will be applied automatically to all action filters, in all controllers; however, if the code in this global exception filter is not specific to action methods, again, we will prefer to use a middleware to do that. We will study this case in Chapter 16, *OWIN and Middleware*.

Using a filter globally versus using a middleware

In this recipe, you will learn how to use a filter globally, and understand the difference between using a filter globally and using middleware.

Getting ready

Let's create an empty web application with VS 2017.

How to do it...

1. First, let's create a ResultFilter class by deriving from IResultFilter:

```
public class MyResultFilter : IResultFilter
{
  public void OnResultExecuting(ActionExecutingContext context)
  {
    // do something before the action executes
  }
  public void OnResultExecuted(ActionExecutedContext context)
  {
    // do something after the action executes
    ViewResult result = context.Result as ViewResult;
    if (result != null)
    {
      result.ViewData["globalMessage"] =
      "Comes from MyActionAttributeFilter at " +
      DateTime.Now.ToLongTimeString();
    }
  }
}
```

2. Next, let's configure this filter to be used as a global filter in `Startup.cs`. We can do this in two ways; by type, or by instance:

```
services.AddMVC(config =>
{
  // FIRST WAY
  config.Filters.Add(typeof(MyResultFilter)); // by type
  // OR
  config.Filters.Add(new TypeFilterAttribute(
  typeof(MyResultFilter))); // by type
  // SECOND WAY
  config.Filters.Add(new MyResultFilter ()); // by instance
});
```

This filter will be applied everywhere on any action or controller in our application without having to use it as an attribute above a controller or an action.

3. Let's add some code in `index.cshtml` to be sure that our global filter works correctly:

```
<!DOCTYPE html>
<html>
  <head>
    <title>Index</title>
  </head>
  <body>
    <div>
      <h1>Message</h1>
      Display message from Global Filter
    </div>
    <footer>
      Message: @ViewData["message"]
    </footer>
  </body>
</html>
```

4. Finally, we can see the result:

5. Alternatively, we can create a class by deriving from `ActionFilterAttribute`. Notice that when inheriting from `ActionFilterAttribute`, we also implement `IActionFilter` and `IResultFilter` interfaces:

```
public class MyActionAttributeFilter : ActionFilterAttribute
{
  public MyActionAttributeFilter() {}
  public override void OnActionExecuting(
  ActionExecutingContext context)
  { }
  public override void OnActionExecuted(ActionExecutedContext
context)
  { }
  public override void OnResultExecuting(
  ResultExecutingContext context)
  { }
  public override void OnResultExecuted(ResultExecutedContext
context)
  {
    ViewResult result = context.Result as ViewResult;
    if (result != null)
    {
      result.ViewData["globalMessage"] =
      "Comes from MyActionAttributeFilter at " +
      DateTime.Now.ToLongTimeString();
    }
  }
}
```

6. Next, let's configure this filter to be used as a global filter in `Startup.cs`. We can do this in two ways; by type, or by instance:

```
services.AddMVC(config =>
{
  // FIRST WAY
  config.Filters.Add(typeof(MyActionAttributeFilter)); // by type
  // OR
  config.Filters.Add(new TypeFilterAttribute(
  typeof(MyActionAttributeFilter))); // by type
  // SECOND WAY
  config.Filters.Add(new MyActionAttributeFilter()); // by instance
});
```

This filter will be applied everywhere on any action or controller in our application without having to use it as an attribute above a controller or an action.

7. Let's add some code in `index.cshtml` to be sure that our global filter works correctly:

```
<!DOCTYPE html>
<html>
  <head>
    <title>Index</title>
  </head>
  <body>
    <div>
      <h1>Message</h1>
      Display message from Global Filter
    </div>
    <footer>
      Message: @ViewData["message"]
    </footer>
  </body>
</html>
```

Filters are code that knows about MVC, and middleware is a more generic code on the pipeline that has no knowledge of MVC. Instead of the global exception filter, we will prefer to use an `Exception` middleware.

There's more...

Deriving from these interfaces, we can create global filters:

- For resource filters: IResourceFilter and IAsyncResourceFilter
- For action filters: IActionFilter and IAsyncActionFilter
- For result filters: IResultFilter and IAsyncResultFilter
- For exception filters: IExceptionFilter and IAsyncExceptionFilter

13
Views, Models, and ViewModels

In this chapter, we will cover the following recipes:

- Creating and using a ViewModel with AutoMapper
- Understanding and using ModelBinding
- Creating our own model binder
- Understanding and using a value provider
- Configuring and using validation

Creating and using a ViewModel with AutoMapper

In this recipe, you will learn how to create and use ViewModel with AutoMapper. AutoMapper is a convention-based object-to-object mapper library (according to http://automapper.org/). We usually use AutoMapper to create ViewModel, **Data Transfer Objects (DTO)**, and more classes from DataModel classes. AutoMapper makes it very easy to instantiate a class and fill the properties from other classes.

Getting ready

We will create an ASP.NET Core MVC Web Application template by going to **File | New | Project | AspNet Core WebApplication**.

How to do it...

1. First, let's add the `AutoMapper` dependency to the project.
2. Next, we will create the `ProductRepository` with fake data. Our `HomeController` will consume the data from this repository. The objects consumed from the repository will be `ProductDto` objects, but we will use them only to transport data between the repository and the controller:

```
public class ProductDataStore
{
  public static ProductDataStore Current { get; } = new
ProductDataStore();
  public List<ProductDto> Products { get; set; }
  public ProductDataStore()
  {
    Products = new List<ProductDto>()
    {
      new ProductDto { Id = 1, Name = "Laptop" },
      new ProductDto { Id = 2, Name = "Phone" },
      new ProductDto { Id = 3, Name = "Desktop" }
    };
  }
}
public interface IProductRepository
{
  ProductDto GetProduct(int id);
  IEnumerable<ProductDto> GetProducts();
  void AddProduct(ProductDto productDto);
}
public class ProductRepository : IProductRepository
{
  public List<ProductDto> Products
  {
    get
    {
      return ProductDataStore.Current.Products;
    }
  }
  public IEnumerable<ProductDto> GetProducts()
  {
    return Products.AsEnumerable();
  }
  public ProductDto GetProduct(int id)
  {
    return Products.Where(p => p.Id == id).SingleOrDefault();
```

```
    }
    public void AddProduct(ProductDto productDto)
    {
        Products.Add(productDto);
    }
}
```

3. Now, we need to create the `ProductViewModel` class, which we will use to send and retrieve properties of it from the view. These `ProductViewModel` objects can sometimes be exactly the same as `ProductDto`, but sometimes not. The `ViewModel` contains all the objects that were displayed in a view, or retrieved from the view. They are objects that can be more complex than the DTO. In this case, they will be identical:

> DTO classes usually have fewer properties than data model classes. For example, the `Employee DataModel` class has `FirstName`, `LastName`, `Email`, and `Password` properties, but the `Employee` DTO model has only `FullName` and `Email` properties.

```
public class ProductDto
{
    public int Id { get; set; }
    public string Name { get; set; }
    public decimal Price { get; set; }
}
public class ProductViewModel
{
    public int Id { get; set; }
    public string Name { get; set; }
    public decimal Price { get; set; }
}
```

4. Each time we get data from the repository, or send data to the repository, we have to do a recurrent job: mapping the data from `Prom ProductViewModel` to `ProductDto`, and vice versa. To achieve this, we have to configure the mappings we want to automate in the `Configure` method in the `Startup.cs` class:

```
public void Configure(IApplicationBuilder app, ...)
{
    ...
    AutoMapper.Mapper.Initialize(mapper =>
    {
        mapper.CreateMap<Models.ProductDto, Models.ProductViewModel>();
        mapper.CreateMap<Models.ProductViewModel, Models.ProductDto>();
    });
```

```
    ...
}
```

5. We will profit from being in the `Startup.cs` class to configure the dependency injection for the `ProductRepository` class and its abstraction, `IProductRepository`, in the `ConfigureServices` method:

```
services.AddScoped<IProductRepository, ProductRepository>();
```

6. Now, we can map `ProductDto` and `ProductViewModel` in both ways in the controller's action methods:

```
public class HomeController : Controller
{
  private IProductRepository _productRepository;
  public HomeController(IProductRepository productRepository)
  {
    _productRepository = productRepository;
  }
  public IActionResult Index()
  {
    var productsDtoFromRepo = _productRepository.GetProducts();
    var model = Mapper.Map<IEnumerable<ProductViewModel>>
    (productsDtoFromRepo);
    return View(model);
  }
  public IActionResult GetProduct(int id)
  {
    var productDto = _productRepository.GetProduct(id);
    if (productDto == null)
    {
      return NotFound();
    }
    var productModel = Mapper.Map<ProductViewModel>(productDto);
    return Ok(productModel);
  }
  [HttpGet]
  public IActionResult AddProduct()
  {
    return View();
  }
  [HttpPost]
  public IActionResult AddProduct(ProductViewModel model)
  {
    if (ModelState.IsValid)
    {
      model.Id = _productRepository
```

```
      .GetProducts().Max(p => p.Id) + 1;
      var productDto = Mapper.Map<ProductDto>(model);
      _productRepository.AddProduct(productDto);
      return RedirectToAction("Index");
    }
    return View(model);
  }
}
```

7. Finally, we will create the Razor views for Index and the AddProduct action method:

- Index.cshtml

```
@model List<ProductViewModel>
<br />
@foreach (var p in Model)
{
  <p>Product @p.Id : @p.Name</p>
}
```

   - AddProduct.cshtml

```
@model ProductViewModel
<p>Let's add a new product</p>
@using (Html.BeginForm("AddProduct", "Home", FormMethod.Post))
{
  <div class="row">
    <div class="col-md-6">
      <div class="form-group">
        @Html.LabelFor(x => x.Name, "Product Name")
        @Html.TextBoxFor(x => x.Name,
        new { @class = "form-control" })
      </div>
      <div class="form-group">
        @Html.LabelFor(x => x.Price, "Product Price")
        @Html.TextBoxFor(x => x.Price,
        new { @class = "form-control" })
      </div>
      <div>
        <input type="submit" value="Add" />
      </div>
    </div>
  </div>
}
```

Understanding and using ModelBinding

In this recipe, you will learn how to use `ModelBinding`. The `ModelBinding` mechanism lets the developer get/set values of UI elements to a class's properties, and vice versa.

Getting ready

We will create an ASP.NET Core MVC web application template by going to **File** | **New** | **Project** | **AspNet Core Web Application**.

How to do it...

1. Let's see how nested types are handled by `ModelBinding`:

```
public class Product
{
  public int Id { get; set; }
  public int Name { get; set; }
  public decimal Price { get; set; }
  public Category Category
  {
    get;
    set;
  }
}
public class Category
{
  public int Id {
    get;
    set;
  }
  public int Name
  {
    get;
    set;
  }
}
@model R2.Models.Product
<form asp-action="Create" method="post">
  <div class="form-group">
    <label asp-for="Id"></label>
    <input asp-for="Id" class="form-control" />
```

```
    </div>
    <div class="form-group">
      <label asp-for="Name"></label>
      <input asp-for="Name" class="form-control" />
    </div>
    <div class="form-group">
      <label asp-for="Price"></label>
      <input asp-for="Price" class="form-control" />
    </div>
    <div class="form-group">
      <label asp-for="Category.Id"></label>
      <input asp-for="Category.Id" class="form-control"/>
    </div>
    <div class="form-group">
      <label asp-for="Category.Name"></label>
      <input asp-for="Category.Name" class="form-control"/>
    </div>
    <button type="submit" class="btn btn-primary">Submit</button>
  </form>
```

The following code will be generated:

```
<div class="form-group">
  <label for="Category_Id">1</label>
  <input type="text" id="Category_Id" name="Category.Id" value=""
  class="form-control"/>
</div>
<div class="form-group">
  <label for="Category_Name">Laptop</label>
  <input type="text" id="Category_Name" name="Category.Name"
value=""
  class="form-control"/>
</div>
```

We will get the `Product` type binded with the preceding form:

```
[HttpPost]
 public IActionResult Create(Product product)
```

2. Let's see how we can change `ModelBinding` on the fly. We can imagine having to post the `Category` object nested into `Product`, and mapping it with another CLR object (C# class) for any reason (for example, we have to create a new category while inserting a new product). We can modify `ModelBinding` on the fly, thanks to the `Bind` attribute:

```
<form asp-action="DisplayCategoryProduct" method="post">
  <div class="form-group">
```

```
  <label asp-for="Category.Id"></label>
  <input asp-for="Category.Id" class="form-control" />
</div>
<div class="form-group">
  <label asp-for="Category.Name"></label>
  <input asp-for="Category.Name" class="form-control" />
</div>
<button type="submit" class="btn btn-primary">Submit</button>
</form>
```

Following code is body of the `DisplayCategoryProduct` action method:

```
[HttpPost]
public IActionResult DisplayCategoryProduct
([Bind(Prefix = nameof(Product.Category))] CategoryProduct
catProduct)
{ ... }
```

3. We could use the `BindRequired` and `BindNever` attributes directly in the class definition to include or exclude some class properties from `ModelBinding`:

```
public class Category
{
  [BindNever]
  public int Id { get; set; }
  [BindRequired]
  public string Name { get; set; }
}
```

4. We can use the `ModelBinder` attribute to override the default model binder. There are a few attributes that help us parametrize the model binding, and add rules or constraints to incoming parameters, especially if we use an API controller.

5. For data coming from the `Body` request, we can use the `[FromBody]` attribute:

```
public IActionResult PostFormApi([FromBody] Product product)
{ ... }
```

`FromBody` is generally used when we post form data by Ajax to an API controller. By default, MVC uses JSON to serialize and deserialize data when a JavaScript client sends data to a controller.

Now, to send data from Ajax, `FromBody` is not required. To make Ajax and the action work together, we should add the following code to the `AddProduct.cshtml` page to send form data with Ajax and jQuery:

```
@section scripts{
  <script type="text/javascript">
    $(document).ready(function() {
      $("#productButton").click(function(){
        $.ajax({
          type: "POST",
          url: "/Home/PostToApiCtrl",
          data : $("#productForm").serialize(),
          dataType: 'json'
          //contentType: 'application/x-www-form-urlencoded;
          charset=utf-8' //default value,
          not mandatory to work
        });
      });
    });
  </script>
}
```

We need to add this code for the controller:

```
public async Task<IActionResult> PostToApiCtrl(Product product)
{
  if (Request.ContentType == "application/x-www-form-urlencoded;
charset=UTF-8")
  {
    IFormCollection jqFormData = await Request.ReadFormAsync();
  }
  return Ok();
}
```

We retrieve the posted form data as a `Product` object, thanks to ModelBinding, but we can also retrieve it as `IFormCollection` using the `Request.ReadFormAsync()` method.

6. For data coming from forms, we will use the `[FromForm]` attribute:

```
public IActionResult PostFormMVC([FromForm]string name)
{ ... }
```

`FromForm` is generally used when we post classic form data to an MVC controller.

7. For data coming from QueryStrings, we will use the `[FromQuery]` attribute. Let's create a reference type to be binded from the QueryString parameters:

```
public class Query
{
  public int ItemsPerPage { get; set; }
  public int CurrentPage { get; set; }
}
public IActionResult GetQueryProduct([FromQuery]Query query)
{ ... }
```

The `Query` class will map with the following URL:
`GET /api/GetItems?ItemsPerPage=10&CurrentPage=7 HTTP/1.1`

8. For data coming from the URL, we will use the `[FromRoute]` attribute:

```
public IActionResult SendDataFromRoute([FromRoute]string name)
{ ... }
```

`FromRoute` is generally used when we send data by any HTTP verb to any type of controller that matches with a URL segment from an existing route in the application configuration (in the `Configure` method of `Startup.cs`), such as `http://www.mysite.com/{name}`.

9. For data coming from request headers, we will use the following lines of code:

```
[FromHeader(Name ="...")] attribute.
public IActionResult SendDataFromHttpHeaders
([FromHeader(Name = "Accept-Language")]string language)
{ ... }
```

The `Name` property in `FromHeader` can be any existing request header, such as Accept-Encoding, User-Agent, or any header we've created.

The following code shows us how to automate ModelBinding with the `FromHeader` attribute inside a class:

```
public class Headers
{
  [FromHeader]
  public string Accept { get; set; }
  [FromHeader]
  public string Referer { get; set; }
  [FromHeader(Name = "Accept-Language")]
  public string AcceptLanguage { get; set; }
  [FromHeader(Name = "User-Agent")]
```

```
    public string UserAgent { get; set; }
}
public IActionResult GetHeadersWithProduct(Headers headers)
{ ... }
```

10. For data coming from configured services with dependency injection (in the
    `Configure` method of `Startup.cs`), we will use the `[FromService]` attribute:

```
public void ConfigureServices(IServiceCollection services)
{
  services.AddScoped<IProductRepository, ProductRepository>();
  services.AddMVC();
}
[HttpGet]
public IActionResult GetDataWithFromServiceParameter
([FromServices] IProductRepository repo)
{
  var products = repo.GetProducts();
  return Ok(products);
}
```

How it works...

The ASP.NET ModelBinding mechanism maps action method parameters to value
providers. Value providers can be form data, route data, QueryString, and files. They can be
any data sent through an HTTP request. We can also create our own value provider, but
that will be explained in the next recipe.

The `Form` value provider is the posted data in an HTTP request. It consists of all the key-
value pairs in the HTTP request body. The ModelBinding mechanism maps the name field
values of the posted form with the properties of the class, to bind as the ActionResult
parameter.

ActionResult parameters can be of the primitive type (`short`, `int`, `double`, `string`, `char`,
and so on), or of simple types (such as Guid, DateTime, or TimeSpan) that have to be
nullable to avoid errors when ModelBinding parses parameters. Also, ModelBinding can
parse from QueryString, or from routing segments defined in the routes definition. They
also can be of complex types; generally, a C# class and any type that couldn't be parsed by
the `.Parse` or `.TryParse` function from a string type.

Creating our own model binder

In this recipe, you will learn what a model binder is, and how to use it.

Getting ready

We will create an ASP.NET Core MVC Web Application template by going to **File** | **New** | **Project** | **AspNet Core Web Application**.

How to do it...

1. First, let's add the `AutoMapper` dependency to `project.json`.
2. After that, we will create the `ProductRepository` with fake data. Our `HomeController` controller class will consume the data from this repository. The objects consumed from the repository will be `ProductDto` objects, but we will use them only to transport data between the repository and the controller:

```
public class ProductDataStore
{
  public static ProductDataStore Current { get; } = new
ProductDataStore();
  public List<ProductDto> Products { get; set; }
  public ProductDataStore()
  {
    Products = new List<ProductDto>()
    {
      new ProductDto { Id = 1, Name = "Laptop" },
      new ProductDto { Id = 2, Name = "Phone" },
      new ProductDto { Id = 3, Name = "Desktop" }
    };
  }
}
public interface IProductRepository
{
  ProductDto GetProduct(int id);
  IEnumerable<ProductDto> GetProducts();
  void AddProduct(ProductDto productDto);
}
public class ProductRepository : IProductRepository
{
  public List<ProductDto> Products
```

```
    {
      get
      {
        return ProductDataStore.Current.Products;
      }
    }
    public IEnumerable<ProductDto> GetProducts()
    {
      return Products.AsEnumerable();
    }
    public ProductDto GetProduct(int id)
    {
      return Products.Where(p => p.Id == id).SingleOrDefault();
    }
    public void AddProduct(ProductDto productDto)
    {
      Products.Add(productDto);
    }
}
```

3. The next step is creating the ProductViewModel class, which we will use to send and retrieve the properties from the view. These ProductViewModel objects can sometimes be exactly the same as ProductDto, but sometimes not. The ViewModel class contains all the properties displayed in a view, or retrieved from the view. They can be properties more complex than the DTO class. In this case, they will be identical:

```
public class ProductDto
{
  public int Id { get; set; }
  public string Name { get; set; }
  public decimal Price { get; set; }
}
public class ProductViewModel
{
  public int Id { get; set; }
  public string Name { get; set; }
  public decimal Price { get; set; }
}
```

4. Each time we get data from the repository, or send data to the repository, we have to do a recurrent job: mapping the data from `Prom ProductViewModel` to `ProductDto`, and vice versa. To achieve this, we have to configure the mappings we want to automate in the `Configure` method in the `Startup.cs` class:

```
public void Configure(IApplicationBuilder app, ...)
{
  ...
  AutoMapper.Mapper.Initialize(mapper =>
  {
    mapper.CreateMap<Models.ProductDto, Models.ProductViewModel>();
    mapper.CreateMap<Models.ProductViewModel, Models.ProductDto>();
  });
  ...
}
```

5. We will profit from being in the `Startup.cs` class to configure the dependency injection for the `ProductRepository` class and its abstraction, `IProductRepository`, in the `ConfigureServices` method:

```
services.AddScoped<IProductRepository, ProductRepository>();
```

6. Now, we need to map `ProductDto` and `ProductViewModel` to the controller's action methods:

```
public class HomeController : Controller
{
  private IProductRepository _productRepository;
  public HomeController(IProductRepository productRepository)
  {
    _productRepository = productRepository;
  }
  public IActionResult Index()
  {
    var productsDtoFromRepo = _productRepository.GetProducts();
    var model = Mapper.Map<IEnumerable<ProductViewModel>>
    (productsDtoFromRepo);
    return View(model);
  }
  public IActionResult GetProduct(int id)
  {
    var productDto = _productRepository.GetProduct(id);
    if (productDto == null)
    {
      return NotFound();
    }
```

```
      var productModel = Mapper.Map<ProductViewModel>(productDto);
      return Ok(productModel);
    }
    [HttpGet]
    public IActionResult AddProduct()
    {
      return View();
    }
    [HttpPost]
    public IActionResult AddProduct(ProductViewModel model)
    {
      if (ModelState.IsValid)
      {
        model.Id = _productRepository
        .GetProducts().Max(p => p.Id) + 1;
        var productDto = Mapper.Map<ProductDto>(model);
        _productRepository.AddProduct(productDto);
        return RedirectToAction("Index");
      }
      return View(model);
    }
  }
```

7. Finally, we will create the Razor views for Index, and the AddProduct action method:

- Index.cshtml:

```
@model List<ProductViewModel>
<br />
@foreach (var p in Model)
{
  <p>Product @p.Id : @p.Name</p>
}
```

- AddProduct.cshtml:

```
@model ProductViewModel
<p>Let's add a new product</p>
@using (Html.BeginForm("AddProduct", "Home",
FormMethod.Post))
{
  <div class="row">
    <div class="col-md-6">
      <div class="form-group">
        @Html.LabelFor(x => x.Name, "Product Name")
        @Html.TextBoxFor(x => x.Name,
```

```
              new { @class = "form-control" })
            </div>
            <div class="form-group">
              @Html.LabelFor(x => x.Price, "Product Price")
              @Html.TextBoxFor(x => x.Price,
              new { @class = "form-control" })
            </div>
            <div>
              <input type="submit" value="Add" />
            </div>
          </div>
        </div>
    }
```

8. Now, we should create `ModelBinder` to map `ProductViewModel` automatically with `ProductDto`. To do this, we have to create two classes: `AutoMapperModelBinder`, which will inherit from `IModelBinder`, and `AutoMapperModelBinderProvider`, which will inherit from `IModelBinderProvider`:

```
public class AutoMapperModelBinder : IModelBinder
{
  public Task BindModelAsync(ModelBindingContext bindingContext)
  {
    ProductDto productDto = new ProductDto();
    var modelType = bindingContext.ModelType;
    if (modelType == typeof(ProductViewModel))
    {
      var model = (ProductViewModel)bindingContext.Model;
      if(model != null)
      {
        productDto = Mapper.Map<ProductDto>(model);
      }
      bindingContext.Result =
ModelBindingResult.Success(productDto);
    }
    return Task.CompletedTask;
  }
}
```

9. `ModelBinder` implements the `BindModelAsync` method, which returns a task. `ProductDto` has to be returned as a parameter of the `ModelBindingResult.Success` method, which is assigned to the `BindingContext.Result` property:

```
public class AutoMapperModelBinderProvider : IModelBinderProvider
{
    public IModelBinder GetBinder(ModelBinderProviderContext context)
    {
        var type = context.BindingInfo.BinderType;
        if (type != typeof(ProductViewModel))
        {
            return null;
        }
        return new AutoMapperModelBinder();
    }
}
```

10. The preceding `ModelBinderProvider` class will assure that the `ModelBinder` will be applied only to the `ProductViewModel` type. We will also need the provider to register `ModelBinder` for the whole application in the `ConfigureServices` method of `Startup.cs`:

```
public void ConfigureServices(IServiceCollection services)
{
    services.AddScoped<IProductRepository, ProductRepository>();
    services.AddMVC(config =>
    {
        config.ModelBinderProviders.Insert(0,
        new AutoMapperModelBinderProvider());
    });
}
```

When we add the new `ModelBinderProvider` class, we have to add it as the first element in the `ModelBinderProviders` list to be sure that it will be executed first.

Understanding and using a value provider

In this recipe, you will learn what a value provider is, and how to use it.

Getting ready

We will create an ASP.NET Core MVC Web Application template by going to **File** | **New** | **Project** | **AspNet Core Web Application (.Net Framework)** | **Web Application**.

How to do it...

The ASP.NET ModelBinding mechanism maps action method parameters to value providers. Value providers can be form data, route data, QueryString, and Files. They can be any data sent through an HTTP request, but not exclusively.

An interesting case to create a custom value provider could be creating a value provider for HTTP headers, cookie values, and so on; however, we could also create a `ValueProvider` class to retrieve `AppSettings`, or `ConnectionString` settings.

1. Let's start by creating a `ValueProvider` class that inherits from `IValueProvider`. This class will implement two methods from `IValueProvider`:
     * `bool ContainsPrefix(string prefix)`, this method tells us whether the `ValueProvider` is able to return a value matching a property of the `ModelBinder`
     * `ValueProviderResult GetValue(string key)`, this method retrieves the value, and returns it through a `ValueProviderResult` class

2. Next, we need to create a `ValueProviderFactory` class that inherits from the `IValueProviderFactory` interface.

    This class implements one method as follows:

    ```
    Task CreateValueProviderAsync(ValueProviderFactoryContext context)
    ```

3. To be sure everything works, we have to add the `ValueProviderFactory` class to the list of `ValueProviders` available in the application. We will do this by adding the following code in the `ConfigureServices` method of `Startup.cs`:

```
services.AddMVC(config =>
{
  config.ValueProviderFactories.Add(new
CustomValueProviderFactory());
});
```

Configuring and using validation

In this recipe, you will learn how to configure and use client-side validation with jQuery, and server-side validation with C#.

Getting ready

We will create an ASP.NET Core MVC Web Application template by going to **File** | **New** | **Project** | **AspNet Core Web Application**.

How to do it...

1. First of all, let's create a class with validation attributes. These attributes will be used on both the client side and the server side:

```
public class ProductViewModel
{
  public int Id { get; set; }
  [Required]
  [RegularExpression(@"^[a-zA-Z]{1,40}$",
  ErrorMessage = "The field must be a string")]
  public string Name { get; set; }
  [Required]
  [Range(0.01, double.MaxValue,
  ErrorMessage = "Please enter a positive number")]
  public decimal Price { get; set; }
}
```

2. In addition to this, we will create a form in order to post the `ProductViewModel`. This is the `Form` version of `TagHelpers`:

```
<form asp-controller="Home" asp-action="AddProduct" method="post"
asp-antiforgery="true">
  <div asp-validation-summary="None"></div>
  <div class="form-group">
    <labelasp-for="Name"></label>
    <inputtype="text" asp-for="Name" />
    <spanasp-validation-for="Name" class="text-danger"></span>
  </div>
  <div class="form-group">
    <labelasp-for="Price"></label>
    <inputtype="text" asp-for="Price" />
    <spanasp-validation-for="Price" class="text-danger"></span>
  </div>
  <div>
    <input type="submit" value="Add" />
  </div>
</form>
```

This is the `Razor` version:

```
@using (Html.BeginForm("AddProduct", "Home", FormMethod.Post))
{
  @Html.AntiForgeryToken()
  <div class="row">
    <div class="col-md-6">
      @Html.ValidationSummary(false)
      <div class="form-group">
        @Html.LabelFor(x => x.Name, "Product Name")
        @Html.TextBoxFor(x => x.Name,
        new { @class = "form-control" })
        @Html.ValidationMessageFor(x => x.Name)
      </div>
      <div class="form-group">
        @Html.LabelFor(x => x.Price, "Product Price")
        @Html.TextBoxFor(x => x.Price,
        new { @class = "form-control" })
        @Html.ValidationMessageFor(x => x.Price)
      </div>
      <div>
        <input type="submit" value="Add" />
      </div>
    </div>
  </div>
}
```

They both generate the same HTML code, and the same data is posted in the controller. For both, we have to add the references to `jquery.validate`:

```
@section scripts{
  <script src="~/lib/jquery-validation/dist/jquery.validate.js">
  </script>
  <script src="~/lib/jquery-validation-
unobtrusive/jquery.validate.unobtrusive.js"
  </script>
}
```

`ValidationSummary` is not mandatory, but the `asp-validation-for` attributes in the `TagHelper` version, and the `ValidationMessageFor` HtmlHelpers in the `Razor` version are mandatory, to enable client and server validation.

3. After that, let's test the client-side validation by entering values in the form. We can see that the validation works without any HTTP request:

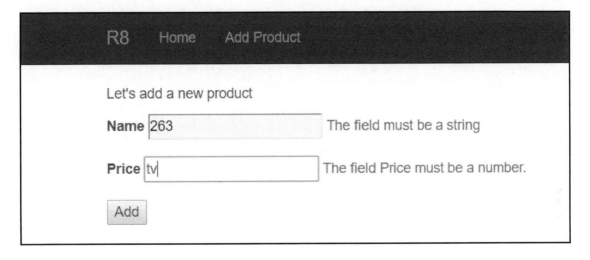

4. Now, let's enter some correct value, and send the form to the controller:

5. We can see that the `ModelState` is valid:

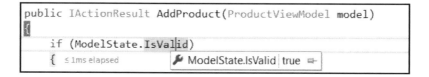

6. Next, we will add a personalized message error, and create the error to see what happens:

```
public IActionResult AddProduct(ProductViewModel model)
{
  if (!model.Name.Contains("tv"))
  {
    ModelState.AddModelError(nameof(model.Name),
    "The model name must contain the word 'tv'");
  }
  if (ModelState.IsValid)
  {
    ...
  }
}
```

7. We realize now that ModelState is not valid anymore with this new constraint added on the fly:

```
public IActionResult AddProduct(ProductViewModel model)
{

    if (!model.Name.Contains("tv"))
    {
        ModelState.AddModelError(nameof(model.Name),
        "The model name must contain the word 'tv'");
    }

    if (ModelState.IsValid)  ≤1ms elapsed
    {                        🔧 ModelState.IsValid  false  ⮌
```

8. In return, we see that the new message has been added on the UI:

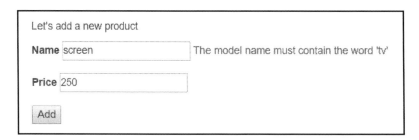

We've just added a constraint and an error message for a `Model` property using the `ModelState.AddModelError` method.

We can also have the validation state for a property, using `ModelState.GetValidationState("PropertyName")`.

14
Razor and Views

In this chapter, we will cover:

- Managing namespaces in views with ViewImports
- Creating a strongly typed Partial view
- Configuring view and area locations
- Using dependency injection in views
- Creating HTMLHelpers

Managing namespaces in views with ViewImports

In this recipe, you will learn how to create and manage namespaces in `Razor` views by creating a `_ViewImport` view to add all the necessary namespaces we need in our application views.

Getting ready

We create an empty web application with a controller and an `index` view with the corresponding folders.

How to do it...

The goal of TagHelpers is to reduce the writing of the views using HTML tags and/or attributes interpreted by Razor. They replace HTMLHelpers with the closest syntax of HTML, allowing integrators to work with MVC views more easily:

1. First, let's add an Insert action method for GET and POST in HomeController.cs, and let's add a break point on the Insert method of POST:

```
        0 references
25      public IActionResult Insert()
26      {
27          return View();
28      }
29
30      [HttpPost]
        0 references
31      public IActionResult Insert(string name)
32      {
33          _repository.CreateProduct(name);
34          return View("Index");
35      }
```

2. Next, let's add the Insert view with TagHelper code for an input to test TagHelpers:

```
<span>MVC 6 :</span>
<form asp-controller="Home" asp-action="Insert" method="post">
    <input type="text" asp-for="Name" />
    <input type="submit" value="Send" />
</form>
```

We can see the asp-for TagHelper added to the input text HTML element.

3. Let's test the POST method, adding a value to the input:

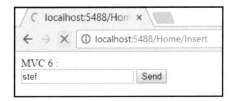

4. We click on the **Send** button to see what happened in the Insert method of POST:

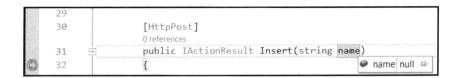

5. The input is null; now, let's rectify that. Add a _ViewImports.cshtml page by right-clicking on the Views folder and selecting **Add | New item | MVC View Import Page**:

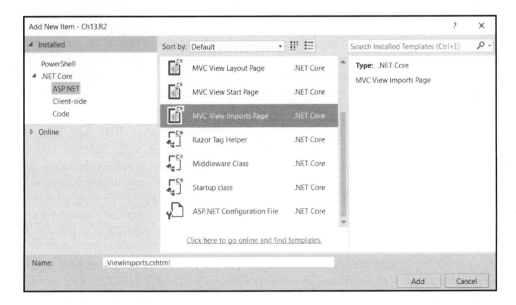

6. Next, we add the following code to `_ViewImports.cshtml` to be allowed to use TagHelpers in `Razor` views, importing the `Microsoft.AspNetCore.Mvc.TagHelpers` namespace:

7. Finally, let's test the `POST` method again in the `Insert` view:

We can see that TagHelpers now works in our views.

Creating a strongly typed Partial view

In this recipe, you will learn what a `Partial` view is, and how to create a strongly typed one.

Getting ready

We will create an empty web application with ASP.NET Core MVC enabled, adding the MVC dependency into the project:

```
"Microsoft.AspNetCore.Mvc": "2.0.0"
```

How to do it...

We can get the benefits of C# compiler with strongly typed Partial views. C# compiler checks names and types of properties. If it detects misuse (such as wrong property names, and so on), it will throw an exception and won't compile the project:

1. First, let's create the `Dto` and `ViewModel` objects:

```
public class ProductDto
{
  public int Id { get; set; }
  public string Name { get; set; }
  public decimal Price { get; set; }
}
public class ProductViewModel
{
  public int Id { get; set; }
  [Required]
  [MaxLength(50)]
  public string Name { get; set; }
  [Required]
  [Range(0.01, double.MaxValue,
  ErrorMessage = "Please enter a positive number")]
  public decimal Price { get; set; }
}
```

2. Next, we create the service layer used by the controller to retrieve the `ProductViewModel`:

```
public interface IProductRepository
{
  IEnumerable<ProductDto> GetProducts();
}
public class ProductRepository : IProductRepository
{
  private List<ProductDto> _products;
  public ProductRepository()
  {
    _products = new List<ProductDto>()
    {
      new ProductDto { Id = 1, Name = "Laptop" },
      new ProductDto { Id = 2, Name = "Phone" },
      new ProductDto { Id = 3, Name = "Desktop" }
    };
  }
  public IEnumerable<ProductDto> GetProducts()
```

```
  {
    return _products.AsEnumerable();
  }
}
```

3. Next, we configure `Startup.cs` to manage the repository life cycle and auto-mapper:

   - In the `ConfigureServices` method:

   ```
   services.AddScoped<IProductRepository,
   ProductRepository>();
   ```

   - In the `Configure` method:

   ```
   AutoMapper.Mapper.Initialize(mapper =>
   {
     mapper.CreateMap<Models.ProductDto,
     Models.ProductViewModel>();
   });
   ```

4. Now, let's create a `ProductController` which consumes the service layer:

   ```
   public class ProductController : Controller
   {
     private readonly IProductRepository _productRepository;
     public ProductController(IProductRepository productRepository)
     {
       _productRepository = productRepository;
     }
     public IActionResult Index()
     {
       var productsDtoFromRepo = _productRepository.GetProducts();
       var model = Mapper.Map
       <IEnumerable<ProductViewModel>>
       (productsDtoFromRepo);
       return View(model);
     }
   }
   ```

5. Now, let's create the `index` view of `ProductController`, which will contain a strongly typed `Partial` view:

```
@model List<ProductViewModel>
<br />
@foreach (var product in Model)
{
  @Html.Partial("ProductPartial", product)
}
```

Here, the code in the `for` loop calls `Html.Partial`. `ProductPartial` is the name of the Partial view. This Partial view has to be located in the `Product Views` folder or in the shared folder. We can see that the second parameter passed is a `product` object.

6. Now, let's see the code in the `Partial` view of `ProductPartial.cshtml`:

```
@model ProductViewModel
<p>Product @Model.Id : @Model.Name</p>
```

Configuring view and area locations

In this recipe, you will learn how to change the view location used per convention by ASP.NET Core MVC.

Getting ready

We will use the previous recipe and add some modifications to use a different view location.

How to do it...

1. First, let's create a new views folder named `ViewsOld`. In this folder, we will copy `_ViewImports.cshtml` and `_ViewSart/cshtml` from the `Views` folder, and cut the `Product` views folder to paste it into the `ViewsOld` folder:

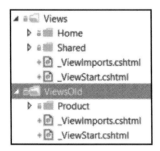

2. Next, we create a folder named `Infrastructure` and create a C# class named `OldViewsExpander.cs`. This class will contain the following code:

```
public class OldViewsExpander : IViewLocationExpander
{
  public IEnumerable<string> ExpandViewLocations
  (ViewLocationExpanderContext context,
  IEnumerable<string> viewLocations)
  {
    // rerturn all classic locations
    foreach (string location in viewLocations)
    {
      yield return location;
    }
    // return new locations
    yield return "/ViewsOld/Shared/{0}.cshtml";
    yield return "/ViewsOld/{1}/{0}.cshtml";
    // now the following locations will be tested
    // "/Views/Home"
    // "/Views/Product"
    // "/Views/Shared"
    // "/ViewsOld/Home"
    // "/ViewsOld/Product"
    // "/ViewsOld/Shared"
  }
  public void PopulateValues(ViewLocationExpanderContext context)
  {}
}
```

2. To include this new configuration in our application, we have to add the new `ViewLocationExpanders` to the list of the `ViewLocationExpanders` application:

```
public void ConfigureServices(IServiceCollection services)
{
  services.AddScoped<IProductRepository, ProductRepository>();
  services.AddMvc();
  services.Configure<RazorViewEngineOptions>(options =>
  {
    options.ViewLocationExpanders.Clear();
    options.ViewLocationExpanders.Add(
    new OldViewsExpander());
  });
}
```

3. We can also modify or add the area locations for the whole application by adding the template views directly to the `ViewLocationFormats` list without using the `OldViewsExpander` class:

```
public void ConfigureServices(IServiceCollection services)
{
  services.AddScoped<IProductRepository, ProductRepository>();
  services.AddMvc();
  services.Configure<RazorViewEngineOptions>(options =>
  {
    options.ViewLocationFormats.Add(
    "/ViewsOld/Shared/{0}.cshtml");
    options.ViewLocationFormats.Add(
    "/ViewsOld/{1}/{0}.cshtml");
  });
}
```

4. To use only the `ViewsOld` folder as the views location for the whole application, we would have to use the following code, clearing the `ViewLocationFormats` list before adding the new locations. Before doing that, we would copy the shared folder and its `_Layout.cshtml` file from the `Views` folder to the `OldViews` folder, in order to not have an error.
   If we don't move Shared folder and `_Layout.cshtml` file, `_ViewStart.cshtml` will search for its layout file in Shared folder and don't use `_Layout.cshtml` as its layout:

```
public void ConfigureServices(IServiceCollection services)
{
    services.AddScoped<IProductRepository, ProductRepository>();
```

```
services.AddMvc();
services.Configure<RazorViewEngineOptions>(options =>
{
  options.ViewLocationFormats.Clear();
  options.ViewLocationFormats.Add(
  "/ViewsOld/Shared/{0}.cshtml");
  options.ViewLocationFormats.Add(
  "/ViewsOld/{1}/{0}.cshtml");
});
}
```

How it works...

To modify or add the View location folder, we created a class, which inherited the IViewLocationExpander interface.

If we did not add the following code, we would not have to include the native Views folder location; we would replace it:

```
foreach(string location in viewLocations)
{
  yield return location;
}
```

The two native folders where the MVC mechanism would search for Views are:

```
"/Views/{ControllerName}"
 "/Views/Shared"
```

Now, with the following code, we will add the new Views locations:

```
yield return "/ViewsOld/Shared/{0}.cshtml";
yield return "/ViewsOld/{1}/{0}.cshtml";
```

We could get the same result without using the OldViewsExpander class by just adding the following code to the ConfigureServices method:

```
services.Configure<RazorViewEngineOptions>(options =>
{
  options.ViewLocationFormats.Add(
    "/ViewsOld/Shared/{0}.cshtml");
  options.ViewLocationFormats.Add(
    "/ViewsOld/{1}/{0}.cshtml");
});
```

Now, the possible folder locations for a view could be:

```
"/Views/{ControllerName}"
 "/Views/Shared"
 "/ViewsOld/{ControllerName}"
 "/ViewsOld/Shared"
```

To complete the job, we need to add a new folder pattern for the legacy areas, as you can see in the following code:

```
services.Configure<RazorViewEngineOptions>(options =>
{
  options.ViewLocationFormats.Add(
  "/ViewsOld/Shared/{0}.cshtml");
  options.ViewLocationFormats.Add(
  "/ViewsOld/{1}/{0}.cshtml");
  options.AreaViewLocationFormats.Add(
  "/AreasOld/{2}/Views/{1}/{0}.cshtml");
  options.AreaViewLocationFormats.Add(
  "/AreasOld/{2}/Views/Shared/{0}.cshtml");
});
Legend:
 // {0} - Action Name
 // {1} - Controller Name
 // {2} - Area Name
```

Using dependency injection in views

In this recipe, you will learn what a dependency injection is and how to use it in ASP.NET Core MVC views. We will see how to inject a list of *category* objects to bind a drop-down list in the AddProduct.cshtml view.

The dependency injection mechanism lets a class get an object through the constructor parameter, instead of calling a factory method, such as the following code:

```
public ClassA (ClassB _object) {
    this.object = _object;
}
```

Use following code instead of preceding code:

```
public ClassA() {
    this.object = FactoryClass.GetObjectB();
}
```

Getting ready

We will create an empty web application with ASP.NET Core MVC enabled by adding the MVC dependency into the project:

```
"Microsoft.AspNetCore.Mvc": "2.0.0"
```

How to do it...

1. First, let's create the Dto and the ViewModel objects:

```
public class ProductDto
{
  public int Id { get; set; }
  public string Name { get; set; }
  public decimal Price { get; set; }
}
public class ProductViewModel
{
  public int Id { get; set; }
  [Required]
  [MaxLength(50)]
  public string Name { get; set; }
  [Required]
  [Range(0.01, double.MaxValue,
  ErrorMessage = "Please enter a positive number")]
  public decimal Price { get; set; }
  [Required]
  public string CategoryName
  {
    get; set;
  }
}
```

2. Next, we create the service layer used by the controller to retrieve the ProductViewModel. The product controller will use this repository. This repository uses a static, hardcoded data store to make the data persistent across HTTP requests:

```
public class ProductDataStore
{
  public static ProductDataStore Current { get; }
  = new ProductDataStore();
  public List<ProductDto> Products { get; set; }
```

```csharp
public ProductDataStore()
{
  Products = new List<ProductDto>()
  {
    new ProductDto { Id = 1, Name = "Laptop" },
    new ProductDto { Id = 2, Name = "Phone" },
    new ProductDto { Id = 3, Name = "Desktop" }
  };
}
}
public interface IProductRepository
{
  IEnumerable<ProductDto> GetProducts();
}
public class ProductRepository : IProductRepository
{
  public List<ProductDto> Products
  {
    get
    {
      return ProductDataStore.Current.Products;
    }
  }
  public IEnumerable<ProductDto> GetProducts()
  {
    return Products.AsEnumerable();
  }
}
```

3. To inject data in the view, we will use another repository which reads data from a JSON file. First, we will create a JSON file at the application root with `No schema selected`.

   The `CategoryJSONDataStore.json` will look as follows:

```json
{
  "Categories": [
  "Computers",
  "Software",
  "Electronics",
  "TV",
  "DVD"]
}
```

4. After that, we create the `CategoryRepository`, which consumes this JSON file and sends it to the view. Obviously, this data should come from a database:

```
public interface ICategoryRepository
{
  List<SelectListItem> GetCategories();
}
public class CategoryRepository: ICategoryRepository
{
  private CategoryFormData _data;
  public CategoryRepository()
  {
    _data = JSONConvert
    .DeserializeObject<CategoryFormData>(
     File
    .ReadAllText("CategoryJSONDataStore.json"));
  }
  public List<SelectListItem> GetCategories()
  {
    return _data.Categories.Select
    (x => new SelectListItem() { Text = x }).ToList();
  }
}
public class CategoryFormData
{
  public List<string> Categories
  {
    get; set;
  }
}
```

5. Next, we configure `Startup.cs` to manage the repository life cycle and `AutoMapper`:

   - In the `ConfigureServices` method:

   ```
   services.AddScoped<IProductRepository,
   ProductRepository>();
   services.AddSingleton<ICategoryRepository,
   CategoryRepository>();
   ```

- In the `Configure` method:

```
AutoMapper.Mapper.Initialize(mapper => {
  mapper.CreateMap<Models.ProductDto,
  Models.ProductViewModel>();
  mapper.CreateMap<Models.ProductViewModel,
  Models.ProductDto>();
});
```

6. Now, let's create a `ProductController` which consumes the service layer:

```
public class ProductController : Controller
{
  private readonly IProductRepository
  _productRepository;
  public ProductController
  (IProductRepository productRepository)
  {
    _productRepository = productRepository;
  }
  public IActionResult Index()
  {
    var productsDtoFromRepo =
    _productRepository.GetProducts();
    var model =
    Mapper.Map<IEnumerable<ProductViewModel>>
    (productsDtoFromRepo);
    return View(model);
  }
  [HttpGet]
  public IActionResult AddProduct()
  {
    return View();
  }
  [HttpPost]
  [ValidateAntiForgeryToken]
  public IActionResult AddProduct(ProductViewModel model)
  {
    if (ModelState.IsValid)
    {
      model.Id = _productRepository.GetProducts()
      .Max(p => p.Id) + 1;
      var productDto = Mapper.Map<ProductDto>(model);
      _productRepository.AddProduct(productDto);
      return RedirectToAction("Index");
    }
    return View(model);
```

```
    }
  }
```

7. Let's add the views for the `Index` and `AddProduct` actions:

- `Index.cshtml`:

```
@model List<ProductViewModel>
<br />
@foreach (var p in Model)
{
  <p>Product @p.Id : @p.Name</p>
}
```

- `AddProduct.cshtml`

```
@model ProductViewModel
@inject
 ICategoryDataStore
 Categories
<br />
<p>Let's add a new product</p>
@using (Html.BeginForm("AddProduct", "Product",
FormMethod.Post))
{
  <div class="row">
    <div class="col-md-6">
      @Html.ValidationSummary(false)
      <div class="form-group">
        @Html.LabelFor(x => x.Name, "Product Name")
      @Html.TextBoxFor(x => x.Name,
      new { @class = "form-control" })
      @Html.ValidationMessageFor(x => x.Name)
    </div>
    <div class="form-group">
      @Html.LabelFor(x => x.Price, "Product Price")
      @Html.TextBoxFor(x => x.Price,
      new { @class = "form-control" })
      @Html.ValidationMessageFor(x => x.Price)
    </div>
    <div class="form-group">
      @Html.LabelFor(x => x.CategoryName, "Category")
      @Html.DropDownListFor(x => x.CategoryName,
      Categories.GetCategories(), "Please select one
category",
      new { @class = "form-control"})
    </div>
    <div>
```

```
        <input type="submit" value="Add" />
      </div>
    </div>
  </div>
  @section scripts{
    <script src="~/lib/jquery-
  validation/dist/jquery.validate.js">
    </script>
    <script src="~/lib/jquery-validation-
    unobtrusive/jquery.validate.unobtrusive.js">
    </script>
  }
```

8. In the `Views` folder, we have to change some code in the `_Layout.cshtml` file and the `_ViewImports.cshtml` file to make the views work correctly:

   - In `Shared/_Layout.cshtml`:

```
<ul class="nav navbar-nav"><li>
  <aasp-area="" asp-controller="Home" asp-
action="Index">Home</a>
</li>
<li>
<aasp-area="" asp-controller="Product" asp-
action="AddProduct">Add Product</a>
</li>
</ul>
```

   - In `_ViewImports.cshtml`:

```
@using R4
@using R4.Models
@using R4.Services
@addTagHelper *, Microsoft.AspNetCore.Mvc.TagHelpers
```

9. If we launch the application, we can now see that the category drop-down list is bound by injecting the `CategoryRepository` directly into the `AddProduct` view, independently from the `ProductController`:

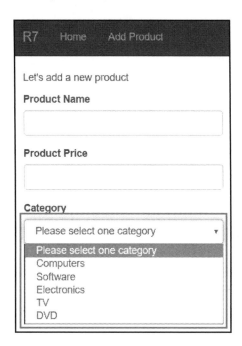

Creating HTMLHelpers

In this recipe, you will learn how to create our own HTMLHelpers. The following code is based on the previous recipe, *Using dependency injection in views*.

Getting ready

We will create an empty web application with ASP.NET Core MVC enabled by adding the MVC dependency into the project:

```
"Microsoft.AspNetCore.Mvc": "2.0.0".
```

How to do it...

Now we can dive deep into dependency injection in views:

1. First, we add an `AddProduct` action method with the corresponding view and associated repository to this template web project. In this example, the *Product* list and the *Category* list come from hardcoded code, but in the real world, it should come from a database (relational or not), a service, or any other data source:

   - Following code is the `Dto` and `ViewModel` classes:

```
public class ProductDto
{
  public int Id { get; set; }
  public string Name { get; set; }
  public decimal Price { get; set; }
}
public class ProductViewModel
{
  public int Id { get; set; }
  [Required]
  [MaxLength(50)]
  public string Name { get; set; }
  [Required]
  [Range(0.01, double.MaxValue,
  ErrorMessage = "Please enter a positive number")]
  public decimal Price { get; set; }
  [Required]
  public string CategoryName
  {
    get; set;
  }
}
```

   - Following code is the `ProductDataStore` service class:

```
public class ProductDataStore
{
  public static ProductDataStore Current { get; }
  = new ProductDataStore();
  public List<ProductDto> Products { get; set; }
  public ProductDataStore()
  {
    Products = new List<ProductDto>()
    {
      new ProductDto { Id = 1, Name = "Laptop" },
      new ProductDto { Id = 2, Name = "Phone" },
```

```
      new ProductDto { Id = 3, Name = "Desktop" }
    };
  }
}
public interface IProductRepository
{
  IEnumerable<ProductDto> GetProducts();
  void AddProduct(ProductDto productDto);
}
public class ProductRepository : IProductRepository
{
  public List<ProductDto> Products
  {
    get
    {
      return ProductDataStore.Current.Products;
    }
  }
  public IEnumerable<ProductDto> GetProducts()
  {
    return Products.AsEnumerable();
  }
  public void AddProduct(ProductDto productDto)
  {
    Products.Add(productDto);
  }
}
```

- Following code is the `ProductController` controller class:

```
public class HomeController : Controller
{
  private IProductRepository _productRepository;
  public HomeController(IProductRepository
productRepository)
  {
    _productRepository = productRepository;
  }
  public IActionResult Index()
  {
    var productsDtoFromRepo =
_productRepository.GetProducts();
    var model =
    Mapper.Map<IEnumerable<ProductViewModel>>
    (productsDtoFromRepo);
    return View(model);
  }
```

```
[HttpGet]
public IActionResult AddProduct()
{
  return View();
}
[HttpPost]
[ValidateAntiForgeryToken]
public IActionResult AddProduct(ProductViewModel model)
{
  if (ModelState.IsValid)
  {
    model.Id = _productRepository.GetProducts()
    .Max(p => p.Id) + 1;
    var productDto = Mapper.Map<ProductDto>(model);
    _productRepository.AddProduct(productDto);
    return RedirectToAction("Index");
  }
  return View(model);
}
}
```

- Following code is the _ViewImport.cshtml file content:

```
@using R5
@using R5.Models
@using R5.Services
@addTagHelper *, Microsoft.AspNetCore.Mvc.TagHelpers
```

- Following code is the AddProduct.cshtml file content:

```
@model ProductViewModel
@inject ICategoryDataStore Categories
<br />
<p>Let's add a new product</p>
@using (Html.BeginForm("AddProduct", "Product",
FormMethod.Post))
{
  <div class="row">
    <div class="col-md-6">
      @Html.ValidationSummary(false)
      <div class="form-group">
        @Html.LabelFor(x => x.Name, "Product Name")
        @Html.TextBoxFor(x => x.Name,
        new { @class = "form-control" })
        @Html.ValidationMessageFor(x => x.Name)
      </div>
      <div class="form-group">
```

```
        @Html.LabelFor(x => x.Price, "Product Price")
        @Html.TextBoxFor(x => x.Price,
        new { @class = "form-control" })
        @Html.ValidationMessageFor(x => x.Price)
    </div>
    <div class="form-group">
        @Html.LabelFor(x => x.CategoryName, "Category")
        @Html.DropDownListFor(x => x.CategoryName,
        Categories.GetCategories(), "Please select one
category",
        new { @class = "form-control"})
        @Html.ValidationMessageFor(x => x.CategoryName)
    </div>
    <div>
        <input type="submit" value="Add" />
    </div>
    </div>
</div>
}
@section scripts
{
  <script src="~/lib/jquery-
validation/dist/jquery.validate.js">
  </script>
  <script src="~/lib/jquery-validation-
  unobtrusive/jquery.validate.unobtrusive.js">
  </script>
}
```

2. Next, we configure `Startup.cs` to manage the repository life cycle and `AutoMapper` to make this work:

   - In the `ConfigureServices` method:

   ```
   services.AddScoped<IProductRepository,
   ProductRepository>();
   services.AddSingleton<ICategoryRepository,
   CategoryRepository>();
   ```

   - In the `Configure` method:

   ```
   AutoMapper.Mapper.Initialize(mapper => {
     mapper.CreateMap<Models.ProductDto,
   Models.ProductViewModel>();
     mapper.CreateMap<Models.ProductViewModel,
   Models.ProductDto>();
   });
   ```

3. Now, we can see the Razor `AddProduct.cshtml` code from the form in detail. See the following code:

```
<div class="form-group">
  @Html.LabelFor(x => x.Name, "Product Name")
  @Html.TextBoxFor(x => x.Name, new { @class = "form-control" })
  @Html.ValidationMessageFor(x => x.Name)
</div>
```

We want to replace the preceding code with this one:

```
<div class="form-group">
  @Html.CustomTextboxFor(x => x.Name, "Product Name")
</div>
```

4. To create this `CustomTextboxFor` HTMLHelper, we have to create a static class with a static extension method named `CustomTextboxFor`. The class name has no importance, but the class namespace has to be the application namespace to be used anywhere in the application:

```
public static class CustomHTMLHelpers
{
    public static IHtmlContent CustomTextboxFor<TModel, TResult>
    (this IHtmlHelper<TModel> htmlHelper,
    Expression<Func<TModel, TResult>> expression,
    string labelText)
    {
        var label = htmlHelper.LabelFor(expression, labelText);
        var textBox = htmlHelper.TextBoxFor(expression,
        new { @class = "form-control" });
        var validation = htmlHelper.ValidationMessageFor
        (expression, null,
        new { @class = "text-danger" });

        var writer = new StringWriter();
        label.WriteTo(writer, HtmlEncoder.Default);
        textBox.WriteTo(writer, HtmlEncoder.Default);
        validation.WriteTo(writer, HtmlEncoder.Default);

        return new HtmlString(writer.GetStringBuilder().ToString());
    }
}
```

5. Now we change the code in the form to the following code, and we can see that it works:

```
@using (Html.BeginForm("AddProduct", "Product", FormMethod.Post))
{
  <div class="row">
    <div class="col-md-6">
      @Html.ValidationSummary(false)
      <div class="form-group">
        @Html.CustomTextboxFor(x => x.Name, "Product Name")
      </div>
      <div class="form-group">
        @Html.CustomTextboxFor(x => x.Price, "Product Price")
      </div>
      <div class="form-group">
        @Html.LabelFor(x => x.CategoryName, "Category")
        @Html.DropDownListFor(x => x.CategoryName,
        Categories.GetCategories(), "Please select one category",
        new { @class = "form-control"})
        @Html.ValidationMessageFor(x => x.CategoryName)
      </div>
      <div>
        <input type="submit" value="Add" />
      </div>
    </div>
  </div>
}
```

6. Next job is, replacing generic drop-down list code with newly created HTMLHelper usage:

```
<div class="form-group">
  @Html.LabelFor(x => x.CategoryName, "Category")
  @Html.DropDownListFor(x => x.CategoryName,
  Categories.GetCategories(), "Please select one category",
  new { @class = "form-control"})
  @Html.ValidationMessageFor(x => x.CategoryName)
</div>
```

Replace the preceding code with this one:

```
<div class="form-group">
  @Html.CustomDropDownListFor(x => x.CategoryName,
  Categories.GetCategories(), "Category")
</div>
```

7. To do that, we add the following extension method to the `CustomHTMLHelpers` class, named `CustomDropDownListFor`:

```
public static IHtmlContent CustomDropDownListFor<TModel, TResult>
(this IHtmlHelper<TModel> htmlHelper,
Expression<Func<TModel, TResult>> expression,
IEnumerable<SelectListItem> selectList, string labelText)
{
  var label = htmlHelper.LabelFor(expression, labelText);
  var dropdownlist = htmlHelper.DropDownListFor
  (expression, selectList,
  "Please select one element on the list",
  new { @class = "form-control" });
  var validation = htmlHelper.ValidationMessageFor(expression,
null,
  new { @class = "text-danger" });

  var writer = new StringWriter();
  label.WriteTo(writer, HtmlEncoder.Default);
  dropdownlist.WriteTo(writer, HtmlEncoder.Default);
  validation.WriteTo(writer, HtmlEncoder.Default);

  return new HtmlString(writer.GetStringBuilder().ToString());
}
```

8. Now the form's code looks like this; we can see that it is less verbose:

```
@using (Html.BeginForm("AddProduct", "Product", FormMethod.Post))
{
  <div class="row">
    <div class="col-md-6">
      @Html.ValidationSummary(false)
      <div class="form-group">
        @Html.CustomTextboxFor(x => x.Name, "Product Name")
      </div>
      <div class="form-group">
        @Html.CustomTextboxFor(x => x.Price, "Product Price")
      </div>
      <div class="form-group">
        @Html.CustomDropDownListFor
        (x => x.CategoryName, Categories.GetCategories(),
"Category")
      </div>
      <div>
        <input type="submit" value="Add" />
      </div>
    </div>
```

```
        </div>
    }
```

How it works...

Let's see, in detail, the static HTMLHelpers `extension` methods. They always return an `IHtmlContent` (an `HtmlString` object which takes a `StringWriter` as a parameter). The first parameter is an `IHtmlHelper<TModel>`, used to attach this method to the `HtmlHelper static` class as an `extension` method. After that, we create, using `HtmlHelper`, all the elements we want to generate (in the current case, a `label`, a `textbox`, and a validation message for one `model` property). We add these elements as a generated string, attached to an HTML encoding format to the `StringWriter` we return.

15
TagHelpers and ViewComponents

In this chapter, we will cover:

- Using Environment, Script, and Link TagHelpers
- Using Form TagHelpers
- Creating TagHelpers programmatically
- Creating a reusable view component
- Creating a view component/controller class

Using Environment, Script, and Link TagHelpers

In this recipe, we will learn how to use the Environment, Script, and Link TagHelpers.

Getting ready

We will use the following TagHelpers:

- The Environment HTML tag
- In the existing Script HTML tag, some TagHelper attributes:
  - `asp-append-version`
  - `asp-src-include`

- asp-fallback-test
- asp-fallback-src
- asp-fallback-src-include

- In the existing Link HTML tag, some TagHelper attributes:
  - asp-append-version
  - asp-href-include
  - asp-fallback-test-class
  - asp-fallback-test-property
  - asp-fallback-test-value
  - asp-fallback-href

How to do it...

We'll dive into using TagHelpers by creating a project that behaves differently in each Environment: Development, Staging, and Production:

1. First, let's use the Environment TagHelper:

```
<environment names="Development">
<link rel="stylesheet"
href="~/lib/bootstrap/dist/css/bootstrap.css" />
</environment>
<environment names="Staging,Production">
<link rel="stylesheet" href=https://ajax.aspnetcdn.com/ajax/
 bootstrap/3.3.6/css/bootstrap.min.css />
</environment>
```

The Environment TagHelper is mapped with an environment variable defined in the application's properties, ASPNETCORE_ENVIRONMENT. This variable is used in the application configuration in Startup.cs as an IHostingEnvironment type. The Environment TagHelper often includes Script and Link HTML tags.

This mechanism helps us to create conditional code with C# in Startup.cs, and with HTML in the _Layout.cshtml file, in order to manage different environments, such as production, staging, and development.

By right-clicking on the project's root and selecting the **Debug** section, we can access the environment variable definitions:

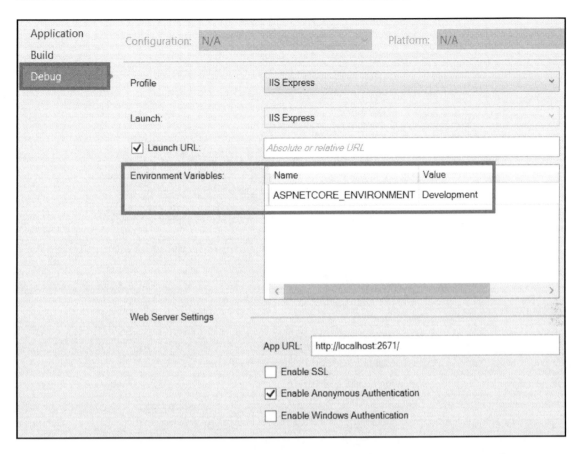

2. Now, to enable this mechanism we have to execute the `.AddEnvironment()` method for the `ConfigurationBuilder` object in the `Startup.cs` constructor. By doing this, we inject the environment variable's into our application through dependency injection:

```
public Startup(IHostingEnvironment env)
{
  var builder = new ConfigurationBuilder()
    .SetBasePath(env.ContentRootPath)
    .AddJsonFile("appsettings.json", optional: true)
    .AddJsonFile($"appsettings.{env.EnvironmentName}.json",
    optional: true)
    .AddEnvironmentVariables();
  Configuration = builder.Build();
}
```

3. Now we can use the `IHostingEnvironment` type in our code to use hosting conditions:

```
public void Configure(IApplicationBuilder app, IHostingEnvironment
env)
{
    ...
    if (env.IsDevelopment())
    {
      app.UseDeveloperExceptionPage();
      app.UseBrowserLink();
    }
    ...
}
```

We can also manage conditions declaratively in the HTML code through the Environment TagHelper:

```
<environment names="Development">
  <script src="~/lib/jquery/dist/jquery.js"></script>
</environment>
<environment names="Staging,Production">
  <script
src="https://ajax.aspnetcdn.com/ajax/jquery/jquery-2.2.0.min.js"></
script>
</environment>
```

4. Now, let's see the TagHelper attributes in the Script HTML tag:

```
<script
src="https://ajax.aspnetcdn.com/ajax/bootstrap/3.3.6/bootstrap.min.
js"
asp-fallback-src="~/lib/bootstrap/dist/js/bootstrap.min.js"
asp-fallback-test="window.jQuery && window.jQuery.fn &&
window.jQuery.fn.modal">
</script>
<script src="~/js/site.min.js" asp-append-version="true"></script>
```

If the value from the `src` attribute coming from a CDN fails, the value of `asp-fallback-src` has to be used instead.
`asp-fallback-test` means that its value (JavaScript code) has to be tested before using the script coming from the CDN.

`asp-src-include` and `asp-src-exclude` are used to include or exclude JavaScript files in the views.

`asp-fallback-src-include` and `asp-fallback-src-exclude` are used to include or exclude JavaScript files in the views if there's a problem with the JavaScript loaded file(s), and if the scripts in `asp-fallback-test` have been tested and not approved.

The `asp-append-version` value (`true` or `false`) decides whether to refresh the cache or not, if the current version of the CDN file we've stored in the browser's cache has been updated since the last upload (if not, no need to download it again, if so, maybe we want to re-download it). This mechanism is called **cache busting**.

5. Finally, let's see the TagHelper attributes in the Link HTML tag:

```
<link rel="stylesheet" href="https://ajax.aspnetcdn.com/ajax/
bootstrap/3.3.6/css/bootstrap.min.css"
asp-fallback-href="~/lib/bootstrap/dist/css/bootstrap.min.css"
asp-fallback-test-class="sr-only"
asp-fallback-test-property="position"
asp-fallback-test-value="absolute"
asp-href-include="~/css/plugins/jasny-bootstrap.min.css" />
<link rel="stylesheet" href="~/css/site.min.css"
asp-append-version="true" />
```

If the value from the href attribute coming from a CDN fails, the value of the `asp-fallback-href` has to be used instead. `asp-fallback-test-class, asp-fallback-test-property`, and `asp-fallback-test-value` means that a CSS class, a CSS property, and its value will be tested to ensure the CDN has been downloaded correctly.

`asp-href-include` is used to include CSS files in the views.

`asp-fallback-href-include` is used to include CSS files in the views if there's a problem when loading the CND file.

The code generated is the following:

```
<link rel="stylesheet"
href="https://ajax.aspnetcdn.com/ajax/bootstrap/3.3.6/css/bootstrap
.min.css" />
<link rel="stylesheet" href="/css/plugins/jasny-bootstrap.min.css"
/>
<meta name="x-stylesheet-fallback-test" content="" class="sr-only"
/>
<script>!function(a,b,c){var
d,e=document,f=e.getElementsByTagName("SCRIPT"),g=f[f.length-1].pre
viousElementSibling,h=e.defaultView&&e.defaultView.getComputedStyle
```

```
?e.defaultView.getComputedStyle(g):g.currentStyle;if(h&&h[a]!==b)fo
r(d=0;d<c.length;d++)e.write('<link rel="stylesheet"
href="'+c[d]+'"/>')}("position","absolute",["/lib/bootstrap/dist/cs
s/bootstrap.min.css"]);</script>
<link rel="stylesheet"
href="/css/site.min.css?v=SZ56l9iAMjwsC3lg_8ONpBnEfYbGculXCgb-
yhj7aKs" />
```

Using Form TagHelpers

In this recipe, we will learn how to use Form TagHelpers.

Getting ready

We will use the following TagHelpers:

- In the existing Form HTML tag, some TagHelper attributes:
    - `asp-controller`
    - `asp-action`
    - `asp-route`
    - `asp-area`
    - `asp-antiforgery`
- In any existing Form element, some TagHelper attributes:
    - `asp-for`
    - `asp-items`
- Associated with any existing Form element, some TagHelper attributes in order to add validation:
    - `asp-validation-summary`
    - `asp-validation-for`

How to do it...

Form TagHelpers make it easier for developers to create reusable components inside CSHTML views.

1. Here is a typical form using the Form TagHelper:

```
<form asp-area="" asp-controller="Product" asp-action="AddProduct"
method="post" asp-antiforgery="true">
  <div asp-validation-summary="All"></div>
  <div class="form-group">
    <label asp-for="Name"></label>
    <input type="text" asp-for="Name" />
    <span asp-validation-for="Name" class="text-danger"></span>
  </div>
  <div class="form-group">
    <label asp-for="Price"></label>
    <input type="text" asp-for="Price" />
    <span asp-validation-for="Price" class="text-danger"></span>
  </div>
  <div class="form-group">
    <label asp-for="CategoryName"></label>
    <select asp-for="CategoryName" asp-
items="@Categories.GetCategories()">
      <option disabled selected value="">Please select one
category</option>
    </select>
    <span asp-validation-for="CategoryName" class="text-
danger"></span>
  </div>
  <div>
    <input type="submit" value="Add" />
  </div>
</form>
```

2. The following is the equivalent in Razor syntax:

```
@using (Html.BeginForm("AddProduct", "Product", FormMethod.Post,
new { area = "" }))
{
  @Html.ValidationSummary(true)
  <div class="form-group">
    @Html.LabelFor(x => x.Name)
    @Html.TextBoxFor(x => x.Name)
    @Html.ValidationMessageFor(x => x.Name)
  </div>
  <div class="form-group">
```

```
      @Html.LabelFor(x => x.Price)
      @Html.TextBoxFor(x => x.Price)
      @Html.ValidationMessageFor(x => x.Price)
    </div>
    <div class="form-group">
      @Html.LabelFor(x => x.Category)
      @Html.DropDownListFor(x => x.Category,
      Categories.GetCategories(), "Please select one category")
      @Html.ValidationMessageFor(x => x.Category)
    </div>
    <div>
      <input type="submit" value="Add" />
    </div>
  }
```

Creating TagHelpers programmatically

In this recipe, we will learn how to create a TagHelper programmatically to display a menu bar.

Getting ready

We create an empty web application, adding `Microsoft.AspNetCore.Mvc` in `project.json`. We also create a `controller` class with an Index View.

How to do it...

It's relatively easy to create a custom TagHelper in C# and use it inside a CSHTML view.

1. First, let's create a `VerticalMenuTagHelper` class, which inherits from TagHelper. We indicate, by using the `HtmlTargetElement` attribute above the class, that we will use vmenu as the HTML element name to use this TagHelper in a view :

```
namespace R3.TagHelpers
{
  [HtmlTargetElement("vmenu")]
  public class VerticalMenuTagHelper : TagHelper
  {
    public List<MenuElement> Elements { get; set; }
    public override void Process(
```

```
      TagHelperContext context, TagHelperOutput output)
      {
        output.TagName = "section";
        string menuElements = "<ul>";
        foreach (var e in Elements)
        {
          menuElements +=
  $@"<li><ahref='{e.Controller}/{e.Action}'><strong>{e.Name}</strong>
          </a></li>";
        }
        menuElements += "</ul>";
        output.Content.SetHtmlContent(menuElements);
        output.TagMode = TagMode.StartTagAndEndTag;
      }
    }
  }
```

2. We also create a `MenuElement` class that will be injected as a parameter to feed our menu bar:

```
public class MenuElement
{
  public string Name { get; set; }
  public string Controller { get; set; }
  public string Action { get; set; }
}
```

The goal is to generate the following code on a page. Of course, in a real context, we inject this code in the Layout page in order to share this menu across the entire application:

```
<section class="menustyle">
  <ul>
    <li><a href='Home/Index'><strong>Home</strong></a></li>
    <li><a href='Home/About'><strong>About</strong></a></li>
    <li><a href='Home/Contact'><strong>Contact</strong></a></li>
  </ul>
</section>
```

3. Next, we create a controller where we will create a viewModel to feed the Index View and the TagHelper:

```
public class HomeController : Controller
{
  public IActionResult Index()
  {
    var model = new List<MenuElement>()
```

```
    {
      new MenuElement
      {
        Name = "Home",
        Controller = "Home",
        Action = "Index"
      },
      new MenuElement
      {
        Name = "About",
        Controller = "Home",
        Action = "About"
      },
      new MenuElement
      {
        Name = "Contact",
        Controller = "Home",
        Action = "Contact"
      }
    };
    return View(model);
  }
}
```

4. Next, we create the Index View to call the tag helper:

```
@model List<R3.TagHelpers.MenuElement>
<html>
  <head>
    <link href="~/css/StyleSheet.css" rel="stylesheet" />
  </head>
  <body>
    <vmenu elements="@Model" class="menustyle" />
  </body>
</html>
```

5. We can see that the `menustyle` class has been added to the TagHelper and the CSS file has been added in the `wwwroot` folder where we store static files. Don't forget to add the `UseStaticFiles` middleware to the `Startup.cs` to allow static files in the application. The CSS code for this class is the following:

```
.menustyle
{}
section.menustyle ul
{
  list-style-type: none;
}
```

```
section.menustyle ul li
{
  display : inline;
  padding : 0 0.5em;
}
```

6. To make all that work, we need to create a `_ViewImports.cshtml`, where we will import all the namespaces we will use in our Views, including the general namespace for TagHelpers, and the namespace of the TagHelper we've just created. We will use the following:

```
@using R3
@addTagHelper *, Microsoft.AspNetCore.Mvc.TagHelpers
@addTagHelper "R3.TagHelpers.VerticalMenuTagHelper, R3"
```

There's more...

In the previous example, the root HTML tag inserted is `section`. We indicate that by giving a HTML tag name as the value to `output.TagName`.
With `output.Content.SetHtmlContent`, we inject HTML into the section element.

Creating a reusable view component

In this recipe, we will learn how to create a view component.

Getting ready

We create an empty web application, adding `Microsoft.AspNetCore.Mvc` in `project.json`. We also create a controller class with an Index View.

How to do it...

View components let developers create a component with both server-side logic and client-side code to render layout.

1. First, add a service and a `TagCloud` class in order to display a list of tag clouds in a reusable component:

```
public interface ITagCloudService
{
  Task<List<Tag>> GetTagsAsync(string userBlog);
}

public class TagCloudService : ITagCloudService
{
  public async Task<List<Tag>> GetTagsAsync(string userBlog)
  {
    return await Task.Run(() => GetTags(userBlog));
  }

  private List<Tag> GetTags(string userBlog)
  {
    return new List<Tag>
    {
      new Tag { Id = 1, Name = "Asp.Net Core" },
      new Tag { Id = 2, Name = "EF Core" }
    };
  }
}

public class Tag
{
  public int Id { get; set; }
  public string Name { get; set; }
}
```

2. In `Sartup.cs`, we configure dependency injection for the newly-created service:

```
public void ConfigureServices(IServiceCollection services)
{
  services.AddMvc();
  services.AddScoped<ITagCloudService, TagCloudService>();
}
```

3. Next, let's create a class `suffixed` with `ViewComponent` and deriving by `ViewComponent`. This class will have to implement an `InvokeAsync` method, which returns a task of `IViewComponentResult`:

```
public class TagCloudViewComponent : ViewComponent
{
  private readonly ITagCloudService _service;

  public TagCloudViewComponent(ITagCloudService service)
  {
    _service = service;
  }

  public async Task<IViewComponentResult> InvokeAsync(string userBlog)
  {
    var viewModel = await _service.GetTagsAsync(userBlog);
    return View(viewModel);
  }
}
```

4. Next, we create a folder named `Components` inside the `Views\ Shared` folder. We have to create a folder with the name of the `ViewComponent` we've just created in the `Components` folder. In this folder, let's create a view named `Default.cshtml`, where we add the following code:

```
@model List<R4.ViewComponents.Tag>
<ul>
  @foreach(var t in Model)
  {
    <li>@t.Name</li>
  }
</ul>
```

5. Now, we can use this view component in two ways:

- One is invoking the view component in a View with the `ViewComponent.InvokeAsync` method. For example, we add the following code to the `HomeController`:

```
public IActionResult Index()
{
  return View();
}
```

Add the following code to `Index.cshtml`:

```
@using R4.ViewComponents

@await Component.InvokeAsync("TagCloud")
```

- The second way is to call the view `Component` directly from the Index `ActionMethod` in `HomeController`, returning a `ViewComponent` instead of returning a View:

```
public IActionResult Index()
{
  return ViewComponent("TagCloud");
}
```

How it works...

A view component can replace a `ChildAction` or a Partial View. It includes more logic.

It will return HTML fragments, encoded or not, that will depend on what type we return from a view component (`ViewComponentResult`, `ContentViewComponentResult`, or `HtmlContentViewComponentResult`).

It can be synchronous or asynchronous.

It can access all the objects a controller can access (`Request`, `RouteData`, `User`, `ViewBag`, `ModelState`, and so on) and the parent View context (through the `ViewContext` object).

It can be called in a View, as a Partial View, or returned by a controller as a `ViewComponentResult`.

A `ViewComponent` is composed of:

- A class that contains logic. This class can derive from the `ViewComponent` and/or the `ViewComponentAttribute` class. Class which act as a `ViewComponent` can't derive from anything other than `ViewComponent` class. Nevertheless, it has to contain an `Invoke()` method.
  This `Invoke()` method can accept parameters from the high-level View.
  This `Invoke()` method can return:
    - A `View` object (for Partial Views)
    - A `Content` Object (for HTML fragments)

- A View (not mandatory).
  If a Partial View is returned by a View Component, it will be searched by Razor in the following locations:
  - `/Views/{ControllerNameWhichContainsTheViewComponent}/Components/{ViewComponentName}/Default.cshtml`
  - `/Views/Shared/Components/{ViewComponentName}/Default.cshtml`

The `ViewComponent` class can be injected by any service configured in the `ConfigureServices` method and can be unit tested.

One inconvenience of `ViewComponent` is that it cannot be updated by Ajax like a partial view. One other inconvenience is that it always belongs to a parent view, but we will see how we can escape this constraint in the next recipe.

Creating a view component/controller class

In this recipe, we will learn how to use/create a hybrid `ViewComponent`/`controller` class.

Getting ready

We will create an empty web application with ASP.NET Core MVC enabled, adding the MVC dependency to the project:

```
"Microsoft.AspNetCore.Mvc": "2.0.0"
```

In this recipe, we will create a basket component and place it in the `_Layout.cstml` file. This way, the basket component will be visible for every page. The basket object will be stored in Session.

How to do it...

1. Let's create all the code we need to display some products to add to the basket. The models will have to be serializable (models, services):

```
[Serializable]
public class Product
{
```

```csharp
  public int Id { get; set; }
  public string Name { get; set; }
  public decimal Price { get; set; }
}

[Serializable]
public class Basket
{
  public List<Product> ListProducts { get; set; }
  public decimal Total { get; set; }

  public Basket()
  {
    ListProducts = new List<Product>();
    Total = 0;
  }
}

public interface IProductRepository
{
  IEnumerable<Product> GetProducts();
}

public class ProductRepository : IProductRepository
{
  private List<Product> _products;
  public ProductRepository()
  {
    _products = new List<Product>()
    {
      new Product { Id = 1, Name = "Laptop", Price = 250 },
      new Product { Id = 2, Name = "Phone", Price = 150 },
      new Product { Id = 3, Name = "Screen", Price = 200 }
    };
  }

  public IEnumerable<Product> GetProducts()
  {
    return _products;
  }
}
```

2. We create the code in order to enable the Session mechanism, some extensions for the ISession object, and some configuration in Startup.cs.

    The ASP.NET Core session mechanism does not include object serialization by default, so we have to create some extension methods to allow us to insert Clr objects in a session. In Startup.cs, we will add the services.AddDistributedMemoryCache() instruction, which enables sessions for our application.
    The services.AddSession() instruction adds a session cookie.
    The services.AddSingleton<IHttpContextAccessor, HttpContextAccessor>() instruction will allow us to access the session object in any class of the application injecting HttpContextAccessor:

```
public static class SessionExtensions
{
  public static T Get<T>(this ISession session, string key)
  {
    var obj = session.Get(key);
    if (obj == null)
    return default(T);
    return Deserialize<T>(obj);
  }

  public static void Set<T>(this ISession session, string key, T
obj)
  {
    if (obj != null)
    session.Set(key, Serialize(obj));
  }

  private static byte[] Serialize(object o)
  {
    if (o == null)
    {
      return null;
    }

    BinaryFormatter binaryFormatter = new BinaryFormatter();
    using (MemoryStream memoryStream = new MemoryStream())
    {
      binaryFormatter.Serialize(memoryStream, o);
      byte[] objectDataAsStream = memoryStream.ToArray();
      return objectDataAsStream;
    }
  }
}
```

```
    private static T Deserialize<T>(byte[] stream)
    {
      if (stream == null)
      return default(T);

      BinaryFormatter binaryFormatter = new BinaryFormatter();
      using (MemoryStream memoryStream = new MemoryStream(stream))
      {
        T result = (T)binaryFormatter.Deserialize(memoryStream);
        return result;
      }
    }
  }
}

public class Startup
{
  ...
  public void ConfigureServices(IServiceCollection services)
  {
    services.AddDistributedMemoryCache();
    services.AddSession(options =>
    {
      options.IdleTimeout = TimeSpan.FromMinutes(30);
      options.CookieName = ".Session";
    });
    services.AddSingleton
    <IHttpContextAccessor, HttpContextAccessor>();
    services.AddScoped<IProductRepository, ProductRepository>();
    services.AddMvc();
  }


  public void Configure(IApplicationBuilder app)
  {
    ...
    app.UseSession();

    app.UseMvc(routes =>
    {
      routes.MapRoute(
      name: "default",
      template: "{controller=Home}/{action=Index}/{id?}");
      });
    }
  }
}
```

3. We create a new Controller named `ProductController`.

To make it a hybrid view component/controller, we have to do two things:

- Decorate the controller with an attribute including a component name that will be the parameter name used when the `Component.Invoke("ComponentName")` is called
- Add an Invoke method to the controller which returns an IViewComponentResult:

```
[ViewComponent(Name = "BasketComponent")]
public class ProductController : Controller
{
  private readonly IProductRepository _productRepository;
  private readonly IHttpContextAccessor
_httpContextAccessor;

  public ProductController(IProductRepository
productRepository, IHttpContextAccessor
httpContextAccessor)
  {
    _productRepository = productRepository;
    _httpContextAccessor = httpContextAccessor;
  }

  [HttpGet]
  public IActionResult Index()
  {
    var products = _productRepository.GetProducts();
    return View(products);
  }

  public IViewComponentResult Invoke()
  {
    Basket basket;
    if (_httpContextAccessor.HttpContext.Session == null)
    throw new Exception("Session is not enabled !");
    else
    basket = _httpContextAccessor.HttpContext
    .Session
    .Get<Basket>("basket");

    if (basket == null) basket = new Basket();

    return new ViewViewComponentResult()
    {
```

```
            ViewName = "BasketData",
            ViewData = new ViewDataDictionary<Basket>(ViewData,
    basket)
        };
    }
}
```

4. We create a view component corresponding to the View returned by the `Invoke` method in the `Views/Shared/BasketComponent/` folder, called `BasketData.cshtml`:

```
@model Basket
<span>
  <span>Basket </span>
  <span>Items : @Model.ListProducts.Count</span>
  <span>Total : @Model.Total</span>
</span>
```

5. We call the view component in the `_Layout.cshtml` View through the following code:

```
@await Component.InvokeAsync("BasketComponent")
```

6. We create the Index View for the `Index` action method of the `ProductController`. This View displays a list of products, but also allow us to add any product to the basket with the `AddToBasket` button. We added the jQuery code to make the AJAX call to the `AddToBasket` method:

```
@model List<Product>
<br />
<div style="width:300px;">
  @foreach (var p in Model)
  {
    <fieldset>
      <div><span>Name: </span><span>@p.Name</span></div>
      <div><span>Price: </span><span>@p.Price</span></div>
      <div>
        <input type="hidden" value="@p.Id" />
        <input type="button" class="basket" value="Add to basket"
/>
      </div>
    </fieldset>
    <br />
  }
</div>
```

```
@section scripts{
    <script>
        $(function () {
            $("input[type=button]").click(function (e) {
                e.preventDefault();
                var id = $(this).prev().val();
                $.ajax({
                    type: "POST",
                    url: "/Home/AddToBasket",
                    data: { "id": id },
                    dataType: 'json',
                    success: function () {
                        window.location.reload();
                    }
                });
            });
        });
    </script>
}
```

7. We add the `AddToBasket` action method to the `HomeController`:

```
public class HomeController : Controller
{
    private readonly IProductRepository _productRepository;
    private readonly IHttpContextAccessor _httpContextAccessor;

    public HomeController(IProductRepository productRepository,
    IHttpContextAccessor httpContextAccessor)
    {
        _productRepository = productRepository;
        _httpContextAccessor = httpContextAccessor;
    }

    [HttpGet]
    public IActionResult Index()
    {
        return View();
    }

    [HttpPost]
    public IActionResult AddToBasket(int id)
    {
        var basket = _httpContextAccessor.HttpContext
        .Session.Get<Basket>("basket");

        if (basket == null) basket = new Basket();
```

```
        var product = _productRepository.GetProducts()
        .Where(p => p.Id == id).SingleOrDefault();

        basket.ListProducts.Add(product);
        basket.Total += product.Price;

        _httpContextAccessor.HttpContext.Session.Set("basket", basket);

        return NoContent();
    }
}
```

8. Finally, we can see the result with the basket updated after each product is added:

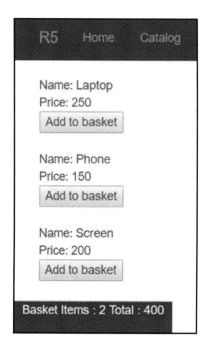

How it works...

A view component/controller is created as a controller inheriting from the `Controller` class. It can be a hybrid object if:

- It's decorated by the `ViewComponent` attribute with a `ViewComponent` name as parameter:

```
[ViewComponent(Name = "BasketComponent")]
public class ProductController : Controller
```

- It contains an `Invoke()` method that returns an `IViewComponentResult`. The `ViewData` property of the `ViewViewComponent` object returned is the name of the `.cshtml` view component:

```
public IViewComponentResult Invoke()
{
  List<string> listeData = new List<string>();
  return new ViewViewComponentResult()
  {
    ViewName = "BasketData",
    ViewData = new ViewDataDictionary<IEnumerable<string>>
    (ViewData, listeData)
  };
}
```

When it is invoked, the searched locations will be:

- /Views/Home/Components/BasketComponent/BasketData.cshtml
- /Views/Shared/Components/BasketComponent/BasketData.cshtml

16
OWIN and Middleware

In this chapter, we will cover:

- Understanding OWIN, Katana, and the new ASP.NET Core HTTP pipeline
- Using inline middleware code as anonymous methods - Use, Run, Map, and MapWhen
- Creating a reusable middleware component
- Migrating an HTTP handler to middleware
- Migrating HTTP modules to middleware

Understanding OWIN, Katana, and the new ASP.NET Core HTTP pipeline

In this recipe, we will get an in-depth look at OWIN, Katana, and the middleware pipeline in ASP.NET Core.

OWIN - an abstraction for decoupling

Open Web Interface for .NET (OWIN) is a standard that defines an interface between web servers and .NET web applications. Implementing OWIN allows us to create an abstraction between web apps, hosts, and servers, and to decouple .NET web applications from IIS. For example, to change the host in WebAPI to be self-hosted in a console application or a Windows service, change ASP.NET MVC or WebAPI with NancyFx.

The host is the process in our OS that loads the server and creates the pipeline. The server listens for the request on specific ports, redirects it to the pipeline, and returns the response to this request generated by the application. The application threads the received request and generates the response.

Katana - the Microsoft OWIN implementation

Before ASP.NET Core, in order to decouple .NET apps from IIS, we could use OWIN. In order to host the ASP.NET Web API outside IIS, we use the Katana project (the Microsoft OWIN implementation).

With Katana, using OWIN-specific libraries, we are still using the Windows environment. ASP.NET MVC 5 is too tight with IIS, nevertheless, OWIN offers us a new HTTP pipeline to be decoupled from IIS.
Since ASP.NET Web API 2, to decouple our APIs from IIS and the ASP.NET pipeline lifecycle, we can use OWIN.

In order to achieve that, using the Katana pipeline and classes, we use a `Startup.cs` file instead of the classic `Global.asax` file to configure our API and change the host to self-hosted (console, Windows service, or Azure worker role).

Another way to decouple .NET apps from the server is to use OWIN as an HTTP pipeline with NancyFx as an alternative to ASP.NET MVC or Web API.
We can use an agnostic method to abstract MVC and WebAPI, replacing both with Nancy. Nancy is a light framework to create HTTP services on Mono, .NET Core, or .NET Framework.

When the request arrives at the host, and before it arrives at the application code, it passes through a pipeline, which is composed by the ASP.NET/IIS pipeline defined by the `HttpApplication` class. It passes through a combination of HTTP handlers and modules. We could aggregate treatments on this pipeline by creating new HTTP modules and handlers, but we won't have a lot of control over it.

A new OWIN implementation with ASP.NET Core

With ASP.NET Core, we are now agnostic from the host and the web server. We use the same philosophy as OWIN, which means using an abstraction between applications, servers, and hosts. The new thing about it is we can compose the pipeline for our application by adding middleware components to this pipeline.

ASP.NET Core respects OWIN principles but is not OWIN. One of the differences is that it maps all incoming data from a request to an HttpContext object available from all middleware (built-in, in line created, or component created). Another difference from the previous versions of ASP.NET is that the HttpContext object is now agnostic from IIS and System.Web, and is more lightweight. Nevertheless, we always have the opportunity to use OWIN libraries, and so use an OWIN pipeline in ASP.NET MVC Core, as we did with ASP.NET Web API 2.2.

The ASP.NET Core pipeline

On the ASP.NET Core pipeline, we can add middleware in two ways: inline code in an anonymous function, or reusable middleware components. Both are added to the pipeline in a sequential way in the Configure() method in Startup.cs.

When the Configure() method is invoked, the HTTP pipeline is prepared and set up to handle incoming requests. These incoming requests are passed into and threaded by each piece of middleware added to the pipeline.

In the next recipe, we will learn how middleware, works with inline code. Inline code for middleware is not the best practice. It's more relevant to create middleware classes and use the app.UseMiddleware method to add them to the pipeline for various reasons (reusability, clarity, and so on). They both work in the same way.

Middleware

In the computer world, middleware is a software component that will interact, interoperate, exchange, and share data across different applications in different ways. There is service, message, or object-oriented middleware.

With ASP.NET Core, middleware will be treatments and components added to the HTTP pipeline represented by the `Configure()` method in `Startup.cs`.

This middleware allows us to gain total control over the pipeline replacing the classic ASP.NET application lifecycle and all the HTTP modules and handlers. We will choose in what order they will be executed.

There's already some built-in middleware but we will have to create our own, or create some to manage the existing ones (authorization, authentication, session, cache, log, routing, exception handling, and so on) with finer granularity.

HTTP modules and HTTP handlers

As opposed to HttpHandlers and HttpModules, middleware is created and used programmatically without a config file. We are now agnostic from IIS and `System.Web`.

Let's look at a few things about `HttpHandlers` and `HttpModules`:

- An `HttpModule` runs for each request before arriving at the handler that generates the response, and/or after it generates the response
- A Handler handles the request and generates the response for a given file extension

Using inline middleware code as anonymous methods - Use, Run, Map, and MapWhen

In this recipe, we will learn how to use inline middleware code in the `Configure()` method of `Startup.cs`.

Getting ready

We create an empty ASP.NET Core web application with Visual Studio, using .NET Core or .NET Framework.

How to do it...

We'll create a new project and use different types of middleware:

1. First, let's use `app.Use`:

```
public void Configure(IApplicationBuilder app)
{
    ...
    app.Use(async (context, next) =>
    {
        await context.Response.WriteAsync
        ("First Inline middleware before Handlen");
        await next.Invoke();
        await context.Response.WriteAsync
        ("First Inline middleware after Handle");
    });
    ...
}
```

`next.Invoke()` will call the next middleware in the pipeline.

We can add as many `app.Use` methods as we want. They will be executed in the order in which they were added on the pipeline.

To make an analogy with an HTTP module, the code executed before await `next.Invoke()` corresponds with the code in the `BeginRequest` method in a class implementing `IHttpModule`, and the code executed after await `next.Invoke()` corresponds with the code in the `EndRequest` method.

The anonymous function inside the `Use()` method has two parameters: the current HTTP context and a delegate called next by convention. This delegate is used to call the next delegate. If we don't call the `next.Invoke()` method inside `app.Run`, we short circuit the pipeline, and the next middleware (inline, static, or custom) that follows will not be executed.

2. Second, let's use `app.Run`:

```
public void Configure(IApplicationBuilder app)
{
    ...
    app.Use(async (context, next) =>
    {
        await context.Response.WriteAsync
        ("First Inline middleware before Handlen");
        await next.Invoke();
        await context.Response.WriteAsync
        ("First Inline middleware after Handle");
    });

    app.Run(async (context) =>
    {
        await context.Response.WriteAsync("Run middleware n");
    });
    ...
}
```

The `app.Run` short circuits the pipeline. The pipeline understands that the code in the `app.Run` method will be the last middleware code executed on the pipeline and the response will be generated. Even if some middleware is added (inline or class) after this code, it will not be executed.

3. Third, we use `app.Map`:

```
public void Configure(IApplicationBuilder app)
{
  ...
  app.Map("/oneurlsegment", (appBuilder) =>
  {
    appBuilder.Use(async (context, next) =>
    {
      await context.Response.WriteAsync
      ("Third Inline middleware before Handle n");
      await next.Invoke();
      await context.Response.WriteAsync
      ("Third Inline middleware after Handle n");
    });
    ...
  }
}
```

The `Map` method will execute a treatment on the URL branch.

4. Fourth, let's use `app.MapWhen`:

```
public void Configure(IApplicationBuilder app)
{
  ...
  app.MapWhen(context =>
  context.Request.Query.ContainsKey("q1"), (appBuilder) =>
  {
    appBuilder.Use(async (context, next) =>
    {
      await context.Response.WriteAsync
      ("Fourth Inline middleware before Handle n ");
      await next.Invoke();
      await context.Response.WriteAsync
      ("Fourth Inline middleware after Handle n ");
    });
    ...
  }
}
```

The `MapWhen` method will execute conditional code checking request parameter(s).

Creating a reusable middleware component

In this recipe, we will learn how to use the Environment, Script, and Link Tag Helpers.

Getting ready

We create an empty ASP.NET Core web application with Visual Studio and .NET Core or .NET Framework.

How to do it...

We'll create a new project and write our first middleware. We can observe the execution mechanism of middleware with this project.

1. First, let's create a `middleware` class:

```
public class MyMiddleware1
{
  private readonly RequestDelegate _next;

  public MyMiddleware1(RequestDelegate next)
  {
    _next = next;
  }

  public async Task Invoke(HttpContext httpContext)
  {
    await httpContext.Response.WriteAsync
    ("Hello from first middleware before Request n");
    await _next(httpContext);
    await httpContext.Response.WriteAsync
    ("Hello from first middleware after Request n");
  }
}
```

A `middleware` class does not inherit from any class or interface, but has to respect some rules:

- Having a `public` constructor that takes a RequestDelegate type as parameter.
- Having a `private` RequestDelegate type property that will be affected by the RequestDelegate variable passed in the constructor.
- Having an asynchronous `Invoke()` method which returns a task and takes a `HttpContext` type as parameter.
- Optionally, inside the `Invoke()` method, execute the _next RequestDelegate with the `HttpContext` as a parameter if this middleware is not the last middleware executed on the pipeline.
- The await _next (httpContext) delegate represents the next middleware defined on the pipeline. The `Invoke` method gets the `HttpContext` in a parameter from the previous middleware on the pipeline.
- The `HttpContext` class contains all the data relative to a request HTTP context (request, session, querystring, route, and many others).

2. Now we add it to the pipeline thanks to the `app.UseMiddleware<MyMiddleware>()` method:

```
public class Startup
{
  ...
  public void Configure
  (IApplicationBuilder app, IHostingEnvironment env)
  {
    app.UseMiddleware<MyMiddleware1>();
  }
  ...
}
```

3. However, a more elegant way is to create an `extension` method for the middleware:

```
public static class MiddlewareExtensions
{
  public static IApplicationBuilder UseMiddleware1
  (this IApplicationBuilder builder)
  {
    return builder.UseMiddleware<MyMiddleware1>();
  }
}
```

Add it to the pipeline, replacing the previous syntax:

```
public class Startup
{
  ...
  public void Configure
  (IApplicationBuilder app, IHostingEnvironment env)
  {
    //app.UseMiddleware<MyMiddleware1>();
    app.UseMiddleware1();
  }
  ...
}
```

4. In this reusable middleware we create, we can add any service or class injected by dependency injection to the middleware constructor in the `ConfigureServices` method of `Startup.cs`:

```
public class Product
{
  public int Id { get; set; }
  public string Name { get; set; }
}

public interface IDataRepository
{
  List<Product> GetAll();
}

public class ProductRepository : IDataRepository
{
  public List<Product> GetPromotedProducts()
  {
    ...
  }
```

```
    }

    public class StoredDataMiddleware
    {
      RequestDelegate _next;
      IMemoryCache _cache;
      IRepository _repo;

      public StoredDataMiddleware(RequestDelegate next,
      IMemoryCache cache, IRepository repo)
      {
        _next = next;
        _cache = cache;
        _repo = repo;
      }

      public async Task Invoke(HttpContext context)
      {
        var products = _repo.GetPromotedProducts();
        _cache.Set<List<Product>>("PromotedProducts", products);
        await context.Response.WriteAsync
        ("I put in cache datas in a middleware n");
        await _next.Invoke(context);
      }
    }
```

In this example, we store a product list in the cache through the middleware.

5. Finally, we see how `Startup.cs` is configured:

```
    public class Startup
    {
      ...
      public void ConfigureServices(IServiceCollection services)
      {
        services.AddMemoryCache();
        services.AddScoped<IDataRepository, ProductRepository>();
      }

      public void Configure(IApplicationBuilder app,
      IHostingEnvironment env, IMemoryCache cache)
      {
        app.UseStoredDataMiddleware();
        //app.UseMiddleware<MyMiddleware2>();
      }
      ...
    }
```

Migrating an HTTP handler to middleware

In this recipe, we will learn how to transform an ASP.NET HTTP handler to ASP.NET Core middleware.

Before anything, let's recap what an HTTP handler is. An HTTP handler handles an incoming request from the ASP.NET/IIS pipeline and generates a response for a given extension file (`.aspx`, `.html`, `.jpg`, and so on.) For ASP.NET MVC, we used a specific handler named `MVCHandler`, which ensures that an `action` method exists in a controller for the specified route in the request URL.

Getting ready

We create an empty ASP.NET Core web application with Visual Studio and .NET Core or .NET Framework.

How to do it...

We'll create a new project and write our first middleware. We can observe the execution mechanism of middleware with this project.

1. First, let's watch the anatomy of an HTTP handler:

```
public class MyHttpHandler : IHttpHandler
{
  public bool IsReusable {  get {  return false;  }  }

  public void ProcessRequest(HttpContext context)
  {
    context.Response.Write("This page pass by MyHttpHandler <br
/>");
  }
}
```

2. Now, let's see the `Web.config` configuration:

```
<system.webServer>
    <handlers>
        <add name="MyReportHandler" verb="*" path="*.report"
type="MyApp.HttpHandlers.MyReportHandler"
resourceType="Unspecified" />
    </handlers>
</system.webServer>
```

We had to specify a name, the authorized HTTP verbs for this Handler, the path, which is the named extension file, and the type, which is the namespace's handler.

3. The equivalent code in ASP.NET Core could be the following: first, we create the middleware corresponding to the handler. We can do that in four ways:

1. Using the `MapWhen` function using inline middleware code calling custom middleware:

```
public class MyReportMiddleware
{
  private readonly RequestDelegate _next;

  public MyReportMiddleware(RequestDelegate next)
  {
    _next = next;
  }

  public Task Invoke(HttpContext httpContext)
  {
      return httpContext.Response.WriteAsync("this .report
file will be              executed and short circuit the
pipeline");
      // we doesn't call next because we want to short
circuit the
      // pipeline in order to act as a classic HttpHandler
      //return _next(httpContext);
  }
}

// Extension method used to add the middleware
// to the HTTP request pipeline.
public static class MyReportMiddlewareExtensions
{
  public static IApplicationBuilder UseMyReportMiddleware
  (this IApplicationBuilder builder)
```

```
      {
        return builder.UseMiddleware<MyReportMiddleware>();
      }
    }

    public void Configure(IApplicationBuilder app)
    {
      ...
      app.MapWhen(
      context =>
      context.Request.Path.ToString().EndsWith(".report"),
      appBranch =>
      {
         appBranch.UseMyReportMiddleware();
      });
      ...
    }
```

2. Using the MapWhen function using inline middleware code calling a static middleware function in Startup.cs:

```
    private static void HandleBranchForReport
    (IApplicationBuilder app)
    {
      app.Run(async context =>
      {
        await context.Response.WriteAsync
        ("this .report file will be executed and short circuit
      the pipeline");
      });
    }

    public void Configure(IApplicationBuilder app)
    {
      ...
      app.MapWhen(
      context =>
      context.Request.Path.ToString().EndsWith(".report"),
      HandleBranchForReport);
      ...
    }
```

3. Using the `MapWhen` function using inline middleware code using the `Run` method inside:

```
public void Configure(IApplicationBuilder app)
{
  ...
  app.MapWhen(
  context =>
  context.Request.Path.ToString().EndsWith(".report"),
  appBranch =>
  {
    appBranch.Run(async (context) =>
    {
      await context.Response.WriteAsync
      ("this .report file will be executed and short
circuit the pipeline");
    });
  });
  ...
}
```

4. Using custom middleware with conditional code inside:

```
// Middleware class
public class MySecondReportMiddleware
{
  private readonly RequestDelegate _next;

  public MySecondReportMiddleware(RequestDelegate next)
  {
    _next = next;
  }

  public Task Invoke(HttpContext httpContext)
  {
    if(httpContext.Request.Path.ToString()
    .EndsWith(".report"))
    return httpContext.Response.WriteAsync
    ("this .report file will be executed and
    short circuit the pipeline");
    else
    return _next(httpContext);
  }
}

// Extension method used to add the middleware
// to the HTTP request pipeline.
```

```
public static class MySecondReportMiddlewareExtensions
{
  public static IApplicationBuilder
UseMySecondReportMiddleware
  (this IApplicationBuilder builder)
  {
    return
builder.UseMiddleware<MySecondReportMiddleware>();
  }
}
```

In the `Startup.cs` file:

```
public void Configure(IApplicationBuilder app)
{
  ...
  app.UseMySecondReportMiddleware();
  ...
}
```

Migrating HTTP modules to middleware

In this recipe, we will learn how to transform an ASP.NET HTTP module in ASP.NET Core middleware.

Before anything, let's brush up on what an HTTP handler is. An HTTP module can add a treatment to an incoming request from the ASP.NET/IIS pipeline before it arrives at the handler, and/or add a treatment to the generated response. It can even transform or generate its own response.

Getting ready

We create an empty ASP.NET Core web application with Visual Studio and .NET Core or the .NET Framework.

How to do it...

We'll create a new HTTP module, and track the starting/ending point of the request. We will also add information to the beginning of the response and end of the response.

1. First, let's see the anatomy of an HTTP module:

```
public class MyHttpModule : IHttpModule
{
  public void Dispose(){}

  public void Init(HttpApplication context)
  {
    context.BeginRequest += (source, args) =>
    {
      context.Response.Write("MyHttpModule BeginRequest");
    };

    context.EndRequest += (source, args) =>
    {
      context.Response.Write("MyHttpModule EndRequest");
    };
  }
}
```

HttpModule has to be configured in the `Web.config` file as follows:

```
<system.webServer>
    <modules>
      <add name="myModule" type="MyApp.HttpModules.MyHttpModule"/>
    </modules>
</system.webServer>
```

2. Now, let's see the equivalent code in ASP.NET core. To transform this module to make it compatible with ASP.NET core, we can create custom middleware and call it, or create inline middleware:

1. The custom middleware is as follows:

```
// Middleware class
public class MyModuleMiddleware
{
  private readonly RequestDelegate _next;

  public MyModuleMiddleware(RequestDelegate next)
  {
    _next = next;
  }

  public async Task Invoke(HttpContext httpContext)
  {
    await httpContext.Response.WriteAsync
    ("MyHttpModule BeginRequest");
    await _next(httpContext);
    await httpContext.Response.WriteAsync
    ("MyHttpModule EndRequest");
  }
}

// Extension method used to add the middleware
// to the HTTP request pipeline.
public static class MyModuleMiddlewareExtensions
{
  public static IApplicationBuilder UseMyModuleMiddleware
  (this IApplicationBuilder builder)
  {
    return builder.UseMiddleware<MyModuleMiddleware>();
  }
}
```

In `Startup.cs`:

```
public void Configure(IApplicationBuilder app)
{
  ...
  app.UseMyModuleMiddleware ();
  ...
}
```

2. Inline code middleware in `Startup.cs` looks as follows:

```
public void Configure(IApplicationBuilder app)
{
  ...
  app.Use(async (context, next) =>
  {
    // This code is equivalent to call the BeginRequest
    // delegate in a HttpModule
    await context.Response.WriteAsync
    ("MyHttpModule BeginRequest");
    await next.Invoke();
    // This code is equivalent to call the EndRequest
    // delegate in a HttpModule
    await context.Response.WriteAsync
    ("MyHttpModule EndRequest");
  });
  ...
}
```

17
Security

In this chapter, we will cover the following topics:

- Authentication in ASP.NET using cookie authentication
- Authentication using authorization servers
- Managing identity
- Securing data with ASP.NET Core
- Hashing
- Encryption

Introduction

In this section, we will take a look at how authentication works in ASP.NET Core.

 All examples in this chapter can be found at https://github.com/polatengin/B05277/tree/master/Chapter17 GitHub repo.

The HTTP protocol is a stateless, *response-for-a-request* based protocol. This means an HTTP server can generate a response once it gets a request, and it never remembers previous requests and their results. Every request is processed separately.

For example, if an application requires you to log in first, a developer should handle the required logic flow to redirect to the user login page if they haven't logged in yet.

So, every request should have all the information to be processed successfully (if a user has logged in or not, who the user is, and their permissions.)

If a bad user sits on the line between the client and the server, they can read packages and easily pretend to be someone else.

Most of the server-side frameworks (ASP.NET, Java, Ruby, and so on) have some mechanism that provides a solution to a developer for storing and accessing this kind of information from server memory.

ASP.NET is no exception, and it has APIs to store/access/process user information from server memory.

> Authentication is the process of determining whether someone or something is, in fact, who or they say they are ,what it says it is: `http://searchsecurity.techtarget.com/definition/authentication`.
>
> Authorization is the process of giving someone permission to do or have something: `http://searchsoftwarequality.techtarget.com/definition/authorization`.

Authentication in the real world

Imagine you lock your home's front door and hide the key under the doormat. The person who finds and uses the key to unlock the front door has access to the entire house.

A simple lock does not have any mechanisms to determine wheather the key holder is the home's owner or a thief.

If you replace a simple lock with an iris scanner, you can both authorize and authenticate the user at the same time.

An iris scanner first determines the user (authentication), and, second, determines permissions (authorization) to allow or deny the user access to the home.

Authentication sample

Let's create a new ASP.NET Core 2.0 web project and see the flow:

 An example project can be found at: `https://github.com/polatengin/B05277/tree/master/Chapter17/0-AuthenticationSample`.

1. First, open Terminal / Command Prompt, and navigate to the folder we want to create the project in. You can find the following project on GitHub (`https://github.com/polatengin/B05277`):

```
dotnet new web -n AuthenticationSample
dotnet restore
```

2. Now we can open the `AuthenticationSample` folder in Visual Studio Code and replace the `app.Run()` method's body with the following code:

```
var list = new[] {
    new { Id=1, Title="Istanbul" },
    new { Id=2, Title="New York" },
    new { Id=3, Title="Madrid" },
    new { Id=4, Title="Rome" },
    new { Id=5, Title="Vienna" },
};
var json = JsonConvert.SerializeObject(list);

context.Response.ContentType = "text/json";
await context.Response.WriteAsync(json);
```

3. We can run the following command in the Terminal / Command Prompt to compile and run the project:

```
dotnet run
```

4. Now we can navigate to `http://localhost:5000` in a browser and see the JSON output of the list variables:

```
✕  Headers │ Preview │ Response  Timing
▼[{Id: 1, Title: "Istanbul"}, {Id: 2, Title: "New York"}, {Id: 3, Title: "Madrid"},…]
  ▼0: {Id: 1, Title: "Istanbul"}
     Id: 1
     Title: "Istanbul"
  ▼1: {Id: 2, Title: "New York"}
     Id: 2
     Title: "New York"
  ▼2: {Id: 3, Title: "Madrid"}
     Id: 3
     Title: "Madrid"
  ▼3: {Id: 4, Title: "Rome"}
     Id: 4
     Title: "Rome"
  ▼4: {Id: 5, Title: "Vienna"}
     Id: 5
     Title: "Vienna"
```

Up to this point, everything went well. But other users can call this endpoint. What if I want to bar unauthorized users?

Authentication in ASP.NET, using cookie authentication

The cookie authentication mechanism sends a secure cookie with authorization info. Every request made from a client to a server contains that secure cookie, and the server-side application can identify the user from the secure cookie.

An example project can be found at: `https://github.com/polatengin/B05277/tree/master/Chapter17/1-CookieAuthenticationSample`.

Getting ready

To work through this example, you need to create a simple ASP.NET Core 2.0 project and add some libraries in it.

How to do it...

We'll create a new ASP.NET Core Web project and add the required libraries to use cookies to hold authenticated user information in it:

1. Let's create a new ASP.NET Core web project and configure it using cookie authentication:

```
dotnet new web -n CookieAuthenticationSample
dotnet add package Microsoft.AspNetCore.Authentication.Cookies
dotnet restore
```

2. Now we need to add the following line in the `Startup.cs` file before the `app.UseMvc()` or `app.UseMvcWithDefaultRoute()` lines in the `Configure()` method:

```
app.UseAuthentication();
```

3. We also need to add the following line in `ConfigureServices()` method, before the `services.AddMvc()` line, as follows:

```
services.AddAuthentication("CookieAuthenticationScheme")
        .AddCookie("CookieAuthenticationScheme", options => {
            options.LoginPath = "/Home/Login";
        });
```

The `LoginPath` property is the redirection point where the user hasn't logged in yet.

4. If you need to return a 401 HTTP status code instead of redirection, this can be easily done by replacing the previous code with the following:

```
services.AddAuthentication("CookieAuthenticationScheme")
        .AddCookie("CookieAuthenticationScheme", options => {
            options.Events.OnRedirectToLogin = (context) => {
                context.Response.StatusCode = 401;
                return Task.CompletedTask;
            };
```

```
    });
```

5. We need a data model to hold user credentials; let's create a folder, name it
   `Models`, and add a `LoginModel.cs` file to it:

```
public class LoginModel
{
    public string Email { get; set; }
    public string Password { get; set; }
}
```

6. Now we're creating a `HomeController.cs` file in the `Controllers` folder and
   adding `Login()` actions to it:

```
[HttpGet]
public IActionResult Login()
{
    return View();
}

[HttpPost]
public async Task<IActionResult> Login(LoginModel model)
{
    if(LoginUser(model.Email, model.Password))
    {
        var claims = new List<Claim>
        {
            new Claim(ClaimTypes.Email, model.Email)
        };

        var identity = new ClaimsIdentity(claims, "login");

        var principal = new ClaimsPrincipal(identity);
        await HttpContext.SignInAsync("CookieAuthenticationScheme",
principal);

        //Redirect user to home page after login.
        return RedirectToAction(nameof(Index));
    }

    return View();
}
```

7. Let's, add the `Login()` action for showing the `Login.cshtml` file in the `Views/Home` folder with the following HTML in it:

```
<form method="post">
    <input type="email" name="email" />
    <input type="password" name="password" />
    <input type="submit" value="Login" />
</form>
```

8. Second, the `Login()` method receives email and password field values and passes them into the following `LoginUser()` method:

```
private bool LoginUser(string email, string password)
{
    //TODO: add DB logic here
    return true;
}
```

The `LoginUser()` method is just a placeholder; you should replace it with database backend logic.

9. If the `LoginUser()` method returns true, `Login()` action creates a new `Claim` and creates a new `ClaimIdentity` using that `Claim`.

   The `HttpContext.SignInAsync()` method (which comes from the `Microsoft.AspNetCore.Authentication.Cookies` NuGet package we installed at the beginning) receives a schema name and `ClaimsPrincipal`.

10. We instantiated a new `ClaimsPrincipal` from `ClaimsIdentity`, which we created before.

It's important that we should provide the correct schema names, which we stated in the `AddAuthentication()` call in the `ConfigureServices()` method in the `Startup.cs` file.

11. After the `HttpContext.SignInAsync()` method, we can redirect the user to a secure page. Every request until the `HttpContext.SignOutAsync()` method can be made to secure pages.

12. The `HttpContext.SignOutAsync()` method clears `AuthenticationCookie` with the provided schema name and, after that, requests to secure pages will fail and redirect to the login page.

13. Now we're ready to mark some pages as secure. It's a relatively easy task; we'll just annotate actions or controllers with the `[Authorize]` class:

```
[Authorize]
public class MailboxController : Controller
{
    public IActionResult Index()
    {
        return View();
    }
}
```

How it works...

Before authentication, the `/mailbox/index` page will redirect to the login page. After authentication, the `/mailbox/index` page will work.

Basically, the app rejects every request made before authentication and redirects them to the login page.

After authentication, the browser receives an authentication cookie and accepts requests that require authentication.

Authentication using authorization servers

If someone tries to access a secure part of your web app and they haven't logged in yet, the app redirects the user to the authorization server to identify themself. Mostly, this means users enter their credentials (username, email, password, and so on.)

The Authorization server one job to do, authenticate the user with their credentials and return claims back.

 Claims are basically granted privileges lists. A user can have multiple claims to use portions of an app, such as viewing billing history, adding a bill, deleting a bill from history are different claims.

Once the authorization server validates the user with the provided credentials, it generates a token that is mapped to the user, and it either issues that token to the user or redirects the user to the app.

If a user tries to access a secure part of your web app, it'll check the token and authorize the user if the token is valid.

Some authorization servers:

- **Azure Active Directory**: https://docs.microsoft.com/en-us/azure/active-directory/active-directory-whatis
- **Auth0**: https://auth0.com
- **Google oAuth**: https://developers.google.com/identity/protocols/OAuth2ServiceAccount
- **Facebook Login**: https://developers.facebook.com/docs/facebook-login

Getting ready

To use authorization servers, we need to create a project, add NuGet packages, and create accounts in authorization server providers.

Some authorization providers need you to create a developer account.

How to do it...

Let's create a new ASP.NET Core web project and add Facebook authentication and Google authentication NuGet packages; to do this, run the following commands:

 An example project can be found at: https://github.com/polatengin/B05277/tree/master/Chapter17/2-FacebookGoogleAuthenticationSample.

```
dotnet new web -n FacebookGoogleAuthenticationSample

dotnet add package Microsoft.AspNetCore.Authentication.Facebook

dotnet add package Microsoft.AspNetCore.Authentication.Google

dotnet restore
```

Using Facebook as an authorization server

Now we need to register our project as a Facebook app in the Facebook Developer Portal (`http://developers.facebook.com`):

1. First, we should enter our Facebook credentials into the Facebook Developer Portal. Create an app using the **Add a new App** button, and fill in the following form:

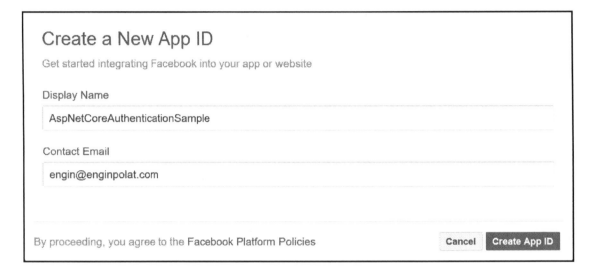

2. After creating an app, we should see the dashboard. On the left-hand side, there is a **+ Add Product** menu; it'll show the **Recommended Products** page when it is clicked on.

3. The **Facebook Login** panel is the one we're looking for. It is responsible for adding a feature to a particular Facebook app for logging in with Facebook credentials.

4. We just need to click on the **Setup** button and tweak some settings; it's that easy:

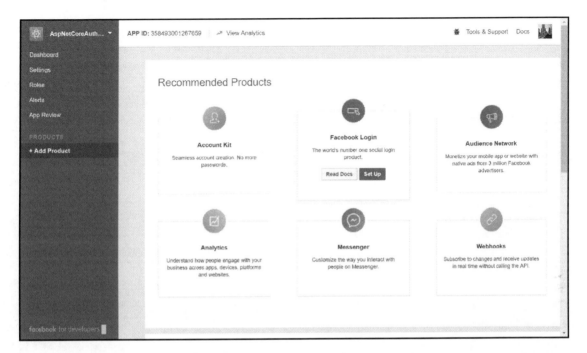

5. In the opening page, just fill in the **Valid OAuth and redirect URIs** textbox with the `http://localhost:5000/signin-facebook` URL. This URL will be our project's endpoint that handles the return value of the Facebook Login.

We should change this URL to our production endpoint before publishing our app in a production environment.

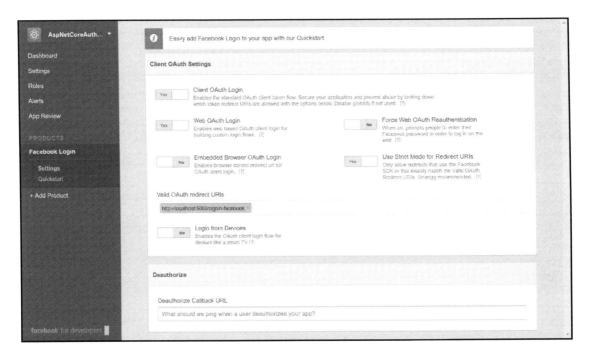

We're not changing other checkboxes or textboxes yet. But, before publishing our project to a production environment, we should revisit the preceding page.

6. After saving the **Facebook Login** page settings, we should go back to the **Dashboard** page of our Facebook application and find the **App ID** and the **App Secret** info:

7. Click on the **Show** button to see the **App Secret**.
8. Now go back to the project. Let's open the `Startup.cs` file and add some code to the `ConfigureServices()` method:

```
public void ConfigureServices(IServiceCollection services)
{
    services.AddDbContext<ApplicationDbContext>(options =>
options.UseSqlServer("Integrated Security=SSPI;Persist Security
Info=False;Initial Catalog=FacebookGoogleAuthenticationSample;Data
Source=."));

    services.AddIdentity<ApplicationUser, IdentityRole>()
            .AddEntityFrameworkStores<ApplicationDbContext>()
            .AddDefaultTokenProviders();

    services.AddAuthentication(
            CookieAuthenticationDefaults.AuthenticationScheme)
            .AddCookie(o => o.LoginPath = new
PathString("/home/login"))
            .AddFacebook(facebook =>
            {
                facebook.AppId = "208906605857885";
                facebook.AppSecret = "90e620f09fbadfaa01f74e2bc3";
            });

    services.AddMvc();
}
```

9. You should change the Facebook **App ID** and the Facebook **App Secret** to your own **App ID** and **App Secret** to your own.

Here are a few important pointers from the code block that was previously provided:

- The first line of the code block configures the connection string to reach the database server.
- The second line is important, and it configures the Identity User class and the `DbContext`.
- The third line is the most important setting in this method. It adjusts CookieAuthentication settings, Facebook AppID, and Facebook AppSecret settings.

 Identity is enabled for the application by calling `UseAuthentication` in the `Configure` method and `AddIdentity` and `AddAuthentication` in the `ConfigureServices` method.

10. In the same file (`Startup.cs`) we should also change the `Configure()` method:

```
public void Configure(IApplicationBuilder app, IHostingEnvironment
env)
{
    if (env.IsDevelopment())
    {
        app.UseDeveloperExceptionPage();
    }

    app.UseAuthentication();

    app.UseMvc((routes) =>
    {
        routes.MapRoute("SigninFacebook", "signin-facebook", new {
controller = "Home", action = "FacebookOK" });
        routes.MapRoute("Default",
"{controller=Home}/{action=Index}");
    });
}
```

Now we have a strong baseline, we can continue with the following:

11. Let's create `Models`, `Views`, and `Controllers` folders, and a `Home` folder in the `Views` folder:

12. We need to create an `ApplicationUser.cs` file in the `Models` folder:

    ```
    using Microsoft.AspNetCore.Identity;

    public class ApplicationUser : IdentityUser
    {
    }
    ```

13. We didn't add custom fields to store in the database. Create the `ApplicationDbContext.cs` file in the `Models` folder too:

    ```
    using Microsoft.AspNetCore.Identity.EntityFrameworkCore;
    using Microsoft.EntityFrameworkCore;

    public class ApplicationDbContext :
    IdentityDbContext<ApplicationUser>
    {
        public
    ApplicationDbContext(DbContextOptions<ApplicationDbContext>
    options) : base(options)
        {
        }
    }
    ```

14. Let's create a `HomeController.cs` file in the `Controllers` folder and add a constructor to it:

    ```
    private readonly SignInManager<ApplicationUser> _signInManager;

    public HomeController(SignInManager<ApplicationUser> signInManager)
    => this._signInManager = signInManager;
    ```

15. With the `_signinManager` variable, we can log users in and out from Facebook. First, return Index View from `Index()` action:

    ```
    public IActionResult Index() => View();
    ```

16. We need an `Index.cshtml` file in the `Views/Home` folder, and it's a relatively easy task:

```
<a href="/home/facebook">Facebook Login</a>
```

17. In the `HomeController.cs` file, add the `Facebook()` action as follows:

```
public IActionResult Facebook()
{
  var properties =
  _signInManager.ConfigureExternalAuthenticationProperties
  ("Facebook", "/Home/FacebookOK");
  return Challenge(properties, "Facebook");
}
```

18. We use the `_signInManager` variable to handle the Facebook `Authentication` process. After **Facebook Login**, the flow will continue with the `FacebookOK()` action:

```
public async Task<IActionResult> FacebookOK()
{
  var info = await
  _signInManager.GetExternalLoginInfoAsync();
  //info.Principal
  //structure that holds Claims, provided by Facebook
  //it includes, Facebook Unique Identifier, Facebook
  Email, Facebook Name, etc.

  //info.ProviderKey
  //Facebook Unique Identifier for logged in user

  return RedirectToAction(nameof(Index));
}
```

19. We use the `_signInManager` variable to get extra info, which the Facebook `Authentication` process will provide us, and then redirect the user to the `Index()` action/page.

20. After this redirection, the user can freely navigate through the app, especially actions/controllers that are marked with the [Authorize] attribute, which they could not navigate before:

```
using Microsoft.AspNetCore.Authorization;
using Microsoft.AspNetCore.Mvc;

[Authorize]
public class MailboxController : Controller
{
    public IActionResult Index() => View();
}
```

Now we have pages open to anonymous users, and pages secured by the Facebook Login mechanism, which open only for logged-in users.

Using Google as an authorization server

Now it's Google authentication time:

1. Let's navigate to the Google Developer Console (https://console.developers.google.com) and log in with Google credentials:

2. After logging into the Google Developer Console, we need to create a project by clicking on the **Create** button and filling in the following form:

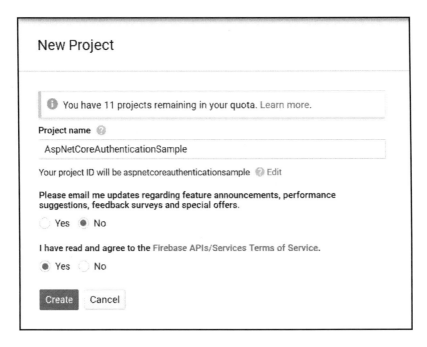

3. When we create our project in the Google Developer Console, it redirects us to the project dashboard immediately.
4. We should click on the **Enable APIs and Services** button, then select the **Google+ API** from the list:

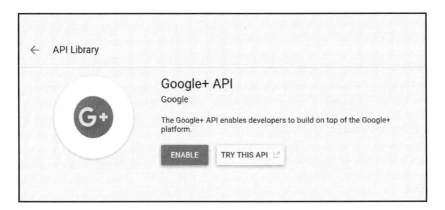

5. With the **Google+ API**, we can enable Google authentication for our projects. Just click on the **Enable** button.

6. When Google finishes enabling the **Google+ API** for our project, it navigates to the **Google+ API** dashboard.

7. We should click on the **Create Credentials** button and fill in the following form:

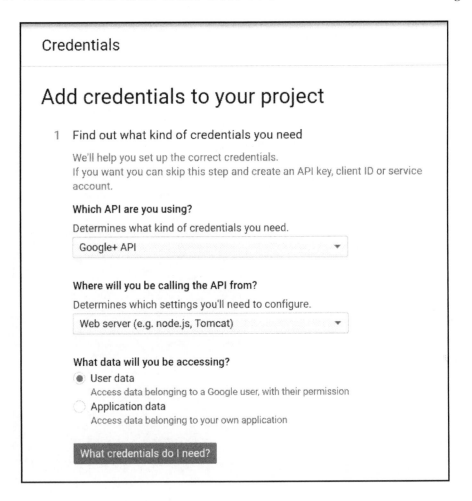

8. When we click on the **What credentials do I need?** button, the Google Developer Console asks the following:

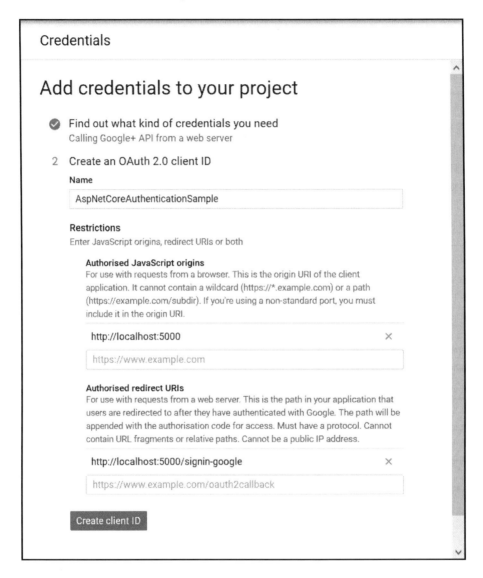

We should change this URL to our production endpoint before publishing our app in a production environment.

There are three important pieces of information on that form:

- **Name**: We should give a meaningful name to our project
- **Authorised JavaScript origins**: We should give the root URL of our project (in this example, I gave it `http://localhost:5000`)
- **Authorised redirect URIs**: We should give an endpoint that handles the Google authentication flow (in this example, I gave it `http://localhost:5000/signin-google`)

5. Now we can click on the **Create client ID** button; after that, we can copy the **Client ID** and download the client credentials file:

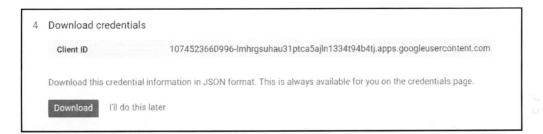

The client credentials file is a JSON format file (`client_id.json`), and it includes `client_id`, `project_id`, and `client_secret` information. We're going to need this information:

1. Let's jump back to our ASP.NET Core project and open the `Startup.cs` file.
2. Change the `ConfigureService()` method, and add the following lines right before the `.AddFacebook()` method:

```
.AddGoogle(google =>
{
    google.ClientId = "1074523660996-
lmhrgsuhau31ptca5ajln1334t94b4tj.apps.googleusercontent.com
";
    google.ClientSecret = "fW3fnRzs7DQa9WEUVbaMhCAL";
})
```

 It is important to change Google **Client Id** and Google **Client Secret** values before publishing to production values.

6. We need to add the following line to the `Configure()` method, right before the `SigninFacebook` line:

```
routes.MapRoute("SigninGoogle", "signin-google", new { controller =
"Home", action = "GoogleOK" });
```

7. Let's open `Index.cshtml` in the `Views/Home` folder and change the content, as follows:

```
<a href="/home/facebook">Facebook Login</a>
<br />
<a href="/home/google">Google Login</a>
```

By doing so, the user can log in with Facebook or Google.

8. Now open the `HomeController.cs` file, and add `Google()` action to it:

```
public IActionResult Google()
{
    var properties =
_signInManager.ConfigureExternalAuthenticationProperties("Google",
"/Home/GoogleOK");

    return Challenge(properties, "Google");
}
```

9. All we need is the `GoogleOK()` method in the `HomeController.cs` file, as follows:

```
public async Task<IActionResult> GoogleOK()
{
  var info = await
  _signInManager.GetExternalLoginInfoAsync();
  //info.Principal
  //structure that holds Claims, provided by Google
  //it includes, Google Unique Identifier, Google Email,
  Google Name, etc.
  //info.ProviderKey
  //Google Unique Identifier for logged in user
  return RedirectToAction(nameof(Index));
}
```

How it works...

Unauthorized requests will respond with the `RedirectToAction()` method and redirect it to Facebook's or Google's login method.

When the user gives permission to an app in the Facebook or Google authorization server (Login page), it carries a token to our app, and we insists that it identifies an individual.

Managing identity

Now we're ready to run our app and let users log in through Facebook login or Google login mechanisms.

Both Facebook and Google return the `ProviderKey` property to identify an individual user. We can hold that info in the database and relate it to another table (such as ShoppingCart, PurchaseHistory, and so on.) This way, we can let Facebook and Google manage users, but we can still reference that user in our database system.

The beauty of ASP.NET Core Identity is that we can easily plug another system into it (such as Linkedin, Microsoft Live, GitHub, Auth0, and so on). It's only adding a library and creating an app in the authorization server system. In ASP.NET Core, we can create an empty project and turn it into a fully fledged application with identity capabilities.

Microsoft published the `Microsoft.AspNetCore.Identity` NuGet package (`https://www.nuget.org/packages/Microsoft.AspNetCore.Identity/`) to help developers create authentication and authorization mechanisms easily.

This package is also part of the `Microsoft.AspNetCore.All` NuGet package (`https://www.nuget.org/packages/Microsoft.AspNetCore.All/`).

New ASP.NET Core web projects already include the `Microsoft.AspNetCore.All` NuGet package, and we don't need anything else to confirm identity in our projects.

 An example project can be found at `https://github.com/polatengin/B05277/tree/master/Chapter17/3-AspNetCoreIdentitySample`.

Getting ready

There is nothing special needed to get ready to manage identity in ASP.NET Core. Just create an empty project and some NuGet packages; that's it.

 It's assumed that the app can reach a SQL Server, with the required permissions.

How to do it...

Let's dive into the code:

1. First, create a new project by running the following scripts in Command Prompt / Terminal:

   ```
   dotnet new web -n AspNetCoreIdentitySample
   dotnet restore
   ```

2. Open `Startup.cs` file, and change the `ConfigureServices()` method, as follows:

   ```
   public void ConfigureServices(IServiceCollection services)
   {
       services.AddDbContext<ApplicationDbContext>(options =>
       options.UseSqlServer("Integrated Security=SSPI;Persist Security
       Info=False;Initial Catalog=AspNetCoreIdentitySample;Data
       Source=."));

       services.AddIdentity<ApplicationUser, IdentityRole>()
               .AddEntityFrameworkStores<ApplicationDbContext>()
               .AddDefaultTokenProviders();

       services.AddMvc();
   }
   ```

3. We set up the connection string and point that to our local database server with the database name, `AspNetCoreIdentitySample`.

It's not a problem if we have no database with that name,
`EntityFrameworkCore` will create it before using it the first time.

4. Also, we declared that we want to use Identity with the `ApplicationUser` class
   and `ApplicationDbContext` database connection layer.

5. Now we need to change the `Configure()` method, as follows:

```
public void Configure(IApplicationBuilder app, IHostingEnvironment
env)
{
    if (env.IsDevelopment())
    {
        app.UseDeveloperExceptionPage();
    }

    app.UseAuthentication();

    app.UseMvcWithDefaultRoute();
}
```

6. Let's create a `Models` folder and add the `ApplicationUser.cs` file to it, as
   follows:

```
using System;
using Microsoft.AspNetCore.Identity;

public class ApplicationUser : IdentityUser
{
    public string CityName { get; set; }

    public DateTime JobBeginDate { get; set; }
}
```

7. We just created a new file to develop the `ApplicationUser` class. We should
   notice that the `ApplicationUser` class should be inherited from the
   `IdentityUser` class, which comes from the
   `Microsoft.AspNetCore.Identity` namespace. The `IdentityUser` class has
   the following properties:

```
public virtual DateTimeOffset? LockoutEnd { get; set; }

public virtual bool TwoFactorEnabled { get; set; }
```

```
public virtual bool PhoneNumberConfirmed { get; set; }

public virtual string ConcurrencyStamp { get; set; }
public virtual string SecurityStamp { get; set; }

public virtual string PasswordHash { get; set; }

public virtual bool EmailConfirmed { get; set; }

public virtual string NormalizedEmail { get; set; }

public virtual string Email { get; set; }

public virtual string NormalizedUserName { get; set; }

public virtual string UserName { get; set; }

public virtual TKey Id { get; set; }

public virtual bool LockoutEnabled { get; set; }

public virtual int AccessFailedCount { get; set; }
```

8. If we need extra information about users, we can add a properties-derived class (in this example it is the `ApplicationUser` class).

9. We added `CityName` and `JobBeginDate` properties.

10. Now we need an `ApplicationDbContext.cs` file in the `Models` folder:

```
using Microsoft.AspNetCore.Identity.EntityFrameworkCore;
using Microsoft.EntityFrameworkCore;

public class ApplicationDbContext : IdentityDbContext<ApplicationUser>
{
    public ApplicationDbContext(DbContextOptions<ApplicationDbContext>
options) : base(options)
    {
    }
}
```

`EntityFrameworkCore` automatically creates a database in the target server, tables in that database, and so on.

11. Create a `HomeController.cs` file in the `Controllers` folder, and add two class-level variables and constructors to it, as follows:

```
private readonly UserManager<ApplicationUser> userManager;
private readonly SignInManager<ApplicationUser> loginManager;

public HomeController(ApplicationDbContext dc,
UserManager<ApplicationUser> userManager,
SignInManager<ApplicationUser> loginManager)
    {
        this.userManager = userManager;
        this.loginManager = loginManager;

        dc.Database.EnsureCreated();
    }
```

12. The `UserManager` and `SignInManager` classes manage the creation of users, logging in, and logging out of the system. Let's create some actions:

```
public IActionResult Index() => View();

[HttpGet]
public IActionResult Register() => View();

[HttpGet]
public IActionResult Login() => View();
```

13. Now we need a `Views/Home` folder with `Index.cshtml`, `Register.cshtml`, and `Login.cshtml` files in it:

- First, we create the `Index.cshtml` file:

```
<a href="/home/login">Login</a>
<a href="/home/register">Register</a>
<a href="/home/logout">Logout</a>
```

- Second, we create the `Register.cshtml` file:

```
<h1>Register</h1>
<form action="/home/register" method="post">
    <table>
        <tr>
            <td>UserName</td>
            <td><input type="text" name="username" /></td>
        </tr>
        <tr>
```

```
            <td>Password</td>
            <td><input type="password" name="password"
/></td>
        </tr>
        <tr>
            <td>Confirm Password</td>
            <td><input type="password"
name="confirmPassword" /></td>
        </tr>
        <tr>
            <td>Email</td>
            <td><input type="email" name="email" /></td>
        </tr>
        <tr>
            <td>Phone Number</td>
            <td><input type="tel" name="phoneNumber"
/></td>
        </tr>
        <tr>
            <td>City Name</td>
            <td><input type="text" name="cityName" /></td>
        </tr>
        <tr>
            <td>Job Begin Date</td>
            <td><input type="date" name="jobBeginDate"
/></td>
        </tr>
        <tr>
            <td><input type="submit" value="Register"
/></td>
        </tr>
    </table>
</form>
```

We're getting enough data from the client to create a user.

 Notice, we're getting `Email`, `PhoneNumber`, `CityName`, `JobBeginDate`

- Third, we create the `Login.cshtml` file:

```
<h1>Login</h1>
<form action="/home/login" method="post">
    <table>
        <tr>
            <td>UserName</td>
            <td><input type="text" name="username" /></td>
        </tr>
        <tr>
            <td>Password</td>
            <td><input type="password" name="password"
/></td>
        </tr>
        <tr>
            <td>Remember Me</td>
            <td><input type="checkbox" name="rememberme"
/></td>
        </tr>
        <tr>
            <td><input type="submit" value="Login" /></td>
        </tr>
    </table>
</form>
```

14. Let's go back to `HomeController.cs` and add a `Login()` action, as follows:

```
[HttpPost]
public async Task<IActionResult> Login(string username, string
password, string rememberme)
{
  var result = await
  this.loginManager.PasswordSignInAsync(username,
  password, rememberme == "on", false);

  return RedirectToAction(nameof(Index));
}
```

We're using a `loginManager` variable to log in a user by calling the
`PasswordSignInAsync()` method. If we are passing `false` as a third parameter,
the user must log in every time they open a new browser. If we are passing `true`
as a third parameter, ASP.NET Core Identity generates a cookie, passes it to the
client, and remembers them when they open a new browser:

15. Logging out is a relatively easier task; use the following code:

```
public IActionResult Logout()
{
    this.loginManager.SignOutAsync();

    return RedirectToAction(nameof(Index));
}
```

We just used the `loginManager` variable and called the `SignOutAsync()` method to successfully log out of the application.

 The `PasswordSignInAsync()` method creates a cookie if the third parameter is true. The `SignOutAsync()` method deletes it, if it exists.

16. The last method is the `Register` method:

```
[HttpPost]
public async Task<IActionResult> Register(string username, string
email, string password, string phoneNumber, string cityName,
DateTime jobBeginDate)
{
    var user = new ApplicationUser()
    {
        UserName = username,
        Email = email,
        PhoneNumber = phoneNumber,
        CityName = cityName,
        JobBeginDate = jobBeginDate
    };

    var result = await this.userManager.CreateAsync(user,
password);

    //TODO: check for
    //result.Succeeded and result.Errors

    return RedirectToAction(nameof(Index));
}
```

The `Register()` method uses the `userManager` variable to create a user. If we provide a password with a second parameter, the user created will have that password. Otherwise, the created user has no password.

In the previous code example, we have the result variable. The `Result` variable either has the `Succeeded` or the `Errors` properties filled. We should iterate the `Errors` property to list errors, such as too short a password, not enough complexity, username or email not provide, and so on.

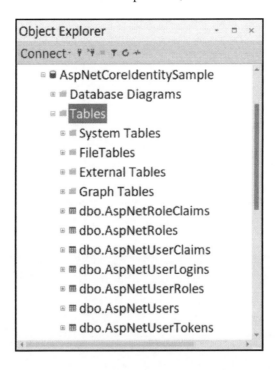

As you can see, the database and all the required tables are automatically created the first time.

Login Register Logout

17. We can click the **Register** link and fill out the form, as follows:

The `AspNetUsers` table in the database will have a new row:

18. Now we can log in and use the entire app:

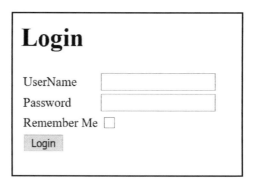

How it works...

Deploy the app to the server and run it. The user can create an account and log in using it. All data is persisted in the SQL Server.

ASP.NET Core Identity makes it very easy to add authentication and authorization mechanisms to our web application using a SQL Server database.

The ASP.NET Core Identity library can be added to the project using the **NuGet Package Manager**.

Basically, the ASP.NET Core Identity library adds different classes to manage users and their permissions for the application. It also includes a mechanism for generating tables to hold a user and related information in the database.

Securing data with Hashing

.NET Core now uses the cryptography API for the following operating systems:

- Apple Security Framework on macOS
- OpenSSL on Linux
- **Cryptography API: Next Generation (CNG)** on Windows

There are two kinds of mechanisms for securing data: hashing and encrypting.

Hashing is a one-way mechanism, and there is no way to return hashed data to its original state.

On the other hand, encryption is a two-way mechanism, and you can return encrypted data to its original state through decryption.

There are a lot of algorithms you can use with ASP.NET Core, such as Hash, SHA256, SHA512, AES, RSA, MD5, and so on. For more information, visit: `https://www.nuget.org/packages/System.Security.Cryptography.Algorithms/`.

 An example project can be found at: `https://github.com/polatengin/B05277/tree/master/Chapter17/4-HashingData`.

Getting ready

There is nothing special to get ready for hashing in ASP.NET Core. Just create an empty project and some NuGet packages; that's it.

How to do it...

In this example, we will use SHA512:

1. Let's create a new project, as follows:

```
dotnet new console -n HashingData
dotnet restore
```

2. Let's open `Program.cs` and change it, as follows:

```
static void Main(string[] args)
{
    var hashed = CalculateHash("Hello World!");
    Console.WriteLine(hashed);

    Console.ReadKey();
}

static string CalculateHash(string input)
{
    using (var algorithm = SHA512.Create())
    {
        var b =
algorithm.ComputeHash(Encoding.UTF8.GetBytes(input));

        return BitConverter.ToString(b).Replace("-", "").ToLower();
    }
}
```

3. We can run this application and see the hashed output:

 There is no way to unhash or restore original data from a hashed version.

How it works...

We can use the `CalculateHash()` method and get a hashed value of the provided text. This is a one-way process, so we can't get the provided text after hashing it.

ASP.NET Core has built-in classes to hash the given data for different algorithms. Hashing is a one-way operation, and the given data cannot be retrived after it has been hashed.

Securing data with Encryption

There are also encryption algorithms in ASP.NET Core, such as AES, Des, 3Des (TripleDes), Rijndael, RC2, and so on. For more information, visit https://docs.microsoft.com/en-us/dotnet/standard/security/cryptography-model.

 An example project can be found at https://github.com/polatengin/B05277/tree/master/Chapter17/5-EncryptDecryptData.

Getting ready

There is nothing special to get ready for encryption in ASP.NET Core. Just create an empty project and some NuGet packages; that's it.

How to do it...

1. Let's create a new project and dive into the code to better understand encryption and decryption in ASP.NET Core:

```
dotnet new console -n EncryptDecryptData
dotnet restore
```

2. Now open the `Program.cs` file, and add the `Encrypt()` and `Decrypt()` methods, as follows:

```
static string Encrypt(string text, string key)
{
    var _key = Encoding.UTF8.GetBytes(key);

    using (var aes = AES.Create())
    {
        using (var encryptor = aes.CreateEncryptor(_key, aes.IV))
        {
            using (var ms = new MemoryStream())
            {
                using (var cs = new CryptoStream(ms, encryptor,
CryptoStreamMode.Write))
                {
                    using (var sw = new StreamWriter(cs))
                    {
                        sw.Write(text);
                    }
                }

                var iv = aes.IV;

                var encrypted = ms.ToArray();

                var result = new byte[iv.Length +
encrypted.Length];

                Buffer.BlockCopy(iv, 0, result, 0, iv.Length);
                Buffer.BlockCopy(encrypted, 0, result, iv.Length,
```

```
encrypted.Length);

                return Convert.ToBase64String(result);
            }
        }
    }
}

static string Decrypt(string encrypted, string key)
{
    var b = Convert.FromBase64String(encrypted);

    var iv = new byte[16];
    var cipher = new byte[16];

    Buffer.BlockCopy(b, 0, iv, 0, iv.Length);
    Buffer.BlockCopy(b, iv.Length, cipher, 0, iv.Length);

    var _key = Encoding.UTF8.GetBytes(key);

    using (var aes = AES.Create())
    {
        using (var decryptor = aes.CreateDecryptor(_key, iv))
        {
            var result = string.Empty;
            using (var ms = new MemoryStream(cipher))
            {
                using (var cs = new CryptoStream(ms, decryptor,
CryptoStreamMode.Read))
                {
                    using (var sr = new StreamReader(cs))
                    {
                        result = sr.ReadToEnd();
                    }
                }
            }

            return result;
        }
    }
}
```

In this example, we used AES encryptor. The `Ecnrypt()` and `Decrypt()` methods get the encryptor key through the method parameters, encrypt or decrypt the provided string, and return the encrypted/decrypted version.

3. All we need to do is change the `Main()` method, as follows:

```
static void Main(string[] args)
{
    var key = Guid.NewGuid().ToString("N");

    var original = "Hello World!";
    var encrypted = Encrypt(original, key);
    var decrypted = Decrypt(encrypted, key);

    Console.WriteLine(original);
    Console.WriteLine(encrypted);
    Console.WriteLine(decrypted);

    Console.ReadKey();
}
```

4. When we run the application, we can see the original, encrypted, and decrypted values as follows:

How it works...

We can use the `Encrypt()` method and get the encrypted value of the provided text. This is a two-way process, so we can get a decrypted value of encrypted text.

ASP.NET Core also has built-in classes to encrypt and decrypt the given data, with different algorithms. Encryption is a two-way operation, and the provided data can be calculated after it has been encrypted using decryption operations with the same algorithm as the encryption.

18
Frontend Development

In this chapter, we will cover the following topics:

- Using Bootstrap
- Writing clean JavaScript
- RequireJS
- Typescript
- Writing and executing unit tests in JavaScript
- Debugging JavaScript code in browsers

All examples in this chapter can be found at the following Github repo:
`https://github.com/polatengin/B05277/tree/master/Chapter18`.

Using Bootstrap

Bootstrap is a matured, frontend framework that helps developers to build responsive (mobile-friendly) websites.

What is Responsive Web Design?

According to W3Schools (World Wide Web Schools: `https://www.w3schools.com/bootstrap/bootstrap_get_started.asp`), responsive web design is about creating websites that automatically adjust themselves to look good on all devices, from small phones to large desktops.

Getting ready

Bootstrap can be downloaded from `https://www.w3schools.com/bootstrap/bootstrap_get_started.asp` or added to a web page from Bootstrap CDN.

Some of the Bootstrap CSS classes require JavaScript code to work on websites.

The most recent version of Bootstrap at the time of writing is Beta.2.

 The example project can be found at `https://github.com/polatengin/B05277/tree/master/Chapter18/0-GettingStartedBootstrap`.

You should add these lines into the head section of the web page in order to use Bootstrap:

```
<script src="https://code.jquery.com/jquery-3.2.1.slim.min.js"
integrity="sha384-
KJ3o2DKtIkvYIK3UENzmM7KCkRr/rE9/Qpg6aAZGJwFDMVNA/GpGFF93hXpG5KkN"
crossorigin="anonymous"></script>
<script
src="https://cdnjs.cloudflare.com/ajax/libs/popper.js/1.12.3/umd/popper.min
.js" integrity="sha384-
vFJXuSJphROIrBnz7yo7oB41mKfc8JzQZiCq4NCceLEaO4IHwicKwpJf9c9IpFgh"
crossorigin="anonymous"></script>

<link rel="stylesheet"
href="https://maxcdn.bootstrapcdn.com/bootstrap/4.0.0-beta.2/css/bootstrap.
min.css" integrity="sha384-
PsH8R72JQ3SOdhVi3uxftmaW6Vc51MKb0q5P2rRUpPvrszuE4W1povHYgTpBfshb"
crossorigin="anonymous">
<script
src="https://maxcdn.bootstrapcdn.com/bootstrap/4.0.0-beta.2/js/bootstrap.mi
n.js" integrity="sha384-
alpBpkh1PFOepccYVYDB4do5UnbKysX5WZXm3XxPqe5iKTfUKjNkCk9SaVuEZflJ"
crossorigin="anonymous"></script>
```

Advantages of using CDN

CDN servers serve only static files and cache them on the client side for a long time period, such as one year.

By doing that, if any user visits that web page, they download the required static files from CDN and cache them.

After that visit, the same user can visit other websites and web pages, and because of the required files cached earlier, the web page uses cached versions of files.

Just processing the files is much faster than downloading the files.

Also, most CDNs have a lot of static file servers around the world and serve required static files from the nearest server to a user.

How to do it...

We'll develop a web page that has responsive capabilities and is adaptive to screen real estate:

1. Let's create a new web page to achieve the following image:

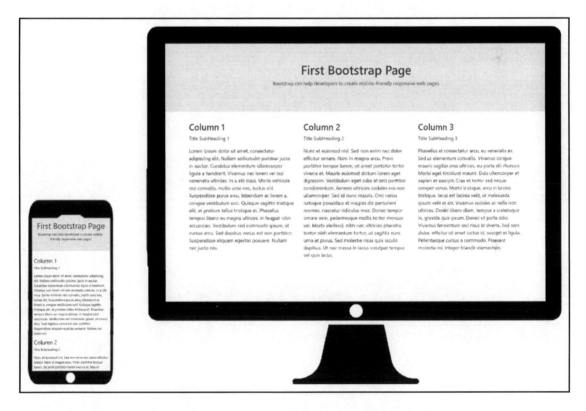

Notice that we'll have a responsive page that displays its content better at different screen sizes.

2. We should create a barebone HTML5 file by creating a new HTML file and naming it `index.html`, as follows:

```
<!DOCTYPE html>
<html lang="en">
<head>
    <meta charset="UTF-8">
    <meta name="viewport" content="width=device-width, initial-
scale=1.0">
    <title>HTML5 Bootstrap</title>
</head>
<body>
</body>
</html>
```

3. After this, we have to add bootstrap files from Bootstrap CDN as follows:

```
<!DOCTYPE html>
<html lang="en">
<head>
    <meta charset="UTF-8">
    <meta name="viewport" content="width=device-width, initial-
scale=1.0">
    <title>HTML5 Bootstrap</title>

    <script src="https://code.jquery.com/jquery-3.2.1.slim.min.js"
integrity="sha384-
KJ3o2DKtIkvYIK3UENzmM7KCkRr/rE9/Qpg6aAZGJwFDMVNA/GpGFF93hXpG5KkN"
crossorigin="anonymous"></script>
    <script
src="https://cdnjs.cloudflare.com/ajax/libs/popper.js/1.12.3/umd/po
pper.min.js" integrity="sha384-
vFJXuSJphROIrBnz7yo7oB41mKfc8JzQZiCq4NCceLEaO4IHwicKwpJf9c9IpFgh"
crossorigin="anonymous"></script>

    <script
src="https://maxcdn.bootstrapcdn.com/bootstrap/4.0.0-beta.2/js/boot
strap.min.js" integrity="sha384-
alpBpkh1PFOepccYVYDB4do5UnbKysX5WZXm3XxPqe5iKTfUKjNkCk9SaVuEZflJ"
crossorigin="anonymous"></script>
    <link rel="stylesheet"
href="https://maxcdn.bootstrapcdn.com/bootstrap/4.0.0-beta.2/css/bo
otstrap.min.css" integrity="sha384-
PsH8R72JQ3SOdhVi3uxftmaW6Vc51MKb0q5P2rRUpPvrszuE4W1povHYgTpBfshb"
crossorigin="anonymous">
</head>
<body>
```

```
</body>
</html>
```

We're ready to develop our first web page using Bootstrap CSS classes.

4. Let's create a `div` element and add a `container` class to it.

```
<div class="container">
</div>
```

 When using Bootstrap, we generally start from container elements because some of the Bootstrap classes require a parent container element. There are two container classes we can choose: the `.container` class provides a responsive fixed width container, and the `.container-fluid` class provides a full width container, spanning the entire width of the viewport.

5. Now we can create a grid system in our page by adding `div` with the `.row` class in it, as follows:

```
<div class="row">
</div>
```

 Bootstrap has a 12-column grid system. The row class creates a horizontal space and we can place 12 columns in it. But, there are some rules about using the row class in Bootstrap, such as, rows must be placed in container classes.

6. We can place up to 12 columns in a row. In this example, we want to put three columns in it. But there is a requirement: we want to place three columns side-by-side on big screens, but if the viewer has a small screen, three columns must be placed vertically.

7. Bootstrap has a set of column classes, such as col, col-2, col-3, col-4, col-5, col-6, and so on. We can use them to sum up to 12 and place them into a row class.

If we want to split a row into two, and if we want the first half to be twice the size of the second half, we can write the following code:

```
<div class="row">
  <div class="col-8"></div>
  <div class="col-4"></div>
</div>
```

Or, we can split a row into four, equal width columns by writing the following:

```
<div class="row">
  <div class="col-3"></div>
  <div class="col-3"></div>
  <div class="col-3"></div>
  <div class="col-3"></div>
</div>
```

We can mix and match the columns to sum up to 12 and achieve the desired layout.

In this example, we want three columns, but the requirement states that on big screens, the columns must be horizontal, and on small screens the columns must be vertical.

Bootstrap covers that scenario as well. The Bootstrap grid system has some media queries and a certain set of column classes as follows:

	Extra small	Small	Medium	Large	Extra large
	<576px	≥576px	≥768px	≥992px	≥1200px
Max container width	None (auto)	540px	720px	960px	1140px
Class prefix	`.col-`	`.col-sm-`	`.col-md-`	`.col-lg-`	`.col-xl-`
# of columns	12				
Gutter width	30px (15px on each side of a column)				

8. So, we can add the following code in the `div` element which has the `.row` class, and achieve the desired requirement:

```
<div class="col-sm-4">
  <h3>Column 1</h3>
  <p>Title SubHeading 1</p>
  <p>Lorem ipsum dolor sit amet...</p>
</div>
<div class="col-sm-4">
  <h3>Column 2</h3>
  <p>Title SubHeading 2</p>
  <p>Nunc et euismod nisl...</p>
</div>
<div class="col-sm-4">
  <h3>Column 3</h3>
  <p>Title SubHeading 3</p>
```

```
    <p>Phasellus et consectetur arcu...</p>
</div>
```

Now, on big screens, the columns will be placed horizontally, and on small screens, the columns will be placed vertically.

How it works...

Bootstrap has evolved over time, along with the web, and is now a mature framework.

By using it from CDN, we can lift the burden of hosting it on our servers. There are thousands of other websites using it over CDN, so we can rely on the fact that users have probably visited some other websites before using ours. Our website can use the pre-cached bootstrap files from disk, so our website can be drawn to the users screens quicker.

Bootstrap has built-in responsiveness, so every out-of-the-box class helps us develop a page that fits on the screen, no matter the size.

Writing clean JavaScript

JavaScript is a powerful language. We can create games, spreadsheet apps, mail clients, and so on, with JavaScript. However, developing applications using JavaScript ends up messy if you aren't careful.

It's a good thing that we are using a JavaScript framework/library to clean up redundant and messy code.

Lodash is one of the most used JavaScript libraries, and it makes it easier to develop JavaScript code, such as walking through arrays, working on objects and their properties, and so on.

According to `https://lodash.com/`, Lodash makes JavaScript easier by taking the hassle out of working with arrays, numbers, objects, strings, and so on. Lodash's modular methods are great for:

Iterating arrays, objects, and strings
Manipulating and testing values
Creating composite functions

Getting ready

First of all, we need to add `lodash.js` to our web page. We can download `lodash.js` from `https://lodash.com/` or add it from CDN (like we did when using Bootstrap).

 It is considered a best practice to use minified versions of CSS and JS files. Almost every framework provides both un-minified and minified versions of CSS and JS files.

 The un-minified versions are suitable for development environments, and minified versions are suitable for production environments.

Let's create a HTML5 file and add `lodash.js` from CDN, as follows:

```
<!DOCTYPE html>
<html>
<head lang="en">
    <meta charset="UTF-8">
    <title>Lodash demo</title>
    <script
src="https://cdn.jsdelivr.net/npm/lodash@4.17.4/lodash.min.js"></script>
</head>
<body>
</body>
</html>
```

 The example project can be found at: `https://github.com/polatengin/B05277/tree/master/Chapter18/1-GettingStartedLodash`.

How to do it...

Now we can add a script tag in the body element and use lodash functions:

```
<script>
var teams = ["Barcelona", "Real Madrid", "Manchester United", "Borissia
Dortmund", "Chelsea",  "Arsenal", "Bayern Munich", "Milan", "Juventus",
"Galatasaray"];
        console.log("First element in teams: ", _.first(teams));
        console.log("Last element in teams: ", _.last(teams));
```

```
var books = [
            { title: "Matrix", price: 40 },
            { title: "Lord of the Rings", price: 30 },
            { title: "Harry Potter", price: 30 },
            { title: "White Fang", price: 5 },
            { title: "Godfather", price: 25 }
        ];

console.log("Name of the cheapest book is ",
_.chain(books).sortBy('price').first().value().title)

console.log("Available chars:", _.times(26, function(x) { return
String.fromCharCode(65+x); }));
</script>
```

In this example, we'll use `first()`, `last()`, `chain()`, `sortBy()`, `value()`, and `times()` functions:

- As the names imply, the `first()` and `last()` methods select the first and last items in a given array
- The `sortBy()` method sorts an array by a given property
- The `times()` method executes a function by the number of times
- The `chain()` method takes an object and turns it into a `lodash` object, which enables other `lodash` method calls to that object
- The `value()` method returns an underlying object that the lodash method wraps

The output of this code is as follows:

Some of the most used `lodash` methods are:

- The `cloneDeep()` method, which creates a deep cloned version of a given object
- The `random()` method, which generates a random number between the given parameters
- The `sample()` method, which picks a given amount of random items from a given array

- The `forEach()` method, which executes a given function for every item in an array
- The `flattenDeep()` method, which generates a one-level deep array from a given array with more levels
- The `filter()` method, which returns an array after the given selector is applied to a given array
- The `shuffle()` method, which returns a shuffled version of the given array

 More documentation can be found at `https://lodash.com/docs/`.

How it works...

Most of the `lodash` methods can be used after the underscore character (_), such as:

```
_.times()
_.first()
_.last()
```

Some of the `lodash` methods can be used after a variable, such as:

```
var chain = _.chain(arr);
var first = arr.sortBy('prop').first();
```

By using lodash, we can write cleaner and less redundant JavaScript code.

RequireJS

RequireJS is a JavaScript file and module loader. We usually use it in browser applications, but it can be used in Node.js applications as well.

The good thing about RequireJS is that it can load files and modules asynchronously. Asynchronous loading makes the web page appear on the screen faster. It basically postpones loading files to whenever they are needed.

By doing asynchronous loading, web pages start with smaller files, and fewer network calls, resulting in quicker startups.

The example project can be found at `https://github.com/polatengin/B05277/tree/master/Chapter18/2-GettingStartedRequireJs`.

If we're developing a large application and it has tens of JavaScript files, it's hard to maintain dependency and load the right file in the right place, for example, in e-commerce applications such as the ones we have; the `shoppingCart.js`, `product.js`, and `customer.js` files.

In the `main.js` file, if we're calling the `purchase()` method from the `shoppingCart.js` file, it requires a method call from the `product.js` file, and it requires calling a function from the `customer.js` file, we end up adding script files to the web page as follows:

```
<script src="customer.js"></script>
<script src="product.js"></script>
<script src="shoppingCart.js"></script>
<script src="main.js"></script>
```

However, it's easy to change the dependency from files, and we should add dependencies to JavaScript files for the web page.

RequireJS solves this problem by loading the required module and calling the `require()` method.

The `require()` method loads the required module if that module is defined in the JavaScript files of the `define()` method.

Getting ready

RequireJS must be added to the web page by CDN, or by downloading the `require.js` file from `http://requirejs.org/docs/download.html`.

In this example, we'll develop a simple to-do list app that looks as follows:

Let's create a simple HTML5 file and add Bootstrap and RequireJS from CDN as follows:

```
<!DOCTYPE html>
<html>
<head lang="en">
    <meta charset="UTF-8">
    <title>Simple ToDo app using RequireJs</title>
    <link rel="stylesheet"
href="https://maxcdn.bootstrapcdn.com/bootstrap/4.0.0-beta.2/css/bootstrap.
min.css" integrity="sha384-
PsH8R72JQ3SOdhVi3uxftmaW6Vc51MKb0q5P2rRUpPvrszuE4W1povHYgTpBfshb"
crossorigin="anonymous">
    <script data-main="scripts/main"
src="http://requirejs.org/docs/release/2.3.5/minified/require.js"></script>
</head>
<body>
</body>
</html>
```

Then, create a scripts folder and add the following JavaScript files to it:

- `main.js`
- `todo.js`

Now we can add the following HTML elements in the body tag:

```html
<div class="container">
    <div class="jumbotron p-4">
        <h1>ToDo App</h1>
    </div>
    <div class="form-group">
        <label>What to do?</label>
        <input type="text" class="form-control" placeholder="Enter what to
do..." autofocus>
    </div>
    <button type="submit" class="btn btn-primary">Add</button>
    <h1>ToDo List</h1>
    <ul class="list-group">
    </ul>
</div>
```

How to do it...

RequireJS can be added to a web page with a simple script tag, as in the previous example. The important thing about this script tag is that it must have a `data-main` attribute to point to the starting point of the JavaScript.

In this example, we determine the starting point as scripts/main, `require()` method adds the missing `.js` extension, and loads the `scripts/main.js` file.

1. First of all, we'll develop the `todo.js` file as follows:

```js
define(function () {
    var list = [];
    return {
        add: function (item) {
            list.push(item);
        },
        renderList: function() {
            var html = '';

            for (var iLoop = 0, len = list.length; iLoop < len;
iLoop++){
```

```
                html += '<li class="list-group-item">' +
list[iLoop] + '</li>';
                }

        return html;
    }
};
});
```

The `todo.js` file defines a module, and that module has a variable named `list` and returns two methods. The first method simply adds an item to the list, and the second method iterates over the list and returns the desired HTML.

2. Now, in the `main.js` file, we'll set a base config and load jQuery from CDN as follows:

```
require.config({
    "baseUrl": "scripts",
    "paths": {
      "jquery": "https://code.jquery.com/jquery-3.2.1.min"
    }
});
```

3. After `require.config({ ... })` method, we'll develop the main module as follows:

```
require(['jquery', 'todo'], function($, todo) {
    $(document).ready(function() {
        $('button').click(function() {
            todo.add($('input').val());
            $('input').val('');
            $('input').focus();
            $('ul').html(todo.renderList());
        });
    });
});
```

The first parameters of the `require()` method are dependencies, the second parameter of the `require()` method is a `callback` function, which will execute after loading dependencies by RequireJS.

We named those dependencies in the same order in the second parameter of the `require()` method.

In the `callback` function of the `require()` method, we are basically calling the corresponding methods of the `todo` module in the `todo.js` file.

How it works...

When `Require.Js` loads a script tag, it first executes a module defined in the `data-main` attribute. If that module has a `config()` method, RequireJS fetches the required files over the network.

Every `define()` method defines a new module with the same name as its filename. Every `require()` method loads the required module over the network asynchronously.

Typescript

JavaScript is around 22 years old, at the time of writing. But still, it lacks some modern software development principles, such as, OOP, strong-type, and more.

OOP usually refers to the ability of encapsulation, abstraction, polymorphism, and inheritance. JavaScript has some techniques that mimic these concepts, but not in a native way, such as interfaces, classes, access modifiers, and so on.

Typescript is a modern way to develop JavaScript applications. Typescript is a superset of JavaScript, and it means that whatever you can do in JavaScript, you can do in Typescript.

Typescript gives you static typing, classes, interfaces, access modifiers, asynchronous execution, and so on, while JavaScript doesn't have those facilities. You can develop a frontend application using Typescript, and the Typescript compiler transpiles your code, turning it into equivalent JavaScript code. After all, the browser only understands JavaScript, so all Typescript code must be converted to JavaScript before publishing to the server.

You can download the Typescript installer from `https://www.typescriptlang.org/`.

After installing the Typescript transpiler, you can create a Typescript file with the `.ts` extension instead of a JavaScript file with the `.js` extension.

The Typescript `transpiler` (`tsc`) can inspect your code, execute some rules, turn your code into the equivalent JavaScript, and save it with the `.js` file extension.

The example project can be found at `https://github.com/polatengin/B05277/tree/master/Chapter18/3-GettingStartedTypescript`.

Getting ready

Let's create a new file with the `.ts` extension, name it `main-0`, and write the following code in it:

```typescript
interface Customer {
    name: string;
    email: string;
    phone: string;
}

let customers: Array<Customer> = [];

customers.push({
    name: 'Engin Polat',
    email: 'engin@enginpolat.com',
    phone: '0123456789'
});
```

As you can see, Typescript allows us to define the interface in the code and add properties in it. Every property can have a type, and all assignments to that property must be that type. Otherwise, the Typescript `tsc` will throw an exception and will not transpile the Typescript code into JavaScript code.

Let's also write the following code and examine it:

```typescript
class Product {
    public title: string;
    public price: number;
    private updatedOn: Date;
}

let ledTV = new Product();
ledTV.title = 'Awesome LED TV with huge screen';
ledTV.price = 1000;
```

Typescript also has a `class` keyword, and it can include properties with access modifiers.

 Like many OOP programming languages, a public keyword means the member can be accessed outside the class, and a private keyword means a member can be accessed only inside the class.

If you execute the `tsc` command over this `main-0.ts` file, the Typescript transpiler turns it into equivalent JavaScript code, as follows:

```
var customers = [];
customers.push({
    name: 'Engin Polat',
    email: 'engin@enginpolat.com',
    phone: '0123456789'
});
var Product = /** @class */ (function () {
    function Product() {
    }
    return Product;
}());
var ledTV = new Product();
ledTV.title = 'Awesome LED TV with huge screen';
ledTV.price = 1000;
```

As you can see, the interface definition has been omitted by the Typescript transpiler, but all assignments are still validated before turning it into JavaScript code.

Now, we'll create a new file, name it `main-1.ts`, and write the following code in it:

```
function logProductNameUsingPromises() {
    return fetch('./data/products.json')
            .then((response: any) => {
                return response.json();
            })
            .then((product: any) => {
                console.log(`${product.title} ${product.price}`);
            })
}
```

If we execute the Typescript transpiler over this code file, it'll turn into the following JavaScript code:

```
function logProductNameUsingPromises() {
    return fetch('./data/products.json')
        .then(function (response) {
        return response.json();
    })
        .then(function (product) {
        console.log(product.title + " " + product.price);
    });
}
```

As you may have noticed, the transpiled code is almost identical. Let's add the following code in the `maint-1.ts` file:

```
async function logProductNameUsingAsyncAwait() {
    let response = await fetch('./data/products.json');
    let product = await response.json();
    console.log(`${product.title} ${product.price}`);
}
```

Typescript makes it easier to develop asynchronous code with an async-await keyword pair.

If we execute the Typescript transpiler over that code, the transpiled JavaScript code will look as follows:

```
var __awaiter = (this && this.__awaiter) || function (thisArg, _arguments,
P, generator) {
    return new (P || (P = Promise))(function (resolve, reject) {
        function fulfilled(value) { try { step(generator.next(value)); }
catch (e) { reject(e); } }
        function rejected(value) { try { step(generator["throw"](value)); }
catch (e) { reject(e); } }
        function step(result) { result.done ? resolve(result.value) : new
P(function (resolve) { resolve(result.value); }).then(fulfilled, rejected);
}
        step((generator = generator.apply(thisArg, _arguments ||
[])).next());
    });
};
var __generator = (this && this.__generator) || function (thisArg, body) {
    var _ = { label: 0, sent: function() { if (t[0] & 1) throw t[1]; return
t[1]; }, trys: [], ops: [] }, f, y, t, g;
    return g = { next: verb(0), "throw": verb(1), "return": verb(2) },
typeof Symbol === "function" && (g[Symbol.iterator] = function() { return
this; }), g;
    function verb(n) { return function (v) { return step([n, v]); }; }
    function step(op) {
        if (f) throw new TypeError("Generator is already executing.");
        while (_) try {
            if (f = 1, y && (t = y[op[0] & 2 ? "return" : op[0] ? "throw" :
"next"]) && !(t = t.call(y, op[1])).done) return t;
            if (y = 0, t) op = [0, t.value];
            switch (op[0]) {
                case 0: case 1: t = op; break;
                case 4: _.label++; return { value: op[1], done: false };
                case 5: _.label++; y = op[1]; op = [0]; continue;
                case 7: op = _.ops.pop(); _.trys.pop(); continue;
```

```
        default:
            if (!(t = _.trys, t = t.length > 0 && t[t.length - 1])
&& (op[0] === 6 || op[0] === 2)) { _ = 0; continue; }
            if (op[0] === 3 && (!t || (op[1] > t[0] && op[1] <
t[3]))) { _.label = op[1]; break; }
            if (op[0] === 6 && _.label < t[1]) { _.label = t[1]; t
= op; break; }
            if (t && _.label < t[2]) { _.label = t[2];
_.ops.push(op); break; }
            if (t[2]) _.ops.pop();
            _.trys.pop(); continue;
        }
        op = body.call(thisArg, _);
    } catch (e) { op = [6, e]; y = 0; } finally { f = t = 0; }
    if (op[0] & 5) throw op[1]; return { value: op[0] ? op[1] : void 0,
done: true };
    }
};
function logProductNameUsingAsyncAwait() {
    return __awaiter(this, void 0, void 0, function () {
        var response, product;
        return __generator(this, function (_a) {
            switch (_a.label) {
                case 0: return [4 /*yield*/,
fetch('./data/products.json')];
                case 1:
                    response = _a.sent();
                    return [4 /*yield*/, response.json()];
                case 2:
                    product = _a.sent();
                    console.log(product.title + " " + product.price);
                    return [2 /*return*/];
            }
        });
    });
}
```

It is now barely recognizable. Obviously, more code means more execution time, but cleaner code means more maintainable code.

How to do it...

In this example, we notice that we can have enums, constructors, instantiating classes, and so on. Let's create a new file, name it `chessboard-sample.ts`, and write the following code:

```typescript
enum PieceColor {
    White = 1,
    Black = 2
}

enum PieceType {
    Pawn = 1,
    Bishop = 2,
    Knight = 3,
    Rook = 4,
    Queen = 5,
    King = 6
}

interface Piece {
    type: PieceType;
    color: PieceColor;
}

class Block {
    isEven: boolean;
    row: number;
    col: number;
    piece: Piece;
    constructor(row: number, col: number) {
        this.row = row;
        this.col = col;
        this.isEven = row % 2 ? !(col % 2) : !!(col % 2);
    }
}

class Board {
    blocks: Array<Block> = [];

    placePieceOnBoard(piece: Piece, row: number, col: number) {
        this.blocks[(row * 8) + (col * 8)].piece = piece;
    }
}

let game = new Board();
for (let iLoop = 0; iLoop < 8; iLoop++) {
```

```
    for (let yLoop = 0; yLoop < 8; yLoop++) {
        game.blocks.push(new Block(iLoop, yLoop));
    }
}
game.placePieceOnBoard({ color: PieceColor.White, type: PieceType.Pawn },
1, 0);
game.placePieceOnBoard({ color: PieceColor.Black, type: PieceType.Pawn },
7, 0);
// more code... removed for brevity
```

This is not a full chess game app, but it's a good starting point.

How it works...

Typescript has two main parts; one is the Typescript language and its superset of JavaScript. It brings OOP and modern app developing paradigm support to JavaScript.

The other part of Typescript is the Typescript transpiler. The transpiler analyzes and converts Typescript code into its JavaScript equivalent.

After all, the browser can only execute JavaScript code, so Typescript code has to be converted to JavaScript.

Writing and executing unit tests in JavaScript

It's important to develop an application over time and not break functionality later. It doesn't matter if the application was developed with C#, Java, Python, or JavaScript.

There are several client-side unit testing frameworks out there, the most prominent ones being:

- Jasmine
- AVA
- Mocha
- Jest
- QUnit

Every testing framework has its ups and downs. We'll use QUnit in this chapter. QUnit was developed by jQuery developers and is used to test jQuery methods. jQuery depends on QUnit not breaking over time, when developers add new functions and break completely non-irrelevant parts of the framework.

 The example project can be found at `https://github.com/polatengin/` `B05277/tree/master/Chapter18/4-GettingStartedQUnit`.

Getting ready

It's so easy to create a basic test setup with QUnit. Let's create a HTML5 file and add several elements to it, as follows:

```html
<!DOCTYPE html>
<html>
<head>
    <meta charset="utf-8">
    <meta name="viewport" content="width=device-width" />
    <title>QUnit Unit Testing Example</title>
    <link rel="stylesheet"
href="https://code.jquery.com/qunit/qunit-2.4.1.css" />
</head>
<body>
    <div id="qunit"></div>
    <div id="qunit-fixture"></div>
    <script src="https://code.jquery.com/qunit/qunit-2.4.1.js"></script>
    <script src="app.js"></script>
    <script src="test-fixture.js"></script>
</body>
</html>
```

This is our test setup; it includes a CSS file to display the test results nicer on the screen. It also includes `test-fixture.js` and `app.js` files. The `app.js` file is our application code, which we want to run tests on. The `test-fixture.js` file is the test file we'll write.

Of course, the `app.js` file will be replaced by our production code file, but in this example, it'll be as simple as possible.

How to do it...

We'll create a basic JavaScript app, and then create some tests to make sure that our app will be functional after making some changes to it.

1. Let's create an `app.js` file and add the following code to it:

```
var App = {
    current: 0,
    increment: function(num) {
        this.current += num || 1;
    },
    decrement: function(num) {
        this.current -= num || 1;
    },
    isEven: function() {
        return this.current % 2 === 0;
    },
    isOdd: function() {
        return this.current % 2 !== 0;
    }
};
```

It simply holds a number, with several functions to manipulate and query their values.

2. Now we can create a new file, name it `test-fixture.js`, and write the following code in it:

```
QUnit.test('This is most basic test', function (assert) {
    assert.expect(1);
    assert.ok(true);
});

QUnit.test('This is another basic test', function (assert) {
    assert.ok(true, 'It works!');
});

QUnit.test('current number is zero', function (assert) {
    assert.equal(App.current, 0);
});

QUnit.test('current number is one after increment', function
(assert) {
    App.increment();
    assert.equal(App.current, 1);
```

```
});

QUnit.test('current number is zero again after decrement', function
(assert) {
    App.decrement();
    assert.equal(App.current, 0);
});

QUnit.test('current number is zero AND even', function (assert) {
    assert.equal(App.current, 0);
    assert.equal(App.isEven(), true);
});

QUnit.test('current number is odd after increment by 5', function
(assert) {
    App.increment(5);
    assert.equal(App.isOdd(), true);
});
```

The `QUnit.test()` method is our test implementation. Each `test()` method has one thing to test. The `test()` methods have two parameters:

- The first parameter is the test's name, and it'll be displayed on the test results page
- The second parameter is the test implementation

The test implementation gets an `assert` object by parameter and uses it to test a variable with the desired value through some methods.

The most used assertion methods are:

- `equal(actual, expected)`: Tests if the actual parameter value is the same as the expected parameter value.
- `deepEqual(actual, expected)`: Tests if the actual parameter value is the same as the expected parameter value. The difference from the `equal()` method is, that the `deepEqual()` method tests objects and traverses through its properties.
- `ok(state)`: Tests state parameter value if it is Boolean `true`.

If we navigate to test fixtures in the browser, we should see the following screen with all tests passed:

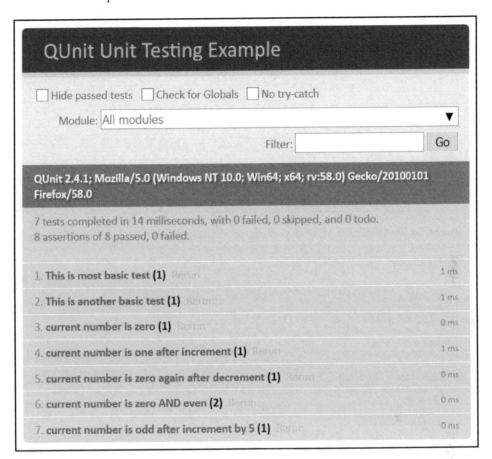

How it works...

The good part of QUnit is that it has no dependencies, works in all browsers, executes QUnit.test() methods, and shows the results on the screen.

Debugging JavaScript code in browsers

JavaScript code is executed in the browser. We (as developers) use intelligent IDEs, intelligent test frameworks, and so on to build an application easily. But sometimes, when the browser executes our intelligently-built code, something we didn't expect happens, and our code breaks.

Bugs can be syntax errors. These kinds of bugs are easy to determine. Most IDEs have some built-in tools to determine syntax errors, and even provide smart fixes.

Some bugs are logical errors. These kinds of bugs aren't easy to determine, yet most IDEs have no support to determine logical errors.

So, we need tools to debug our code in the execution environment, namely, the browser.

 The example project can be found at `https://github.com/polatengin/`
`B05277/tree/master/Chapter18/5-GettingStartedDebugging`.

Getting ready

All browsers have an inner mechanism that understands and executes JavaScript code. This mechanism is called the JavaScript Engine.

The main job of a JavaScript Engine is to take the JavaScript code that we developed, and convert it to fast, optimized code that can be interpreted by a browser.

Some of the most popular JavaScript Engines are:

- Google V8
- Mozilla Spidermonkey
- Microsoft Chakra

How to do it...

Let's examine several methods to debug code. The first one is the JavaScript `console.log()` method:

1. Create a new file, name it `index.html`, and write the following code:

```html
<!DOCTYPE html>
<html>
<head>
    <meta charset="utf-8">
    <title>Debugging</title>
</head>
<body>
    <script>
        var num1 = 5;
        var num2 = 8;

        var sum = num1 + num2;

        console.log(sum);
    </script>
</body>
</html>
```

2. After navigating to this web page, press the *F12* key on the keyboard and click on the **Console** tab. You should see **13** as follows (the screenshot is taken from the Google Chrome browser, but it's almost identical in other browsers):

If we want to see a variable's value, we can add the `console.log()` method and print a variable's value into the **Console** tab.

 Usually, the *F12* key opens the Developer Panel, which includes several debugging tools such as JavaScript Debugger, Console, DOM Elements, and so on.

Also, all modern browsers have a built-in JavaScript Debugger. In the debugger window, you can set breakpoints in the JavaScript code.

We can add breakpoints at each JavaScript line; JavaScript will stop executing on that line and let you examine variable's values.

After examining the values, you can resume the execution of code (typically with a play button), and you can also resume execution from a certain point in the code.

As you can see in the following screenshot, you can set breakpoints on some code lines, and the Watch panel lets you see and change the variables' values:

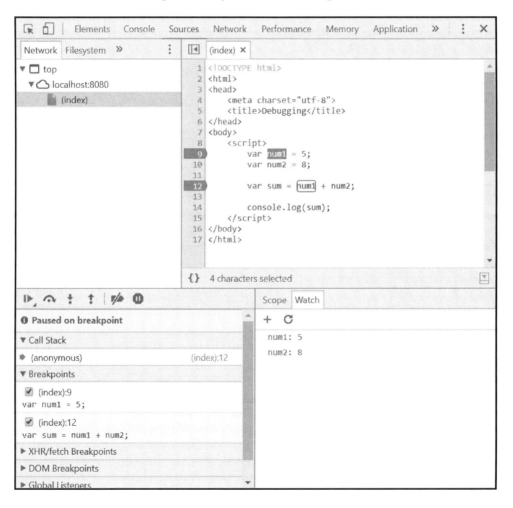

The browser stops executing the JavaScript code when it hits the breakpoint line, and displays a notification: **Paused in debugger**. We can resume execution by clicking the play button:

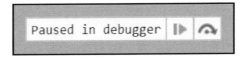

If we want to set up a breakpoint based on some variable's values or code execution path, we should use the debugger; keyword as follows:

```
if(sum > 10) {
  debugger;
}
```

How it works...

The browser fetches HTML first, then interprets it and determines the required external files (image, CSS, JavaScript files).

The browser fetches the required external files and processes each downloaded file separately.

The JavaScript files and JavaScript codes in the HTML file will be processed by a special unit in the browser, the JavaScript Engine.

The JavaScript Engine takes the JavaScript code, or JavaScript file, as an input, performs some analysis and validation on it, then compiles it into fast and optimized machine code, which executes on the CPU through the browser.

19

Deployment and Hosting

In this chapter, we will cover the following topics:

- Deployment options
- Hosting an ASP.NET Core web app on IIS
- Hosting an ASP.NET Core web app on Kestrel
- Hosting an ASP.NET Core web app on Azure
- Hosting an ASP.NET Core web app in Docker containers

 All examples in this chapter can be found at the following GitHub repo:
`https://github.com/polatengin/B05277/tree/master/Chapter19`.

Deployment options

During/after the development of a .NET Core project, we deploy it to the desired
environment, such as test, staging, pre-prod, or prod.

.NET Core applications can be deployed to an environment using the following options:

- Optimization options
  - Debug
  - Release
- Build options
  - Framework dependent
  - Self-contained

Getting ready

There are two different build modes in .NET: Debug and Release.

The .NET Core compiler can do a lot of optimization if it goes for the Release mode. The Debug mode includes a lot of extra code in the compiled assembly to make it easier for a developer when debugging the application. The Release mode is a stripped and extra optimized version of Debug mode.

Generally, we use the Debug mode for debugging the project, and the Release mode for the final build for the production environment.

Let's create a sample project by executing the following command in the project's folder and examining the differences between these options:

```
dotnet new web
```

 The example project can be found at https://github.com/polatengin/
B05277/tree/master/Chapter19/0-GettingStarted.

How to do it...

1. Create a new file named `Deploy.sh` and add the following line to it:

```
dotnet run
```

2. Run the `Deploy.sh` file in a Terminal/Command Prompt window with the following command:

```
./Deploy.sh
```

The `dotnet run` command compiles the project, starting from the `csproj` file, and includes all `.cs` files in the compilation process. After executing the `dotnet run` command, the Terminal/Command Prompt window should display the following message:

```
Hosting environment: Production
Content root path: C:/B05277/Chapter19/0/-GettingStarted
Now listening on: http://localhost:5000
Application started. Press Ctrl + C to shut down.
Application is shutting down...
```

This message shows us that the application is up and running on
`http://localhost:5000` now.

The `dotnet run` command compiles the project in **Debug** mode, but does
not create compiled artifacts/assemblies on disk.

3. If we want to create DLL files after the compilation process, we should run the
following command:

dotnet build

Usually, we want to create deployment files in the project folder, copy
them into the necessary environment, then run it in that environment.

After executing the `dotnet build` command, we should see the following
output:

```
Microsoft (R) Build Engine version 15.5.179.9764 for .NET Core
Copyright (C) Microsoft Corporation. All rights reserved.
Restore completed in 60.76 ms for C:/B05277/Chapter19/0-
GettingStarted/GettingStarted.csproj.
GettingStarted -> C:/B05277/Chapter19/0-
GettingStarted/bin/Debug/netcore/app2.0GettingStarted.dll
Build succeeded.
0 Warning(s)
0 Error(s)
Time Elapsed 00:00:01.79
```

The `dotnet build` command creates the `bin/Debug/netcoreapp2.0` folders in
the project folder and creates DLLs in it. If the project has no dependencies, only
the project DLL will be created, otherwise the project DLL and all dependency
DLLs will be created in that folder.

If nothing is declared, the `dotnet build` command compiles the project to the
hosting environment, such as Win7-x86, Win10-x64, Ubuntu.17.10-x64, OsX.10.12-
x64, and so on.

> The whole Runtime Identifier Catalog is at: `https://docs.microsoft.com/en-us/dotnet/core/rid-catalog`

You can compile the project without hosting an environment if you want, just by declaring the runtime environment.

4. You can declare the runtime environment in the `csproj` file as follows:

```
<PropertyGroup>
  <TargetFramework>netcoreapp2.0</TargetFramework>
  <RuntimeIdentifier>win7-x64</RuntimeIdentifier>
</PropertyGroup>
```

The other way to declare a runtime environment is with the `.NET Core CLI` command switch, as follows:

```
dotnet build --runtime ubuntu-x64
```

After compiling the .NET Core project to a specific environment using runtime environment identifiers, we can copy artifacts (DLLs) according to the environment, and run the application.

Also, we can compile the project in **Release** mode.

> It's a best practice that every app that is going to be deployed to a prod environment should be compiled in Release mode.

There is also a `.NET Core CLI` switch we can use to change the optimization mode to **Release**, as follows:

```
dotnet build --configuration Release
```

We can find the compiled versions in the `bin/Release/netcoreapp2.0` folder.

> If we used the runtime environment identifier, there will be another folder in the `netcoreapp2.0` folder: the runtime environments folder.

If we want, we can mix and match `.NET Core CLI Commands` as follows:

```
dotnet build --runtime ubuntu-x64 --configuration Release
```

If we can install .NET Core to a computer, it ends up in a dedicated folder, such as `C:/Program Files/dotnet` in Windows, and so on.

In that folder, there is a folder named `shared` which includes all the .NET Core libraries required to run .NET Core applications.

We can deploy compiled artifacts of our project into a .NET Core pre-installed computer and run the application in it.

This is called **Framework Dependent Deployment**.

We can deploy our project to a computer that does not have .NET Core pre-installed. All we need to do is add all the required .NET Core libraries in our project's deployment folder.

This is Self-Contained Deployment, and it can be done through the following .NET Core CLI command:

```
dotnet publish --self-contained
```

After executing the previous command, there will be a `bin/Debug{or Release}/netcoreapp2.0/publish` folder. This folder will include all the .NET Core and project-related dependency DLLs, and our project's executable file (`.exe`).

We can copy the folder to a computer that has no .NET Core installed, and we can still run the application.

`dotnet publish` can have `--runtime`, `--configuration` as well.

How it works...

The .NET Core CLI has all the required commands to build and deploy our project.

Debug and Release modes are the same in terms of executing the application, but they are very different in terms of performance and optimization.

The bundle size is very different in Framework Dependent Deployment and Self-Contained Deployment. This is because Framework Dependent Deployment deploys only the application DLLs, and not the .NET Core related DLLs, which should be deployed if you use a Self-Contained Deployment model.

The Self-Contained Deployment model can free us to pre-install the required .NET Core version on the computer.

Hosting an ASP.NET Core web app on IIS

IIS (Internet Information Server) has been Microsoft's Application Server since 1995. An application server serves static or dynamic content by a HTTP request.

IIS is a flexible and general-purpose application server that runs on Windows.

We can deploy our project to IIS basically by deploying the project in a folder and creating an IIS website pointing to that folder.

Getting ready

IIS should be installed before starting this section. IIS can be freely installed and used; we just need to enable it by opening the **Turn Windows features on or off** window in **Control Panel**:

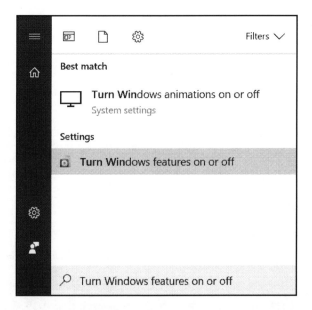

We should configure the **World Wide Web Services** and the **IIS Management Console** to have IIS on the computer:

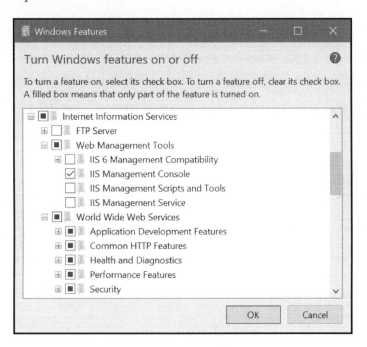

After clicking on the **OK** button, Windows will enable IIS on the computer and we can use it to serve web applications.

Also, we need to install the .NET Core Windows Server Hosting bundle (we can download the setup from `https://docs.microsoft.com/en-us/aspnet/core/publishing/iis?tabs=aspnetcore2x`):

 Example project can be found at: `https://github.com/polatengin/B05277/tree/master/Chapter19/1-HostingIIS`.

How to do it...

1. Let's create a new ASP.NET Core project and serve it in IIS:

   ```
   dotnet new web
   ```

2. Open the `Program.cs` file and look for the following code block:

   ```
   public static IWebHost BuildWebHost(string[] args) =>
   WebHost.CreateDefaultBuilder(args)
   .UseStartup<Startup>()
   .Build();
   ```

3. We should add a `UseIISIntegration()` method call in that function as follows:

```
public static IWebHost BuildWebHost(string[] args) =>
WebHost.CreateDefaultBuilder(args)
.UseStartup<Startup>()
.UseIISIntegration()
.Build();
```

 The `UseIISIntegration()` method call is important and required if we're going to deploy our project to IIS.

`UseIISIntegration()` method makes the ASP.NET Core application to use IIS as a reverse-proxy and specify which port will be listened, and so on.

When a website is created in IIS, it'll read the configuration from the `web.config` file placed in the project root folder.

4. Now we're creating a `web.config` file in the project root folder. Write the following code in it:

```
<?xml version="1.0" encoding="utf-8"?>
<configuration>
  <system.webServer>
    <handlers>
      <add name="aspNetCore" path="*" verb="*"
modules="AspNetCoreModule" resourceType="Unspecified" />
    </handlers>
    <aspNetCore processPath="%LAUNCHER_PATH%"
arguments="%LAUNCHER_ARGS%" stdoutLogEnabled="false"
stdoutLogFile=".logsstdout" forwardWindowsAuthToken="false" />
  </system.webServer>
</configuration>
```

The preceding code tells IIS to serve website content from the ASP.NET Core application. This file and its content is required for hosting the ASP.NET Core application on IIS.

5. Let's deploy the project with the following .NET Core CLI commands:

```
dotnet publish -c Release
```

This will create a publish folder, with some DLL files in it, and display the following output:

```
C:/B05277/Chapter19/1-HostingIIS> dotnet publish -c Release
Microsoft (R) Build Engine version 15.5.179.9764 for .NET Core
Copyright (C) Microsoft Corporation. All rights reserved.
Restore completed in 69.62 ms for C:B05277Chapter191-
HostingIISHostingIIS.csproj.
HostingIIS -> C:/B05277/Chapter19/1-
HostingIIS/bin/Release/netcore/app2.0HostingIIS.dll
HostingIIS -> C:/B05277/Chapter19/1-
HostingIIS/bin/Release/netcore/app2.0publish
```

6. Now we can open the IIS Management Console to create a new website:

7. First, delete the default website by right-clicking on it and clicking **Remove**.
8. To create a new website, right-click on the `Sites` folder on the left-hand side and click on **Add Website**.

9. Fill the new window by giving the website a name and selecting the compiled project folder:

 We compiled the project with the -c Release option, and it generated Release mode artifacts in the `bin/Release/netcoreapp2.0/publish` folder.

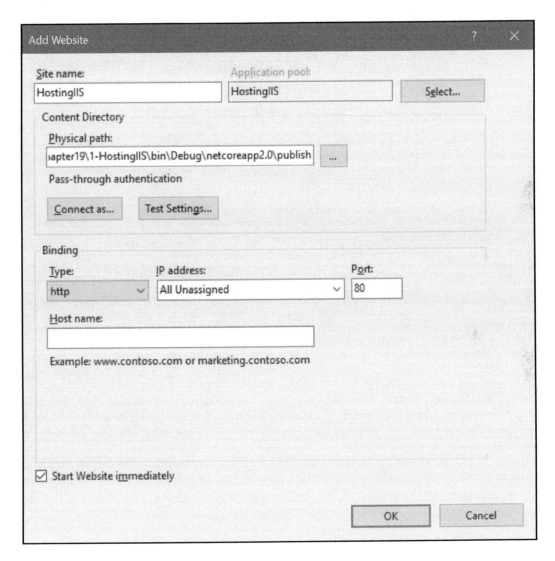

10. The next step is to change the default value of .NET Framework to No Managed Code in Application Pool Basic Setting. We should click on the `Application Pools` folder on the left-hand side of the IIS Management Console, and then double-click on the website name from the list:

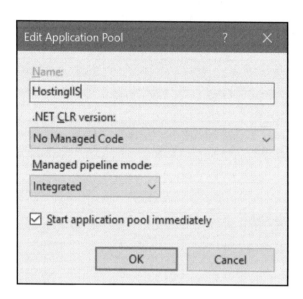

11. Now, we can launch the preferred web browser, navigate to the `http://localhost` address, and see the result as follows:

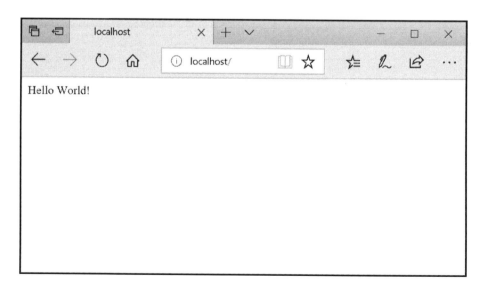

How it works...

IIS can serve ASP.NET Core applications. By default, it'll assign port 80 to the first created website; we can change this default port to whatever we want/need in the bindings settings of the website:

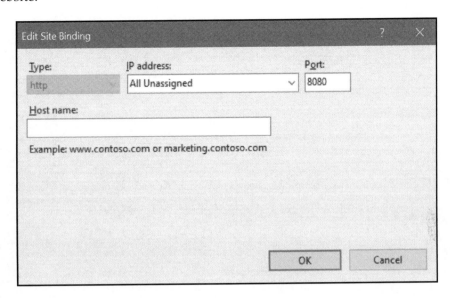

If we want, we can set the Host name in the same window. The Host name is a domain name of that website, such as microsoft.com or google.com.

 IIS uses the ASP.NET Core Windows Server Hosting bundle to serve the application. If we don't install the required bundle, IIS will display a HTTP500.19 error page instead of our application.

Hosting an ASP.NET Core web application on Kestrel

Kestrel is the latest application server developed by Microsoft. The main purpose of Kestrel development is supporting Linux and macOS operating systems.

By doing that, Microsoft ensures that all ASP.NET web developers can use Linux or macOS systems to develop and serve the application.

Kestrel is developed with cross-platforming in mind, but it is also developed with new architecture and patterns.

Getting ready

Kestrel is a dependency package of the ASP.NET Core web project, and is installed by the NuGet Package Manager. .NET Core CLI (`dotnet.exe`) will be installed when you install .NET Core on your computer.

`dotnet.exe` is the starter of any .NET Core application on any platform, such as Windows, Linux, or macOS.

Let's create a new **ASP.NET Core Web Application** and launch the application by excuting the following command:

```
dotnet new web
```

 Example project can be found at: `https://github.com/polatengin/B05277/tree/master/Chapter19/2-HostingKestrel`.

How to do it...

1. Open the `Program.cs` file and look at the `public static void Main(string[] args)` method call; this is the main entry point of any .NET Core application.

   The `Main` method calls the `BuildWebHost()` method to do some groundwork to serve the application in one of the application servers, such as IIS, Kestrel, and so on.

The `BuildWebHost()` method creates a new web host and starts its services from the `Startup` class:

By default, the `Startup` class can be found in the `Startup.cs` file; you can change it to whatever file you want.

```
using System;
using System.Collections.Generic;
using System.IO;
using System.Linq;
using System.Threading.Tasks;
using Microsoft.AspNetCore;
using Microsoft.AspNetCore.Hosting;
using Microsoft.Extensions.Configuration;
using Microsoft.Extensions.Logging;

namespace HostingKestrel
{
    public class Program
    {
        public static void Main(string[] args)
        {
            BuildWebHost(args).Run();
        }

        public static IWebHost BuildWebHost(string[] args) =>
            WebHost.CreateDefaultBuilder(args)
                .UseStartup<Startup>()
                .Build();
    }
}
```

2. We can start the project by calling .NET Core CLI commands, as follows:

dotnet run

We can also deploy and publish the project as we saw at the start of this chapter.

After starting the project, we should see the following output in the Terminal/Command Prompt window:

```
C:/B05277/Chapter19/2-HostingKestrel> dotnet run
Hosting environment: Production
Content root path: C:/B05277/Chapter19/2-HostingKestrel
Now listening on: http://localhost:5000
Application started. Press Ctrl+C to shut down.
```

The web application binds itself on port 5000 by default.

We can change the default port by adding some parameters to the `dotnet run` command:

```
In Windows Powershell Window
C:/B05277/Chapter19/2-HostingKestrel>
$env:ASPNETCORE_URLS="http://*:4000"; dotnet run
Hosting environment: Production
Content root path: C:/B05277/Chapter19/2-HostingKestrel
Now listening on: http://[::]:4000
Application started. Press Ctrl+C to shut down.

In Windows Command Window
C:/B05277/Chapter19/2-HostingKestrel> SET
ASPNETCORE_URLS=http://*:4000 && dotnet run
Hosting environment: Production
Content root path: C:/B05277/Chapter19/2-HostingKestrel
Now listening on: http://[::]:4000
Application started. Press Ctrl+C to shut down.

In Linux, MacOS Terminal Window
C:/B05277/Chapter19/2-HostingKestrel>
ASPNETCORE_URLS="http://*:4000" dotnet run
Hosting environment: Production
Content root path: C:/B05277/Chapter19/2-HostingKestrel
Now listening on: http://[::]:4000
Application started. Press Ctrl+C to shut down.
```

3. We can navigate to `http://localhost:4000` with our favorite browser and see the application is running:

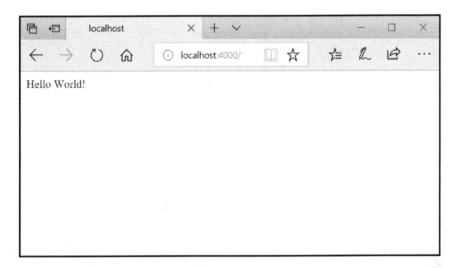

Now, we can set up the load balancer, DNS server, and so on, and bind any domain name to our server with the port number `4000` and serve the application to the world.

How it works...

`dotnet.exe` runs the application from the main entry point (public static `Main()` method in the `Program.cs` file).

First, it creates a new web host by calling the `WebHost.CreateDefaultBuilder()` and the `Build()` methods.

 The `CreateDefaultBuilder()` method applies some default parameters and method calls, such as; using Kestrel as a web server, loading `IConfiguration` from different locations, enabling IIS Integration, configuring log output to console, and so on.

The `CreateDefaultBuilder()` method includes the `UseKestrel()` method within itself. The `UseKestrel()` method is an `ExtensionMethod` provided by the `Microsoft.AspNetCore.Server.Kestrel.dll` assembly.

We can see the only NuGet dependency of the project is `Microsoft.AspNetCore.All` (`https://www.nuget.org/packages/Microsoft.AspNetCore.All`) by opening the `csproj` file.

The `Microsoft.AspNetCore.All` dependency is an empty library with some dependencies, such as; `Microsoft.AspNetCore.Server.Kestrel`, `Microsoft.AspNetCore.Session`, `Microsoft.AspNetCore.StaticFiles`, `Microsoft.EntityFrameworkCore`, `Microsoft.Extensions.Logging.Console`, and so on.

The last line of the `BuildWebHost()` method is the `Build()` method call, and it basically runs Kestrel as a web server.

Hosting an ASP.NET Core web app on Azure

Cloud providers make sure that developers can easily scale their applications.

For example, we could have developed a social network application, but we can't be sure how many resources we need.

Mostly, we'll estimate based on the collected sample usage data, educated guesses, and so on.

During the fetching resources phase, we increase the required resources in case of high demand. Of course, increasing resources also increases the cost of owning an application.

The application's usage pattern will never be a flat line, so we never need the same number of resources. The resources needed will vary on a day-to-day, or even; hour-to-hour, basis.

Cloud providers make it easy to have only the required number of resources at that point in time.

This is very economic, and makes sense when we can't estimate the usage of a startup application, for example.

Getting ready

We need an Azure subscription to host an ASP.NET Core web application. We can easily create a subscription from the following site: `http://azure.com`.

Until we bind a credit card and enable the transaction, Azure will not generate bills and runs in a free trial. The free trial mode gives us lots of Azure services for free, but not all of them.

After creating a subscription, let's log in with our credentials to the Azure Portal by navigating to `http://portal.azure.com`:

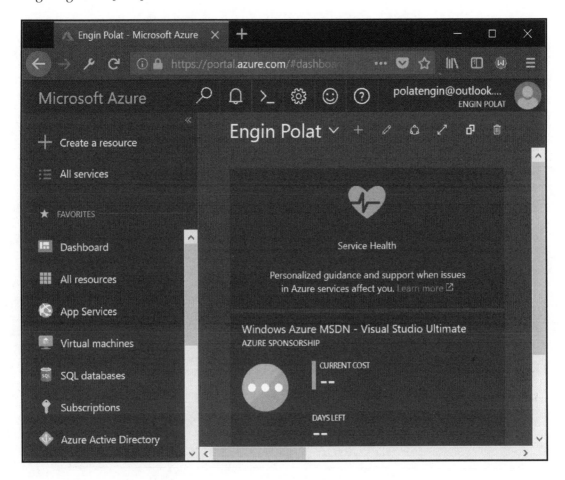

We'll need a new website for this example, so let's create one.

Click on the **+ New** button on the left-hand side; it'll open the New Resource blade. Next then click on the **Web + Mobile** menu item:

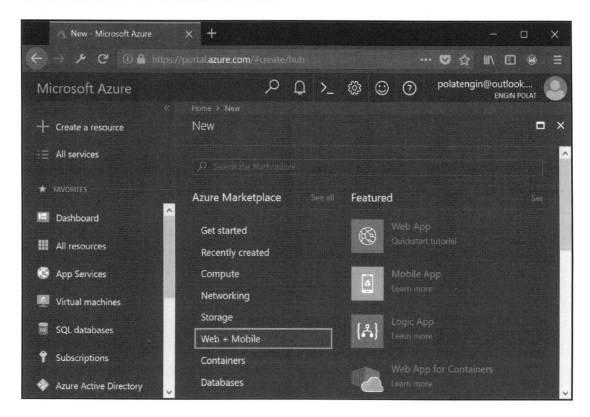

Now, click on **Web App**; it'll open the **Create Web App** blade. Fill the empty textboxes and create a new web app by following the guidelines (https://docs.microsoft.com/en-us/azure/app-service/app-service-web-overview):

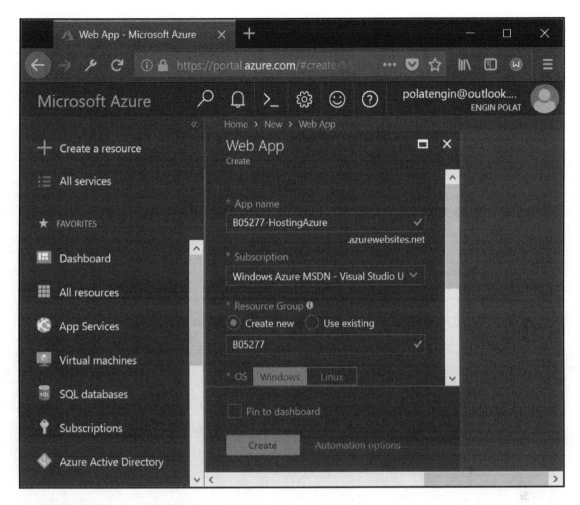

Azure will create a new web app, and in a few seconds, we'll have a new web app in Azure.

Let's create a new ASP.NET Core web app:

```
dotnet new web
```

 Example project can be found at: https://github.com/polatengin/
B05277/tree/master/Chapter19/3-HostingAzure.

How to do it...

Now we need to deploy it to Azure. There are several ways to do it, such as using Visual Studio, using Visual Studio Code, using TFS, GitHub with continuous deployment options, FTP, and so on.

Deploying an ASP.NET Core web app to Azure with Visual Studio Code

According to `http://code.visualstudio.com`, Visual Studio Code is a code editor redefined and optimized for building and debugging modern web and cloud applications. Visual Studio Code is free, and available on your favorite platform—Linux, macOS, or Windows.

After installing Visual Studio Code from `http://code.visualstudio.com`, we can add the Azure App Service Tools extension to it:

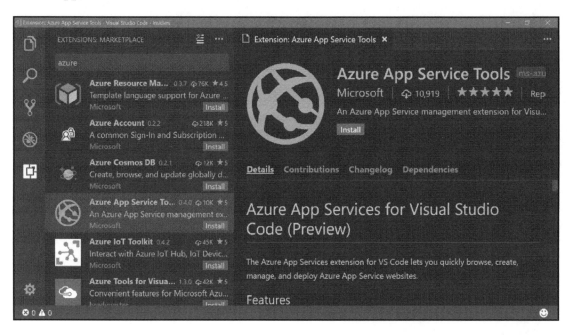

1. We need to add a `web.config` file before publishing the project to Azure with the following content:

```xml
<?xml version="1.0" encoding="utf-8"?>
<configuration>
  <system.webServer>
    <handlers>
      <add name="aspNetCore" path="*" verb="*"
modules="AspNetCoreModule" resourceType="Unspecified" />
    </handlers>
    <aspNetCore processPath="dotnet" arguments=".HostingAzure.dll"
stdoutLogEnabled="false" stdoutLogFile=".logsstdout" />
  </system.webServer>
</configuration>
```

 Notice the arguments parameter of the `aspNetCore` element. It should contain the deployed assembly name. You should change it if the project's name is different.

2. It's time to deploy the project to a local disk with .NET Core CLI commands:

   `dotnet publish -c Release`

   This command will create a `bin/release/netcoreapp2.0` folder with the deployed project.

3. Let's open Visual Studio Code with the `bin/release/netcoreapp2.0` folder. You should see the Azure App Service panel in the **Explorer** tab. After logging in to your Azure subscription, you can see the web app created previously.
4. Right-click on it and click the **Deploy to Web App** menu item.

This will package the local deployment and publish it to Azure:

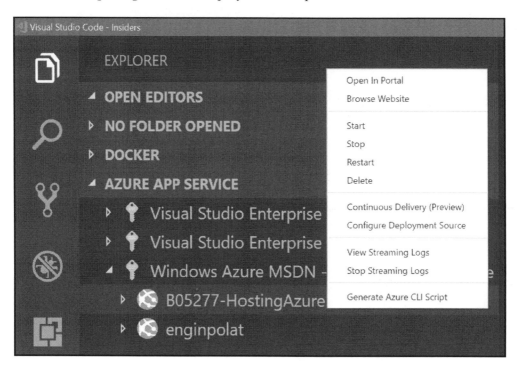

After publishing is successful, you can see a deployment completed message in the **OUTPUT** panel:

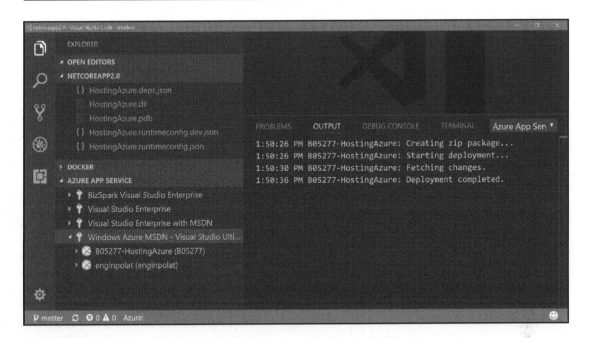

 If the `web.config` file didn't include the `netcoreapp2.0` folder, you should add this file manually.

5. After these steps, you can navigate to the URL of the web app you created in Azure and you will see the application.

Deploying an ASP.NET Core web app to Azure with Visual Studio Community Edition

Visual Studio is one of the top-rated IDEs of all time. The Community Edition is a free-of-charge version of Visual Studio and can be downloaded from `https://www.visualstudio.com/vs/`.

Once you have downloaded and installed the Visual Studio Community Edition, you can create/open ASP.NET Core Web Application projects:

1. To load a previously-created ASP.NET Core web application project, simply double-click on the `.csproj` file in the project root folder.

   It is easy to publish a project to Azure in the Visual Studio Community Edition.

2. First, right-click on the project row in **Solution Explorer** and click **Publish**:

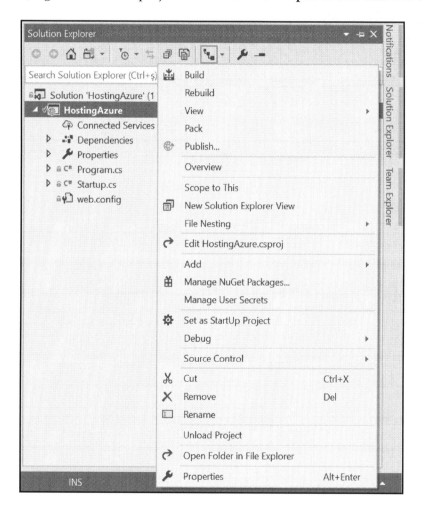

3. In the opened window, we should select the **Microsoft Azure App Service** option, select the **Select Existing** option, and click on the **Publish** button:

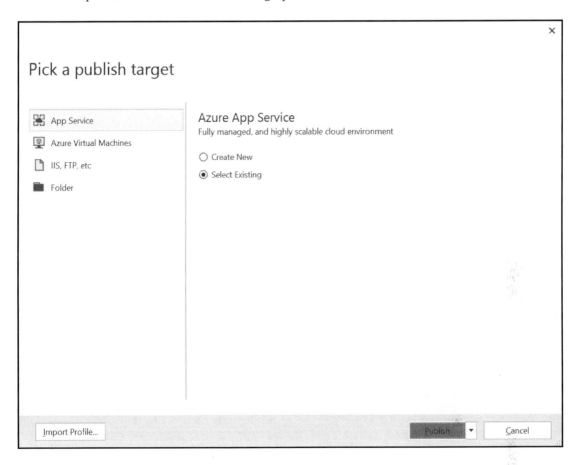

4. In the newly-opened dialog, we can see and select previously-created web apps from Azure Portal:

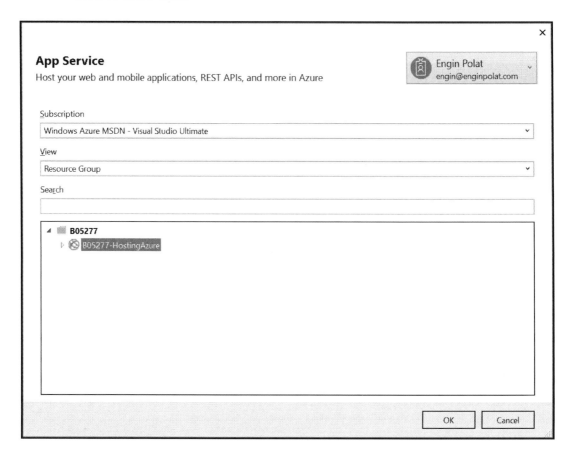

5. After clicking the **OK** button, Visual Studio will take care of packaging and publishing the project to Azure.

How it works...

Azure has different options to allow developers to publish their ASP.NET Core web app projects.

Hosting an ASP.NET Core web app in Docker containers

If you publish the project in a local data center, it's not so easy to deploy and configure the ASP.NET Core web application. Before Docker, developers usually deployed their applications to Virtual Servers.

First, they need to provision a Virtual Server, install the full OS on it, then install the required services on it, such as IIS, SQL Server, and so on.

After all these steps, the developer can deploy the application and configure it to run in that Virtual Server. It's not uncommon that projects need different environments, such as dev, test, staging, prod, and so on.

Also, at some time, developers usually differentiate the environment specs and resources, such as port numbers, database connection strings, and even underlying operation systems.

Docker makes it easy to create an environment and configure it with a human-readable text file. This text file is called a DockerFile. We can create an environment and declare its configuration by creating a DockerFile.

The Docker CLI can compose a Docker image by that DockerFile, deploy the project into it, and make a Docker image of it. The Docker CLI can also instantiate a Docker container from a Docker image. Imagine a Docker image as blueprints, and Docker containers as instances of blueprints. So, the Docker CLI can instantiate a Docker image into a Docker container several times. We should install a Docker daemon before using it; the installer can be downloaded from `https://www.docker.com/community-edition`.

A Docker daemon is cross-platform, so you can download, install, and run it on whatever operating system you have.

Getting ready

Let's create a new ASP.NET Core web app project:

```
dotnet new web
```

Open the newly-created project in Visual Studio Code and create a new file called
DockerFile.

Notice that the filename is **DockerFile**, with no file extension.

We can be sure Docker is installed and running properly by opening a Terminal/Command
Prompt window and executing the following commands:

```
docker --version
docker info
```

Example project can be found at: `https://github.com/polatengin/`
`B05277/tree/master/Chapter19/4-HostingDocker`.

How to do it...

DockerFiles must start with a Docker image as the base. In our case, this base image is a
.NET Core 2.0 Docker image developed by Microsoft.

We can see all the images by Microsoft at: `https://hub.docker.com/r/`
`microsoft/ aspnetcore-build/`.

Our DockerFile must begin with the `FROM microsoft/aspnetcore-build` line.

If we want, we can build our own Docker image from an operating system
baseline, but there are a lot of things we should do before deploying the
project to it, such as installing HTTP libraries, SSL libraries, .NET Core
Runtime, and so on. We can see layers of a DockerFile of aspnetcore-
build:2.0 at `https://hub.docker.com/r/microsoft/dotnet/~/`
`dockerfile/`.

The second line in the `DockerFile` is the working directory; in our case it is `WORKDIR` `/app`.

Then we should add a line in the `DockerFile` to copy all project files into, another line to run the `dotnet publish` command, and another line to run the .NET application.

An example of `DockerFile` content is given here:

```
FROM microsoft/aspnetcore-build AS builder
WORKDIR /app

# copy csproj and restore as distinct layers
COPY *.csproj ./
RUN dotnet restore

# copy everything else and build
COPY . ./
RUN dotnet publish -c Release -o out

# build runtime image
FROM microsoft/aspnetcore
WORKDIR /app
COPY --from=builder /app/out .
ENTRYPOINT ["dotnet", "HostingDocker.dll"]
```

1. Now we can open a Terminal/Command Prompt window and execute the following command:

   ```
   docker build -t hostingdocker .
   ```

 The `docker build` command can take a Docker image name with the `-t` argument. Also note the `.` character at the end of the command.

The output of the Docker command should look something like the following:

```
C:/B05277/Chapter19/4-HostingDocker> docker build -t hostingdocker
.
    Sending build context to Docker daemon  603.1kB
    Step 1/10 : FROM microsoft/aspnetcore-build AS builder
    latest: Pulling from microsoft/aspnetcore-build
    3e17c6eae66c: Already exists
    fdfb54153de7: Pull complete
    a4ca6e73242a: Pull complete
    93bd198d0a5f: Pull complete
```

```
    6030a6f9bb3e: Pull complete
    3244c708b1c9: Pull complete
    675a274a8d69: Pull complete
    5c16d1951794: Pull complete
    e0c6c215cec5: Pull complete
    c8a448f88b0b: Pull complete
    7c41433694e9: Pull complete
    0f54f547def2: Pull complete
    Digest:
sha256:393f83b0e5e3b880a97b7a4118c7663a0fd3463433fc9672026710ccbc5f
db88
    Status: Downloaded newer image for microsoft/aspnetcore-
build:latest
     ---> e421e10eaa5d
    Step 2/10 : WORKDIR /app
     ---> c1c98dc2991d
    Removing intermediate container 86d31c5a3e46
    Step 3/10 : COPY *.csproj ./
     ---> a4e35715c569
    Step 4/10 : RUN dotnet restore
     ---> Running in c0dc80c24979
      Restoring packages for /app/HostingDocker.csproj...
      Generating MSBuild file
/app/obj/HostingDocker.csproj.nuget.g.props.
      Generating MSBuild file
/app/obj/HostingDocker.csproj.nuget.g.targets.
      Restore completed in 563.85 ms for /app/HostingDocker.csproj.
     ---> e921c6f6c55e
    Removing intermediate container c0dc80c24979
    Step 5/10 : COPY . ./
     ---> 0af6a5882bf6
    Step 6/10 : RUN dotnet publish -c Release -o out
     ---> Running in 23f8a5c9f5e3
    Microsoft (R) Build Engine version 15.4.8.50001 for .NET Core
    Copyright (C) Microsoft Corporation. All rights reserved.
      HostingDocker ->
/app/bin/Release/netcoreapp2.0/HostingDocker.dll
      HostingDocker -> /app/out/
     ---> 458c871a3416
    Removing intermediate container 23f8a5c9f5e3
    Step 7/10 : FROM microsoft/aspnetcore
     ---> 01d033b55240
    Step 8/10 : WORKDIR /app
     ---> Using cache
     ---> 3cb4029d92c4
    Step 9/10 : COPY --from=builder /app/out .
     ---> 7574cfa0f543
    Step 10/10 : ENTRYPOINT dotnet HostingDocker.dll
```

```
  ---> Running in cd6120f3325f
  ---> fd60e8356b33
Removing intermediate container cd6120f3325f
Successfully built fd60e8356b33
Successfully tagged hostingdocker:latest
```

Now we can list all Docker images by executing the `docker images` command:

```
C:\WINDOWS\system32\cmd.exe
Microsoft Windows [Version 10.0.17046.1000]
(c) 2017 Microsoft Corporation. All rights reserved.

C:\Users\EnginPolat>docker images
REPOSITORY                    TAG          IMAGE ID        CREATED          SIZE
hostingdocker                 latest       fd60e8356b33    3 minutes ago    299MB
<none>                        <none>       458c871a3416    3 minutes ago    1.9GB
<none>                        <none>       bc3d115f00b1    11 minutes ago   299MB
microsoft/aspnetcore-build    latest       e421e10eaa5d    10 days ago      1.9GB
microsoft/aspnetcore          latest       01d033b55240    10 days ago      299MB

C:\Users\EnginPolat>
```

2. We can create a Docker container from the `hostingdocker` Docker Image by executing the following command:

    ```
    docker run -it -p 5000:80 hostingdocker
    ```

```
C:\WINDOWS\system32\cmd.exe - docker run -it -p 5000:80 hostingdocker
Microsoft Windows [Version 10.0.17046.1000]
(c) 2017 Microsoft Corporation. All rights reserved.

C:\Users\EnginPolat>docker images
REPOSITORY                    TAG          IMAGE ID        CREATED          SIZE
hostingdocker                 latest       fd60e8356b33    3 minutes ago    299MB
<none>                        <none>       458c871a3416    3 minutes ago    1.9GB
<none>                        <none>       bc3d115f00b1    11 minutes ago   299MB
microsoft/aspnetcore-build    latest       e421e10eaa5d    10 days ago      1.9GB
microsoft/aspnetcore          latest       01d033b55240    10 days ago      299MB

C:\Users\EnginPolat>docker run -it -p 5000:80 hostingdocker
Hosting environment: Production
Content root path: /app
Now listening on: http://[::]:80
Application started. Press Ctrl+C to shut down.
```

The -p switch attaches internal port number 5000 to external port number 80.

3. Finally, we can launch our favorite browser, navigate to http://localhost, and see if the application is up and running:

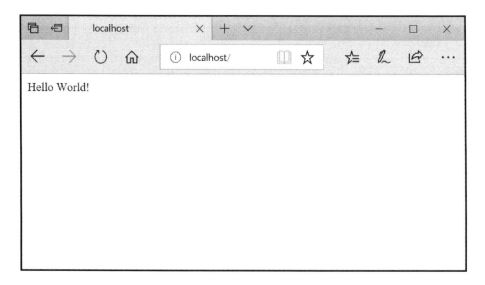

How it works...

Docker makes it easy to isolate the application and deploy it with the desired configuration.

Configuration can be declared as a text file, which enables the developers to create a pipeline to release the new version of a project by compiling the project and creating a new environment from a DockerFile.

All these steps are called Continuous Deployment.

Other Books You May Enjoy

If you enjoyed this book, you may be interested in these other books by Packt:

ASP.NET Core 2 High Performance - Second Edition
James Singleton

ISBN: 978-1-78839-976-0

- Understand ASP.NET Core 2 and how it differs from its predecessor
- Address performance issues at the early stages of development
- Set up development environments on Windows, Mac, and Linux
- Measure, profile and find the most significant problems
- Identify the differences between development workstations and production infrastructures, and how these can exacerbate problems
- Boost the performance of your application but with an eye to how it affects complexity and maintenance
- Explore a few cutting-edge techniques such as advanced hashing and custom transports

ASP.NET Core 2 and Angular 5
Valerio De Sanctis

ISBN: 978-1-78829-360-0

- Use ASP.NET Core to its full extent to create a versatile backend layer based on RESTful APIs
- Consume backend APIs with the brand new Angular 5 HttpClient and use RxJS Observers to feed the frontend UI asynchronously
- Implement an authentication and authorization layer using ASP.NET Identity to support user login with integrated and third-party OAuth 2 providers
- Configure a web application in order to accept user-defined data and persist it into the database using server-side APIs
- Secure your application against threats and vulnerabilities in a time efficient way
- Connect different aspects of the ASP. NET Core framework ecosystem and make them interact with each other for a Full-Stack web development experience

Leave a review - let other readers know what you think

Please share your thoughts on this book with others by leaving a review on the site that you bought it from. If you purchased the book from Amazon, please leave us an honest review on this book's Amazon page. This is vital so that other potential readers can see and use your unbiased opinion to make purchasing decisions, we can understand what our customers think about our products, and our authors can see your feedback on the title that they have worked with Packt to create. It will only take a few minutes of your time, but is valuable to other potential customers, our authors, and Packt. Thank you!

Index